NEWSLETTERS FROM THE CAROLINE COURT, 1631–1638: CATHOLICISM AND THE POLITICS OF THE PERSONAL RULE

NEWSLETTERS FROM THE CAROLINE COURT, 1631–1638: CATHOLICISM AND THE POLITICS OF THE PERSONAL RULE

edited by
MICHAEL C. QUESTIER

CAMDEN FIFTH SERIES
Volume 26

CAMBRIDGE
UNIVERSITY PRESS

FOR THE ROYAL HISTORICAL SOCIETY
University College London, Gower Street, London WC1 6BT
2005

Published by the Press Syndicate of the University of Cambridge
The Edinburgh Building, Cambridge CB2 2RU, United Kingdom
40 West 20th Street, New York, NY 10011–4211, USA
477 Williamstown Road, Port Melbourne, VIC 3207, Australia
Ruiz de Alarcón 13, 28014 Madrid, Spain
Dock House, The Waterfront, Cape Town 8001, South Africa

First published 2005

A catalogue record for this book is available from the British Library

ISBN 0 521 854075 hardback

SUBSCRIPTIONS. The serial publications of the Royal Historical Society, *Royal Historical Society Transactions* (ISSN 0080–4401) and Camden Fifth Series (ISSN 0960–1163), volumes may be purchased together on annual subscription. The 2005 subscription price which includes print and electronic access (but not VAT) is £77 (US $124 in the USA, Canada and Mexico) and includes Camden Fifth Series, volumes 26 and 27 (published in July and December) and Transactions Sixth Series, volume 15 (published in December). Japanese prices are available from Kinokuniya Company Ltd, P.O. Box 55, Chitose, Tokyo 156, Japan. EU subscribers (outside the UK) who are not registered for VAT should add VAT at their country's rate. VAT registered subscribers should provide their VAT registration number. Prices include delivery by air.

Subscription orders, which must be accompanied by payment, may be sent to a bookseller, subscription agent or direct to the publisher: Cambridge University Press, The Edinburgh Building, Shaftesbury Road, Cambridge CB2 2RU, UK; or in the USA, Canada and Mexico; Cambridge University Press, Journals Fulfillment Department, 100 Brook Hill Drive, West Nyack, New York, 10994–2133, USA.

SINGLE VOLUMES AND BACK VOLUMES. A list of Royal Historical Society volumes available from Cambridge University Press may be obtained from the Humanities Marketing Department at the address above.

Printed and bound in the United Kingdom at the University Press, Cambridge

CONTENTS

ACKNOWLEDGEMENTS

The newsletters reproduced in this volume are preserved among the papers of the English Catholic secular clergy in the archives of the archdiocese of Westminster. I would like to record my gratitude to Westminster Cathedral's archivist, the Reverend Ian Dickie, who has been unfailingly helpful with the resources in his charge.

Several people were so kind as to read through the text, notably Kenneth Fincham, Caroline Hibbard, and Thomas McCoog, who all made many extremely helpful suggestions.

Among those who supplied references were: Joseph Bergin, Loic Bienassis, Lyn Boothman, Caroline Bowden, Thomas Cogswell, Pauline Croft, Gabriel Glickman, Donna Hamilton, Simon Healy, Peter Lake, Mark Nicholls, Geoffrey Scott, Jeanne Shami, and Nicholas Tyacke.

I was also fortunate enough to be able to make use of the research notes of Antony Allison, a meticulous scholar who studied this material for many years. Without his work, in both manuscript and published form, it would have been virtually impossible to edit this material and present it for publication.

NOTE ON THE TEXT

The manuscripts published in this volume are printed in full with routine openings and terminations, and endorsements and annotations. (The endorsements are usually, though not invariably, in the hand of the recipient of the letter.) The original spellings have been retained,[1] except that modern usage is employed for *u* and *v*, and for *i* and *j*. Most abbreviations have been expanded through the use of italics and square brackets.

In my volume of Catholic letters from the period 1609–1614, *Newsletters from the Archpresbyterate of George Birkhead* (Camden Society, fifth series, XII, 1998), I retained both original punctuation and capitalization. This was done in order to preserve the very different styles of writing of the various clerics who were sending their newsletters to Rome – some hasty and scribbled, others more considered – reflecting the temperaments and purposes of the senders. By contrast, the majority of the letters in this volume were written by only two men, John Southcot and George Leyburn. Their writing style and presentation are quite uniform and far more formal than that of the letters printed in the earlier volume. It seemed unnecessary therefore to preserve completely the original form of the text. Thus, I have modernized capitalization and part-modernized (or rather, tidied up) the punctuation of these newsletters, while leaving the original spelling intact. Interlineations are indicated by the use of brackets <thus>. Deletions (where the deleted word is still legible) are indicated ~~thus~~. Other deletions and obliterations are noted in square brackets.

Cross-references to other letters printed here are made by citing in italic type the number of the letter, e.g. *Letter 23*.[2] Underlining of words and passages of text in these letters has been preserved.

The letters are printed in chronological sequence. In the absence of other evidence, I have assumed that letters which were written on the Continent were dated according to the New Style and those written in England were dated Old Style. However, it is clear that, by this period, some English Catholics were dating their letters according to the New Style even when they were in England.[3] (With Old-Style dates, I take the year as beginning on 1 January and not 25 March.)

---

[1] In these newsletters, 'whether' is frequently written as 'whither', 'than' as 'then', and 'two' as 'tow'. I have changed the spelling in these cases so as to aid the sense.

[2] Thus used, the term 'letter' refers to both actual letters and to items which strictly speaking are advice or position papers, rather than letters, but which were sent to Rome for the same purpose as the newsletters (i.e. *Letters 67, 69, 78, 79*).

[3] See Codignola, *CHL*, p. 65.

In my editing of this material I have tried to indicate the identity, where I am certain of it, of all of the individuals cited. When individuals are first mentioned in the text I have usually identified them via a footnote. Thereafter, if they are mentioned in the text in such a way as may obscure who they are, for example via an alias, they are again identified by means of a footnote, though only the first time that they are thus mentioned in each letter. (I have not, however, regularly listed each individual's alias or aliases when his name is cited in the footnotes unless an unusual form of the alias is used in the text.) I have not generally attempted to add standard biographical information about the Catholic clergy cited here; I simply refer to the usual Catholic sources, unless such information is directly relevant to the text of the letter.

ABBREVIATIONS

AAW	Archives of the Archdiocese of Westminster
ABSJ	Archivum Britannicum Societatis Jesu
Albion, *CI*	G. Albion, *Charles I and the Court of Rome* (London, 1935)
Alexander, *CLT*	M. van Cleave Alexander, *Charles I's Lord Treasurer* (Chapel Hill, NC, 1975)
Allison, JG	A.F. Allison, 'John Gerard and the Gunpowder Plot', *RH*, 5 (1959–1960), pp. 43–63
Allison, Q J	A.F. Allison, 'A question of jurisdiction: Richard Smith, bishop of Chalcedon and the Catholic laity, 1625–1631', *RH*, 16 (1982), pp. 111–145
Allison, RS	A.F. Allison, 'Richard Smith, Richelieu and the French marriage: the political context of Smith's appointment as bishop for England in 1624', *RH*, 7 (1964), pp. 148–211
Allison, RSGB	A.F. Allison, 'Richard Smith's gallican backers and Jesuit opponents', I (*RH*, 18 (1987), pp. 329–401), II (*RH*, 19 (1989), pp. 234–285), III (*RH*, 20 (1990), pp. 164–206)
Anglia MS 1	Letters of the Jesuit general to members of the English province of the Society of Jesus (summaries at ABSJ, XLVII/3 (I: 1605–1623), XLVII/4 (II: 1624–1632) and XLVII/5 (III: 1633–1641))
Anstr.	G. Anstruther, *The Seminary Priests*, 4 vols (Ware and Great Wakering, 1968–1977)
Anstruther, *Vaux*	G. Anstruther, *Vaux of Harrowden* (Newport, 1953)
ARCR	A.F. Allison and D.M. Rogers, *The Contemporary Printed Literature of the English Counter-Reformation between 1558 and 1640*, 2 vols (Aldershot, 1989–1994)
ARSJ	Archivum Romanum Societatis Jesu
Bellenger, *EWP*	D.A. Bellenger, *English and Welsh Priests 1558–1800* (Bath, 1984)
Berry, *Sussex*	W. Berry, *County Genealogies: Pedigrees of the Families in the County of Sussex* (London, 1830) [copy at the

	West Sussex Record Office annotated by J. Comber]
BIHR	*Bulletin of the Institute of Historical Research*
Birch, *CT*	T. Birch, *The Court and Times of Charles I*, 2 vols (London, 1948)
BL	British Library
BS	*Biographical Studies*
CD 1628	R.C. Johnson, M.F. Keeler, M.J. Cole, and W.B. Bidwell (eds), *Commons Debates 1628*, 6 vols (London, 1977–1983)
Codignola, *CHL*	L. Codignola, *The Coldest Harbour of the Land: Simon Stock and Lord Baltimore's Colony in Newfoundland, 1621–1649* (Montreal, 1988)
CRS	Catholic Record Society
CRS, 1	*Miscellanea I* (CRS, 1, 1905)
CRS, 10–11	E.H. Burton and T.L. Williams (eds), *The Douay College Diaries* (CRS, 10–11, 1911)
CRS, 22	*Miscellanea XII* (CRS, 22, 1921)
CRS, 41	L. Hicks (ed.), *Letters of Thomas Fitzherbert 1608–1610* (CRS, 41, 1948)
CRS, 54–55	A. Kenny (ed.), *The Responsa Scholarum of the English College, Rome*, 2 vols (CRS, 54–55, 1962–1963)
CRS, 74–75	T.M. McCoog (ed.), *English and Welsh Jesuits 1555–1650*, 2 vols (CRS, 74–75, 1994–1995)
CSPD	R. Lemon and M.A.E. Green (eds), *Calendar of State Papers, Domestic Series*, 12 vols [for 1547–1625] (London, 1856–1872)
CSPV	H.F. Brown and A.B. Hinds (eds), *Calendar of State Papers, Venetian Series*, 11 vols [for 1581–1625] (London, 1894–1912)
DNB	*Dictionary of National Biography*
Dockery, *CD*	J.B. Dockery, *Christopher Davenport* (London, 1960)
ESRO	East Sussex Record Office
Foley	H. Foley, *Records of the English Province of the Society of Jesus*, 7 vols (London, 1875–1883)
GEC	G.E. Cokayne, *The Complete Peerage*, 13 vols (London, 1910–1959)
Havran, *CC*	M. Havran, *Caroline Courtier: The Life of Lord Cottington* (London, 1973)
Hibbard, *CI*	C. Hibbard, *Charles I and the Popish Plot* (Chapel Hill, NC, 1983)
Hughes, *HSJ*	T. Hughes, *History of the Society of Jesus in North America, Text*, 2 vols (London, 1907–1917), vol. 1

Hughes, *RCR*	P. Hughes, *Rome and the Counter-Reformation in England* (London, 1942)
JPN	W. Powell (ed.), *John Pory (1572–1636)* (Chapel Hill, NC, 1977) [John Pory's newsletters on microfiche]
Knowler, *ESLD*	W.D. Knowler (ed.), *The Earle of Strafforde's Letters and Dispatches* , 2 vols (London, 1739)
Larkin, *SRP*, II	J.F. Larkin (ed.), *Stuart Royal Proclamations: Royal Proclamations of King Charles I 1625–1646* (Oxford, 1983)
Lunn, *EB*	D. Lunn, *The English Benedictines, 1540–1688* (London, 1980)
Milton, *CR*	A. Milton, *Catholic and Reformed* (Cambridge, 1995)
NAGB	M. Questier, *Newsletters from the Archpresbyterate of George Birkhead*, Camden Society, fifth series, XII (Cambridge, 1998)
nd	no date (of publication)
np	no place (of publication)
ODC	Order of Discalced Carmelites
OFM	Order of Friars Minor
OP	Order of Preachers
OSB	Order of St Benedict
Pastor, *HP*	L. Pastor, F.I. Antrobus, R. Kerr, E, Gray, and E.F. Peeler (eds), *The History of the Popes*, 40 vols (London, 1891–1953)
PD	Nunziatura d'Inghilterra 3a, Vatican Archives, Gregorio Panzani's Diary 1634–1637 (transcript and translation at ABSJ)
PRO	Public Record Office (National Archives)
RH	*Recusant History*
RPCS	D. Masson *et al.* (eds), *The Register of the Privy Council of Scotland*, 2nd series, 8 vols [for 1625–1660] (Edinburgh, 1899–1908)
Sharpe, *PR*	K. Sharpe, *The Personal Rule of Charles I* (London, 1992)
SJ	Society of Jesus
TD	M.A. Tierney, *Dodd's Church History of* England, 5 vols (London, 1839–1843)
Tyacke, *AC*	N. Tyacke, *Anti-Calvinists* (Oxford, 1987)
VA	Vatican Archives
VCH Surrey	H.E. Malden *et al.* (eds), *The Victoria History of the County of Surrey*, 4 vols (London, 1902–1967)

INTRODUCTION

The newsletters and their historical context

The present series of newsletters comes from the archives of the archdiocese of Westminster – Series A (volumes XXIV and XXVI–XXIX), Series B (volumes 27 and 47), and Series OB (volume 1). They have their origin in the journey from London into exile in France of Richard Smith, bishop of Chalcedon, in 1631.

Bishop Smith had been appointed to his titular see in late 1624 at the behest of the French king, Louis XIII, and Smith's own patron, Cardinal Richelieu. (Smith's predecessor, William Bishop, first bishop of Chalcedon, had died in April 1624, after little more than a year in office.) Smith's promotion was a key move in the Bourbon regime's strategy to secure the Anglo-French dynastic alliance of 1624–1625. It was believed that he would be able to secure English Catholic support for the treaty.[1] Soon after he was consecrated (in Paris in January 1625) he returned to England. He and his allies among the secular clergy had, for a long time, harboured plans and projects to reform the structure and practice of Catholicism in England. William Bishop had already made a stab at implementing some of them. Now, with the same objectives in mind, Smith began a co-ordinated and aggressive campaign to enforce his authority over the entire English Catholic community, and particularly over the religious orders (notably the Jesuits and the Benedictines) and their patrons. Many of the religious and their benefactors were already his irreconcilable enemies and had no intention of acknowledging his claims.

It was a consistent line of Bishop Smith's friends and supporters that his conduct in office was peaceful, beneficent, and fruitful, and that there was no opposition to him until the point, in 1627, when he turned his attention to the (allegedly) small procedural matter of 'approbation', the (theoretically automatic) licensing of missionary priests in England to hear the confessions of their ghostly children. The quarrel escalated rapidly when it became clear that his policy was part of a much wider drive for conformity (to episcopal authority

---

[1] For the background to Richard Smith's appointment, and its significance, see Allison, RS; M.C. Questier, *An English Catholic Community? Aristocratic Politics and Confessional Conflict, c. 1550–1640* (forthcoming).

and various hierarchical norms and Tridentine practices) among the English Catholic clergy. Numerous memoranda and position papers on the issue were soon circulating back and forth within the Catholic community.[2]

To many of Smith's enemies it appeared that his claims about the extent of his episcopal authority (and the various functions associated with such claims, in particular the setting-up of a 'tribunal' or quasi-consistory court to judge matrimonial and probate cases) were potentially offensive to the State. They argued that the exercise of such aspects of his authority would risk the increase of 'persecution' of English Catholics by the State. Representations made to the Caroline regime by Smith's Catholic opponents probably contributed to the regime's decision to issue a proclamation against him on 11 December 1628.[3] The proclamation denounced Smith as a traitor for persuading the king's subjects away from their allegiance, for usurping 'to himself exercise of episcopall jurisdiction from Rome', discharging this usurped authority within the realm, and holding continual intelligence with the king's enemies.[4] Matters had, of course, been greatly complicated by the Stuart regime's recent military enterprise against Louis XIII.

Catholics supposed that this was largely show on King Charles's part. 'When these matters were in hoatest treaty', related the priest John Southcot, 'the State was certainly informed where the bishop was and could have then apprehended him if they had meant it really'. Southcot said that 'the lord that was known ordinarily to harbour him had express warning sent him by order from the king to look to him self'. In other words, Charles was merely trying to head off the inevitable stream of anti-popish comment which would start when parliament next assembled. (It was scheduled to meet on 20 January 1629.) Charles was also, speculated Southcot, trying 'to terrify the French and perhaps to bring them on in their treaty of peace which is now in hand, the king being informed that the bishop hath bin a dependent of Cardinal Richelieu'.[5]

On the other hand, some members of the privy council, notably Sir John Coke, were far from happy about Bishop Smith's encroachments on the king's authority. A concerted effort had in fact been made in

---

[2] For the approbation controversy, see Allison, Q J.

[3] See AAW, A XXII, no. 154, p. 665; Allison, Q J, pp. 126–127; cf. D. Lunn, 'Benedictine opposition to Bishop Richard Smith (1625–1629)', *RH*, 11 (1971–1972), pp. 1–20, at pp. 14, 20, n. 163. Antony Allison comments that 'although Smith consistently denied ever having attempted to prove the public wills of Catholics, he later admitted that his tribunal dealt with [. . .] private wills', in which there were 'legacies for pious uses'; Allison, Q J, p. 127.

[4] AAW, A XXII, no. 153, p. 663; Larkin, *SRP*, no. 104.

[5] AAW, A XXII, no. 154, p. 665.

1628 to arrest some of Smith's leading officials.[6] Edmund Arrowsmith was executed, and George Fisher believed that he was going to suffer the same fate.

Temporarily, the storm passed. Charles entirely failed to live up to the expectations of the anti-papists in the 1629 parliament. Smith, for his part, was now back-pedalling furiously on the scope of his authority. He tried to counter his enemies' jibes that he was a cat's-paw of the French. In a letter to the queen of 19 December 1628, he had admitted that he had been a pensioner of Richelieu, but he claimed that since he had arrived in England he had not taken a penny from the cardinal. Nor had he received any missive from him, nor written to him more than once or twice since the time when most of Henrietta Maria's French attendants had been forcibly repatriated by Charles. And before that he wrote to the cardinal for no other end than to move him to intercede with the French king that Catholics might now enjoy the tolerance which they believed had been guaranteed to them by the Anglo-French dynastic treaty. He would not concede that his authority prejudiced that of the crown. He denied that he had set up a 'new tribunal' for proving wills, or 'any other kind of tribunal than St Paul did when he excommunicated the incestuous Corinthians, or regular superiors do when they correct their brethren'. Nor had he 'all these 4 yeares exercised any authority at all over any lay person'.[7]

Nevertheless, a second royal proclamation, dated 24 March 1629, was issued against the increasingly beleaguered bishop. This was clearly intended to answer some of the crown's critics in the recent parliament.[8] Still no effective attempt was made to arrest Smith himself. But such repeated public denunciations were severely damaging to Smith's credibility and reputation.

[6] In October 1628 Humphrey Cross and Richard Tomlins were ordered by Viscount Conway to make a thorough search of the London prisons. In itself, this was nothing unusual, but on this occasion Conway prefaced the warrant with the observation that 'there is information and probable suspition of some undutifull combination or practise against the peace of the goverment of this kingdom and that the same is founded upon a supposed power from Rome and from thence communicated to severall persons within this realme', among them several 'prissonners [. . .] about the cittie of London'. In particular, Cross and Tomlins were directed to harass Smith's officials – William Harewell in the New Prison and George Fisher in the Gatehouse; PRO, SP 16/118/25, fo. 34r.

[7] AAW, A XXII, no 154, p. 665; Allison, Q J, p. 129. Smith asserted also, in a letter of 31 December 1629 to an unnamed lady at court, that his authority was only spiritual; *ibid.*, pp. 127–128. Although Smith's new thoughts on his authority were widely circulated, and his officials seemed on the verge of fixing up an accommodation between their master and his opponents, this prospective *détente* failed because Smith's enemies demanded that he should issue the supposedly private thoughts in these two letters as a public statement of his acceptance of the limits on his authority, and this he refused to do; *ibid.*, pp. 131–132.

[8] AAW, A XXIII, no. 93; AAW, SEC 16/1/4; Larkin, *SRP*, no. 109.

Frantic attempts were made to shore up Smith's position, including a conference, in August 1629, to try to make peace with his Catholic opponents.[9] By now, however, Smith had been driven to take refuge in the French embassy in London. Sir George Calvert, 1st Baron Baltimore, returned from the New World in 1630. He assumed control of the campaign against Smith and revived the text of one of the principal polemical pieces that had, back in 1627, been circulated against Smith, the so-called 'letter of the three gentlemen'. In March 1631 it was issued again, now entitled 'The Declaration of the Lay Catholicks of England'.[10] It was presented to the Catholic ambassadors in London, and, in April, to the Spanish diplomat, Carlos Coloma, as he was returning to Spain by way of Brussels. Coloma went as far as to sign a statement that the documentation shown to him was factually accurate and genuine.[11]

Smith's supporters retaliated. They collected, from September to November, affidavits from the Catholic laity that they had not even heard of the 'Declaration'.[12] The French ambassador, François Duval, marquis de Fontenay Mareuil, was initially chary about supporting them. But he eventually signed, in late June 1631, an amended version of a document (of 31 May)[13] to this effect. It was printed at Paris under the title *Général Désadveu des Catholiques Lais d'Angleterre, contre une Déclaration qui a esté faussement publiée à leur Nom.*[14]

The bishop's position, however, had deteriorated beyond repair. He left the country on 24 August 1631. George Leyburn conducted him as far as Calais before returning to London.[15] The final straw had been the papal breve *Britannia* (issued on 29 April/9 May 1631).[16] It

---

[9] AAW, A XXIII, no. 126, p. 455.

[10] AAW, A XXIV, no. 77, p. 297; *Letter 3*. See also AAW, A XXIV, nos 72, 78, 85, 86, 155; Hughes, *HSJ*, pp. 200–201.

[11] *The Attestation of [. . .] Don Carlos Coloma* (St Omer, 1631); ARCR, II, no. 191; Hughes, *RCR*, pp. 382, 384. The 'Declaration' had signatures appended to it, though when it came out in print (in both English and Latin) the signatures were omitted; Allison, Q J, p. 134.

[12] See e.g. AAW, A XXIV, no. 113 (Essex). For general declarations in favour of Smith by the laity, some of which also mention the 'Declaration', see AAW, A XXIV, nos 155 (Wales), 157 (Lincolnshire), 158 (Staffordshire), 159 (Oxford [diocese]), 160 (Essex), 161 (Wells [diocese]), 163 (Hampshire), 164 (Northamptonshire), 165 (Yorkshire), 166 (Staffordshire and Cheshire), 167 (Sussex), 168 (Berkshire), 171 (Durham), 174 (Durham), 175 (Hampshire), 177 (Suffolk), 178 (Northamptonshire), 181 (Cambridgeshire), 182 (Norfolk), 183 (Derbyshire), 184 (Worcestershire and Shropshire), 187 (London and Middlesex), 188 (Yorkshire), 189 (Yorkshire), 203 (Kent). See also AAW, A XXIV, nos 186, 190, 192, 210.

[13] Entitled 'Abrenunciatio Catholicorum Laicorum Angliae in Declarationem quandam sub ipsorum nomine false editam', AAW A XXIV, no. 98.

[14] Allison, Q J, pp. 134–135; AAW, A XXIV, no. 99, p. 401.

[15] Anstr., II, p. 193.

[16] AAW, A XXIV, no. 93, p. 381; Hughes, *RCR*, pp. 378–380.

pronounced on the issues in dispute between him and his enemies, mainly in favour of his enemies, at least on the question of approbation.

Smith arrived in Paris and promptly resigned his episcopal title, thinking thereby to shame his enemies and push the pope into appointing another bishop in his place, or possibly more than one.[17] Urban VIII accepted Smith's retirement but then, with classic Roman indecision, left things as they were. By the time Smith realized he had made a tactical error, and tried to withdraw his resignation, it was too late.[18] He was never again to exercise the overarching power which he and his friends had craved within the English Catholic community. Smith's exile enraged his followers. They kept him and Peter Biddulph[19] (Smith's representative at Rome from 1631) supplied with a stream of newsletters, memoranda, and petitions, in order to try to persuade the papal curia to restore Smith, or at least to grant episcopal authority over English Catholics to one of their party.

These newsletters and other documents supply the material for this volume. I have decided to print in their entirety virtually all the letters in the Westminster archdiocesan archives which were written, between December 1631 and May 1638, by Smith's two faithful lieutenants in London, John Southcot and George Leyburn. I have included a few other letters as well – written by Richard East (*Letter 33*), William Case (*Letter 58*), Richard Smith himself (*Letter 71*), and Anthony Champney (*Letter 95*), and also some memoranda drawn up by Smith's supporters (*Letters 67, 69, 78, 79*) which describe the state of religion in England in the mid-1630s. Some of Biddulph's dispatches are extant in copies in the Westminster archive, and many of Smith's own letters to Biddulph (mainly for the period 1632–1634) are bound in the final volume (B 27) of the Westminster archive's 'Roman letters' series. (I have used these principally to edit and annotate Southcot's and Leyburn's letters.)

We can get, therefore, an accurate glimpse from these letters of an active Catholic clerical traffic of information and exhortation, a glimpse which allows us to discern the aims and ambitions of one of the most powerful and determined English Catholic clerical factions of the day, a faction struggling not just to exert its authority over English Catholics but also to affect decisively substantial areas of the Caroline regime's ecclesiastical and foreign policy. These newsletters also allow us to see a good deal of the internal politics of the English Catholic community, in particular the way in which these clerics tried to appropriate and retain the aristocratic and gentry patronage on

[17] AAW, A XXIV, no. 179, p. 671.
[18] See AAW, A XXIV, no. 214; *Letter 14*; AAW, A XXVI, nos 21, 29.
[19] Better known by his alias of Fitton.

which their claims to and assertion of authority and superiority so heavily relied.

Bishop Smith and his friends alleged that he enjoyed the support of the majority of English Catholics, particularly those whose social status added weight to their opinions. In a report to the Congregation for the Propagation of the Faith (De Propaganda Fide) of 14/24 June 1631, he insisted that a paltry 'seven, or eight at most, English notables came to see the French ambassador' on the issues in dispute, in order to express opposition to Smith, 'nor could others have been to see his Spanish colleague' for that purpose. Of these 'notables', two (Cashel and Baltimore) had Irish, not English, titles. Another (Herbert) was 'not a peer of the English parliament'. Yet another had now withdrawn his opposition. Smith stated that, since there were in total twenty-four Catholic peers, the malcontents were an unimpressive number 'in comparison with the whole body'.[20] The pro-episcopal lobby collected attestations and affidavits about the extent of aristocratic support for Smith. Letters were obtained from, for example, the marquis of Winchester, who protested his respect and reverence for the bishop.[21]

This battle for support among the leading aristocratic patrons of the community came out into the open with the 'Protestatio Declaratoria' of October 1631. This new attack on Smith was delivered shortly after he had withdrawn in disgust to Paris. It was dispatched to Rome, with additional documentation and lists of subscribers and supporters from among the Catholic nobility. Twelve nobles had signed the protestation itself. Five others had registered their assent but did not actually put their signatures to it. It was claimed that only one peer (Baron Arundell) was completely committed to Smith's cause. Two others were basically supportive of him but did not think that episcopal jurisdiction should be restored at that time. Another two were not committed to either side. Three hundred gentlemen were alleged to have signed the document, and even more were said to have sanctioned it.[22]

What all this suggests is that there was a fairly even balance between Smith's supporters and his opponents, and that noble and gentry opinion about the rights and wrongs of his cause was fluid and changeable. In short, there was still all to play for, even after Smith had gone into exile. If those nobles and their families who positively supported the conformist line spun by the clergy in sympathy with Smith were rather few in number, Smith was still able to protest that

[20] Hughes, *RCR*, pp. 382–383; Hughes, *HSJ*, p. 219.
[21] AAW, A XXV, no. 21, p. 39.
[22] Allison, *QJ*, pp. 138–139; Hughes, *HSJ*, p. 225. See also AAW, A XXVI, no. 98, p. 273; no. 122, p. 339; no. 123, p. 341.

his enemies' claim that virtually none of the aristocracy supported him was false.[23] Whatever such people actually said when they were besieged and badgered for their support by leading clergy on both sides, Smith's backers may well have been right to think that things were much more evenly balanced than the 'Protestatio Declaratoria' claimed. They certainly argued, with some confidence, that if Smith were restored, or if another bishop were to come in his place, many of those Catholics who currently resisted episcopal authority would desist from their opposition.[24]

On the surface, of course, these spats and disputes do generally look rather pernickety and tedious. But they were one of the central processes by which Catholicism in England was identified, defined, and redefined, and through which its meanings and significance were hammered out, during this period. Also, these newsletters, which describe these quarrels in such detail, are a crucial key to the structure of the community which gave rise to them. For example, they delineate some of the tight familial and kin networks which sustained the leading clerical protagonists in these quarrels. John Southcot was himself a cousin of another of Smith's friends and leading clerical officials, Richard Broughton, and also of the influential political theorist, Thomas White (better known by his alias of Blacklo), a relationship which tied Southcot into the wider kinship circle of the lord treasurer, Sir Richard Weston, created earl of Portland in February 1633, whose daughter had married Thomas White's brother Richard.[25] George Leyburn was a cousin of the influential priest, Henry Holden. The foundation in the mid-1630s of an Augustinian convent at Paris for English Catholic women (under the patronage of Cardinal Richelieu and Louis XIII) recruited personnel from among the families of the convent's English clerical sponsors. Relatives of Richard Smith and John Colleton were among the first to be professed there. On 28 October 1636 Smith noted that his niece, Mary Gildon, was 'to be clothed' in the new convent 'on Al[l] Saintes daye when I am to preach'.[26]

[23] AAW, B 27, no. 107; *Letter 13*.
[24] See AAW, A XXVII, no. 131, pp. 407–408.
[25] See *Letter 26*.
[26] AAW, A XXVIII, no. 176, p. 569. See A.F. Allison, 'The English Augustinian convent of Our Lady of Syon at Paris: its foundation and struggle for survival during the first eighty years, 1634–1713', *RH*, 21 (1993), pp. 451–496, at pp. 458–459; *Letter 66*; F.-M.-Th. Cédoz, *Un Couvent de Religieuses Anglaises à Paris de 1634 à 1884* (London, 1891), p. 32. Kinship did not, however, necessarily lead to ideological affinity and harmony. As is made clear in these letters, there were sharp divisions even within leading Catholic families. Peter Biddulph's father and John Southcot's father were both patrons of the Jesuits and seriously disapproved of what their sons were doing. Southcot's cousin Thomas White's mother was Mary, the

But, just as significantly, the ways in which the Caroline Catholic community argued with itself about how it should be governed actually informed the relationship between English Catholicism and the Caroline State. These newsletters' rehearsals of the to-and-fro, and tit-for-tat squabbles between different factional groups among the clergy are also the substance of a narrative of the changing fortunes of Catholicism as a political issue during the 1630s.

What were the issues at stake between Bishop Smith and his opponents?

The arguments aired in the approbation controversy were not in themselves particularly new. Conflict between the diocesan authorities in national churches and the members of religious orders was endemic in Europe at this time, especially in France. But the strife caused by such arguments within the English Catholic community reached a new stage of intensity during the 1620s, when local episcopal authority was instituted among and over the English Catholics for the first time since the Reformation.

Since the appointment of the archpriest, George Blackwell, in 1598 there had been disputes and quarrels about how far the Catholic missionary clergy in England were conforming to the godly patterns and ideals which were desirable for men of their profession. As is well known, some of the secular clergy accused the religious of corrupting the ideals of the English 'mission' as it had been inaugurated during Elizabeth's reign, and of draining, for their own selfish purposes, the English Catholic community of men and financial resources. The religious, particularly the Jesuits, retaliated by alleging that their critics were only a small fraction of the secular clergy – embittered, ambitious, and failed men who were jealous, or 'emulous', of the success of the regulars in evangelizing the kingdom, and were now campaigning against them only in order to cosy up to the State in the hope of obtaining a measure of toleration (though only for themselves and, in effect, at the expense of the majority of English Catholics). But, with the restoration of episcopacy and the appointment of a secular priest as a bishop, the secular clergy who had spearheaded the appeals to Rome against George Blackwell now had the instruments of disciplinary authority to start enforcing one version of what those

daughter of the lawyer Edmund Plowden, and thus a cousin of the influential lawyer, Francis Plowden, who was an opponent of Bishop Smith.

godly patterns and ideals were, to the possible exclusion of other versions.[27]

Crucially, as we shall rehearse in more detail shortly, this was happening at almost exactly the same time that certain Church-of-England men (often described by historians as avant-garde conformists or Laudians) were making almost precisely the same kind of bid to enforce conformist patterns of godly behaviour in the Church of England, and were using not dissimilar weapons to do it. In both cases, the agency making the bid claimed to be moderate and mainstream, restoring, not revolutionizing, the Church, and acting entirely in conformity with the traditions which all members of their Church could presume to have inherited from the time of its inception.

We may, of course, conclude that the bid by English Catholic avant-garde conformists failed while the bid by avant-garde conformist elements in the Church of England succeeded (at least in the short term). This was in large part because of structural differences between the two. (The English Catholic conformist impulse was reliant on resources a lot more limited than those available to the Laudians.) Many of the letters printed in this volume lament the lack of success of the secular clergy in making their case to the authorities in Rome, and they deplore the continued stubborn delinquency of their opponents in England. But it is clear that these secular priests did have the ear of the queen and prominent courtiers. And for much of the 1630s it seemed to them, and to their enemies as well, that local episcopal rule might well be restored by Rome over Catholics in England and Scotland. As these letters show, for a time in the early 1630s, the seculars believed that, even if Smith was forced finally to step aside, the Roman curia might invest one of his colleagues (or more than one) with episcopal authority.

In addition, the often apparently rather petty arguments aired in the controversies between different Catholic factions were part of a much wider, and widely recognized, contemporary rhetoric of order and discipline. To dominate this rhetoric was absolutely essential for those who aspired to any kind of controlling authority within the English Catholic community. The conflict at the rhetorical heart of these debates over episcopacy was about what the Catholic clergy in England were supposed to be doing. In some senses it was quite obvious: to dispense the sacraments and, indeed, to perform all the services to the faithful that a good missionary priest should. But if it was accepted, as in theory it was, by all these clerics, that the purpose

---

[27] For an excellent summary of the issues in controversy among the English clergy at this time, see E. Duffy, 'The English secular clergy and the Counter-Reformation', *Journal of Ecclesiastical History*, 34 (1983), pp. 214–230.

of the Catholic missionary clergy was to roll back the tide of Protestant heresy, then there was more to it. This was because, in contemporary English Catholic thought, there was reckoned to be more than one way of achieving the 'conversion' of England.

In fact, the action of 'converting' (evangelizing, sanctifying, and saving) one's fellow man (Catholic as well as Protestant) was capable of causing deep divisions among Catholics. John Bossy has described how the modes of evangelization which the Society of Jesus adopted were likely to antagonize others who only partly shared the Society's goals or view of the world.[28] As one typical memorandum concerning episcopal government (sent to Rome by the secular clergy in July 1627) stated,

> [...] the necessity of having this authority here well established and continued is apparent to any indifferent judge, both for the comfort of the good and for the correction of the bad. For without this authority the wisest men, that understand the case of England truly, are of opinion that this great work of the conversion of our country will advance nothing at all, and never be achived, and that the abuses and inward impediments, which have hitherto chiefly hindered the same, will rather grow and encrease daily, as by experience we see they doe.

At this point the author of the memorandum launched into a recitation of the normal catalogue of 'intolerable abuses' which lack of episcopal control was reckoned to have caused. Some priests

> [...] have come into England, and have practised their priestly function without a lawfull mission. Others have practised beiond the extent of their faculties. There are divers particular religious men here that do acknowledg[e] no superiour in England. Some have committed notorious and daungerous indiscretions. Some live scandalously, and the like.[29]

It is clear that, for all the overt polemical overtones of these remarks, those seculars who were in favour of an immediate restoration of local episcopal jurisdiction among English Catholics knew that they had identified a live issue when they floated their claims to authority on a polemic of decorum and order in the Church. Thomas McCoog's research has shown that there were doubts, even from the inception of the English Jesuit mission, about how far the Society's vocation and purposes were being realized and fulfilled in England. In the 1570s, the Jesuit general, Everard Mercurian, had hesitated about authorizing an English mission precisely because of the foreseeable difficulties which Jesuits would experience in living there in accordance with

---

[28] J. Bossy, *The English Catholic Community 1570–1850* (London, 1975), section 1.
[29] AAW, A XX, no. 102, p. 354.

their institute.[30] Such concerns were the inevitable result of not being able to wear clerical dress, live openly as Catholic clergymen, and benefit from the discipline exerted by the priests' immediate superior – since the hunted life of priest-missioners did not easily allow for regular visitation, renewal of vows, and the like. And, of course, the political activities of some leading English members of the Society gave their enemies the opportunity to criticize them for provoking the wrath of the State against all English Catholics.

Privately, the Jesuits continued to air their worries about how well they fulfilled their apostolic mission, how difficult it was for a mission superior to visit his community and provide spiritual and other direction, and even about apparently rather minor questions such as how their devotions were to be carried out, and how much time during each day was to be spent in prayer. McCoog notes that, in 1626, i.e. just before the approbation crisis broke, the Jesuit general, Muzio Vitelleschi, 'issued a series of ordinances and regulations for the religious life of the missioners in England'.[31]

Similarly, the Benedictines had begun their mission in 1603, as David Lunn points out, 'with very little formal organization'. More reliance was placed on the charisma and ability of the local superior than on any very developed chain of command. When the local superior was, like Thomas Preston (head of the Cassinese Benedictines in England), refractory on an important political issue such as the oath of allegiance, or generally incapable of keeping order, as was Leander Jones (the vicar general of the Spanish congregation of the Benedictines in England), then this could cause serious difficulties. The result was a series of anxieties and discussions, similar to that which McCoog traces among the Jesuits, about how to regularize the often rather irregular aspects of the Benedictine mission in a country where there were no cloisters.[32]

In 1615, for example, there was a draft Benedictine proposal for a structure for their missionaries' lives, virtually identical in some of its suggestions to what the Jesuits were recommending. It counselled two hours of mental prayer each day, as well as the normal liturgical routine which the monks were supposed to perform. It also advised the appointment of additional officials ('provincials') who would, in effect, go on visitation in order to guarantee that monks were not

---

[30] T.M. McCoog, *The Society of Jesus in Ireland, Scotland, and England 1541–1588: 'Our Way of Proceeding?'* (Leiden, 1996); *idem*, 'The religious life of the English Jesuits' (forthcoming).
[31] *Ibid.*
[32] For the reconstitution of the English Benedictine congregation, see Lunn, *EB*, p. 147; *idem*, 'Benedictine opposition', pp. 4–6.

involved in commercial ventures or in politics.[33] A number of codes followed in subsequent years. A set of rules was drawn up for the newly united Benedictine Congregation in England in 1617, and there was another series in 1633.[34] It is clear, however, that there remained real difficulties.[35] In consequence, the pro-episcopal lobby could fashion a *prima facie* convincing critique of the regulars' alleged irregularities.

A significant branch of the pro-episcopal, or hierarchalist, priests' propaganda concentrated on proving, however, that their censures of the regulars did not imply that they were opposed to religious orders *per se*. In fact, they tried to show that, in seeking to police and regulate the religious orders, the secular clergy could claim to be assisting the regulars' own purposes and best interests. Even if Richard Smith and his friends evinced no specific concern about whether the Jesuits and Benedictines completed prescribed annual retreats, renewed their vows, and so on, the pro-episcopal lobby could convincingly parade their interest in promoting a culture of order and discipline as a benefit to all the clerical groups on the English Catholic mission.

For this reason, it was in the interests of the pro-episcopal secular clergy to be able to show that they retained the friendship of the well- or better-intentioned among the regulars. Since the revival of the Order of St Benedict's mission in England, the seculars had got on reasonably well with the Spanish Benedictine congregation.[36] Among the regulars who were prepared to support Smith actively was the Carmelite, Thomas Dawson. In October 1627 he wrote to the Congregation for the Propagation of the Faith asking permission to live under the authority of Smith as bishop of Chalcedon, instead of that of his own order.[37] The leading secular priest, John Jackson's Franciscan brother, Bonaventure, was also well regarded by Smith's friends.[38] There were even a few Jesuits of whom they approved. One was Edmund Arrowsmith who served, until his arrest and execution (see above), as one of Smith's officials in the north of England.

[33] Lunn, *EB*, p. 147.
[34] *Ibid.*, p. 148.
[35] David Lunn suggests that 'the loose, Jesuit-type organization, which had its heyday among the Benedictines between 1603 and 1619, was less advantageous to all concerned than might be supposed', and he speculates that 'it might have been better, at least for the laity, if the regulars had submitted to the ordinary jurisdiction of Bishop Richard Smith in the 1620s'. There were a number of 'rebellions' against the imposition of authority on monks in England, and 'even after 1619, quite apart from the rebels, it has to be said that proper discipline, monastic observance and supervision were unsolved problems'; *ibid.*, p. 148. Failings in the order's loose missionary organization 'were spotlighted' in the approbation controversy; *ibid.*, p. 151.
[36] *NAGB, passim.*
[37] AAW, A XX, no. 138, p. 503; Hughes, *RCR*, pp. 342, 363.
[38] Dockery, *CD*, pp. 22, 26, 27, 29, 41, 117.

Smith's agent in Rome, Thomas White, was advised in July 1627 to inform the curia that

> [...] not only the secular priests of England, but also the religious them selves of all orders (the Jesuitts only excepted) togeather with the archbishop of Rehemes [William Gifford OSB], the college of Doway, the English residence at Paris, with all the Catholicks of England (save only such as depended upon the Jesuitts) did all jointly concurr to sue to his Holinesse for a bishop.[39]

Here, then, we have a rhetorical as much as a strictly jurisdictional dispute over what was the best way to maintain and promote a godly ministry within the English Catholic community. The approbation controversy was always more than a technical debate about the precise legal extent of Smith's powers. It was also informed by a number of crucial contemporary anxieties about the relationship between clergy and laity.

In the first place, patronage dispensed from the upper echelons of the community to seminarist chaplains always threatened to create conflicts of interest. Gentry and aristocratic largesse could imply clerical obedience, even subservience, on the chaplains' part. As Thomas McCoog asks, 'would the patron take advantage of his position and demand that the priest involve himself in occupations inappropriate for a religious?' And, generally, 'there would be an ever-present temptation' for the clergyman 'to ape the behaviour and style of [...] [his] hosts'. If 'the exigencies of the English mission and the demands for concealment required the clergy to pose as [...] stewards and gentlemen, where did the necessity end and self-indulgence begin?' Would such role-playing corrode the cleric's 'religious fervour and apostolic zeal'? The real problem was that, heavily reliant upon the support of lay gentry patrons, priests were often very much at their patrons' beck and call. The patron might compel his chaplain into seigneurial service in a way which would cramp his clerical style and damage the structure and original purpose of the 'mission'.[40]

It was unavoidable that the social tensions and frictions caused by many Catholic clergymen's status and duties should be incorporated into the struggle between the different factions which were fighting for political dominance within the community and for the right to represent themselves to the State as the true spokesmen of that community. The perceived lack of regulation and discipline among both clerics and laity became a central topic of argument between these factions. The regulars claimed that their own institutional

[39] AAW, A XX, no. 102, pp. 354–355.

[40] McCoog, 'Religious life', citing Bossy, *English Catholic Community*, p. 259. Cf. W. Gibson, *A Social History of the Domestic Chaplain 1530–1840* (Leicester, 1997), pp. 38–42, 44.

structures guaranteed the integrity of their mission against the temptations generated by the style of life lived in the houses of their patrons. The clergy who saw episcopal regulation as the key to raising clerical standards and ensuring discipline argued that, without the mechanisms of episcopal government, godly Catholicism was likely to be corrupted, not just among the clergy but among the laity as well.

One document, from July 1627, enumerated the 'fruict' of William Bishop's and Richard Smith's own episcopal 'endeavours' under twelve separate heads. Stress was laid on the fact that 'the hierarchy hath bin sett up in an orderly and dew manner, by making vicar generalls, archdeacons, rurall deanes and other officers belonging therunto'. 'Ecclesiasticall discipline, which was utterly decaied, doth begin hereby to florish againe.' The effects of that discipline were then listed. Disorderly priests had been 'corrected and reclaimed from their bad courses'. Those who had subscribed to the 1606 oath of allegiance had been made to recant. Many of the laity had received the sacrament of confirmation 'to their singular comfort and encouragement'. The 'gravity, good example and zealous exortations of the bishops' had 'helped very much to confirme the Catholickes in that constant profession of their faith', and in a 'true devotion and obedience to the Sea Apostolicke'. Smith had not only 'taken particular care to determine of the feasts and fasts proper to our country', and started to collate a definitive martyrology, a true record of English Catholic witness to the faith, but also, 'by his authority', he had 'donn many good offices to reconcile divers discontented wives and husbands, who lived ordinarily before a sunder', and had even sought to make peace between the warring clerical factions.[41]

The Jesuit authorities' own warnings about the dangers of relying too heavily upon lay patronage accurately anticipated and tried to deflect the kind of charges which were being levelled against the Society by its enemies. As early as January 1607, an admonitory letter was sent by the Jesuit general, Claudio Acquaviva, to the English mission. He advised that, in place of external poverty, where it could not be practised, an interior one should be cultivated instead. The fact that the Jesuits could not simply apply to their superior for financial supply meant that they would have to be even more careful about their calling of evangelical poverty. And they should avoid familiarity with the patron's family in order to fend off threats to chastity.[42] The English Jesuits' vice-provincial congregation of 1622 issued instructions which advised the Jesuit missioner to extract himself from any kind of

[41] AAW, A XX, no. 102, pp. 355–356.
[42] McCoog, 'Religious life'; cf. Gibson, *Social History*, pp. 49–52.

involvement in 'marital and domestic arguments'.[43] A memorial in 1630, codifying the rules which, in theory, governed Jesuit missioners' lives in England, set out ways of avoiding conflict with patrons. As McCoog remarks, 'no matter how great the cause, no Jesuit should ever complain to his host about food and lodging'. And there were strict warnings against 'involvement both in the management of the house and the inner workings of the marriage'.[44]

But the Jesuits' opponents frequently alleged that the religious did not balk at such meddling. The involvement of the Jesuits in such disputes was, as the secular clergy's correspondence and newsletters during the 1620s and 1630s make clear, used to fuel accusations that the religious disrupted the life of the Catholic community. In 1636 the Jesuit Henry More forwarded to Rome various complaints against the Society, notably concerning the Jesuits' allegedly 'excessive involvement in the financial affairs of laymen'.[45] Of course, the Society's general congregations did legislate on such issues (though their deliberations and decisions were obviously not limited to England alone). But, as far as many leading secular clergymen were concerned, here was evidence which showed that the loose life and morals of the regulars not only set Catholics against each other but also gave public scandal and turned people away from the Catholic Church back towards the Church of England. This was a dreadful distortion of the 'conversion of England', which was the proper function of the Catholic missionary clergy.

In this context, it is possible to see the English Jesuits' annual letters not just as upbeat reports of the Society's activities in their own country, but also as carefully crafted polemical replies to their enemies' accusations. At the Jesuits' residence at Clerkenwell in March 1628, government searchers seized, among other papers, a list of points to be incorporated in the Society's annual report for the English province. This list included not just numbers of baptisms and 'generall confessions', but also how many had been reconciled and converted, in particular 'straunge and notable conversions'; 'how many have bene recalled or kept from taking the oath [of allegiance] or falling otherwise'; 'what p[ar]ticuler benefitts have happened for the good of the Society'; 'how many have bene directed to the seminaryes, or religious howses, men or women'; 'how many prisoners, or what p[er]secution hath befallen us or our freinds'; and 'what reliefe prisoners or pore Catholikes have had by our meanes'; 'what good example or edification hath bene given by us or our freindes in life

---

[43] McCoog, 'Religious life'.
[44] Ibid.
[45] Ibid.

or death'; and 'what opinion the Society hath in those [...] parts'; 'what charity or almes hath bene given to the Society'; and 'how many attonm[en]ts have bene made by those who were at dissension'.[46] The results of such surveys would inevitably be taken, by a significant section of the Catholic community, as direct challenges to the claims of the pro-episcopal lobby which had often implied that the religious, and the Jesuits in particular, did none of these things properly, if at all.

The accounts written by the hierarchalist clergy of devout and selfless secular priests serving large numbers of all social ranks or classes (while, implicitly or explicitly, we are led to understand that the religious avoided such service) were themselves generated by the logic of the controversies between these factions, as each tried to represent itself as the true basis for a rebuilding of the Catholic Church in England. We can see this clearly in e.g. Thomas Green's well-known memorandum of 1635 (printed as *Letter 78*). Of the Jesuit, Thomas Keel, Green noted that he 'calls himselfe the pore mans p[riest] and takes at tymes a long circuite', but the fact remained, said Green, that he 'performeth not well that office', because he inconveniently turned up on 'working days', 'well horst', and because 'his fashion of habitt suteth not with [...] Gods pore'. Here was the classic indictment, first perfected during the notorious 'appellant' controversy, of the, as it were, 'society' Jesuit, too much on his high horse, or here, literally, on a horse, to have even the faintest understanding of the spiritual needs, crude as they might be, of the labouring poor. In the polemical context that Green wrote, the fact that it was equally hard to imagine Richard Smith or his well-born agents and officials, John Southcot, George Leyburn *et al.*, in this role of the poor man's priest seems to have been neither here nor there.

As we have already mentioned, the polemical and ideological significance of the feud among English Catholics over Richard Smith's authority was not confined within the boundaries of the English Catholic community. The debates and quarrels about Smith's powers both fed into and fed off similar debates and quarrels raging in the contemporary French Church. Smith and his enemies both had patrons among the French clergy and they appealed to them for support. They represented their own concerns as part of the larger struggle between a contemporary species of gallican sentiment and a virulent ultramontane critique of that sentiment. Smith's cause, championed by English writers such as Matthew Kellison, was taken up by French gallican theorists in order to attack the papalist Jesuits.[47]

[46] Foley, I, pp. 127–128.
[47] Allison, RSGB, I, p. 330.

It was crucial for Smith to win, and be seen to win, the plaudits of those French clergymen who could be taken, by at least some English Protestants, as representative of a national Church which, though Roman Catholic, was not antithetical to the English one.[48] What French churchmen wrote in his favour was circulated in England. In August 1632, Southcot noted that twenty copies of a tract by the Abbé de Saint-Cyran (Jean Duvergier de Hauranne) which supported Smith had been brought across from France and were now being distributed via the secular clergy's network.[49]

But English Catholics' interest in mainland Europe was not limited to the concerns of their gallican friends. As Antony Allison has shown, the approbation controversy of the later 1620s was a continuation of the political passions aroused among Catholics by the Stuart regime's negotiations with the Spaniards and the French in the early 1620s (leading, finally, to the Anglo-French dynastic treaty of 1624–1625, and the marriage of Charles to Henrietta Maria). The opportunity for improving the political fortunes of English Catholics had been raised by the prospect of one dynastic match, with Spain. But the desired amelioration of their situation was then (in part) achieved by a completely different treaty, i.e. with the French. This fractured the political coherence of the Catholic community in a way that would not have happened if the accommodation with the State for which all Catholics hoped had been achieved via the attempt to forge an alliance with Spain. As we might expect, the new authority claimed by Bishop Smith came to be seen as an adjunct of a royal foreign policy which increasingly was viewed by some English Protestants as a betrayal of the pan-European Protestant cause. Ironically, it was also believed by many Catholics to be contrary to the interests of the Spaniards who, they thought, alone had the true interests of English Catholics at heart. In the 1630s the spectacle of Catholic powers pitted against each other, as the Thirty Years War dragged on, allowed the different English clerical factions to accuse each other of confused and misdirected loyalties. In particular, the Jesuits' enemies argued that the Society was criticizing the pope, Urban VIII, for siding with the French against the Habsburgs.[50]

---

[48] For the Laudians' attitudes to the French Church, see Milton, *CR*, pp. 264–269. Anthony Milton shows that, although some English Protestants believed gallican Church theory was simply a lesser version of the general evils represented by the Church of Rome, others, such as Richard Montagu, took its moderation, or at least aversion to high papalism, to represent the basis for a reunion between the Church of England and the Church of Rome.

[49] See *Letter 25*.

[50] See e.g. *Letter 3*. Urban VIII had been nuncio in Paris during the reign of Henri IV; Hibbard, *CI*, p. 42. For perceptions that he was biased against the Habsburgs and the

Catholics and English politics in the 1630s

However, were the jurisdictional concerns of these warring Catholic clerical factions more than a rather minor branch of the relationship between the Caroline regime and the leading European Catholic powers? The answer may well be that they were.

There is, as is well known, a consensus among historians that Catholicism was a substantial cause of the Caroline regime's political difficulties during the 1630s and was partly responsible for its collapse in 1640–1642. Professor Hibbard's superb monograph, *Charles I and the Popish Plot*, shows that there appeared, to many contemporaries, to be convincing proof of a 'popish' conspiracy to subvert substantial areas of the law and, of course, the crown's stewardship of the Church of England. Kevin Sharpe concedes that 'what perhaps alone served to connect the religious issues of 1640–2' with William Laud and the Caroline regime 'was the fear of popery', and 'more than anything else it was the solvent that eroded trust in the king'.[51] But Professor Sharpe calls this 'paranoia'. He suggests that it was ridiculous for John Pym (and many others) to characterize Laud as a covert papist. And, indeed, it is hard to see the general run of English Catholics as any kind of fifth column. Allegations of 'popery' look, primarily, like a running commentary on the regime's supposed mishandling of foreign policy, the rise of 'Arminianism' and a host of other 'commonwealth' issues.

It is therefore worth asking again, and trying to explain, why such Catholics as the ones who wrote and featured in the newsletters printed in this volume were, in fact, part of the 'popery' equation in the 1630s. One reason was that their aims and ambitions clearly coincided with what many historians have seen as a series of new, even revolutionary, directions in royal, and especially royal ecclesiastical, policy-making in the 1630s, even though, as is clear from these letters, it is not the case that the Catholic pro-episcopal lobby suddenly threw themselves into the arms of the Laudians or were even necessarily personally acceptable to Laud and like-minded Church-of-England men.

Rather, as contemporaries themselves observed, the ideological circumstances and assumptions of certain sections of the English Catholic community and certain sections of the Church of England's clergy started, in the 1630s, to look distinctly analogous. Anthony Milton has demonstrated how many disputes and debates within the

---

imperial cause, see Albion, *CI*, pp. 160, 177–178. But, as Hibbard points out, with France's engagement in the Thirty Years war against the Habsburgs involving financial pressure on the French clergy for increased tax contributions, the curia became increasingly less Francophile in the second half of the 1630s; Hibbard, *CI*, p. 47.

[51] Sharpe, *PR*, pp. 938, 939.

Church of England at this time took the Roman Church as a focal point. Those who wanted to put, what for shorthand purposes might be called, an anti-Calvinist or avant-garde conformist case naturally played up certain positive aspects of the relationship between the two Churches which much English Protestant polemical thought tended to describe entirely negatively.[52] Certainly, the structure of political conflict within the English Catholic community invited Smith, and those who sympathized with him, to make comparisons between their ideals and those of conformist Church-of-England clergy who were trying to bring about extensive changes in the discipline and the doctrine of the established Church.

Of course, those comparisons were not, of themselves, necessarily 'true'. However, when certain Catholics decoded the rhetoric of clergymen such as Laud, they accurately concluded that there was enough in such rhetoric for them to be able to claim that all their interests and concerns were in some sense in alignment, and that the Caroline regime could take this as a sign that Catholicism was now both an acceptable, and even desirable, force to be, if not quite incorporated, then at least positively tolerated within the wider, monarchically-governed English Church, as well as around the person of the sovereign himself.

After Smith had been forced into exile, his friends continued to lobby the privy council and powerful courtiers. Not all members of the regime who were thus approached were likely to be sympathetic to the, allegedly Francophile, secular clergy leadership. Sir Richard Weston and Sir Francis Cottington were generally regarded as Hispanophiles and were probably hostile to Smith's pretensions.[53] Cottington was regarded as a friend of the Society.[54] But John Southcot believed that they should be lobbied as hard as any other councillor. Smith himself petitioned Weston over the travails of Jean Arismendy (a retainer of the 3rd Viscount Montague) in 1633.[55]

One privy councillor in whom they enthusiastically placed their confidence was Edward Sackville, 4th earl of Dorset.[56] At the end of June 1634, the aged priest, John Colleton, formerly one of Smith's

---

[52] Milton, CR.

[53] See e.g. Letters 9, 17; AAW, A XXVI, no. 86, p. 237. For Weston's and Cottington's political relationship, see Havran, CC, ch. 6f, and esp. ch. 10, and p. 123. For their position at the centre of the 'Spanish faction' in the 1630s, see A.J. Loomie, 'The Spanish faction at the court of Charles I, 1630–8', BIHR, 59 (1986), pp. 37–49.

[54] AAW, B 27, no. 101. For Cottington's crypto-Catholicism, see Havran, CC, p. 77. Cottington's brother, Edward (d. 1602), had joined the Jesuit novitiate; ibid., p. 3.

[55] See Letters 52, 53.

[56] For an assessment of the 4th earl of Dorset's religious opinions, see D.L. Smith, 'Catholic, Anglican or puritan? Edward Sackville, 4th earl of Dorset and the ambiguities of

officials, dined with Dorset. Dorset told Colleton that he sympathized with Smith's position, and indeed had kept him from harm. Allegedly, Dorset believed that the 'puretans did not persecute the byshop soe much as the regulars did'.[57] (Here the pro-episcopal lobby could proudly point to a prominent member of Henrietta Maria's circle mouthing that much-repeated dictum from appellant times onwards – namely that the English Catholics' troubles were caused principally by the ill humours within their own community rather than by the malice of the State.)

Dorset intervened in the notorious Worthington–Parkins marriage dispute, a case which was recorded in its full and disgusting details by John Southcot and George Leyburn. Dorset could be admired here as an agent of royal justice who was, in effect, enforcing the discipline which a Catholic bishop should and would exercise over English Catholics if only he were allowed to. (Smith remarked that 'if no [episcopal] justice be setled there, men will seek justice at heretiks hands'.)[58]

In 1633, during the fuss over the satirical anti-regular play, *Hierarchomachia or the Anti-Bishop*, Smith noted with glee how some privy councillors had actually thought well of the piece. Although it had not been published as such, the Jesuits' friends 'prosecute the matter hotely at the councel table, and have brought thither one who was 8 years a Jesuit and priest for to know of him who is the author'.[59] But their malice backfired, Smith observed in June, for 'the Jesuits, having got a copie of the comedie, spred it but to their shame, and giving one to the councel, hoping therby to get the author punished, the councel recreated them selves with the comedie, and wil have it plaied in Oxford'.[60]

With other prominent royal servants it was more difficult to argue that they naturally sympathized with Catholics. One such was William Laud, whose rise and rise consistently fascinated the secular clergy. They had, of course, no real illusions about Laud's attitudes to Rome. They lamented in May 1636 that, when Cottington was urging Charles not to compel court Catholics to take the oath of allegiance, Laud weighed in to tell Charles that they should definitely be coerced into

religion in early Stuart England', *Transactions of the Royal Historical Society*, 6th series, 2 (1992), pp. 105–24.

[57] *Letter 61*.
[58] AAW, A XXVII, no. 61, p. 179. For the Worthington–Parkins case, see *Letters 9, 10, 11*.
[59] AAW, B 27, no. 118.
[60] AAW, B 27, no. 121.

taking it.[61] As the Venetians noted, what Laud's critics interpreted as his quasi-Romanism was not how Laud interpreted the beliefs and practices which he wished to inculcate into the English Church.[62] But this did not mean that it was not possible for Catholics to represent Laud as, at the very least, 'a religione Catholica [. . .] haud aversi'.[63] In 1632, Southcot observed how the new secretary of State, Sir Francis Windebank, who was so favourable to Catholics, had achieved his promotion by Laud's means as well as Weston's.[64] Colleton affected to believe that Laud was not unsympathetic to the Catholics who wanted to see a bishop restored in the realm.[65]

Catholics, the queen, and the court

More important, for Catholics, than any individual councillor was, of course, the queen. Several scholars have remarked on the religious pluralism of Henrietta's entourage. Known for her often rather pushy

---

[61] *Letter 60.* For the political friction between Laud, on the one hand, and Cottington and Weston, on the other, see Havran, *CC*, p. 89, and *passim*. Havran notes that Laud accused Weston and Cottington of being overly lax towards Catholics; *ibid.*, p. 121.

[62] The Venetian ambassador, Anzolo Correr, observed in May 1637 that although Laud 'is pronounced by the generality to be the protector of the Catholic party' because he 'not only does nothing against them, but [. . .] seems to make a very close approach to the rites of the Roman Church', 'the well informed know that his aims are very different, and [. . .] he lets things run with their present freedom not from inclination but from a forced connivance'. This was because 'he aims at destroying the party of the puritans, which has grown so much as to cause apprehension to the government. In order to abase them he can only adhere to those forms which are most objectionable to them'; *CSPV, 1636–1639*, p. 217. See also *ibid.*, pp. 151, 358. (For a good evocation of Laud's attitude to conformity, and hatred of 'puritanism', see Sharpe, *PR*, pp. 288–292.) For Laud's attitude to the Church of Rome, and his efforts to strike anti-Romish poses, see e.g. Albion, *CI*, pp. 188–189, ch. 9; Hibbard, *CI*, pp. 6–7. The archbishop, at his trial, cited the occasions when he had persuaded Catholics to convert to the Church of England. And, at various times, he enforced the law against recusants, protested about Catholics at court (and particularly about courtiers' conversions to Rome), tried to take the eldest sons of Catholics to be bred up as Protestants, restricted the circulation of Catholic books, and even arrested the occasional priest, and, finally, attacked Catholics via the canons of 1640; Hibbard, *CI*, pp. 58, 257, 261; Milton, *CR*, pp. 86–87; Sharpe, *PR*, pp. 305–306, 648–649; *CSPD, 1637*, p. 78; *CSPV, 1636–1639*, p. 359. Sharpe argues that the claim that Laud was a crypto-Catholic 'is a charge completely without foundation' because 'Laud proceeded vigorously against recusants in the country and at court, and alienated the queen by his outspoken opposition to the attendance of English Catholics at her private chapel'; Sharpe, *PR*, p. 285.

[63] AAW, A XXVIII, no. 5, p. 23.

[64] *Letter 17.* For Windebank, see Hibbard, *CI*, p. 34. Windebank was the primary instrument for securing liberty and protection for priests from the operation of the penal statutes, Hibbard, *CI*, pp. 41–42. For the protection warrant issued by Windebank in February 1636 for Southcot, see AAW, A XXVIII, no. 91. In May 1635 Leyburn noted how two priests had recently been arrested, but were released again, and Windebank sent for one of the pursuivants involved, and 'did chid[e] him fearefully'; *Letter 72.*

[65] *Letter 34.*

Catholicism, she nevertheless extended her patronage beyond her Catholic friends and retainers. One of her court favourites was the earl of Holland, who, on many contemporary accounts, was a puritan.[66] Holland was one of a group of hot Protestant, or puritan, notables who, by 1635/1636, felt that even a France which had quite recently crushed the Huguenots was a necessary ally in the fight against the Empire and Spain. These included Robert Rich, earl of Warwick; Francis Russell, earl of Bedford; and members of the Providence Island Company (such as John Pym, John Hampden, Lord Brooke, and Viscount Saye and Sele). Holland was a 'court link' for Warwick and other proponents of a French alliance who did not have such immediate access at the court.[67] As Hibbard shows, this group engaged in an entirely traditional commonwealth polemic, which included a fair dose of anti-popery. They stressed the wisdom of calling parliament; their capacity to help the crown to the levels of financial supply that it required; and the need to reform the Church of England (and get rid of Laudian innovation).

We might not expect Catholic suitors for the favour of the queen to be particularly enthusiastic about her entertainment of such people. But, as Hibbard also demonstrates, Henrietta attracted other supporters of a French alliance who were not so thoroughly opposed to Laud, anti-Spanish but not actual zealots, and not so committed to calling parliament. These people were essentially an aristocratic entourage based on the Percy family, and included Robert Sidney, earl of Leicester.[68] This group was a more pleasing prospect for Catholic observers. The earl of Leicester was one of Richard Smith's contacts in Paris. The earl served there as an ambassador in 1636, and advocated closer diplomatic and military Anglo-French ties (for the purpose of regaining the Palatinate for Charles Louis).[69]

---

[66] R.M. Smuts, 'The puritan followers of Henrietta Maria in the 1630s', *English Historical Review*, 93 (1978), pp. 26–45; Sharpe, *PR*, pp. 164–165.

[67] Robert Philip, Henrietta Maria's Oratorian chaplain, pointed out to Gregorio Panzani that the queen 'se la teneva più con li puritani, che con li Protestanti', but this was only because of her hatred of Weston; VA, PD, fo. 49r.

[68] Hibbard, *CI*, pp. 32–33.

[69] *Letter 75*; Sharpe, *PR*, pp. 525f; Hibbard, *CI*, p. 73. As Sharpe points out, Leicester did not see eye to eye with Viscount Scudamore, the resident ambassador, who was also a confidant of Smith. For Scudamore, see I. Atherton, 'Viscount Scudamore's "Laudianism": The religious practices of the first Viscount Scudamore', *Historical Journal*, 34 (1991), pp. 567–596, esp. pp. 587–588, 590–591; *idem, Ambition and Failure in Stuart England* (Manchester, 1999), ch. 6.

The 'French option' in British foreign policy drew support from several different points on the spectrum of contemporary English/British political opinion, both Catholic and Protestant. It allowed Catholics an *entrée* into the deliberations of court and council where, in other circumstances, they might not have been expected to have had a voice. Henrietta

The Catholic secular clergy's newsletters of this period show how the queen was approached as a patron and supporter of their projects and ambitions.[70] Smith, of course, was one of Richelieu's chaplains, and he had expected to benefit personally and politically from the peace concluded with France in 1629. Considering how much Henrietta basically disliked Richelieu, it is easy to see why the pro-episcopal lobby's Catholic enemies should have chosen to blacken Smith's name by harping on the close personal link between him and the cardinal. Smith's associates, however, consistently represented the Jesuits and their friends as Hispanophiles and enemies of the Queen.[71] A report compiled by the seculars to be sent to Rome alleged that

Maria was never one of Cardinal Richelieu's most enthusiastic supporters, but the death of Lord Treasurer Weston in 1635, and the real possibility of some kind of alliance with France to assert the young elector Charles Louis's claim to the Palatinate, led to a spectacular U-turn on Henrietta's part. She decided to support Richelieu, partly in order to see her mother Marie de Médicis, one of Richelieu's severest critics, honourably repatriated, and partly because the now open war between Bourbon and Habsburg reduced Henrietta's freedom to deal with Hispanophiles at the English court; Sharpe, *PR*, p. 538. Sharpe notes how the 'Spanish' faction at court and on the council fragmented, with Cottington intimating that he was open-minded about the possibility of doing a deal with France; *ibid.*, pp. 539–540. By 1635 the French were fully committed to fighting the Habsburgs. (A formal declaration of war was made in Valencia on 29 April/9 May 1635; *ibid.*, *PR*, p. 510.) In 1635 the arrival in England of a new French ambassador, Henri de Ferté Nabert, marquis de Senneterre, was the occasion and means of arranging *détente* between Henrietta and the cardinal; and Henrietta started to urge English participation in the war; Smuts, 'Puritan followers', pp. 35, 38. It was only later, when the negotiations for some more permanent Anglo-French diplomatic and military understanding came to nothing, that Richelieu's enemies were able to take advantage of the disintegration of the British Isles' internal political coherence. In 1637, as the Scots rebelled, Henrietta realigned herself so as to support the intrigues against the cardinal and started to agitate on Spain's behalf, and (with the arrival in England of Marie de Médicis and then of Strafford) the queen's 'puritan' friends were finally discomfited; Smuts, 'Puritan followers', pp. 41–43; Sharpe, *PR*, pp. 175, 837f.

[70] In 1631, George Leyburn, via the good will and recommendations of Henrietta's closest clerical advisers, notably Robert Philip and William Thompson OFM, was in effect installed as one of her chaplains. He was sworn 'provisor' of her chapel on 9 August (though this was a purely formal appointment); Anstr., II, p. 193; BL, Harleian MS 1219, no. 108, fos 373r–v, 374r. He does not appear on any of the queen's establishment or pension lists. (I am very grateful to Caroline Hibbard for this point.) In early 1641, when a list of exemptions was being compiled after the king was forced to agree to the exile (before 7 April 1641) of all Catholic clergy except for the queen's chaplains, those who figured prominently on this list included Leyburn, and the secular priest George Gage, who was the secretary of the secular clergy's episcopal chapter; Hibbard, *CI*, p. 186. Walter Montagu's additions to the list included Anthony Champney and six other priests who were members of the chapter, implying that they were in some sense regarded as being in Henrietta's service; Anstr., II, p. 122; Hibbard, *CI*, p. 191. Montagu had claimed, in March 1637, that Peter Biddulph, Smith's agent in Rome, would receive a pension directly from the queen; AAW, A XXIX, no. 15, p. 31.

[71] As Loomie points out, the Peace of Madrid (1630), negotiated with the Spaniards, was predicated on a Spanish acceptance that there was nothing they could do now to assist the English Catholics. Olivares had, in July 1630, received advice from John Knatchbull (one

the Jesuits 'affect not the person of our most religious and Catholike queene as appeareth by the perpetuall muttering against her of their cheif adherents; and calling her the head of the puritan faction'.[72] Smith, however, informed Biddulph in November 1632 that Robert Philip

> [...] told me that she never missed daye to heare Masse since she came to England, but the twoe dayes of her deliverie of child. That everie moneth she confessed and communicated besides other principal feasts, and that she told him that she never had the least tentation to change her religion. Fie upon such admirations. Who can be free from them if such a queene be not?[73]

Whether they were imps of Richelieu or not, the pro-episcopal lobby worked hard to influence the queen. They expected her to campaign on their behalf at Rome, and she did. They made every attempt to cultivate her Scottish Oratorian confessor, Robert Philip (although they were hostile to some of her Capuchin chaplains). Philip seems to have been consistently supportive of Smith and his friends.

In mid-1636 Sir William Hamilton was sent to Rome to function as a diplomat there on behalf of the queen (in place of the deceased Arthur Brett).[74] In Rome, Hamilton's first audience with the pope was a great success, and Cardinal Francesco Barberini presented him with a gift of '2 very fair horses for his coach'. Hamilton kept correspondence with Windebank by means of the Benedictines' letter-carrying network.[75] Smith and his friends believed that Hamilton would negotiate at Rome on their behalf, though, as Smith learned in August 1636, Hamilton would not do so without specific instructions from the queen.[76]

---

of the enemies of the pro-episcopal lobby) that although Philip IV was the true protector of English Catholics, Henrietta Maria was beginning to exert a claim over those Catholics' loyalties, 'and would even do them harm' if they continued to look to Spain. Prominent Catholics told Knatchbull that it was in their best interests to conceal their Hispanophile tendencies altogether; A.J. Loomie, 'Olivares, the English Catholics and the peace of 1630', *Revue Belge de Philologie d'Histoire*, 47 (1969), pp. 1154–1166, quotation at p. 1162. Henrietta was noted by George Con as saying in January 1637 that the English Catholics, meaning, of course, those who were Hispanophiles, 'would think little of Heaven itself, unless they got it at the hands of Spain'; Albion, *CI*, p. 164.

[72] AAW, A XXV, no. 98, p. 369; cf. Smuts, 'Puritan followers'.

[73] AAW, B 27, no. 132.

[74] Albion, *CI*, pp. 154f. For the issues which Brett, as agent, was directed, by the king (though he went as the representative only of the queen), to deal with principally – the question of the appointment of a bishop, and the oath of allegiance, see *ibid.*, pp. 155–156. As Albion points out, Sir William Hamilton was brother of the earl of Abercorn, and a relative of the marquis of Hamilton, the duke of Lennox, and the king himself; *ibid.*, p. 157.

[75] AAW, A XXVIII, no. 139, p. 467; *Letter 83*.

[76] AAW, A XXVIII, no. 151, p. 509. One of Hamilton's functions in Rome was to persuade the papal curia, especially Cardinal Barberini, that the oath of allegiance demanded nothing

In return a series of papal representatives was dispatched to Henrietta Maria–Gregorio Panzani, George Con, and Carlo Rossetti. The first two in particular became a prime focus for the secular clergy leadership's attention. Panzani was well liked by the seculars; they regarded him as no friend to the Society.[77] Con, however, was viewed by them in a different light. The seculars sometimes complained that he listened too much to the Jesuits. However, for Con to keep, as he did, in Charles's good books, it would have been very difficult for him to evince any kind of overt sympathy towards the Society. (From time to time, the seculars themselves affected to believe that he was opposed to the Jesuits' ambitions.)[78]

Clearly, the papal agents had concerns and issues to consider other than the factional disputes among the English Catholic clergy. Panzani, in particular, is well known for having pushed his curial masters towards considering the possibility of reunion of the Church of England with the Church of Rome.[79] Panzani and Con were both very keen to report every sign that the culture of the English Church had changed, and that Charles had decisively rejected much of his Jacobean ecclesiastical inheritance. Every irenic sermon, every uncensured Catholic-sounding doctrine, every insult flung at the 'puritans', every glance cast favourably by Charles towards his Catholic subjects, the Catholic ambassadors in London, or towards Rome itself, were all picked up on, committed to paper, and then sealed up to be sent to Rome. Here, of course, the papal agents were doing much the same kind of thing as the English Catholics, who were reporting that the regime had turned a tolerant corner, and that the ecclesiastical temper of the Church of England was now markedly less anti-popish than it had formerly been. Undoubtedly, English Catholics and the papal agents fed off each other's enthusiasm for the new order of things. Many of the 'advices', preserved in the secular clergy's Roman agent's papers, which describe the allegedly tolerant climate of the 1630s, are very similar to Panzani's and Con's reports; they may even have been written in part to assist the papal agents' work.[80]

---

more than temporal loyalty, and to explore whether Rome might be persuaded to recognize it as a lawful oath; Albion, *CI*, p. 264.

[77] Panzani was more pro-active in pushing for the restoration of Smith, or at least some secular priest in episcopal orders, to rule over the English Catholics; *CSPV, 1636–1639*, pp. 68, 69, 302.

[78] See e.g. AAW, A XXVIII, no. 177, p. 571; no. 178, p. 575; *Letter 80*.

[79] Albion, *CI*, ch. 7.

[80] Hibbard, *CI*, pp. 66–67.

Catholic loyalism and the oath of allegiance

During the mid-1630s, there were several high-level attempts to modify the oath of allegiance in order to make it acceptable to English Catholics and to Rome. The Benedictine monk, Leander Jones, tried to hammer out a compromise on the oath, and several Catholics (including the 2nd Baron Baltimore and Sir Tobie Mathew) devised new formulations of the oath which they believed Charles might also find admissible.[81] This bargaining process did not, initially, bear fruit, at least not in any formal sense. The alterations to the oath which Charles suggested in negotiation with George Con were not well received at Rome, as the king probably anticipated. The Catholics who tried to frame variations of the oath inevitably ran into royal demands that they should concede more than they were in fact prepared to do. Simultaneously, they ran the gauntlet of criticism from co-religionists who tended to claim that they made too many concessions to the regime. As Gordon Albion points out, in early March 1638 a long accusatory letter had been received by the committee in Rome which was considering the question of a joint papal-monarchical revision of the 1606 oath. The letter was very hostile to Con himself, who had got as far as any Catholic ever had in moderating the demands made of Catholics by the crown over the question of allegiance.[82]

The secular clergy leadership's public position on the oath was that it ought not to be taken under any circumstances. Their official line was still that Pope Paul V's condemnation of it must be honoured and obeyed. They rejected allegations that they exhibited any weakness on this score. And they attacked the religious and their patrons for cutting and running over this issue.[83] The 2nd Baron Baltimore's variant of the Jacobean oath was described by his critics as, in effect, a capitulation to the State's unjust demands that Catholics should violate their consciences in order to prove their loyalty to the king.[84]

---

[81] See G. Sitwell, 'Leander Jones's mission to England, 1634–1635', *RH*, 5 (1960), pp. 132–182; VA, PD, fo. 117r.

[82] Albion, *CI*, pp. 272–281.

[83] Smith's friends compiled long lists of those (mainly the religious and their sympathizers) who, they alleged, had compromised over the oath. See e.g. AAW, A XXVIII, no. 68.

[84] See AAW, A XXV, no. 100. This undated document is endorsed 'Lord Baltimores oath', and is a version of the 1606 oath of allegiance. It contains some important modifications. For example, whereas the original oath condemned as 'impious and heretical', 'this damnable doctrine' that 'princes which be excommunicated and deprived by the pope may be deposed or murdered by their subjects' (J.P. Kenyon, *The Stuart Constitution* (London, 1966), p. 459), Baltimore's oath omitted the word 'deposed'. Baltimore was trying to prevent the Catholic's declaration of loyalty to the crown being understood as a condemnation of the papal deposing power. Baltimore, a friend by turns to both Jesuits and seculars, drew up the oath for his Maryland colony; Hughes, *HSJ*, pp. 355–359. Panzani recorded in his diary on

Although the secular clergy were themselves desperate to come to an accommodation with the regime on the question of Catholics' loyalty to the crown,[85] they sought to show that the papacy would never allow their enemies' compromises with the regime, for example those proposed by the 'irenic' monk, Leander Jones. Smith was delighted in July 1632 that Jones was 'dejected in mynde, perhaps becaus[e] his writing in favour of the oathe is not wel taken [. . .] [in Rome] as in truthe it deserveth'.[86] By April 1634 the Benedictines were incensed against Smith and the seculars for attacking Jones's attempted compromises on the oath.[87] The seculars continued to censure Thomas Preston (who, in 1634, under the pseudonym of William Howard, published *A Patterne of Christian Loyalty* in favour of the oath).[88]

The problem, though, was this. If the regime was as broad-minded and ready to compromise on the loyalty issue as some Catholics enthusiastically said it was, to accuse those Catholics of, as it were, betraying the cause actually added to their credit with the regime. What might then transpire was a situation where such people would achieve a genuine understanding with the State, and finally square the loyalism circle. In August 1635 John Southcot was preparing a damage limitation exercise to minimize the benefits which he feared the Jesuits were about to reap by negotiating with the regime over the oath of allegiance.[89]

What was obviously crucial here was the change in personal style which marked Charles off from his father. There was a good deal of semi-public irenicism in the talks between Charles and Con. As Albion remarks, 'Charles's intimacy with the papal agent was no backstairs affair conducted only in the privacy of his own or the queen's apartments'.[90] In other words, even if Charles's alleged admissions (to Con) that the Church of England was arguably schismatic, and that reunion was, if not immediately practicable, then at least theoretically desirable, were more the stuff of light-hearted banter than deep

---

4 December 1635 that George Leyburn came on that day 'a discorrere della formola del Baltimoro'; VA, PD, fo. 121r.

[85] See e.g. *Letter 69*.

[86] AAW, B 27, no. 101. For Leander Jones's attempts to persuade Rome that Charles's intentions in retaining and enforcing the 1606 oath of allegiance were different in kind from those of James I, and so should not be condemned now in the terms employed by Paul V, see Albion, *CI*, pp. 146–147, 255–257.

[87] See *Letter 70*.

[88] See *Letters 60, 64*. For Preston's long career as an apologist for the regime on this issue, see *NAGB*, *passim*; P. Milward, *Religious Controversies of the Jacobean Age* (London, 1978), pp. 103–113.

[89] *Letter 75*; AAW, A XXVIII, no. 33, p. 135; no. 34, p. 137.

[90] Albion, *CI*, p. 236. See also Hibbard, *CI*, p. 50.

theological and ecclesiological discussion, this must unavoidably have created a swirl of rumour and expectation, and perhaps not just among Catholics, that the king really thought along such lines.[91] This must have been the case if Charles was so careless as to drop hints to such prominent Catholics as Edward Somerset, heir to the earl of Worcester, that, as Con related it to Barberini in 1637, 'the oath as it stood contained a scandalous proposition, and that he had to sympathize with those who refused it'. By November 1636, Charles was himself drawing up possible modifications to the oath formula.[92]

'Toleration'

Many contemporaries (and not just Catholics) believed, therefore, that in this period the English Catholic community was edging towards the enjoyment of some kind of official tolerance, even if not necessarily a full legal toleration. Of course, in the 1630s there were still high-profile incidents where the regime looked rather intolerant towards Catholics. Foreign diplomats in London reported fisticuffs and swordplay when the regime tried, as it did in March 1630, to prevent English Catholics from going to the chapels of the Catholic ambassadors in London, and to the queen's chapel as well.[93] In 1633 the Irish friar, Arthur McGeoghan was executed for treasonous words (though clearly Richard Smith, for one, was not heartbroken at the demise of a member of a religious order at the hands of the State).[94]

But, as the 1630s progressed, it became clear not only that many of the Catholic clergy were now enjoying a *de facto* tolerance quite contrary to the intentions of the Elizabethan treason statutes, but also that the system of punishment of Catholic recusants for their nonconformity was changing quite radically. This was because of the introduction of a formal system of compounding for recusancy debts, a system which had been instituted in the later 1620s but which had taken a little time to become established.[95]

Kevin Sharpe argues that the Caroline measures against recusant separatists in the 1630s were not lenient: 'even those recusants who

---

[91] See Albion, *CI*, ch. 10. Hibbard describes very well the 'genuine intimacy' between Charles and Con; Hibbard, *CI*, pp. 17, 38–39, 49.

[92] Albion, *CI*, pp. 264–271. For the negotiations over the oath between Charles and the Roman curia via the two agents, Con and Hamilton, see *ibid.*, ch. 11; Hibbard, *CI*, pp. 69, 265.

[93] *CSPV, 1629–1632*, pp. 304, 308, 314, 315, 319; A.J. Loomie, 'London's Spanish Chapel before and after the Civil War', *RH*, 18 (1987), pp. 402–417, at p. 403.

[94] *Letter 53*; AAW, B 27, no. 113.

[95] For the compounding policy, see Havran, *CC*, pp. 120–121; K.J. Lindley, 'The lay Catholics of England in the reign of Charles I', *Journal of Ecclesiastical History*, 22 (1971), pp. 199–221, at pp. 209–214.

pursued their faith privately and quietly in the country were not left alone'; Charles was 'not prepared to treat recusancy lightly'. For Sharpe, the compounding policy was not just to provide a cash-starved crown with revenue. 'The fines were intended as punishment and disincentive' as well. Sharpe points to some of the well-known recusant family heads whose composition payments were pretty hefty.[96] And Sharpe is undoubtedly right that the amounts which the State derived from compositions for recusants' debts shot up during this period.

But, as the newsletters printed in this volume make clear, the issue here was also about whether the State would, in return for recusants' compositions, do as it promised and call off its attack dogs, the low-life army of private operators who harried recusant Catholics. There was widespread sentiment among Catholics that, whatever the composition arrangements were, they would be worth it if the petty and sometimes brutal harassments by 'pursuivants' and other officials were to be brought to an end. (The deal was also that the continuous exchequer reassessments of recusants' property would stop.)[97]

Some Catholics in the early 1630s complained that the new policy was not being properly implemented.[98] But, by November 1632, Smith was saying that he believed the pursuivants were at last being reined in. Pests such as the self-proclaimed convert from Catholicism, James Wadsworth, were still arresting Catholics, but proceedings against them went no further.[99] In October 1633 Smith believed that the New Prison was 'quite empt[i]ed'. In particular, his friend George Fisher had been released, and in fact any imprisoned priest in London who wanted his liberty could have it.[100] The compounding scheme seemed, at last, to be working.[101]

Of course, precisely what the Catholic community still did not have was a toleration in the sense that most of the community's tolerance discourses had envisaged ever since the accession of James VI in 1603. Even in May 1636, a report compiled by the seculars was compelled to gloss over the occasional harassments of Catholics that were still taking place.[102] But it made political sense for Catholics to characterize the compounding policy as essentially lenient even when certain recusants were having to fork out quite large sums for

---

[96] Sharpe, *PR*, pp. 302–303. For exchequer accounts in the 1630s concerning the composition payments made by Catholics, see PRO, E 101/630/4, 5; PRO, E 101/629/3, 4, 6.

[97] See e.g. AAW, A XXVIII, no. 66, p. 279; *Letter 49*.

[98] See e.g. *Letters 6, 20, 28*; AAW, A XXVI, no. 105, p. 293.

[99] AAW, B 27, no. 113.

[100] AAW, B 27, no. 131.

[101] See e.g. *Letters 32, 41, 44, 45, 49, 51*.

[102] *Letter 79*.

the privilege of being left in peace. (After all, sour puritan critiques of royal policy towards Catholics were saying precisely that it was very lenient.) The Catholic clerical perspective on the issue was, in any case, not primarily concerned with the material wellbeing of individual Catholics. The secular clergy's interest was in the creation of a public climate of tolerance, via political change, in order to persuade Rome that the secular clergy's programme for institutional change and reform within the English Catholic community could be successfully and safely implemented. As Smith wrote to Peter Biddulph in July 1633, 'though we had a cardinal of our nation, yet we should get little' from Rome, 'unles there were present hope of the conversion of our countrie. And, if you remember, my predecessor', William Bishop, 'was made when there was great hope by reason of the Spanish ma[t]ch then treated, and I was made when the French [match] was made, and, unles some such hopeful times come agayne, I doubt you labour in vayne and wil be paid with delaies' by the Roman curia.[103]

The king, the Church of England, the Catholics, and the puritans

This climate of (potential) tolerance, then, was the context for Catholics' accounts of royal sympathy for them. They claimed that the king evinced not just a tolerance of Catholic ideas and practices but also engaged in a biting critique of certain kinds of Protestants within the Church of England. Catholic newsletter writers seized avidly on stories about the king's aversion to puritans. Just before Charles set off for Scotland in March 1633, for a coronation which was conducted along lines which were offensive to the Scottish kirk,[104] he had discoursed on the 'severitie of the Inquisicion', and that 'the Inquisicion was good to keep an uniformitie of religion'.[105] (Smith opined, with the thoughts obviously connected in his mind, that 'there was never greater calme for religion than now, and [. . .] it were the fittest time to send in a [Catholic] bishop'.)[106]

It is not difficult to see why these Catholic clerical *engagés*, with their hierarchalist agenda, should have taken up and repeated so emphatically and enthusiastically the claim that Charles's regime had detected a threat to itself from 'puritans' within the Church of England. For here they were able to tap into and share the 1630s Church-of-England rhetoric of anti-puritanism, at least as it has been described by one school of modern historians. According to these scholars, the Laudians widened the meaning of the word 'puritan',

[103] AAW, B 27, no. 123.
[104] D. Smith, *A History of the Modern British Isles, 1603–1707* (London, 1998), p. 101.
[105] AAW, B 27, no. 117; *Letter 44*.
[106] AAW, B 27, no. 117.

and swept into it practices and attitudes which the alleged 'puritans' would have regarded as merely 'orthodox' and acceptably conformist, but which avant-garde conformists were determined to consign to the dustbin of heresy.[107]

The secular clergy collected and retailed stories that 'puritans' were opposed to Charles's ecclesiastical vision. In October 1633 they tut-tutted at a 'book printed by puritans' against Laud, entitled '*Flagellum Pont.*', the work, of course, of John Bastwick. Earlier in the year, they noted the prosecution of the Feoffees for Impropriations and of Henry Sherfield. In 1637 they applauded the condemnation of Bastwick, Henry Burton, and William Prynne.[108] A famous public occasion on which Catholics believed they could detect royal anti-puritanism was the well-known visit made by the king to Oxford in August 1636, during which Charles and Henrietta watched an explicitly anti-puritan play, written by one of Laud's protégés, incorporating, for example, criticism of those who were opposed to the collection of Ship Money.[109]

These Catholic accounts of the 'puritan' threat to monarchical authority and the ecclesiastical establishment fed neatly into their analysis of their own need for episcopal government. A paper in Peter Biddulph's hand bluntly states that,

> [...] the goverment of the Catholikes by a bishop is conformable to the goverment established in the [...] Church of England, and therefore the Protestant bishops have no reason to be offended with it, especially considering that the Catholike bishop beeing only a titular bishop he standeth in no competencye with them, nor trencheth at all upon their autority.

None would be elected except such as should be thought fit by the king. And the bishop elected would take an oath of allegiance of the kind taken to the crown by former Catholic bishops in England, and by bishops in other Catholic countries, by which oath he would be obliged to discover all disloyal attempts by Catholics. And he would force all priests to take the same oath. 'Lastly he shall make known to his Majestye his arrivall at his first comeing over, and his usuall place of abode in the countrye' so that he could be called to answer at any

---

[107] See N. Tyacke, 'Puritanism, Arminianism and counter-revolution', in Conrad Russell (ed.), *The Origins of the English Civil War* (London, 1973), pp. 119–143; Tyacke, *AC*, p. 186 and *passim*; Hibbard, *CI*, p. 21. For a critique of the same, see J. Davies, *The Caroline Captivity of the Church* (Oxford, 1992), esp. ch. 2; Sharpe, *PR*, ch. 6. Ironically, one of the best accounts of Laud's programme for enforcing conformity in a variety of venues, from the parish upwards, combined with an explanation of how that vision of uniformity of worship was described by Laud himself as an essay in anti-puritanism, is to be found in *ibid.*, pp. 288–292, 649–654.

[108] See *Letters 34, 35, 93*; AAW, B 27, no. 131.

[109] See *Letter 83*. Cf. Sharpe, 'Archbishop Laud', pp. 156–157, 160.

time, and give an account of all priests 'that come from tyme to tyme into England'.[110]

Catholics argued that moderate Protestants should not only find nothing offensive here but should positively welcome these Catholic efforts to reinstitute episcopacy within the Catholic community. Such efforts were analogous to the reform programme currently being implemented in the Church of England.

Another issue where self-proclaimed Catholic enthusiasts for hierarchalist conformity and episcopal government could draw a contrast between their own loyalism and the alleged disloyalty of those Protestant critics of the crown who claimed that the Caroline regime was resorting to unwarranted innovations in the practice of government was the question of royal revenue. Picking up on the religious overtones of the quarrels in the parliaments of the late 1620s about the extent and limits of royal revenue-raising powers, some Catholics intimated that a Catholic bishop would side with the king in such disputes. In one position paper of 1634, alongside all the good 'commonwealth' effects which it was alleged a Catholic bishop would have (everything from the suppression of 'excesse [...] drinking' to the prevention of 'inordinat recourse to forreine ambassadors'), it was added that 'a Catholick bishop, being tolerated by the State, by his gravity and authority may perswade Catholickes, more forcibly than any other can, to graunt extraordinary contributions or benevolences when they shalbe required for the supply of his Majest[i]es [...] occasions'.[111]

The main point, therefore, of this stream of Catholic advice to the Caroline regime was that the enemies of the Caroline vision for the Church of England and the enemies of loyalist Catholics were substantially the same. The Catholic avant-garde conformists also identified 'puritans' in their own community. In another advice paper, compiled to demonstrate the wisdom of tolerating a restored Catholic episcopate in England, it was alleged that 'as the State and Church of England have ever thought it fitt to maintaine hierarchicall government against the puritans, so may it be thought lickwise behoofull, in regard of safty, to permitt the Catholicks to have their hierarchie also supported by a bishop against the opposers thereof'.[112] It was even possible to allege that the shape and structure of the Church of England were to be commended precisely because the Henrician Reformation had wiped out the religious houses and their

---

[110] AAW, A XXIV, no. 43, pp. 138–139. See also *Letter 67*.

[111] *Letter 67*.

[112] AAW, A XXVII, no. 207, p. 731, cited in *Letter 67*.

parasitic privileges. In March 1632 John Jackson reflected at length on the misdemeanours of the religious and concluded that

> [. . .] it is a great greif to many of us to think of the time we spende in bemoaning our selves one to an other, in complayning to superiors in petitioning, in defending our selves from their slanders in informing etc., all which we might fruitfully bestowe in reading, studying, writing or converting of sowles or defending our religion etc. And it is a shame to see what bookes and volumes the Protestants set owt, of sermons, discourses of pietie, according to their maner, and how they imploy their time in learning, because they have noe regulars in their religion to troble them or hinder them, as our regulars doe us.[113]

We find Richard Smith writing, on 26 March/25 April 1635, to Archbishop William Laud himself in order to emphasize what he and Laud had in common, and where their common interest lay.[114] Among the other Church-of-England men whom the Catholic pro-episcopal lobby regarded as allies was Brian Duppa. In April 1635 George Leyburn enthused about a recent sermon by Duppa in front of the king, on Good Friday, the day after Duppa became tutor to Prince Charles.[115] Not surprisingly, Richard Montagu (who, of course, was known to be anti-Jesuit) was viewed in a similarly favourable light by the English Catholics who most admired Laud's style of Church government.[116]

Smith and his friends claimed to believe that the realignments and epistemic shifts which they perceived in the upper echelons of the Caroline Church were not in fact limited to a few senior churchmen at court. Southcot recorded stories about disgruntled and disappointed university men and provincial clergy who held the same opinions.[117] In addition, Smith's friends collected and played up the news of more general changes in attitudes towards doctrine, church fabric, and the sacraments (especially confession).[118]

A long report, compiled by the seculars in 1636, on the condition of the Church of England, constitutes an accurate guide to the political significance of all these scattered observations.[119] The writer wanted

---

[113] AAW, A XXVI, no. 33, p. 107.

[114] *Letter 71.*

[115] See *Letter 70.*

[116] For Gregorio Panzani's discussions with Richard Montagu, see Albion, *CI*, p. 182. In the secular clergy's Roman agent's papers there is an account of one of Panzani's meetings with Richard Montagu; AAW, A XXVII, no. 182. The account incorporates a description of Montagu's London chapel.

[117] *Letter 17.*

[118] See *Letters 48, 49, 50, 61.* For the best modern evocation of the collective ideological thinking behind the 'beauty-of-holiness' aspects of Laudianism, see P. Lake, 'The Laudian style', in K. Fincham (ed.), *The Early Stuart Church* (London, 1993), pp. 161–185, at pp. 164–168.

[119] *Letter 79.*

to portray a Church which had changed so utterly, and so quickly too, as to be virtually unrecognizable from the Jacobean one. Here, for his own purposes, the writer of this report is reproducing some of the essential catch-phrases about puritanism which were uttered at the extreme end of the avant-garde conformist/'Arminian'/Laudian spectrum. As Peter Lake writes, 'it is only when the Laudian project', in the sense of its positive liturgical claims and innovations, 'is set over against this polemically constructed image of puritan deviance and subversion that the full polemical and political resonance of the Laudian project can be recovered'.[120] The same sort of conclusion could quite reasonably be drawn about the English secular clergy's account of the, as it were, 'nonconformist' tendencies of those who opposed the hierarchalist programme for reform and renewal of the Catholic Church's structures in post-Reformation England.

In some ways, none of this should surprise us. After all, for years, Catholic commentators had been looking for signs of splits and dissensions in the higher reaches of the established Church. The hierarchalist secular clergy desperately wanted to show that some 'moderate' Church-of-England men were moving closer to Rome on some issues. Occasionally they allowed themselves to speculate about how 'further union and reconciliation' might take place.[121] But what is significant here is that these secular clergy newsletter writers do not use evidence of this kind of rapprochement simply to anticipate the reunion of the Churches. Indeed, the topic of reunion, at least as it was discussed by clerics such as the Franciscan Christopher Davenport, generally got short shrift from the pro-episcopal priests. Where they do mention the ideas and writings of Davenport it is usually with derision.[122] The seculars were well aware that Laud was not in favour of talk about reunification.[123]

---

[120] Lake, 'The Laudian style', p. 180.

[121] See *Letter 79*.

[122] For Davenport, see Dockery, *CD*. The seculars attacked Davenport for too easily reconciling the two religions (even while their own memoranda and advice papers to Gregorio Panzani and others said that the new conformist outlook in the Church of England was potentially compatible with the religion of the Church of Rome). In April 1633, Southcot believed Davenport's approach would hinder conversions to Catholicism; *Letter 44*. Panzani reported, evidently on the basis of advice which he was being fed by the secular clergy, that Davenport's famous tract, *Deus, Natura, Gratia*, was regarded by some as 'far too condescending to schismatics and heretics'; Dockery, *CD*, p. 76. Although Laud refused to licence Davenport's book, Leyburn believed that the State would take advantage of its admissions that, in effect, Catholics both admitted that Protestants practised true religion and conceded the validity of the Church of England's ministry and orders; *Letter 59*.

[123] Contact with Davenport placed Laud and his protégés, such as Jeremy Taylor, in an uncomfortable position. Laud tried to deny at his trial that he had ever had much dealing with Davenport; Dockery, *CD*, pp. 81, 54, 59–60; cf. *ibid.*, p. 91.

So the hope, entertained quite seriously by such people as Gregorio Panzani, of an ever closer union between the two Churches, was not really the issue for the most committed of the Catholic clergy who meddled at the court and had access to the ear of the queen and also of a number of cardinals at Rome. What they saw and enthused about was the impact of the Laudian shifting of the boundaries of what was considered orthodox belief in the Church of England, and the way in which conformity was glossed and enforced. Here they saw opportunities not so much to assist some grand but ultimately rather fanciful reunification project but rather to assert and justify their own dominance within the Catholic community by stressing, ironically, how much they shared certain conformist ideals with the 'best' kind of Church-of-England clergy, and by extension the king, thus proving their loyalty to the regime, and reversing the evil effects of the years of conflict between Catholics and the State.

It was not surprising, then, that the pro-episcopal lobby cast hostile glances at the Jesuit polemicists of the 1630s. There had, of course, always been a certain amount of carping by various Catholic factions at their Catholic opponents' attempts to select and deploy the right polemical tone when confronting the Protestantism of the established Church. It was as easy to depict (some) Catholics' zeal as intemperance and disloyalty as it was to portray (some) Catholics' moderation as lukewarmness and compromise. But in the 1630s the hierarchalist secular clergy excoriated, increasingly loudly, the regulars for alienating the hearts and minds of moderate Protestants (thus, impliedly, hindering the 'conversion of England'). So, for example, Leyburn condemned Matthew Wilson SJ's *A Direction to be Observed by N.N.* This tract was penned in defence of Wilson's own *Mercy & Truth. Or Charity Maintayned by Catholiques*, written in reply to Christopher Potter's *Want of Charitie* (itself a reply to the Jesuited Sir Tobie Mathew's *Charity Mistaken*).[124] The seculars were well aware that Potter was a creature of Laud.[125]

At the same time, however, we can see how potentially threatening the rhetoric of the pro-episcopal lobby might also appear to many Protestants. It was hardly a secret how ambitious the secular clergy's schemes for a 'tolerated' Catholic episcopal presence in England actually were. One of the assurances which the pro-episcopal secular clergy had trumpeted during the first half of the 1620s, as they manoeuvred to secure the appointment first of William Bishop and then of Richard Smith as bishop of Chalcedon, was that a Catholic bishop in England would be titular only, i.e. he would not style

---

[124] *Letters 87, 88*; Hibbard, *CI*, pp. 67–68.
[125] *Letter 50*; Milton, *CR*, pp. 155–157.

himself bishop of any of the established English sees. (This was part of the secular clergy's claim that they were pursuing a merely spiritual programme of reform within the English Catholic community, and that they were in no way challenging the crown's authority in ecclesiastical matters as far as the Church of England was concerned.) But in the 1630s they were actively considering having bishops who *would* use the names of established English sees for their titles. Briefly they speculated that one of them might even use the title of archbishop of Canterbury.[126] They petitioned Rome to grant them not just one but three (or more) bishops in England to replace Smith.[127] In mid-June 1633, Smith's friends thought that he might even be made a cardinal. They had petitioned Cardinal Richelieu for Smith to be accorded this honour, though Smith himself believed that it would be taken as a sign of 'ambition' and should be postponed until more English bishops had been appointed by Rome.[128]

The religious, according to John Southcot, retaliated by noising it about that the seculars would have '3 bishops and an archbishop'; and 'a certaine Jes[uit] pr[iest] demanded of an other pr[iest] that had ben a Jes[uit] (hearing that we were to have more bishops)', whether it were 'a mortall sin to seek to hinder it by meanes of the State, by which it appeares how these men are minded and how strangely they are bent against episcopall power'.[129] Southcot would, however, have confirmed Smith's enemies' worst fears when he wrote that,

> [...] perhaps in time and by degrees we shall come to have them [i.e. bishops], and no doubt it were needful for the good government of this Church that so many were made, bycause neither the regulars nor the State would then have any hope to suppresse episcopall authority, being setled in so many, and, the faculties of missionaries being once well ordered, they would quickly bring all things here to a good passe and the laity to some conformity and unity of minds, who are now pittifully divided amongst themselves by reason of their ghostly fathers differences.[130]

Conclusion

We can see here, then, how a series of different issues and concerns seriously divided the English Catholic community during the Caroline

---

[126] See *Letters 3, 4, 5.*

[127] See e.g. *Letters 5, 14, 17, 18, 26, 28, 29, 45, 46, 85.*

[128] AAW, B 27, no. 133.

[129] *Letter 45.*

[130] *Ibid.* There was, in fact, a partial reconciliation between the seculars' leaders and some of the religious in late 1635, brokered by Panzani, but the Jesuits either kept or were kept out of it. See *Letter 76.*

period, but these ideological tensions and collisions were not merely or only the result of personal bitterness and antagonism. Rather, the airing of Catholic political aspirations and ambitions, particularly around the court and the queen, was a highly articulate and sophisticated polemical exercise, performed in order to attract and retain support both within and outside the community and also to attack and damage a number of enemies, both Catholic and Protestant, in a high-stakes game which many contemporaries were well aware might result in a complete reversal of the legal and political orthodoxies which had framed the Reformation settlement and had proscribed many aspects of Roman Catholicism within the English Church and polity.

THE NEWSLETTERS

1. [John Southcot] to [Richard Smith], 13 December 1631

[*AAW, A XXIV, no. 213, pp. 769–770*]

Most hon[ored] master,

I have yours of the 1 and 8 of December which came both togeather and in the former there were divers enclosed for others which made it come open to my hands, the party that receaved it at the French house being desirous to give M^ris Salisbury[1] hers before her departure from thence. Wherfor, if it please you, lett your letters to me come always single and sealed by them selves. I ame sory to see what Mr Fitton[2] writes of the Fr[ench] ambassadors[3] absence from court and discontent, which wilbe a great hinderance to his negotiation for the present. As for Ingolos[4] opinion of your going to R[ome] I know not on the suddaine what to say to it, but I could easily be induced to think that some of the court have sett him on to propose it by way of freindship out of a feare perhaps <and jealousy> they have of your remaining in France and joyning with the French bishops. Neither do I think that your presence in R[ome] would hasten but rather protract matters longer beside the charges of your maintenance there, which, if it be as Mr Fitton writes, I know not how we shalbe able to procure it from hence. Neither is it liked by some of our brethren here that Mr Fitt[on] should be silent concerning the breve[5] being procured uppon so false information. For although he seek not to destroy the regulars exemption from approbation, yet there are wherin perhaps

---

[1] For a possible identification of Mrs Salisbury, see J.H. Pollen (ed.), *Unpublished Documents* (CRS, 5, 1908), p. 393.

[2] Peter Biddulph. See Allison, RSGB, I, pp. 360–361. Biddulph had gone to Rome in July 1631 as Richard Smith's representative and agent for the secular clergy. He remained there until March 1638.

[3] Jean de Gallard, baron de la Rochebeaucourt et de Brassach, French ambassador at Rome.

[4] Francis Ingoli, secretary of the Congregation for the Propagation of the Faith (De Propaganda Fide), and a friend of the English secular clergy leadership. See Hughes, *RCR*, pp. 341, 342, 363–365, 385, 387, 389, 397, 400, 402–406; Hughes, *HSJ*, p. 183.

[5] The papal breve *Britannia*, issued by Pope Urban VIII on 29 April/9 May 1631.

it will not be needful to stirr more, yet there <u>are divers other</u> points touched in the supplication,[6] <u>whi</u>ch <u>are not to</u> be wholy smothered up in silence, and especially that of the ap<u>pellants cond</u>emnation as tracti a Diabolo,[7] about w<u>hi</u>ch M[r] Charnock, as I heare, hath written something briefly in the appellants defence.[8] But it is well liked that M[r] Fitton should inculcat those other points for the <u>declaration of my lor</u>ds[9] authority over the laity, and for the 3 parochialls,[10] and shewing of letters patents and faculties. And we intend to <u>moove the Italian</u> Capucin[11] that is now here concerning tho<u>se points, and to</u> desire him to write to Rome about them, w<u>hi</u>ch M[r] Laborne, <u>who hath talked with</u> him, thinkes he may be soon persuaded to doe, finding him very freindly to us, and [*p. 770*] opposit to our chief adversaries.

Concerning the mony w<u>hi</u>ch Fa[ther] <u>Leander</u>[12] saieth that that M[r] Skelton[13] had, I have requested M[r] Laborne <to write> to M[r] Skelton about it. What S<u>i</u>r Fr[ancis] Inghilf[ield][14] gave was left to M[r] Shelleis[15] disposing, wherof I suppose he hath given you an account.

---

[6] The 'Humillima Supplicatio Cleri Saecularis' of 6/16 July 1631 (AAW, A XXIV, nos 127, 128), which asked Urban VIII to delay publication of the breve *Britannia* in which the pope announced his decision over Smith's dispute with his opponents in England.

[7] See AAW, A XXIV, no. 127, p. 503.

[8] On 19/29 March 1632 Richard Smith reported to Biddulph that Robert Charnock, who, with William Bishop, had led the secular clergy's first appeal against the archpriest George Blackwell in 1598, 'hath written the storie of his and <my> predecessors [i.e. William Bishop's] going to R[ome] and their emprisonment there by F[ather] Persons'. Smith planned to dispatch it as soon as he could and would 'call upon the*m* in England to send you other books of the appellants'. Smith had in his possession 'an excellent booke of that matter written by M[r] Colleton', i.e. John Colleton's *Iust Defence of the Slandered Priestes* (London, 1602), 'but it is in English'; AAW, B 27, no. 107. In the end Smith sent two appellant books 'which cost me here very dear'; AAW, B 27, no. 116. See also AAW, B 27, no. 128.

[9] Richard Smith.

[10] See *Letters 13, 15, 29*.

[11] Alessandro d'Ales, alias Francesco della Rota, for whom see Albion, *CI*, pp. 111–115. This Capuchin correspondent of Cardinal Francesco Barberini was prone to recite the alleged ills and moral laxity within the English Catholic community largely as they would have been phrased by Richard Smith and his friends. The Capuchin, however, advised the appointment in England of an Italian rather than an Englishman as a bishop, as a way to keep the peace among English Catholics. A similar recommendation was made by the queen's almoner, Jacques le Noël Du Perron. See also Hibbard, *CI*, p. 43.

[12] John (Leander) Jones OSB.

[13] Simon Skelton. See Anstr., II, p. 296.

[14] Sir Francis Englefield had died on 26 October 1631. See Berry, *Sussex*, p. 354.

[15] William Shelley. See Anstr., II, p. 293.

I cannot gett the Vindiciae[16] nor the Queremonia.[17] Simbolum Jesuitaru*m*[18] I send hereinclosed, and I have Examen Juridicu*m*[19] to send by the first good opportunity. The Apologie of Fludd[20] in Latin may be had in Paules church yard.

If your health serve you this winter, I think it would be to much purpose if you pleased to write some short treatises in English concerning mattrimony and baptisme as I remember you once intended to do. I wish also that you would finish y*our* treatise De Optimo Confessario, and De Aequivocatione, while you have the help of bookes there. And were it not to seem to overpresse to[o] much, I and others do desire that somwhat were written by y*our* penn by way of exhortation or admonition to the Cath[olics] of England with inculcation of Gods judgments uppon such as have resisted epi*scop*all authority by examples taken out of Church history. Such a treatise would do infinitt good, and the true way to draw men of[f] from this opposition is to deale with them by way of conscience as we find by experience.[21] M*r* Hare[22] and I have made an attestation under o*ur* hands and seales w*h*ich if you please you may print, not putting in our names at length but only the first letters. For my own part I see no great inconvenience in printing the attestations so that the priests names be not sett down ad longum, for that p*er*haps would prove dangerous to them.

This is all for the present, but only my woonted dutie.

No address.

[on p. 769]

Endorsed: 13 Decemb[er] 1631

[16] Thomas Bacon, *Vindiciae pro Nicolao Smithaeo contra Censuram Nomine Facultatis Parisiensis editam in eius Librum, cui Nomen, Modesta & Brevis Discussio, &c [...]* (Liège, 1631); ARCR, I, no. 34.

[17] John Floyd SJ, *Ecclesiae Anglicanae Querimonia Apologetica de Censura Aliquot Episcoporum Galliae, in Duos Libros Anglicanos, &c. Authore Hermanno Loemelio* (St Omer, 1631); ARCR, I, no. 488. See Allison, RSGB, I, pp. 374–375.

[18] John Floyd SJ, *Censura Symboli Apostolorum ad Instar nuperrimae Censurae quarundam Propositionum [...]* (Paris, 1631); ARCR, I, no. 484. See Allison, RSGB, I, pp. 374–375.

[19] Francis O'Mahony OFM, *Examen Iuridicum Censurae Facultatis Theologicae Parisiensis* (Frankfurt [imprint false; printed at Louvain?], 1631); ARCR, I, no. 861. See Allison, RSGB, I, p. 367.

[20] John Floyd SJ, *An Apolagy of the Holy Sea Apostolicks Proceeding for the Government of the Catholicks of England during the Tyme of Persecution* (Rouen, 1631); ARCR, II, no. 292. See Allison, RSGB, I, pp. 356–359.

[21] For the treatises on the scope of his episcopal authority which Richard Smith wrote in 1631 while he was in France, see Allison, QJ, pp. 135–138.

[22] This may be the priest Robert Hare (not listed in Anstr.) who was a prisoner in the New prison in 1632; AAW, A XXVI, no. 164, p. 495. (In December 1633 he petitioned successfully for release; *CSPD, 1633–1634*, p. 329.)

2. [George Leyburn] to [Richard Smith], 20 December 1631

[*AAW, A XXIV, no. 207, pp. 749–752*]

Most honored sir,

This daye I receaved a packett from Mr Plantyne²³ of the 16 of December in which ther was onely one inclosed from you unto Signor Antoni[n]o.²⁴ The regulars continue in ther violence and more than ever move the lay-Cath[olics] against you. The Lord Baltomore,²⁵ Brudenall²⁶ and Sir Basile Brooke²⁷ had soe delt with my Lord Morley²⁸ that they had made him of a friend an enenimy [*sic*]. The Lord

---

²³ Lawrence Platt. Both Lawrence and his brother Francis used the alias of Plantin; Anstr., II, pp. 247–248. John Southcot's diary notes that Lawrence 'went agent to Paris 15 August [1631]', CRS, 1, p. 107. Francis Platt was subsequently cited in a list of allegedly disreputable priests who favoured the Jacobean oath of allegiance and/or led loose lives, although it was added that he had reformed; AAW, A XXVIII, no. 68, p. 287. In May 1632 Lawrence lamented the recent beheading of Louis de Marillac 'specially [...] because he was my good friend, and once I had the honour to be his cha[plain]'; AAW, A XXVI, no. 74, p. 209. In August 1633 Richard Smith noted that 'the elder Platt is come hither to read in a monastery', and 'the younger is come over to be [a] guide to young gentlemen'; CRS, 22, p. 183. In January 1655 Peter Biddulph nominated Lawrence to succeed him as the English secular clergy's agent at Rome; Anstr., II, pp. 247–248.

²⁴ John Southcot.

²⁵ Sir George Calvert, 1st Baron Baltimore, for whose opposition to Richard Smith, see Allison, QJ, *passim*.

²⁶ Sir Thomas Brudenell, 1st Baron Brudenell, the future 1st earl of Cardigan.

²⁷ In 1635 the English secular clergy reported disapprovingly of Sir Basil Brooke, 'totus immersus est negotiis secularibus et contentiosis praesertim monopoliis, circa metallia, silvas, saponem, et similia'. (See *Letter 65*.) However 'ex se magis propendet in clerum secularem quam in regulares, et amicissimum se exhibuit tum priori episcopo (qui in eius aedibus prope Londinum, quae communiter vocantur Aula episcopi [i.e. Bishopshall], diem suum obiit) tum etiam moderno, ante incaeptam controversiam de approbatione regularium, sed postea a Ploydeno [Francis Plowden] tractus est in partes opponentium episcopum, una cum Thoma Brudenello, qui modo est baro [...] contra propriam inclinationem, nullo alio magis motivo, quam amicitiae erga Ploydenum, vel certe, aurae cujusdam popularis, cui jure deditus est, quia opponentes episcopum se ostendabant, pro sapientioribus et praecipuis Angliae Catholicis. Postquam vero immersit se huic oppositioni, nullis fuit illo violentior aut acerbior contra episcopum'. He was entirely Hispanophile and had taken, as his second wife, Frances, the daughter of Henry Mordaunt, 4th Baron Mordaunt, the widow of Sir Thomas Neville, 'cuius intuiti magis quam antea mancipat se obsequio Jesuitarum et Jesuitam modo alit domae suae quod nunquam hactenus fecit'; AAW, A XXVIII, no. 58, p. 224. See Allison, QJ, pp. 120–121, 141; CRS, 1, p. 100. (Brooke was a close friend, and executor, of the 9th earl of Shrewsbury, who was a patron of the Jesuits; B. FitzGibbon, 'George Talbot, ninth earl of Shrewsbury', *BS*, 2 (1953), pp. 96–110, at p. 102.) In January 1635, however, Brooke told the Oratorian priest and papal envoy, Gregorio Panzani that he would approve the restoration of local Catholic episcopal authority over English Catholics, provided that the restored bishop's powers were restricted and he had the king's approval; VA, PD, fo. 68r.

²⁸ Henry Parker, 14th Baron Morley and Monteagle. In the early 1630s Morley had employed, as a chaplain, the secular priest William Hargrave, who in 1634 became

Brudenall told <u>him that if he</u> did adhere unto you he would <u>endangere</u> his estate, he would be excomunic<u>ated living s</u>eperated <from his wife>, and he would be deprived of his good man [*sic for* name] at your pleasure in soe much that my lord was strangely carryed away and they did inveye much against your person. But now I have satisfyed my lord and have hindered ther <u>designe</u> upon him w*hi*ch was to procure <u>his hand aga</u>inst you. And moreover I am to goe to morrowe unto the Lord ~~Brudenall~~ <Baltamore> to expostulate concerning what was sayd unto my Lord Morley and <u>my lord haith</u> promised to goe w*i*th me. Mr Collenton[29] is now come to the towne but will not be drone to residenc[e]. Our chef friends here are unspeakeably trubled w*i*th the contents of Mr Fittons[30] letter from Rome. He writeth of a favorable audience, of the readines of the French ambassa[dor][31] to assist him in regarde of her Majestyes letter,[32] of the great hopes he harbored of wish[e]d successe. But, after, he signifieth that you have written a letter unto his Holines[33] w*hi*ch doth hinder all successe in your affayres, because you <u>resigne unto him</u> your authority in soe much that all for the present is dashed and he cannot negotiat any farther.[34] This letter of yours is taken greatly to hart here by your friends and if ther be tyme ther will be written a common letter to

president of the college of Saints Peter and Paul at Lisbon; Anstr., II, p. 146. The secular clergy's January 1635 survey of the Catholic nobility noted with satisfaction that 'favet clero specialiter, et aegre tulit se delusum fuisse a barone de Baltimore defuncto, per falsas informationes circa authoritatem ep*iscop*i Chalcedon*en*sis quare sub chyrographo suo una cum Marchione Wintonensi [John Paulet, 5th marquis of Winchester] negavit se ullo modo adstipulari adversariis ep*iscop*i'. It was noted also that, from a life of youthful excess, he had turned to one of frugality; AAW, A XXVIII, no. 3, p. 15. (AAW, A XXVIII, no. 3 is a summary of the dispositions of the English Catholic peers. Along with AAW, A XXVIII, no. 58, it was probably drawn up for Gregorio Panzani. He repeats some of the contents of both documents in his 'Relazione' of the state of religion in England, an account which largely endorses the views of the English secular clergy leadership (VA, Barberini MS LVI, 136 (a.n. 2450): 'Relazione dello stato della religione Cattolica in Inghilterra data alla Santita di N.S. Urbano VIII da Gregorio Panzani nel suo ritorno da quel regno l'anno 1637' (transcript and translation at ABSJ)). Panzani noted on 25 February 1635 that George Fisher and John Southcot had come to see him, 'et attesimo alla relatione'; VA, PD, fo. 8or.

[29] John Colleton. See Anstr., I, pp. 82–84.

[30] Peter Biddulph.

[31] Jean de Gallard, baron de la Rochebeaucourt et de Brassach, French ambassador in Rome.

[32] See *Letter 5*.

[33] Pope Urban VIII.

[34] For the circumstances of Richard Smith's resignation as bishop of Chalcedon, see Allison, QJ, pp. 138–139, 144; AAW, OB I/ii, no. 128; *Letter 16*. Smith, who had been living in the French embassy in London for two years, left the country on 24 August 1631. (George Leyburn conducted him as far as Calais.) The papal breve *Britannia* (29 April/9 May 1631) had pronounced on the issues in dispute between him and his enemies mainly in favour of his enemies, at least on the question of 'approbation' (for which events see the Introduction in this volume). (For a printed copy of the breve, see AAW, A XXIV, no. 93.) Leyburn

wish you to undertake the charge agayne. I have told Mr Hammon[35] what you wish[e]d me if it may doe any good. It would be a great comfort unto our friends to heare that those 3 ther wer well united together and deuly furnished with ther rents [?] for Mr Hamon to supplye ther wants, and this would be if all the moneys were at your disposing. Agayne, I could have gotten ther moneys, thought [*sic for* though] with much difficulty, if Mr Plantyn as I wish[e]d him would have been advised by me and abstayned from to[o] much officiousnes in his informations to Mr Hamon. I protest unto you faithfull[y] this want of union amongst many of ours doth soe truble me that I am wearie and out of hart to do any thing. Few occurrences only. Our State is thinking of breaking with Spane. On Fridaye last did dye Doctour Price, subdiene of Westminster,[36] receaved 3 dayes before into the Catholike Church, in soe much that ther was holden a consultation not to burie him but at last it was determined that he should be buried.[37] He was one of ours that did receave him into the Church. This example is like to doe great good.

This is all. And I am not furnish[e]d with leasure.

December 20 1631.

[*on p. 752*]

Addressed: For my maister.

Endorsed: Lords dealing against Chalced[on].

---

set out for his master further reasons why he had become *persona non grata* in England. '1. The Spanish divines hath [*sic*] declared against you. 2. You have a pension of the Cardinal Richelieu. 3. You [...] make a faction amongst the Catholics, having been sent for their comfort. 4. You have been the cardinal's [...] chaplain. 5. Your controversy is a French plot devised by the French to hinder the increase of Catholics for their own politic ends, or at least to frenchify them and avert them from Spain'; Anstr., II, p. 193.

35 John Jackson, alias Hammond and Nelson. Jackson was described by a French Capuchin in July 1622 as 'l'ausmonier du Baron d'Arondel [Thomas Arundell] Catholique'; AAW, A XVI, no. 122, p. 496. In December 1634 Jackson came to the papal agent Gregorio Panzani in a carriage in order to take him to see his patron Arundell; VA, PD, fo. 43r.

36 Theodore Price. See Albion, *CI*, p. 197; K. Fincham, 'William Laud and the exercise of Caroline ecclesiastical patronage', *Journal of Ecclesiastical History*, 51 (2000), pp. 69–93 at pp. 80–81.

37 John Pory reported that Price, 'at the hower of his death received extreme unction [...]. Whereupon I have heard my lord chamberlain [the earl of Pembroke] should saye to the king: is this the orthodoxe man your Majesty would have made a bishop last yeare?'; JPN, p. 190. Pory noted also that 'the custome of Westminster Abby is, when a prebend dye, some other prebend must undertake to bury him'. 'But all of them being ashamed to undertake this d[octo]rs buriall in respect of his religion last of all professed, hee laye some 6 or 7 dayes above grown[d]e', untill the dean allowed one Mr Frost, 'a singing man of the kinges chappell', to 'undertake so muche'. Price's livings were worth £600 p.a., and 'they saye he preacht but once in all his life'; *ibid*. See also *Letter 3*.

3. Clerk [John Southcot] to [Peter Biddulph], 20 January 1632

[*AAW, A XXVI, no. 20, pp. 63–66*]

Sir,

I have y*ou*rs of the 30 Novemb[er] having continewed my weekly writing to you for these 3 weekes and more, and therfor shall be glad to heare that all mine are come safe to y*ou*r hands.

With these you shall receave the last part of the catalogue of knights, wherin you will find no markes but of such as are knowen to me to be Cath[olic]. Perhaps there may be many more that I know not.

Many here are also of opinion that we should demaund b*isho*ps with titles in England, and I was ever of that opinion my self even from the begining, for we shall never els have things rightly setled here, wherfor I do not see but that, as you find occasion offered there, you may propose it and solicit it as effectually as you can. Only be careful to carry the matter secret that o*u*r adversaries, if it be possible, may not heare of it till it appeare how likely it is to be effected, least they seek to hinder it both here and there. Why might not my Lord of Chalced[on][38] or some other be made archb[ishop] of Canterbury and reside ordinarily in Rome as the Irish Metropolitan doth, and then some other two b*isho*ps more be made with subordination to him to reside in England?[39]

But as for confraternities to be erected by the clergy,[40] I find that o*u*r brethren here do not relish any such motion, but they desire to go on the ordinary way as they have [*p. 64*] begunn and would gladly have his Hol[iness] to confirme o*u*r deane and chapter as it is, w*hi*ch both this b*isho*p[41] and his predecessor[42] sett on foot and have approoved by the advise of good lawiers both in France and Flanders, and I do not see what should hinder the validity of it. Yet we must do as we may, and as that court will permit, w*hi*ch you know better than we do here. Therfor do as you see cause. Y*ou*r commission is very ample, and there needs no particuler one for any thing you are to treat for the clergies good.

---

[38] Richard Smith.
[39] See *Letter 5*.
[40] i.e. the English secular clergy.
[41] Richard Smith.
[42] William Bishop.

I suppose amongst other forbidden bookes you will gett the lay Cath[olics'] Declaration[43] to be putt in, as also the Answer to the Demaunds of a Great Prelatte sett forth in French then in English 1625.[44] And we hope you will gett the Hierarchie[45] excepted, which if it should be condemned I assure you it would make a great mutiny here and I have heard some already speake bigg words uppon that occasion.

Some of the Theatines[46] best freinds and followers here do speake very scurvily of his Hol[iness] in many places by occasion of Swedens victories in Germany.[47] It were good that notice were given of it in that court, for it makes his Hol[iness's] person and authority little

[43] Sir George Calvert, 1st Baron Baltimore, former secretary of State to James I, had returned in 1630 from his colony in Newfoundland and placed himself at the head of the opposition to Bishop Smith. (See the Introduction in this volume.) He put into circulation again the well-known attack on Smith of November 1627, usually referred to as the 'letter of the three gentlemen', and solicited signatures to it from Catholic nobility and gentry. By March 1631 the document was known as 'The Declaration of the Lay Catholicks of England'. With numerous signatures appended to it, the document was taken to the Catholic embassies in London, and to the Spanish diplomat Carlos Coloma in Brussels, and then went into print. Smith's supporters wrote an 'Abrenunciatio Catholicorum Laicorum Angliae in Declarationem quamdam sub ipsorum nomine false editam' (AAW, A XXIV, no. 98) to counter the 'Declaration', and, with the signatures of leading lay Catholics added to it, a translation of it was presented to the French ambassador, François Duval, marquis de Fontenay Mareuil, who, at the end of June 1631, signed a new rendition of it. A version was then printed at Paris, entitled *Général Désadveu des Catholiques Lais d'Angleterre, contre une Déclaration qui a esté faussement publiée à leur Nom* (Paris, 1631); ARCR, I, no. 362. See Allison, QJ, pp. 134–135; Hughes, *HSJ*, p. 188; AAW, A XXIV, no. 99. For the 'Declaration', see AAW, A XXIV, no. 77; and for confutations of it, see AAW, A XXIV, nos 78, 80, 81, 85, 86. For Thomas Arundell, 1st Baron Arundell's reply to the 'Declaration', describing it as 'a fitt discourse to be annexed to the incredible history of the invisible Church', see AAW, A XXIV, no. 87, p. 363.

[44] Etienne Binet, *An Answer to the Demands of a Great Prelate. Touching the Hierarchy of the Church. And the Just defence of Privileged, and Religious Men* (Rouen, 1626); ARCR, II, no. 885. This tract was a translation, probably by a Jesuit, of Binet's *Response aux Demandes d'un Grand Prelat [. . .]*, published in 1625 under the pseudonym of François de Fontaine. The prelate of the title was Sebastien Zamet.

[45] Matthew Kellison, *A Treatise of the Hierarchie and Divers Orders of the Church against the Anarchie of Calvin* (Douai, 1629); ARCR, II, no. 473. For Kellison, see Anstr., I, pp. 193–194. On 7/17 April 1632 Smith advertised Biddulph that 'I have showed D[octor] Kellis[on's] Hierarchie to the archb[ishop] of Toulouse', Charles Montchal, a friend of Cardinal de La Valette (who had supported Smith's appointment as bishop of Chalcedon, and who had held the see of Toulouse before Montchal); AAW, B 27, no. 108; J. Bergin, *The Making of the French Episcopate 1581–1661* (London, 1996), pp. 672–673. See also AAW, A XXVI, no. 36, p. 117 (Kellison's letter to Biddulph of 29 February/9 March 1632, thanking him for the 'care' of his book 'which I hope to send the next post unto you, as also to Paris, the bishops there having called for it so often'; AAW, B 27, no. 127).

[46] i.e. the Jesuits.

[47] On 3 January 1632 William Case, chaplain to John Paulet, 5th marquis of Winchester, had informed Biddulph that he believed it very probable that Richard Smith's opponents 'have some desperat designe against [Pope] Urban [VIII], because they goe about to possess

regarded [*p. 65*] amongst Catholickes now a daies. [*two words erased*] Non fuit sic ab initio. Waunt of authority well setled amongst us hath brought us to great remissenesse already, and ere long will bring all to utter confusion if it be not prevented the sooner. And I pray make it appeere there how ridiculous a thing it is for the Jes[uits] to cry out as they do of the impossibility of the practise of episcopall authority here in these times, whenas they and other religious do practise things far lesse profitable, and with much more daunger. For the Jes[uits] practise their sodalities where many meet togeather and combine. They teach schooles also both in London and the country which cannot be done without concourse and some noise.[48] The others

the mindes of the best Catholikes [...] that hee seekes the ruin of the emperour, that hee rejoyced at the overthrow' of the count of Tilly by Gustavus Adolphus at Breitenfeld on 7/17 September 1631 and 'would have had publique signes of joy, but that hee was by the advise of some hindred; that hee invited the k[ing] of Sweden to come in for th*e* distraction of the emperour; and that hee could not but see what advantage the Turke would hereby take for the subversion of Christianity', and they 'denigrate alsoe the French king by saying that hee assisteth heretiks and resisteth the progress of Catholike religion'; AAW, A XXVI, no. 17, pp. 57–58; CRS, I, p. 107. On 9 May 1632 Case reported to Smith that his opponents were trying to discredit him by linking him with the opponents of the imperialists: 'they calumniat you by saying that you are a French man, the cardinalls [i.e. Richelieu's] creature, a stirring man, a stubborne man etc. They calumniat the cardinall by saying that hee is a fautor of haeretiks, nay as badd or worse than Sweden. They calumniat the pope by saying that hee hath beene colde in resisting haeretiks, and that hee hath thought it necessary for the howse of Austria to bee shockt'; AAW, A XXVI, no. 69, p. 193. For Urban VIII's attitudes to the conflicting interests of the Bourbon and Habsburg dynasties, see Pastor, *HP*, XXVIII, pp. 24–25, 30, 55f. His election as pope had been greeted favourably in Paris. Throughout his pontificate it proved difficult for him to maintain a pose of impartiality between France and Spain; *ibid.*, pp. 278f, 339f; R. Bonney, *The European Dynastic States 1494–1660* (Oxford, 1991), p. 68.

[48] Edward Bennett, one of Richard Smith's officials, had in January 1627 berated Richard Blount SJ concerning a school opened by the Jesuits at Holywell in Wales. Bennett wrote that 'lately there hath bin a complaint made unto me that one of your fathers should keepe a schoole at Greenfeild Abbey hard by St Wenefrides well which may breed no litle inconvenience in that place', because, alleged Bennett, this would provoke the authorities into persecution of Catholics. The 'whole countrey thereaboutes therefore intreated him to desist', but the Jesuit ignored this, so the district's archdeacon asked Bennett to intervene; AAW, A XIX, no. 111, p. 391. On 17 May 1627 one Edward Pennant informed Bennett that the fact that a certain Catholic, 'Mr Prichard', 'taught at Gree[n]field is as sure as that there is a schoole at Eaton'. This man Pritchard had 'schollers that mett there to the number of vii this last winter. The same was not soe privat, but the vicar of the parish (whoe keepes schoole at the church) tooke notice thereof and grumbled to me therat'. One 'great magistrat in the neibourhood [...] complayned to me of great indiscretion and overboldnes for his teachinge'; AAW, A XX, no. 82, p. 291. See also AAW, A XX, no. 83 (an affidavit, dated 20 May 1627, made by several people, including the priest Thomas Pennant, a brother of Edward Pennant, that Pritchard had taught at Holywell since November 1626); T.M. McCoog, 'The Society of Jesus in England, 1623–1688: an institutional study' (Ph.D. thesis, University of Warwick, 1984), pp. 286–287. For complaints in 1635 about the Jesuits' keeping of schools, at Anne Vaux's house at Stanley Grange and also near Wolverhampton,

have their capitular meetings often times, they practise the giving of scapulars, girdles and the like, and com*m*end them to their penitents much more than they do the sacrament of confirmation, w*h*ich they rather slight and extenuat. What will this come to in the end? You may confidently assure them there that nonn in England do or would much oppose the [*word deleted*] practise of episcopall authority here but some religious men and Catholickes their adherents, for if these would be silent and quiett [*p. 66*] the State would never so much as take notice of it or be seen to dislike it. This is certainly true.

For newes there is little stirring. I heare that we have made over to Sweden six score thousand pounds sterling already and bequeathed 80 thousand more ~~that~~ <the same> way, w*h*ich France oweth us.[49]

Doctor Fludd,[50] a Cath[olic] doctor of phisick, hath bin questioned by the king this Christmasse about Doctor Price the k[ing's] chaplaine his dying Catholick, for they <two> were freinds and country men. But Doct[or] Fludd answered the matter very discreetly and well and in that conference the king expressed him self so far as to say that he hated neither the papists nor their religion, and that (notwith-standi[n]g they were more under the lash of the law) he would be as gratious to them as to his other subjects, and so dismissed Doct[or] Flud very graciously from him. He saied also that he did beleeve that the Church doth not erre. This doct[or] is o*u*r great freind and my phisitian and freind in particular.[51]

---

at Mr Leveson's, see *CSPD, 1635,* pp. 303, 539, 545–546, 590, 608; Anstruther, *Vaux,* pp. 460–462.

[49] *CSPV, 1629–1632,* p. 597.

[50] Dr Robert Floyd. See T.H.B.M. Harmsen (ed.), *The Foot out of the Snare (1624)* (Nijmegen, 1992), p. 295.

[51] See AAW, A XXIX, no. 41 (an extract from a (no longer extant) letter of 18 January 1632 by Southcot concerning Floyd and Theodore Price). Southcot 'visited D*o*ct*o*r Fludd this morning, who told me that the king had sent for him to examine him about Doctor Price his death, and charged him upon his alleageance to answere him truely to what he should aske him, saying before that he had heard him often by many comended to be an honest man, and that he did so beleeve him to be. First he asked him whether he brought any priest to D*o*ct*o*r P[rice]. D*o*ct*o*r Flud answered no, and truly. 2. Whether he had seen him in the compaghnie of any priest. He answered, yea oftentimes, at least such as he thought to be priests. 3. Whe[ther] he saw any priest do any priestly function about him at his death or before? He answered no. And truly. 4. Whether he died a papist. He answered that he thought he did because he had often heard him say he would saile to eternity rather in St Peters shipp than in John Calvins boat. To w*h*ich the king replied in these words: so had I to[o]. For we do not hould that Calvin could not err as you doe that the pope cannot. The d*o*ct*o*r replied that he did not hould that the pope (scilicet as a privat man) could not erre, but ecclesia non errat, that the Church did not err. So doe I hould to[o], saied the king, and then saied further that he neither hated the papists nor their religion, and would be as gratious and mercifull to them as to his other subjects'. An account of Price's conversion was translated in order to be read in Rome; Albion, *CI,* p. 197, n. 3. See also *CSPD, 1631–1633,* p. 205; Birch, *CT,* II, p. 21.

The counsell are now buissy about the examination of a certai[n]e apprentise of 20 yeares of age taken in Salisbury who tould one of his compagnions that he meant to kill the king with a pistoll, and that the Divill one [n]ight had appeared unto him in the shape of a man and incited him therunto. Perhaps this devill was some puritan that made him self a divill for this purpose. More I have not what to write.

Adieu. 20 Januar[y] 1632.

No address.

Endorsed: 20 Jan[uary]. Antonino. Clerk.
About the Jesuitts speaking against the pope.
That the regulars practise things more dangerous than episcopall auctority.

4. [George Leyburn] to Fitton [Peter Biddulph], January/February 1632

[*AAW, A XXVI, no. 22, pp. 71–72*]

Worthie deare sir,

I have receaved yours of the 20 of December. All our friends were more trubled with my maisters resignation[52] than I can expresse as you will perceave by a former from me. But I hope that her Majestyes second letter wherin is inclosed the supplication[53] of the Catholiks of this country will open the way agayne to your negotiation.[54] Our friends did meet 3 dayes aggoe in my chamber. The poynts resolved: Mr Lovell[55] will imparte they are for canonicall and ordinarie authority and therfore mislike your propos[it]ion concerning a congregation. My maister writeth that at Ro[me] the Jesuists informeth [*sic*] that ther is a great peace and quietnes in this country since his departure. But the contrarie is most true, nothing but disorder and confusion. And assure your selfe that the best and most of the councell would willinglie winke at a bishop. Your propositions for more bishops doth [*sic*] much take. But then his Holynes must style them bishop

---

[52] See *Letter 2* for Richard Smith's resignation as bishop of Chalcedon.
[53] See *Letter 1*.
[54] For Henrietta Maria's letters, on Richard Smith's behalf, to the French ambassador in Rome and to Urban VIII, see *Letters 5, 18, 24*.
[55] John Southcot.

of Yorkeshire, bishop of Lancheshire, determining the dieces, or, if he would make 3, one to have the jurisdiction ~~of~~ <over> all Catholikes on this syde of Trent, the other over all on the other syde of Trent, and the third [to be] bishop of Walles.[56] I had thought to have writte[n] unto S*ig*nor Georgio[57] concerning the 4 cheef opposers of episcopal authority, w*h*ich are the Lord Baltamoore, Sir Nicho[las] Fortescue,[58] Sir Toby[59] and Ployden.[60] Sir Toby you knowe well. Ployden is the Catho[lic] common executour wherfore he feareth th*a*t in matter of wills he should be cal[le]d [in]to question.[61] The report is th*a*t he haith marryed [h]is owne made and keepeth it privately. Baltamoore after his first wifes d[eath] did marrie his wifes kitchin made,

---

[56] See *Letter 3* for Southcot's views on this topic of titular and established sees. Leyburn argues, in this letter, for non-established sees. For the scheme for three bishops, see *Letter 5*; and, for a 1634 petition concerning the same, to be directed via the queen to Gregorio Panzani, see AAW, A XXVII, no. 201.

[57] George Con. Con was a Scottish cleric who rose to prominence in the household of the cardinal secretary of State, Francesco Barberini. Leyburn had written to Con on 15 November 1631; AAW, A XXIV, no. 206. See Hibbard, *CI*, pp. 47–48, and *passim*.

[58] See *DNB, sub* Fortescue. Sir Nicholas was a grandson of one of Henry VIII's groom porters. He had briefly fallen under suspicion after the discovery of the gunpowder plot. He obtained a number of government posts from 1610 onwards, including a chamberlainship of the exchequer. He died in Fetter Lane on 2 November 1633. The secular priest, Edward Johns, recorded in December 1633 that Fortescue in his last illness had recanted his opposition to Smith. He denied having assisted with the composition of the 'letter of the three gentlemen' but acknowledged that he had consented to its publication; CRS, 22, pp. 185–186.

[59] Sir Tobie Mathew. He had been one of the principal opponents of Richard Smith in England during the 1620s. Smith's supporters made polemical use of the fact of Mathew's priesthood, conferred on him via a secret ordination, the clandestine nature of which allowed him to masquerade in England as a lay courtier. One account of Smith's opponents described Mathew's affectations and appetites, and said that 'rursus a nonnullis estimatur ut vafer nebulo, ab aliis (praesertim faeminis) ut magnus sanctus', but, either way, he was very vain and affected Spanish manners; AAW, A XXVIII, no. 58, p. 233. See *Letter 57*. In January 1635 Gregorio Panzani reported that Charles I believed that Mathew was mad; VA, PD, fo. 67r.

[60] Francis Plowden (1588–1661), who lived at Aston-le-Walls, in Northamptonshire, was a well-known Catholic lawyer. He used his professional expertise to assist other Catholics. He was a favourer of the Society, and his Jesuit brother Thomas resided with him; Allison, *QJ*, p. 142; B. Stapleton, *A History of the Post-Reformation Catholic Missions in Oxfordshire* (London, 1906), pp. 309–313.

[61] Plowden specialized in probate work, and would inevitably have viewed with hostility Richard Smith's intention to set up a tribunal to deal with, *inter alia*, probate cases. According to the secular clergy, he was 'ingenii turbulentissimum ac litium amantissimi propriae opinionis ac voluntatis tenacissimus' and 'assiduus sectator fori contentiosi'. He was depicted unfavourably in the play *Hierarchomachia* (see *Letter 32*). He was also 'author et fautor praecipuus diversorum monopoliorum seu inventorum quorundam lucrosorum, ob quae hodie Catholici nostrates magno in odio habentur a Protestantibus'; AAW, A XXVIII, no. 58, pp. 223–224.

and having [*ms torn*] her in the New Found Land[62] haith lately marry-
yed him selfe unto his doughters chambermaide.[63] He did first sollicite
her and, when he could not prevaile, he did give her money to buy
a ring and when he had the ring he did marrie her, notwithstanding
the mayde, fearing least this was not sufficient, being not done by
a pr[iest], she would not permitt him to consummate, wherupon
he told her that now she was bound. Notwithstanding he could not
prevaile untill she had been with Fa[ther] Knott[64] whom he kept and
told him her case, to which he replyed with a smile ~~this~~ that her lord
would not wish her to any thing which is unjust, wherupon she went
and did consummate the act with him. Since,[65] this good lord would
goe backe pretending that there was a spirituall kindered betwixt him
and her which did make the marriage invalide and this was because
his wife was god mother to this maide: a foule and scandalous busines
when it shall be brought upon the State, as infallibly it will. The
Jesuists now persuadeth her to goe to religion.[66] For Sir Nicholas, it

[62] For Baltimore's second wife, Joan, who died in 1630 when shipwrecked while returning
to England, see GEC, I, p. 393; Hughes, *HSJ*, p. 176; Codignola, *CHL*, pp. 46, 53–54, 165,
168, 170; L.C. Wroth, 'Tobacco or codfish. Lord Baltimore makes his choice', *Bulletin of the
New York Public Library*, 58 (1954), pp. 523–534, at pp. 529–531; *Letter 5*.

[63] According to AAW, A XXVII, no. 111, p. 321, her name was Mary Wynne. She was
the daughter of Captain Edward Wynne, who had been the leader of the first group of
settlers whom Sir George Calvert sent out to Newfoundland, and who landed at Ferryland
in August 1621; Codignola, *CHL*, p. 10; VA, PD, fo. 79r.

[64] Matthew Wilson SJ.

[65] i.e. since that time.

[66] On 27 February 1632 John Jackson sent an account of the business to Richard
Smith, who urged Biddulph, 'if you could there get an answer to that case it would be
to great purpose'; AAW, B 27, no. 107. The seculars argued that Baltimore's marriage was
clandestine, and therefore against the canons of the Council of Trent. See *Letters 4, 5, 8*.
Jackson wrote further that she had refused intercourse 'till she acquainted Fa[ther] Knot
and asked his opinion. He sayd she might be assured that my lo[rd] wold aske nothing of her
that was unlawfull, therupon they consummated mariage. When this was knowne to some
it trobled them. And there was a consultation of 12 Jes[uits]', including 'Fa[ther] Blunt', and
'Fa[ther] Knot or Smith'. And Mary Wynne was 'removed from him'. 'They first laboured
to have her enter in[to] religion. Then they found a means to make it noe mariage and
drew this case. Isabella post matrimonium contractum et consummatum cum Antonium levat
de sacro fonte Catholicam mortua Isabella Antonius cum eadem Catharina clam contrahit
in Anglia pro verba de praesenti absque sacerdote vel testibus et consummant. Quaeritar
utrum talis contractus inter Antonium et Catharinam sit validus. They conclude it is not.'
But they 'will not have it knowne and say if it come to be knowne to the priests, they will
not medle with it'. Baltimore's son, Cecil, shortly to become the 2nd baron, who had, noted
Jackson, 'maried your best ladies daughter' (Anne, daughter of Thomas Arundell, 1st Baron
Arundell of Wardour and his wife Anne), 'offred the made or rather his now mother in law
a 100[li] and that his fa[ther] shold give her 50[li] to relinquish'. But the maid 'will not but
keeps the ring as a testimonie. There is means made to see if any pr[iest] will be of opinion
that it is noe mariage in regard of cognatio spiritualis, seing the Councel of Trent, say they,
is not here receyved.' It was believed that Wilson had gone to see the nuncio at Brussels

is well knowne how lude ever he haith been. Besyds he maryed his own made, and keepeth her obscurely in the country. Is ther not great need of a bishop? Aske Signor Georgio to whom remember my table service. I did deliver his last unto Fa[ther] Philip[67] wherin his facultyes were inclosed.

Addressed: A Mons*ieur* Monsieur [*sic*] Fitton. Rome.

Endorsed: [*on p. 71*] M[r] Fitton.
      [*on p. 72*] About my Lord Baltamour and the 3 chief adversaryes my lord hath.

5. Antonino [John Southcot] to [Peter Biddulph], 3 February 1632

[*AAW, A XXVI, no. 23, pp. 73–76*]

Sir,

I wrote not the last week to you, but referred all to M[r] Lab[orne] who shewed me yours of the 20 Decemb[er] wherin you make no mention of the ~~two~~ writing or omitting to write by the two precedent posts, and yet the last w*h*ich we receaved from you bore date 30th of November, by w*h*ich account two weekes letters are lost if you wrote by both those posts.

    I have written divers letters unto you since the 30 of November which was the first time I began to write, two in Decemb[er], of the 2 and 16, and three in January of the 6, 13 and 20th, of the receipt of all w*h*ich I shalbe glad to heare, having as yet heard nothing therof, but especially of the receipt of that of the 2 of Decemb[er] with w*h*ich we sent you the priests and Catholickes petition to his Hol[iness] accompaghnied with a letter fro*m* the queen to Mons*ieur* Brissac,[68]

---

about the case, and would lobby against Smith at the same time; AAW, A XXVI, no. 32, p. 105. See also Jackson's account of the affair sent to Biddulph on 1 March; AAW, A XXVI, no. 33. For the presentation of this material about Baltimore to the Congregation for the Propagation of the Faith, see Hughes, *HSJ*, pp. 229–230. George Fisher related the case to Gregorio Panzani in February 1635; VA, PD, fo. 79r.

  [67] Robert Philip, the queen's Scottish Oratorian chaplain. When Henrietta Maria's Oratorians and Theatines were summarily dismissed by Charles in 1626 she retained the services of only two priests, both Oratorians (Robert Philip and Pierre Viette), and a Scottish chapel clerk, until 1630 when a number of Capuchins (eight priests and two lay brothers) were permitted to attend her; Dockery, *CD*, p. 37; Hibbard, 'Henrietta Maria', *The Court Historian*, 5 (2000), pp. 15–28, at pp. 26–27.

  [68] Jean de Gallard, baron de la Rochebeaucourt et de Brassach, French ambassador in Rome. For a French version of the petition, of 31 December 1631, sent by the English

which is the thing you desire in this letter to M[r] Laborne, and which I hope will put my lord[69] right againe in that court.

We have receaved the printed coppy of the jubily,[70] but it wantes authentication, as the breve you sent before also did. ~~But~~ Hereafter I pray send such things ever authenticated by some notary.

The regulars I heare do informe there that all is quiett here now the bishop is gonn, [two words deleted] seeking therby to hinder his rettourne, but the petition we sent will shew the contrary. To which you may add that many cry out for the sacrament of confirmation[71] and speake and write bitterly against those that have caused my lord to fly and, if there be such outward quietnesse here as they now bragg of, it is bycause they them selves forbeare to make so great a busseling, now my lord is gonn, [p. 74] as they did before, bycause they were the only causes of the unquietnesse that was then made. But assure your self the inward discontents are more now and further extended by much [word deleted] since my lords departure, and it is to be feared they will break out into some disorder shortly if my lord rettourne not the sooner to us againe. And therfor hasten his rettourne, or at least the substitution of some other in his place all you can. The disorders and abuses against religion and manners both in clergy, some secular ~~reg~~ some regular, and in the laity are incredible, and if authority be not quickled [sic] setled they wilbe incurable. M[r] Muscot[72] knowes many particulers in this kind which you may do well to write unto him to sett down, or rather wish my lord bishop to injoine him to sett down, in writing all he knoweth, and to send it to you. The sight of those things will moove more than anything els in that court.

We have consulted a little concerning the buissenesse of making bishops with English titles. And there are 3 waies in deliberation. 1. to give ould titles such as were in the time of the first Saxons. 2. to divide England according to the present division of administring justice, videlicet, all shires on this side the river of Trent, the Presidentship of the North, and the Presidentship of Wales, and according to this division to settle 3 bishops with subordination to one as archbishop.[73] 3. To give moderne titles as of Canterb[ur]y, York, London etcetera.

Catholics to the pope, with a copy, in George Leyburn's hand, of the queen's letter to Brassach, also dated 31 December 1631, see AAW, A XXIV, no. 217.

[69] Richard Smith.

[70] By a bull of 5/15 December 1631 Urban VIII had proclaimed a universal jubilee to invoke God's assistance for the Church in the circumstances of the current European conflict; Pastor, *HP*, XXVIII, p. 279; CRS, I, p. 107.

[71] For the politico-ecclesiastical significance of the sacrament of confirmation, see Allison, RS, pp. 156, 160; Allison, RSGB, I, pp. 341–342.

[72] George Fisher. See Anstr., II, pp. 102–109.

[73] Smith wrote in November 1631 to Biddulph that he had petitioned Urban VIII for '3 bishops, one for the Southe at Dorchester by Oxford where S. Birin[us] was bishop',

Which of these three waies is best we [*p. 75*] cannot agree but leave it to you to propose any. And surely the last is that which we must come unto in the end wherin there is no other difficulty but feare of offending the State,[74] which may be prevented two waies. First by assuring that Protestants are exempted and that the bishop shall have only spirituall and not temporall power over Catholickes, and consequently can have no pretences against the k[ing's] right. Secondly by procuring the thing to be donn first and then before it be made publick to gett some foraine prince to dispose the k[ing] to be content with it with such reasons as may be alleaged for that purpose. There might be also a third way, which is this: to give the title of Canterbury to my lord of Chalcedon <really>, but to will him not to use it, but to use still that of Chalcedon. Consult these things with our freinds there, and do as you think good, for all is left to your dispatch and prudent resolution. I send you two points more, suggested by Mr Button[75] the archd[eacon] of Staffordshire, wherof you may have use there.

For newes I cannot say much. It is reported and hoped that our queen is again with child. Pursevants are still buissy. A minister is to be censured shortly in the starr chamber for saying that there was but

another at Hexham 'where there was a bishop in S. Bedes time', and a third in Wales (at Caerleon) 'where [there] was a bishop in the Britons time'. Smith's thinking was that 'if his Holiness [shall] restore thes three old bishoprics which long since are decayed he shall no more prejudice the bishops in England than by making bishops in partibus infidelium, and yet shall make them ordinaries'. On 10/20 May 1632 he wrote to Biddulph that he had advised Urban VIII that the bishop for the South 'should either be archb[ishop] or have archiepiscopal authoritie over the other two of the North and of Wales'; AAW, B 27, no. 109; Allison, RSGB, II, p. 236. See AAW, A XXV, no. 114 (a paper in Latin suggesting the division of England into three Catholic bishoprics), no. 115 (a paper in Italian recommending the appointment of an archbishop and two bishops, and suggesting candidates, including John Southcot, John Jackson, Cuthbert Trollop, George Fisher, Edmund Lechmere and Thomas White). Smith had recommended them all separately, with Richard Franks, to Urban VIII on 10/20 May; AAW, B 27, no. 109.

[74] A project for granting titles to English Catholic bishops based on the existing sees of the Church of England had caused considerable trouble during the early 1620s. At the end of August 1622 Edward Bennett had reported to Rome that 'our adversaries', despairing of victory in the curia, 'have not omitted to stir up coals here, and, as is very probably thought, have stirred up the king and State to oppose in the business'. The lord keeper, Bishop John Williams, 'hath been lately with the Spanish ambassador [Carlos Coloma] complaining, as from the king, that the pope went about to set up bishops in his kingdom against his will, which, in former ages, was not wont to be done but by the prince's nomination; and withal signified that he understood they should be created with titles of Canterbury, Lincoln, &c; which must need cause great exasperation in the State, and would by no means be suffered'; TD, V, pp. 90–92, ccxlix; AAW, A XVI, no. 133, p. 535; no. 153, p. 595.

[75] Richard Button. See Anstr., I, p. 60. He had been one of the leading appellant priests in the protests against the archpriest George Blackwell. He was a founding member of William Bishop's episcopal chapter, and in June 1625 became archdeacon of Staffordshire and Cheshire. In August 1636 Button was resident with Lady Isabel Stafford; AAW, A XXVIII, no. 135, p. 457.

a paire of shires between the Church of Rome and that of England.[76] The cause of the two Scotts[77] which hath bin long in triall before my lord of Lenox[78] [*word deleted*], <made> High Cunstable for that purpose, and other lords is not yet ended, but it wilbe shortly, and it is thought it will end by [*p. 76*] banishing Ramsy[79] who accused the other that is a Scottish lord (his name I have forgotten)[80] to have drunke to the health of James the 7th of Scotland (meaning the marquis [of] Hamilton), but as it seemes can not proove it sufficiently against him. Once it was to have been tried by single combat but now it seemes not.

Three Jesuitts were lately released and banished at the instance of [the] queen mother[81] who sent hither a gentleman to see the queen.[82] One of these Jes[uits] is Fa[ther] Knott.[83]

For conclusion lett me tell you that the Lord Baltimor, quondam Sir Georg Calvert, secretary of State, who is now become a great champion for the Jes[uits] by Toby Mathewes persuasion and a great antibishoper, since the losse of his second wife[84] at sea, coming from

---

[76] John Pory recorded on 4 February 1632 that on the previous Wednesday (1 February) 'one Mr Carrier a minister was censured in the starr chamber at £500 fine, and imprisonment during the kinges pleasure, and referred over to the high commission', for saying, among other things, that 'they haste but a payer of shires between our religion and popery, and that it skilled not which of the twoe a man professed'; JPN, p. 205. For the prosecution of Richard Carrier with others in star chamber, see S.R. Gardiner (ed.), *Reports of Cases in the Courts of Star Chamber and High Commission* (Camden Society, new series, 39, 1886), pp. 89–108. I am grateful to Kenneth Fincham for this reference.

[77] For the prosecution, beginning in July 1631, of James Stuart, Lord Ochiltree, on account of the charges which he had brought against James Hamilton, 3rd marquis of Hamilton and others (including the earls of Haddington, Roxburgh, and Buccleugh), see *RPCS, 1630–1632*, pp. viii, xliii, xliv, 263, 269, 352 and *passim*; A. Searle (ed.), *Barrington Family Letters 1628–1632* (Camden Society, fourth series, XXVI, 1983), p. 197; JPN, pp. 165, 184, 186, 191.

[78] James Stuart, 4th duke of Lennox. For Lennox, see D. Smith, *Constitutional Royalism and the Search for Settlement, c. 1640–1649* (Cambridge, 1994), pp. 39–42.

[79] David Ramsay, a gentleman of the privy chamber, who had served as the marquis of Hamilton's intermediary with Gustavus Adolphus. See *RPCS, 1630–1632*, p. xliv.

[80] Donald MacKay, Lord Reay. For the dispute between Reay and Ramsay, see *CSPD, 1631–1633*, pp. 251, 252, 270, 311, 343, 400; *RPCS, 1630–1632*, pp. xliv, 388, 412; JPN, pp. 177, 184, 186, 191, 197, 199–200, 202, 209, 213, 215, 219, 229, 243, 245, 261, 265, 271, 277, 305. The Venetian ambassador in England, Giovanni Soranzo, reported on 18 July 1631 that 'the Scots who were arrested bore testimony against the marquis that he had designs and practices against the king and prince, to make himself king of Scotland. They based their calumny upon his followers in that kingdom and his near blood relationship to the crown', *CSPV, 1629–1632*, p. 526. His raising of levies for Gustavus Adolphus was alleged to be part of his intended treason. See Sharpe, *PR*, p. 168; *CSPD, 1631–1633*, p. 437. Ochiltree's trial was indefinitely postponed, and he was kept in prison until 1652; *RPCS, 1633–1635*, p. xliv.

[81] Marie de Médicis.

[82] For the arrival of Marie de Médicis's envoy, Biscara, to visit Henrietta Maria, see *CSPV, 1629–1632*, p. 576.

[83] Matthew Wilson SJ.

[84] Joan Calvert. See *Letter 4*.

Virginia, hath gone about to marry an other waiting maide that
was his last wifes goddaughter. He first married her with a ring per
verba de praesenti but clandestine, as I take it, and then solicited
consum*m*atione with her, after w*h*ich obtained, he pretends now
he cannot marry her without dispensation from Rome, wherin the
Jes[uits] seeke to abett him uppon pretence of spirituall alliance which
the Councell of Trent hath abrogated. It seemes God will humble and
punnish o*u*r adversaries with shame. The case is secrett, and in secrett
I write it to you, as I meane to do to my lo*r*d wherfor name not me
hereafter if it co[me] to light, but you may lett it be knowne there
what this man is whom they so much rely uppon, and whose children
they seek to preferr to [*word obscured*], as I heare, in that court.

Adieu.

No address.

[*on p. 73*]

Endorsed: 3º Februar[y] 1632. 3 Feb[ruary]. Antonino.
        About 3 b*is*ho*p*s more. About Baltamore.

6. Antonino [John Southcot] to [Peter Biddulph], 24 February 1632

[*AAW, A XXVI, no. 30, pp. 97–100*]

Sir,

I wrote unto you the last weeke according to custome. But as yet we
heare nothing from you of the receipt of our former letters w*h*ich we
much desire to doe, being in paine for feare of some miscariage.

M*r* Laborne is gonn into Lascashire [*sic*] about some buissenesse
of his own, and he desired M*r* Hare and me to supply in his absence.
He receaved yours of the 3 of January, and as touching Fa[ther]
Philip[85] we do conceave that Sig*n*or Agostino[86] is mistaken in him, for

---

[85] Robert Philip seems to have been consistently supportive of Smith and his friends in
their quarrel with the regulars. See *Letter 22*. Gregorio Panzani noted, however, that Philip
admitted to him in December 1634 that there was fault on both sides of the dispute, and
that Smith had boasted in France 'di volere tribulare li Giesuiti'; VA, PD, fo. 40r. In January
1635 Philip told Panzani that if the secular clergy lobbied him for the return of Smith,
he, Panzani, should dissuade them because Smith had alienated both the regulars and the
State; *ibid.*, fo. 58r. Nevertheless, the Jesuit Robert Jenison informed Panzani in the same
month that Smith had, in 'lettere intercette', instructed his friends to get Philip invested
with episcopal authority (although Philip pointed out that, as he was Scottish, it would be
impossible); *ibid.*, fo. 63r.
[86] Girolamo Agostini, secretary to Alvise Contarini, Venetian ambassador.

he was our freind before Agostinos coming and did us good offices with Chasteauneuf[87] and others. Perhaps he might in freedom of speach say to him that my lords[88] demaund was intempestiva, but we can not inferr of that any aversion in the man against my lord bycause many of the clergy <and> of my lords best freinds did think as much. We rather thinke that Agostino ~~was~~ is no freind of my lords bycause he communicated with my lords adversaries an informa-tion which was given him <here> in privat touching the laity, as we wrote unto you heretofore, which was called Vera et Sincera Infor-matio de Affectionibus Catholicorum erga Episcopum Chalcedoniensem etcetera.[89]

The narration[90] and supplication,[91] which I mentioned to you in my last letter, to his Hol[iness] from the clergy is not yet [*p. 98*] coppied out but I purpose to have a coppy ready by the next week and will send it to my lord for you. It is long and containes much matter but you may abreviat it and alter it at your discretion.

We intend also the next week to send you a letter[92] from the chapter to his Hol[iness] in conformity of those points which you proposed to Card[inal] Ginetti[93] where we will touch uppon that point of a successor in Fa[ther] Fitzherberts place.[94]

We certified you in some of our former letters of a disgracefull accident happened of late to one of my l[ord] bishops chief opposers, namely my Lord Baltimor.[95] The Jesuitts have undertaken to breake

[87] Charles de l'Aubespine, marquis de Chateauneuf, French ambassador in England.
[88] Richard Smith.
[89] This document is now AAW, A XXI, no. 42 (which Allison, QJ, p. 142, dates to c. 1627). It accuses Francis Plowden and Sir Tobie Mathew of being behind the agitation against Richard Smith, influencing others such as Sir Basil Brooke and Thomas Brudenell, 1st Baron Brudenell (whose first cousin Audrey (d. 1623) had been Brooke's first wife). On 7/17 April 1632 Smith reminded Biddulph to 'be not too confident of Signor Agostino', for Southcot had written that he 'played him a trick in England, and his accusing of F[ather] Phil[ip] increaseth the suspicion'; AAW, B 27, no. 108. By January 1633 Smith heard from Biddulph that Agostini was now to be trusted again; AAW, B 27, no. 115.
[90] See *Letter 7*. This item appears to be the 'Humillima Narratio' referred to by Southcot in *Letter 17*.
[91] The 'Humillima Supplicatio'. See *Letter 1*.
[92] This appears to be AAW, A XXVI, no. 31, a petition (dated 26 February 1632) from John Colleton, dean of the chapter, and countersigned by George Leyburn, to Urban VIII, urging the restoration of Richard Smith and episcopal government over English Catholics, and arguing that the control of the English college in Rome should return to the secular clergy now that, the petition (mistakenly) said, the rector of the college, Thomas Fitzherbert, was dead.
[93] Cardinal Martio Ginetti, major-domo of Urban VIII.
[94] Thomas Fitzherbert remained as the rector of the English college in Rome until his death in August 1640.
[95] See *Letters 4, 5*.

the mach[96] and to worke it by the nuncio of Brusselles[97] meanes. But perhaps the clergy wilbe of an other opinion when the case shalbe proposed unto them, it being now in handling in Fa[ther] Knott.[98] He gave the maide (who was his penitent) straunge councell, as I heare, for he led her [to] be assured that my L[ord] Balt[imore] would moove her to nothing but what she might lawfully doe wherupon she gave way to consummacion, as my lord had mooved before. I was tould this day that Fa[ther] Knott is much [p. 99] vexed <and troubled> [word deleted] hereat, now fearing (it seemes) that he shalbe accounted to have given very imprudent and ungodly counsell to the maide. You shall heare more of this hereafter.

Here is arrived one M[r] Chambers, a Scottish priest, whom you have seen perhaps in Paris. He goeth into Scotland[99] shortly and at his rettourne he desireth to carry with him some information from hence to the nonce of Paris[100] touching our affaires which we will in the meane time think of. Some think that he is a bishop and sure it is that he was to have bin made bishop for Scotland, but that the Theatines,[101] hearing of it, sought to crosse it. Yet perhaps he was privatly consecrated, which if it be soe, it will be a great strengthning to us and our bishop. He heares that two things are objected against you in Ro[me]. The one is that you were dismissed the college,[102] the other that you were the chief agent in procuring the Sorbon censures[103] whereat, they say, the pope is offended. And he seems to feare that these two consideration[s] will

---

[96] i.e. the marriage of Sir George Calvert, 1st Baron Baltimore, and Mary Wynne.

[97] Fabio de Lagonissa, archbishop of Conza.

[98] Matthew Wilson SJ.

[99] On 1 March 1632 John Jackson reported to Biddulph that 'Mr David Chambers is in towne. I have him once a day with me. He prepares to go to Scot[land] where the Jes[uits'] proceedinges doe much hurch [sic for hurt]'; AAW, A XXVI, no. 33, p. 107. For Chambers, see M.V. Hay, *The Blairs Papers, 1603–1660* (London, 1929), pp. 111–12; Allison, RSGB, I, p. 362. He had connections with the Paris Oratory, and had campaigned for the appointment of Catholic bishops in Scotland. He enjoyed the patronage of Urban VIII's nephew, Cardinal Francesco Barberini, and was a cousin of Thomas Chambers, the well-known nephew of George Con and almoner to Cardinal Richelieu; Hay, *Blairs Papers*, pp. 122–129; Hibbard, *CI*, pp. 125, 269, 288; I. Atherton, *Ambition and Failure in Stuart England* (Manchester, 1999), p. 205.

[100] Cardinal Alessandro Bichi.

[101] Jesuits.

[102] This is a reference to Peter Biddulph's part in the so-called 'Fitton rebellion' at the English college in Rome. On 15/25 October 1623 five students, including Biddulph, were expelled from the college by the rector Thomas Fitzherbert; Anstr., II, p. 25.

[103] i.e. *Censura Propositionum quarundam, tum ex Hibernia Delatarum, cum ex duobus Libris Anglico Sermone Conscriptis in Latinum Bona Fide Conversis Excerptarum [. . .]* (Paris, 1631); ARCR, I, nos 683–685, which condemned *inter alia* two English tracts written by Jesuits (Matthew Wilson SJ, *A Modest Briefe Discussion of some Points taught by M. Doctour Kellison in his Treatise of the Ecclesiasticall Hierarchy* (Rouen [imprint false; printed secretly in England], 1630); ARCR, II, no. 822; Floyd, *An Apolagy of the Holy Sea Apostolicks Proceeding [. . .]*).

much hinder th*e* progresse of y*o*ur negotiation, as proceeding from
one whose person is not gratefull. But I tell him [*p. 100*] that the first
is ~~fals~~ far otherwise than as it is reported, and the second, were it true,
can be no prejudice unto you or us bycause by the event the pope and
cardinalls will see our intentions wh*ich* will cleer all in time.

Newes we have nonn. Carleton Vicount Dorchester[104] died on
Ashwednesday last, and the secretariship is not yet given to an other.
Many are in competency for the place as Lo*r*d Cottington,[105] S*i*r
Kellam Digby,[106] Lo*r*d Aston,[107] S*i*r Dudly Digg[es], Watt Mountague[108]
and others.[109] Pursevants are still buissy. Compositions are not yet
~~finished~~ <accorded> for recusants. The king and queen are gonn
to Newmarkett for a month or 3 weekes. I heare the mony is stayed
now wh*ich* should have bin [*word deleted*] <sent> to <the k[ing] of>
Swedland.[110] We are in hand to recover o*u*r fishing out of the
Hollanders hands.[111] The kings going to Scotland houldeth not for this
yeare.

This is all I have to say. So in hast, adieu. 24 Febr[uary] 1632.

Yours,

Antonino.

No address.

Endorsed: 24 Feb[ruary]. Antonino. About my Lo*r*d Baltamour his case.

7. [John Southcot] to [Richard Smith], 28 February 1632

[*AAW, B 47, no. 59*][112]

Most hon[oured] m*a*ster,

M*r* Laborne being gon into the North about buissenesse of his own,
and not to rettourne till Easter, I receaved two packetts from you

---

[104] Sir Dudley Carleton, 1st Viscount Dorchester.
[105] Sir Francis Cottington, created Baron Cottington in July 1631.
[106] For the secular clergy's relationship with Sir Kenelm Digby, see A.F. Allison, 'An English
gallican: Henry Holden, (1596/7–1662): part 1 (to 1648)', *RH*, 22 (1995), pp. 319–349, *passim*.
[107] Sir Walter Aston, 1st Baron Aston of Forfar.
[108] Walter Montagu, younger son of Henry Montagu, 1st earl of Manchester. See Hibbard,
CI, passim.
[109] Cf. Birch, *CT*, II, p. 169.
[110] See *Letter 3*; cf. *CSPV, 1629–1632*, p. 597.
[111] Cf. *ibid.*, p. 612.
[112] AAW, B 47 is unpaginated.

since his departure, the first of 23 of February, and the later 1° Martii. And in the later there was one to me, with M[r] Fittons[113] to your self enclosed in it, but wheras M[r] Fitton saies in that letter that he sends you ~~the~~ a coppy of <u>the second information</u> w*h*ich he gave to Card[inal] Ginetti, y*our* letter makes no mention therof, and we should be glad to see it also, that we may proceed from hen<u>ce in conformity therunto</u>, wherfor I beseech yo<u>u cause M[r] Plantin</u>[114] to write a coppy for us by the next post.

We will procure <u>the best information</u> we can to satisfy M[r] Fitton in those points which he mentioneth in his letter and heretofore some of them were [*word deleted*] touched in o*ur* former letters. He <u>hath bin weekly written</u> unto ever since the <u>begining of December and</u> I hope they will all come safe, bycause in his last to M[r] Laborne he writes that M[r] Skinner[115] receaved that week a letter from hence dated the 18 November, wherby it appeares that o*ur* letters come but slowly.

For my part I do not like that the nonce[116] should <u>be so importunat with you to go to</u> R[ome].[117] It argues some feare <they have> of y*our* stay in France, and a desire to prolong the bui<u>ssinesse and weary</u>

---

[113] Peter Biddulph.

[114] Lawrence Platt.

[115] Edward Skinner. In February 1630 Thomas White recommended that Skinner should succeed him as Smith's agent at Rome; AAW, A XXIV, no. 5, p. 13. Edward was the second son of Anthony Skinner of Shelfield Park, Aston Cantlow, Warwickshire, and Elizabeth, daughter of Edward Gage of Bentley, Framfield, Sussex (a patron of the secular clergy until his death in 1614). He was a brother of the priests Andrew and James Skinner. (James became the secular clergy's agent in Rome in 1646. His sister Eleanor was one of the first members of the new Augustinian convent at Paris, founded with the assistance of leading secular clergymen. See Anstr., II, pp. 296–297; William Camden, *The Visitation of the County of Warwick in the Year 1619*, J. Fetherston (ed.) (Harleian Society 12, 1877), p. 295; *Letter 46*; F.-M.-Th. Cédoz, *Un Couvent de Religieuses Anglaises à Paris de 1634 à 1884* (London, 1891), p. 28.) On 7/17 April 1632 Smith informed Biddulph that 'Mr Skinner [. . .] is this day gone for England', by way of Dieppe, 'in companie of the L[ord] Grandison [William Villiers, Viscount Grandison], but in very weak case for healthe'; AAW, B 27, no. 108. (By May Smith had heard that Skinner was 'much mended'; AAW, B 27, no. 109. Cf. AAW, A XXVI, no. 142, p. 385, XXVII, no. 27, p. 71.) In London, Skinner continued to receive news from France, particularly from Lawrence Platt (see e.g. AAW, A XXVI, no. 74, p. 209), and from Biddulph in Rome (see AAW, A XXVI, *passim*), until his death in early 1633; *Letter 32*.

[116] Cardinal Alessandro Bichi.

[117] On 19/29 March, Smith reported to Biddulph that his patron Cardinal Richelieu, who was 'exceeeding forward to help our cause', had offered Smith £500 to go to Rome. Smith had successfully persuaded Richelieu that he (Smith) and his leading supporters in England believed that Smith would be 'detained [there] under some honorable com*mendati*on', and in effect prevented from carrying on his struggle. They thought that he should stay in Paris until the suit against his opponents was successful, and then return to England. The nuncio Cardinal Bichi, however, thought Smith's presence was needed in Rome 'because the Jes[uits] send 20 re*lati*ons for every one of ours'; AAW, B 27, no. 107. See also AAW, B 27, nos 108, 109.

you out. Others here are of my opinion also, and therfor it is wished by us that you ~~should~~ would not seem to give him any hope therof but put it fairely of[f] with some good excuse, as of y*our* age and of the charge etc*etera* and we conceave that the feare they have of your stay in France (if it be well mannaged) may moove them to dispatch you the sooner, especially if y*our* freinds write effectually for you from thence, and the b*isho*ps second it, by way of entreaty and intercession, and no otherwise, as we never desired they should to the least prejudice of the Sea Apostolick or his Hol[iness's] authority.

I have inquired who those two English ambassadors are at Civita Vecchia of whom Mr Fitton writeth in his last letter, and I understand they are two brothers called Nappers, the elder wherof goes to R[ome] uppon a wager being to receave 5 for one at his rettourne.[118] Whether the Jes[uits] will make use of ~~the~~ him there I know not, and perhaps they will, bycause he hath used them here divers times, and is thought to tend that way. He is a bould man and hath a good witt. Therfor it were good Mr Fitton were advertised therof. It is now more than ever desired that you should see o*ur* ambassador[119] there, bycause he is the likliest man to be made secretary in Carletons place. It is sufficient that the nonce is not against it.

Mr Price[120] hath gotten a protection under 6 of the councells handes by S*ir* John Langworths meanes,[121] who wrought it by a clerk of the councell uppon some considerations w*hi*ch I know not what they were.

Two pr[iests] are discovered that ~~live pretend~~ live in the shew of wedlock. The one I heard of but yesterday being a young man of 30 yeares of age of 3 yeares standing here, wherof two he hath led in this sacrilegious manner. He studdied at Sivil, and of a marchants factor there was made a scoller and pr[iest] and now keepeth a ~~wharf~~ wharf about Milford Lane. His name is Crispe.[122] He went by the name of Cary. But he is yet knowen to few, yet I feare the Jes[uits] will know it, bycause one Tipper, S*ir* John Wintours man, hath bin <lately> tould (by mischaunce) that he was a priest w*hi*ch before he knew not, and it is like he will not conceale it from the Jes[uits]. The other is Anth[ony] Smith[123] whom [*sic*] when I acquainted [him] with that

[118] Christopher and William Napper, two of the sons of William Napper and Isabel Powell, are both recorded as having been in Rome in January 1632; A. Davidson, 'Roman Catholicism in Oxfordshire from the late Elizabethan period to the Civil War c. 1580–1640' (Ph.D. thesis, University of Bristol, 1970), p. 207; CRS, 1, p. 133.

[119] Sir Isaac Wake. See *CSPV, 1629–1632*, p. 598. Smith recorded that Wake was a 'moderate' man and a good friend; AAW, A XXVII, no. 61, p. 177.

[120] William (Benedict) Jones OSB.

[121] The Langworths were patrons of the Benedictines; ARSJ, Anglia MS 32/ii, fo. 401r.

[122] See Anstr., II, pp. 75–76.

[123] For Anthony Smith, alias Pole, see Allison, JG; Codignola, *CHL*, pp. 43–45.

report made of him, he humd and hawd and spake little consequently
or to the purpose. And since that time, which was a month agoe, I
have neither seen him nor heard from hime. I feare it is to[o] trew,
and some say that he hath two wives, one a Protest[ant] and an other
Cathol[ic]. God help them bothe and mend them.

Mr Spence <u>alias Chambers</u>[124] is come. Mr Hammon[125] thinkes him
to be a <u>zealous clergy man, and</u> doubts whether he be actually bishop
or noe; but takes no notice to him, nor speakes of it to others, bycause,
if it be so, it is very secrett. He desires <u>to have an information</u> from us
at his rettourne out of Scotland after two or 3 months, thinking to go
over againe.

I send you <now> the long <u>narration and supplication</u> which I
mentioned before,[126] and when M^r <u>Plantin or some other hath</u> taken
a coppy you may please to send it to Mr Fitton who may reduce it into
a shorter forme.

This week <u>we send our common letter</u>[127] to his Hol[iness] in conformity of those points which Mr Fitton gave to Card[inal] Ginetti.

We heare not yet <u>of Mr Haslewoods</u>[128] arrivall here.

You may please to write still to Mr Laborne by the <u>name of Fontaine</u>,
only the outward cover must be to <u>Monsieur Heyne</u>.

Thus with woonted duty remembred, I rest.

28 Febr[uary] 1632.

No address or endorsement.

8. [John Southcot] to [Richard Smith], 14 March 1632

[AAW, A XXVI, no. 38, pp. 121–124]

Most hon[oured] master,

I have yours of the 8 of this month wherin you make no mention yet of
visiting our ambassador there,[129] a thing so behoofull in many respects
that your freinds here would not have it omitted by any meanes.

---

[124] David Chambers. See *Letter 6*; cf. Anstr., II, pp. 340–341.

[125] John Jackson.

[126] See *Letters 1, 4, 6*.

[127] Presumably a reference to AAW, A XXVI, no. 31 (John Colleton to Urban VIII, 26
February 1632).

[128] James Haselwood. See Anstr., II, pp. 150–151. He eventually became chaplain to
Viscount Stafford.

[129] Sir Isaac Wake. See *Letter 7*.

We wrote the last week to the Inquisit[ion] and the week before [to the] pope, and now we send duplicates of them by the way of Paris which you will receave togeather with these. M[r] Laborne is still out of town. M[r] East[130] is sick of an ague in the country. He writeth to me very earnestly to have his case proposed to the assembly of bishops there and him self justified by their verdict which M[r] D[octor] Seton[131] promised to do who carried the case with him drawen by M[r] East him self. I send you that parcell of M[r] Easts letter to me which concerns that buissenesse and I beseech you lett M[r] Plantin[132] call uppon D[octor] Seton for the case and, when the assembly is, lett it be proposed, and followed to M[r] Easts desire and satisfaction, whom we have all <reason> to keep our freind as much as we can. M[r] Ploydon,[133] Sir Basil[134] and that crew do give it out here that my lord bishop is coming over againe shortly, perhaps to hinder [*two words obliterated*: his coming (?)] <if they can> fearing indeed that he shall come unexpectedly uppon them ere long by some order from the citty.[135] They beginn now to give out that the Catholickes are willing to have a bishop but with no tribunal, or forum externum.

I heare that Fa[ther] John Floid and Fa[ther] Rudesindo[136] have given their verdict at large in writing uppon the lords case,[137] and pronounce that it is no marriage, giving only for reason the not reception of the Councell of Trent here which hath taken away that impediment of compaternity derived from the wife to the husband.[138] I have seen Fa[ther] Floids verdict but I could not gett a coppy of it, for, it seemes, they are loath to lett anything be seen under their

---

[130] This appears to be the cleric Richard East who wrote to Richard Smith in April 1632 with news about John Floyd's recently published reply to Sir Humphrey Linde (*A Paire of Spectacles [. . .]* (Rouen, 1631); ARCR, II, no. 298), criticizing Floyd's tract for 'not carrying with it the gravity of a divine', and for making jokes at Smith's expense; AAW, A XXVI, no. 52, p. 157. See also *Letters 25, 32, 33*; AAW, A XXVI, no. 24, p. 77. East had been ordained at Arras in April 1631 and was sent to England in June 1632; Anstr., II, p. 92.

[131] Dr William Seton had been a friend of the secular clergy while he was in Rome during the 1620s; AAW, B 26, no. 70. Thomas More described him as 'nere of kin to the late chanceler of Scotland', Alexander Seton, earl of Dunfermline (d. 16 June 1622); AAW, A XVIII, no. 55, p. 337.

[132] Lawrence Platt.

[133] Francis Plowden.

[134] Sir Basil Brooke.

[135] On 7/17 April 1632 Richard Smith complained to Peter Biddulph that 'Mr Ploiden and his fellows give out everie where that I am to returne shortly and that speech did first rise from the Capucins in England', though 'whence they had that I know not'. Smith speculated that the rumour might have come from François Joseph le Clerc du Tremblay (Père Joseph); AAW, B 27, no. 108.

[136] William (Rudesind) Barlow OSB.

[137] Baron Baltimore's marriage to Mary Wynne. See *Letters 4, 5, 6*.

[138] Southcot refers here to the fact that Baltimore's third wife was god-daughter to his second wife.

hands wherin they oppose the reception of the Councell. The clergy[139] consulted of this case the last week, and resolved that the mariage was good, but nothing in writing. Indeed John Floids reasons ~~are~~ and answers are but fallacies, as far as I could judg of them hearing them read but once over by an other body who was charged not to lett that coppy go out of his hands.

I ame sory you yeald to Mr Colletons request of not abiding ordinarily in London, for now we have no hope to draw him from his brother and kinred who I feare will gett all he hath when he dieth. And, besides, his superiority[140] [p. 122] is of small use to us or to the Catholickes while he is not ordinarily at hand to be spoke withall.

For my self I humbly thanke you for the care you shew of my health and indeed I was fain to use some prevention this Lent fearing the like consequence as ~~that~~ happ[ened] [he]re last Easter by occasion of Lenten diett. I ame now somwhat better than I was, but still in phisick and not yet confirmed in healthe and strength, soe as I dare ride half a dozen miles. Neither have I bin able yet to go down to my fathers house in Surrey,[141] but after Easter I will beginn to make a triall.

This book of Petronilla[142] is wonderfully well liked of, and many coppies are wished for here.

As for your going to R[ome], all here are against it and not without good reason for that were to beginn your buissenesse againe, and <to> putt your self and us to needlesse charges and perhaps to hinder your rettourne hither for ever. Our freindes will not give their consents unto it by any meanes.[143]

Doctor Flud[144] tould me the other day that one in the country saied unto him I had forsworne [my] self in attesting the Disclaime[145] wherfor I could wish that the attestations were printed, with the two first letters of the pr[iests'] names, for Mr Hares justification and mine in that point.

[139] i.e. the secular clergy.

[140] Colleton was dean of the episcopal chapter.

[141] The Southcot residence was at Merstham (Albury Manor); *VCH Surrey*, III, p. 216; CRS, I, pp. 98–99.

[142] P.S.P., *A Discours Hapned. Betwene an Hermite called Nicephorus & a yong lover called Tristan, who for that his mistresse Petronilla entred into religion would faine become an hermite* (Paris, 1630); ARCR, II, no. 586. This work is a translation of Jean-Pierre Camus, bishop of Belley's romance entitled *Pétronille. Accident Pitoyable de Nos Jours*, written in 1626. It was a polemic directed against some of the regular clergy.

[143] See *Letter 7*.

[144] Dr Robert Floyd. See *Letter 3*.

[145] *Général Désadveu des Catholiques Lais d'Angleterre [. . .]*. See *Letter 3*.

Thus, with all woonted duty, I rest. 14 Martii 1632.

[on p. 124]

Addressed: For my maister at Paris.

No endorsement.

9. [John Southcot] to [Richard Smith], 11 April 1632

[AAW, A XXVI, no. 54, pp. 161–162]

Most hon[oured] master,

Even now I receaved yours of the 12 of Aprill to which there occurreth not much to answer in particuler. Mr Nelson[146] hath sent for Mr Dade[147] to deliver him the generals letter, but he hath putt off his coming once or twice. I cannot yet heare that Doct[or] Haillers book[148] is come hither. It <u>is pitty Dire</u>cteur Spirituel[149] is not in English and Latin pro bono communi, for I conceave it would do much good in all places. I heard Mr Plantin[150] <u>was</u> in hand with it <once> and I wish he had made an end of it ere he had given it over.[151]

A good freind of yours and ours tould me that he understood from a privy <u>counseller</u> for certaine that my <u>Lord Peter</u>[152] <u>and others</u> had

---

[146] John Jackson.

[147] Thomas Middleton OP, Superior of the English Dominicans.

[148] François Hallier, *Defensio Ecclesiasticae Hierarchiae, seu, Vindiciae Censurae Facultatis Theologiae Parisiensis, adversus Hermanii Loemelii Spongiam* (Paris, 1632); ARCR I, no. 499. For Hallier, whom Allison terms a 'moderate gallican', and his links with the English secular clergy, see Allison, RSGB, III, pp. 165–166. On 7/17 April Smith recorded that a member of the Sorbonne 'told me that it is thought D. Halliers book will be put in the Indice'; AAW, B 27, no. 108.

[149] Jean-Pierre Camus (bishop of Belley), *Le Directeur Spirituel Désinteressé* (Paris, 1632).

[150] Lawrence Platt.

[151] Lawrence Platt in 1633 did, in fact, publish his translation of Jean-Pierre Camus's book *Le Directeur Spirituel Désinteressé* as *The Spirituall Director Disinteressed* (Rouen [imprint false; printed at Paris], 1633); ARCR, II, no. 648. This work argued for the superiority, as confessors, of parochial clergy over the religious orders. See E. Duffy, 'The English secular clergy and the Counter-Reformation', *Journal of Ecclesiastical History*, 34 (1983), pp. 214–230, at p. 224.

[152] William Petre, 2nd Baron Petre. Via a notarial instrument drawn up by William Case on 11 May 1632, the marquis of Winchester described how he found Petre to be a violent opponent of Catholic episcopal authority in England; AAW, A XXVI, no. 71, p. 199. In January 1635, the seculars described Petre with venom thus: 'totius est a partibus Jesuitarum, et alienissimus ab episcopo Chalcedonensi quamvis in pueritia fuerunt una condiscipuli. Hic baro ex illis est, qui credunt nihil doctum, nihil prudens, nihil pium esse in toto terrarum orbe, nisi quod proficiscitur a Jesuitis, pro quibus est zelosissimus ne dicam factiosissimus, vir alioquin pius'; AAW, A XXVIII, no. 3, p. 16.

geven up somwhat to the k[ing] by my lord <u>treasurers</u>[153] <u>meanes in</u> writing a good while since ag*ai*nst the bishop.[154] <u>But this freind,</u> <u>defend</u>ing the b*isho*p in his answer to the saied counsellor, and retorting all objections uppon the b*isho*ps adversaries, shewing that the daunger to the State was greater on their part than on the b*isho*ps, bred a good opinion in the counsellor of the b*isho*p and his authority, which he promised to informe the k[ing] of. I suppose you will ghesse at the parties though I name them not. Mr Fountaine[155] and I will do o*u*r best to <u>gett a coppy of</u> that writing or at least to learne the contents therof.

There hath happened this weeke an other foule buisinesse which ma[y] [*ms torn*: argue (?)] the want of authority here, and serve as a testimony of Gods [*ms torn*: judgements] ~~uppon the~~ withall in some kind. The buissenesse is this. M[r] Worth[ington],[156] clayming interest in a young gentlewoman,[157] daughter to my Lady Perkins,[158] lately profest at Gaunt,[159] and having used many waies to gett her from thence both before and since her profession, pretending that she is his lawfull wife, and consequ*en*tly that her profession is void, but after much labour and charge having profited nothing in the buissenesse, nor yett anything by following it so eagerly but scorne and derision from his adversaries and their freinds, without hope to prevaile any other way, at length resolved uppon this course, videlicet to cause M[r] Gibbons al*i*as Wakeman,[160]

---

[153] Sir Richard Weston, 1st Baron Weston, created earl of Portland in February 1633.

[154] Richard Smith.

[155] George Leyburn.

[156] William Worthington was the son of Thomas Worthington of Blainscow Hall, and Mary, daughter of George Allen of Rossall Grange (and thus a niece of Cardinal William Allen). William was a great-nephew of Thomas Worthington DD, the former president of Douai college. He was also a brother-in-law of Peter Biddulph (*Letter 10*), for he had previously been married to Helen, daughter of Richard Biddulph of Biddulph Hall, Staffordshire, Peter Biddulph's father. Richard Biddulph was himself regarded as a favourer of the Society of Jesus. (Thomas Worthington DD, who had entered the Society in 1626, died at Biddulph Hall in 1626 or 1627; Anstr., I, p. 388.) In June 1633 Richard Smith informed Biddulph that 'they write that' the Jesuit John Worthington, the Biddulph family chaplain, 'who is to goe to R[ome] as procurator of their order, giveth out that he is to com*m*and you from *your* father to give over y*ou*r office'; AAW, B 27, no. 121. However, entries in Gregorio Panzani's diary for February and May 1635 suggest that John Worthington was not as hostile to Richard Smith and the seculars as many other Jesuits were; VA, PD, fo. 91r. See also PRO, 31/9/17B (transcript of Panzani's letter to Cardinal Francesco Barberini of 13 May 1635).

[157] Penelope Parkins.

[158] Mary Parkins.

[159] Ghent.

[160] John Wakeman. Biddulph noted that Chrysogona Wakeman (a member of Mary Ward's Institute) was sister to John Wakeman and to Thomas Wakeman SJ. On 7/17 April 1632 Biddulph reported to Edward Skinner that there were 'two Jesuitesses' who had left Rome for Paris via Marseilles, 'one M[rs] Ratclif and M[rs] Wakeman who is my kinswoman.

the concealed <u>Theatin,</u>[161] <u>to be appr</u>ehended by a messenger of my
lord of Dorsetts,[162] having first petitioned to the k[ing] and gotten the
reference to be made unto his lordship, and carried before my lord, who,
examining the matter in the presence of them both, in fine committed
<u>Gibbons close prisoner to</u> the Gatehouse where he is at this present,
and there likely to ly, for ought I see, till M[r] Worthington gett his
<u>wife whom Gibbons</u> carried over and persuaded to be a nunn. This
matter haith bread a great clamour against Worthington and a great
scandall to all.[163] And it were fitt that M[r] Fitton[164] certified the pope
[*p. 162*] and cardinalls therof, as I suppose you will do the nonce[165]
there.

Mr Calvert[166] is much disgusted, and sweareth that he hath seen it
written from <u>Paris that</u> the clergy hath certified <and divulged> his
fathers case there, to his ignom[in]y, by one who saieth that he had the
letter in his hand <u>which was wr</u>itten to <u>my lord</u>[167] <u>him</u> self from hence
about that matter.[168] Either he doth this out of cunning, and to see
what we will say to it, or els, if it be true, we cannot but think that my
lord hath some untrusty persons about him that seek to do ill offices
which his lordship may quickly ~~know~~ perceave.

She came lately from Naples. Her brother is one of the priests'; AAW, A XXVI, no. 57,
p. 167.
  [161] i.e. Jesuit.
  [162] Edward Sackville, 4th earl of Dorset, whom the secular clergy identified as a supporter
of Richard Smith.
  [163] This was a long-running case concerning a broken marriage agreement between
William Worthington and Penelope Parkins (daughter of Sir George Parkins, the recorder
of Nottingham, and his wife Mary, daughter of Edward Isham); G.W. Marshall (ed.), *The
Visitations of the County of Nottingham in the Years 1569 and 1614* (Harleian Society 4, 1871),
pp. 159–160; P.W. Hasler (ed.), *The House of Commons 1558–1603*, 3 vols (London, 1981), III,
p. 176. William alleged that Penelope had been compelled to go abroad and enter a house
of religion; AAW, A XXIV, no. 185, p. 687; XXVI, nos 1–14, no. 24, p. 63, no. 88, p. 255,
no. 95, p. 261, no. 101, p. 279, no. 111, p. 311, no. 147, p. 401; XXVII, no. 147, p. 449; *Letters
10, 11, 12, 20*; Anstr., II, p. 331. See also AAW, A XXVII, no. 5 for copies of documents
relating to Worthington's suit. He claimed that he was 'deluded of the certane promises
[which] were given unto me by M[rs] Parkins in the way to Dover for her speedie returne,
she pretending that jorney partly to avoyd her mothers and friends importunitie in pressing
her to marrie an Irish man, partly to avoyd her indignation against the mariage with me',
since 'her fortunes depended wholie upon her mother'. Worthington believed he had John
Wakeman's promise that Penelope would return, but 'in the end [Wakeman] broake his
oath', and 'cloathed her in a religious habitt'. Worthington's threats against Wakeman and
the Jesuit Matthew Wilson were to no avail, and he went over to Ghent to seek redress there;
AAW, A XXVI, no. 4, p. 23.
  [164] Peter Biddulph.
  [165] Cardinal Alessandro Bichi.
  [166] Cecil Calvert, who, four days after the date of this letter, would become the 2nd Baron
Baltimore, following the death of his father, Sir George Calvert; GEC, III, p. 393.
  [167] Richard Smith.
  [168] Sir George Calvert, 1st Baron Baltimore's marriage to Mary Wynne. See *Letters 4, 5, 6*.

It were to be wished in my opinion that my lord treasurer and Lord Cottington were particulerly writen unto in my lords behalf by my lord ambassador there,[169] seeing those two have bin made the chief instruments to informe the k[ing] against him.

I should have informed you long since in secrett, as I did M[r] Fitton, that Signor Angelo[170] the Italian <and> musitian to the king tould me he was to goe to Chichester to treat with the bishop[171] there about his conversion, and to make him an offer of provition from the resident of Spaine[172] here in his Majesties name for his maintenance according to his degree beyond seas. What the ground should be of this I know not, or whether he tould it me only to [en]deer him self unto me, but he conjured me to great secrecy, and as a secrett I beseech you to keep it till we heare further.

Thus with my sisters[173] humble duty remembred, and my own, I rest.

11 Aprill 1632.

No address or endorsement.

10. Antonino [John Southcot][174] to Fitton [Peter Biddulph], 13 April 1632

[*AAW, A XXVI, no. 55, pp. 163–164*]

Sir,

I wrote to you the last weeke according to my custom, since which time I receaved yours of the 3 of March by M[r] Skinner who is, God be thanked, safe arrived in Sussex, ~~and~~ as he writeth to me, and intendeth to be in London within a fortnight. We will all be ready to do with curtesy as you desire, and [*word deleted*] shew our selves thankfull for the paines he hath taken there in our affaires. The last we had from you was of the 13th of March wherin you sent Card[inal]

---

[169] Sir Isaac Wake, who died in June 1632; *CSPV, 1629–1632*, p. 626.

[170] This is presumably the 'musitian' called Angelo whom Sir George Calvert noted in January 1623 as being in Charles's service. Angelo had caused a scandal by assisting with the 'musique' at 'midnight masse' in the Spanish embassy in London at Christmas in 1622; Bodl., Tanner MS 73, fo. 270r.

[171] Richard Montagu, bishop of Chichester.

[172] Juan de Necolalde y Martinez de Barrenechea. See A.J. Loomie, 'The Spanish faction at the court of Charles I, 1630–8', *BIHR*, 59 (1986), pp. 37–49.

[173] This may be a reference to John Southcot's sister-in-law Elizabeth (Seaborne); W.C. Metcalfe (ed.), *The Visitations of Essex*, 2 vols (Harleian Society 13–14, 1878–1879), I, p. 492.

[174] For Southcot's change of his alias, see *Letter 14*.

Borgia his speech made in open consistory[175] and wrote the passages
briefly of that buissenesse to M[r] Laborne but I hope which we were
all sory to heare of. In requitall of that newes M[r] Lab[orne] will
certify you of a scandalous action happened here since Easter between
one John Green, alias Gibbons, alias Wakeman a pretended sec[ular]

[175] For the speech delivered by Gasparo Borgia, archbishop of Seville and Toledo, on 27
February/8 March 1632, see AAW, A XXVIII, no. 74; Pastor, *HP*, XXVIII, pp. 287–290;
JPN, pp. 251–252. In December 1631 Borgia, who had replaced the count of Monterey as
the Spanish ambassador in Rome, had been instructed to represent forcefully to the pope
the necessity of aiding the emperor financially, and to allow Philip IV to levy taxation on the
Spanish clergy for that purpose; and, if Urban VIII refused (as he, in fact, did), to deliver a
strong protest; *ibid.*, pp. 281–282. Southcot noted in his diary that Borgia 'spake in public
consistory to the pope by commandment of the king of Spain protesting the king to be
free and the pope to be to blame if any harm came to religion by the wars of Germany';
CRS, 1, pp. 107–108. See also AAW, A XXVI, no. 42, p. 131 for Biddulph's information of
10/20 March 1632 that, following his performance in the consistory, Borgia 'is held here
to have incurred excommunication for his disobedience and insistent proceeding against
the pope, insomuch that now he neither frequenteth congregacion nor chappels. He came
last week to the congregacion of the Holy Office before his Holiness, allthough he was
not warned to come as the custome is, and then the pope asked him what he did there,
seeing he was not sent for, and tould him that he was excommunicated, and that he should
looke unto it, because he would not absolve him from it, yett, because the congregacion
concerned the good of the Church, he would not for that time forbid him to stay and be
present at it'. Afterwards the pope told Borgia that he would no longer receive him as
Spanish ambassador. Biddulph believed that Borgia and 'those who were authors of that
protestation, have done the pope greate wrong [. . .] for they should rather have thanked' the
pope; for the pope had 'some 7 or 8 dayes before [. . .] apppointed [. . .] a congregacion' of
former nuncios to France, Spain, and Germany to consider 'the business of the emperour'
and 'to doe what they should think fitt for his assistance'. This congregation was to meet
on the very day that Borgia delivered his protest, 'and they have met often since'. However,
'I doubt not butt many in England will augment these matters, and draw all they cann in
the worst sense to calumniate his Holines, and make the world believe that there were some
greater division than indeed there is'. See also Pastor, *HP*, XXVIII, pp. 290–291. On 29
May 1632 Biddulph recorded that 'the Spanish embass[ador], who was so long expected,
is now arrived at his Holiness sollicitation, who could not endure that Borgia should be
any more embass[ador]', although 'last night there arrived an extraordinarye currier from
Spaine with order that Borgia should remaine still ordinarye embass[ador]' and the other
should 'be only as extraordinarye'; AAW, A XXVI, no. 78, p. 219. On 23 June/3 July 1632
Biddulph noted that Cardinal Borgia and the pope were reconciled; AAW, A XXVI, no. 91,
p. 251. However, on 7/17 July Biddulph wrote that Borgia had been refused audience by
the pope on the grounds that there was already a Spanish ambassador in Rome; AAW, A
XXVI, no. 94, p. 259.
    For Borgia's continuing troubles at the papal court, and his return to Spain in early 1636,
see AAW, A XXVIII, no. 86, p. 337. On 9/19 July 1636 Biddulph reported that Borgia, who
had abandoned his palace in Rome (AAW, A XXVIII, no. 135, pp. 458–459), had 'taken a
very faire pallace in Madrid, haveing before been lodged in a monasterye' which indicated
that he would not be coming back to Rome. Philip IV showed him 'extraordinarye favour'
and used 'his counsell in all businesses of State', so much so that Olivares had started to
take against him; AAW, A XXVIII, no. 139, p. 467. But on 5/15 August Biddulph noted
that Borgia's 'long stay in Madrid' offended the pope, who would proceed against him with
'rigour' if he did not go to his archbishopric; AAW, A XXVIII, no. 150, p. 505.

priest but commonly thought a concealed Jes[uit] whom I suppose you knew there in the college,[176] and a brother in law of yours, one M[r] Will[iam] Worthington who married your sister. There hath bin a buissenesse depending between these two about two yeares and more concerning the Lady Perkins her daughter,[177] whom Worthington claimeth as his lawfull wife, being (as he saieth <he> can proove) contracted unto her and having bedded with her. This gentlewoman Gibbons notwithstanding persuaded to be a nunn, and carried her over to the English Benedictine nunns at Gaunt, where she was lately profest contrary to Worthingtons will and clayme, which clayme he prosecuted partly by himself and partly by a procurator before the bishop of Gaunts officiall even till the time of her profession.[178] And finding no meanes to prevaile there as he expected, but suffering rather much trouble and disgrace by the manifould practises of the freinds of that house both in his person and in his reputation, he thought he had no other remedy but to cause Gibbons to be apprehended by a messenger, which he did by order from the earle of Dorsett, having first petitioned to the king, who made the reference to Dorsett. But withall he hath used such caution as that Gibbons shalbe questioned upon no other point but this, as indeed he was not, when he appeared togeather with Worthington upon the 8 of this month before my lord of Dorsett, who, finding him guilty of what the other accused him, committed him close prisoner to the Gatehouse where it is intended he shall ly till Worthington have his wife from Gaunt, but he is not so close but that he hath the liberty of the house, and free accesse of his freinds unto him. Of this case you may make good use to shew the necessity of episcopall authority here, and withall the judgments of God uppon them that oppose it, for Worthington was alwaies leaning to that side, and hath ever bin the Jes[uits'] penitent. The other[179] is a Jes[uit] in hart, and is wholy used and [em]ployed in their buissenesses both here and beyond seas against my lord[180] and Doct[or] Champney.[181] [p. 164]

I understand for certaine that there was a writing presented to the k[ing] against my lord bishop by some Catholickes a good while since. My Lord Peter was named in particuler for one and no doubt but my

---

[176] John Wakeman was admitted at the English college in Rome in October 1615 and was ordained in December 1620. He would have known Biddulph, who entered the college in October 1619; Anstr., II, pp. 331, 25.

[177] Penelope Parkins, daughter of Sir George and Mary Parkins. See *Letters 9, 11.*

[178] See AAW, A XXVI, no. 101.

[179] i.e. John Wakeman.

[180] Richard Smith.

[181] Anthony Champney; see Anstr., I, pp. 70–71. On 26 February 1635 Wakeman visited Gregorio Panzani, and represented himself as 'molto indifferente' concerning the issue of episcopacy, but said he believed that a restored bishop should have restrictions placed on his jurisdiction; VA, PD, fo. 80r.

Lord Baltimor, Savage[182] and others were consenting therunto also by meanes of my lord treasurer[183] and Lord Cottington; but I cannot learne what was contained in the writing nor gett a coppy of it although I have used some diligence already therin. This was tould by a privy counsellor to a Cath[olic] freind of ours who spake much in my lords behalf to that counsellor and gave him good satisfaction concerning his claime and person wherof the counsellor saied he would informe the k[ing].[184]

I should have tould you before that this action of Worthington hath caused a great noise and scandall here amongst Catholickes, and if the matter be not taken up quickly it may be of very daungerous consequence and bring many Cath[olics] in question for sending over their children unto monasteries which is ~~made~~ premunire by a law made in K[ing] Charles his time.[185] It is reported that Worthington hath the hands of some pr[iests] for the justification of this action and to warrant the lawfulnesse therof and Ghibbons (as I heare even now) hath bin so imprudent and so uncharitable as not only to suspect me for one of those pr[iests] but also to write it to my father, and yet I protest sincerly that I neither allow of the action, nor ever knew of it till it was past and donn, neither do I think that any other seculer pr[iest] hath his voice or hand in it, and I ame sure all the better sort here in London are utterly against it, yet I doubt not but information wilbe given there to the contrary which you must seek to prevent or forestall if you can.

Other occurrences I must referr to Mr Laborne. Adieu in haste. 13 Aprill 1632.

Addressed: Pour Monsieur Fitton a Rome.

Endorsed: Dated 13 Aprill. Antonino.
About my brother Worthington his busin[ess]. [*ms obscured*] petition put up by [*ms obscured*] to the king against my lord.

---

[182] Thomas Savage, 1st Viscount Savage, Henrietta Maria's chancellor. The secular clergy's 1635 survey of the nobility noted that Savage 'non vult se immiscere oppositioni adversus episcopum, licet aliquoties solicitatus fuerit, nam fatetur eiusmodi negotia omnio relinquenda esse Sedis Apostolicae dispositioni'; AAW, A XXVIII, no. 3, p. 15. See Hibbard, *CI*, p. 40.

[183] Sir Richard Weston, 1st Baron Weston, created earl of Portland in February 1633.

[184] See *Letter 9*.

[185] On 19 March 1628, after the return of the Commons from the opening of parliament, 'there was read (as of form in other parliaments hath been usual) one bill', which had failed in 1626, entitled 'An act to restrain the passing or sending of any to be popishly bred beyond the seas'. It passed into law as 3 Charles I, c. 3. It received the royal assent on 26 June 1628. See *CD 1628*, II, pp. 12, 25; IV, p. 481; *The Statutes of the Realm*, 11 vols (London, 1810–1828), V, pp. 25–26.

11. Laborn [George Leyburn] to [Peter Biddulph], 13 April 1632

[*AAW, A XXVI, no. 56, pp. 165–166*]

Worthie deare sir,

I receaved yours with a copie inclosed of Cardinal Borgia his speech in the consistorie which was to[o] plane and bitter.[186] You write comfortably concerning my maisters[187] busines. Sweet Jesus send a speedie and wish[e]d conclusion. Our cheef friends mett on Tuseday last together in my chamber and they desired me to commend unto you divers particulars of busines which they assure them selves by your assistance may be effected to ther contents. First is that you please to endevour to procure that ordinarie facultyes of missionaryes may be equall and that order may be taken with the Jesuists ejects which are many in this country and much disordered, as alsoe order may be taken to hinder them[188] from making ignorant and simple priests, which they doe with intention to make a dishonorable and contemptible clergie. The second was to wish you to put up a petition that the congregation will be pleased to take into ther owne hands all regular missionaries and that they may be examined de vita et moribus. Third was that you send alwayse your breves authenticated and more than one copie. The fourth that no particular indulgence might be granted unto particular persons. Here you may touch of the Jesuists sodalities.[189] The fift that noe bookes may be printed without licence from the ordinarie of England. The sixt is a long busines which causeth great scandall, which is thus. Your brother Worthington some 3 yeares aggoe did marrie him selfe unto a doughter[190] of the Ladie Perkins without her notice and

---

[186] See *Letter 10*.

[187] Richard Smith.

[188] i.e. the Jesuits.

[189] See AAW, A XXVI, no. 81, p. 225, for John Jackson's report of 6 June 1632 to Biddulph about the alleged use of sodalities by Jesuits to supplant secular priests. Jackson claimed he had received 'diverse lettres out of <diverse parts of> the country, reporting the regulars erecting and spreading of new sodalities', and 'if some order be not taken with these sodalities many abuses will growe upon their use of them'. Jackson said he had been told 'of a gentleman who maintained a <sec[ular]> preist', and the Jesuits, 'knowing the use they cold make of him and his wealth, watched an opportunitie, and, when the sec[ular] pr[iest] was gone upon some business abroad, one of them came to him, moved him to be of a sodalitie, and being thereupon to make a generall confess[ion] it had been held incongruent if he had not made the same to any but one that cold advise him into that sodality', and thus 'they gained him and others by him'. See also AAW, A XXVI, no. 141 (Thomas Hill OSB's information to George Fisher, to be forwarded to Biddulph in Rome, concerning the Jesuits and their sodalities).

[190] Penelope Parkins.

after did lye with her and as he sweareth did consummate ex sue
parte although she, a mayd at that tyme, could not be penetrated,[191]
and sodainely after her mother had notice and, being a creature of
the Jesuists, did consult with them, much offended with this marriage;
wherupon they (whether moved with charity or a good peece of money
I will not sweare) wrought with the doughter and wonne her to goe
over to Gant wher they did cloth her and after her nov[ic]eship did
intend to professe her, of which [p. 166] the king, who haith a great
morall goodnes, is much offended with this proceeding of the Jesuists
and says that he will write over to the infanta[192] that the gentleman M^r

[191] In July 1632 Penelope Parkins made a statement admitting that she had spent one night
with Worthington in her chamber in Drury Lane, but her maid was present throughout,
and could testify that no intimacy had taken place. She claimed that she 'never made any
publicke or private sponsalls with Mr Worthington nor ever expressed my self unto him by
words or signes of promise of future marriage nor of any prefixed day or time to marry him.
Yet once being tyred out and forced by his importunity seeking then to ridd my self of him,
I said to satisfy him at that time that wee would talke againe of that matter on Wednesday
following but, I never intending it, wee mett not that day, and at our next meeting I gave him
a flatt deniall to marry him, bidding him to cease from further troubling of mee therewith.'
Subsequently she met Worthington and a priest 'in Lincolnes Inn Fields (as I was coming
from my mothers going to my grandmothers with whome I then lived withall)'. The priest
advised her 'that it was needeles to expect my mothers consent', but Penelope replied
that 'though my mothers consent were not necessary yet of this am I resolved, without
my mothers consent will I never accept of any man in marriage'. She swore that, 'M^r
Worthington neyther had any carnall knowledg of mee, neyther did I ever comitt act or
suffer act comitted by him by which I might any waies suspect carnall knowledg betweene
us for that I never suffered him to attempt the same soe as I never had the least scruple of
any such act had with him.' She denied Worthington's claim that she had on one occasion
lured him to see her, 'for I incited him not but he came up to my chamber against my will,
nor would by any perswations depart at that time of night, yet made promise confirmed by
oathes that he would not attempt any thinge dishonest, and withall threatened to make a
noise that my mother should know of his presence unles I would remayne in the chamber
and be quiett, wherupon he staied all that night. But by my commaund the mayde who was
ever present with mee lay downe at my back, and went not from mee at all that night till
morning following [...] at her riseing. Mr Worthington takes leave of mee and made great
boasts and ostentation of his fidelity kept and performed unto mee that night.' Subsequently
he became more bold, and 'would have had an other kynde of admittance than the former
was', but she told him he was 'unworthy in demaunding a thing soe prejudiciall to my fame
and honour'. She swore also that Worthington admitted 'immediately before my coming out
of England in presence of my mother and Mr Gibbons that, for any carnall knowledg hee
had of mee, I was as innocent as the child new borne [...] [and] for ought he knew I was a
virgin'. Lastly she alleged that she was 'not [...] compelled, drawne or urged to this course
of religion which I professe, either by my mother, Mr Gibbons, or any other what soever, but
have freely undertaken it, through Gods sole guift of his divine grace and inspiration of the
Holy Ghost, and that my mother gave mee her free consent to marry with Mr Worthington
rather than that I should depart out of England discontentedly'; AAW, A XXVI, no. 95,
pp. 263–264.
[192] Isabella Clara Eugenia, archduchess of Austria, and ruler of the Netherlands.

Worthington may have justice.[193] If Winter[194] had not been gon over he had been apprehended as well as Gibbins.[195] I heare that the Jesuists, by some friends who are inward with the treasurer and Cottington, have caused a petition to be preferred unto the king against my lord,[196] and one of the cheef in the councell, hearing of it, sayd that he would informe against that information.[197] I cannot furnish you with more occurrences for the present, onely that now it is generally thought that our queen is with child.[198] The king is never willinglie from her.

[193] William Worthington counterclaimed that Penelope Parkins was relying upon 'the opinion of some [...] divines [...] who speake very largely of a womans power to sweare in this case for her honors sake when she is induced rather to lett her actions be framed as dishonest than in the way of marriage'. 'Mr Edward Silisdon and Mr Gibbons [...] intimated inspection as the best way for clearing of this point. But divines and phisitians will tell us many reasons why this can bee noe clearing to her, or barr to my pretention which way soever it fall, and yet gives scope enough of occasion to both partes of this deposicion. And therefore I shalbe loath to enter into the examinacion of this point by particuler interrogatories till wee come before some judge that must determine the matter, leaving every one to their more charitable opinion both of her and mee, upon such circumstances and passages as wilbe made manifest by the proofe of witnesses.' She 'sweares the mayde lay at her backe whilst I was in the chamber but shee saith nothing in what parte of the chamber I was, at the same tyme, and where I lay both then and after when the mayde was departed thence'. Worthington insisted also that she was forced to enter religion; AAW, A XXVI, no. 111, pp. 312–313. Worthington alleged further that 'the mayde Catherine Nunn [daughter of John Nunn of Norfolk], who (as hee hath heard heertofore) was induced to sweare falsly before the eearle [sic] of Dorsett touching the concubitus, hath lately written a letter of repentance [...] out of remorse of conscience', and it was hoped that she would 'declare who induced her to that perjurie'; AAW, A XXVI, no. 8, p. 37; no. 1, p. 17. (Richard Worthington, William's brother, who became a chaplain at the Venetian embassy in London, also said the maid had been proved a liar. He claimed on 13/23 August 1632 that, in Ghent, Penelope Parkins was now tiring of the spiritual exercises which she was put to by the Jesuits, although Edward Weston and the abbess of the convent had promised her that she might herself one day become abbess there. She had confessed to Richard Worthington that she and William 'had layne one night together, and how extraordinarye her love was to my brother, and that so much as that shee would have preferred him in mariage before a king or an emperor, and that shee loved his person yet verye well, though shee disallowed of his pretences'; AAW, A XXVI, no. 11, pp. 45, 44.) On 7 October 1632 William Worthington informed Biddulph that he believed Penelope Parkins was secretly in England, and the earl of Dorset was now not so favourable to his cause as he had hoped. Worthington had, by then, negotiated for a match between himself and the daughter of one of Henrietta Maria's servants, Françoise de Monbodiac, wife of Jean Garnier, and had used an intermediary 'to interest' Henrietta Maria's 'confessor in it on my behalf'. But she had then contracted herself to a Frenchman to whom she was now married; AAW, A XXVI, no. 147, p. 402. For Richard Worthington, see Anstr., II, p. 365.

[194] Robert Winter, brother of Sir John Winter.

[195] John Wakeman.

[196] Richard Smith.

[197] See Letters 9, 10.

[198] This rumour was untrue. See Letter 15.

I heare that the countesse of Buckinghame is dead or dying.[199] The countesse of Shroseberry is buryed.[200] The Lord Brudenell is very sick. Sir Luis Treshame went post yesterdaye towards [*word illegible*]. I should have written this in D[octor] Champneys letter.

Here are many unnaturall sutes amongst the gostlie children of Jesuists and <of> some other regulars: Ployden and his sonne,[201] M[rs] Corame and hers, M[rs] Perkins and hers, <M[r]> Cuffolde[202] and his, and many more, and that fowle busines of the Lord Baltamoore,[203] as alsoe this of Worthingtons, toucheth nearly the Jesuists, both of them, especially Baltamoore, being ther creatures.

No address.

Endorsed: 13 April. Laborn.
> About divers points that the clergy would have mee to sollicite.
> About strang[e] suites amongst the Jesuitts paenitants.
> M[r] Worthingtons case.
> 13 Apr[il]. Lisbon.

[*in margin on p. 165*]

Your brother Worthington, having notice, did goe over him selfe to Bruxells and did claime her for his wife of the bishop, wherupon the Jesuists did cite him to the bishops court;[204] and being many and powrefull, and he but one and destitute of friends, they did what they listed them selfes <and put M[r] Worthingtons [*sic*] in prison at

---

[199] Mary Beaumont, who had married successively Sir George Villiers, Sir William Rayner, and Sir Thomas Compton, and had been created countess of Buckingham in July 1618. She died on 19 April 1632.

[200] Mary (Fortescue), wife of John Talbot, 10th earl of Shrewsbury. She died, in fact, in December 1635 and was buried on 6 January 1636; GEC, XI, p. 718. The earl's second wife was Frances, daughter of Thomas Arundell, 1st Baron Arundell and his second wife Anne (Richard Smith's patrons).

[201] For the litigation between Francis Plowden of Shiplake and his son Edmund over a now disputed former award made, in previous chancery proceedings, concerning maintenance promised as part of a marriage settlement for Edmund and his wife Mabel (Mariner), daughter of the Hampshire recusant Dorothy Mariner, see PRO, C 2/Charles I/P40/59, P65/22, P79/14, P93/17; A. Mott, 'A dictionary of Hampshire recusants: tempo Eliz', (typescript at ABSJ), pp. 261–262.

[202] Identity uncertain. For the Cuffaud family of Hampshire, see Mott, 'Dictionary', pp. 152–156. In May 1635 Alexander Cuffaud and his nephew William presented their arguments to Gregorio Panzani in favour of Richard Smith; VA, PD, fo. 93r.

[203] See *Letters 4, 5, 6*.

[204] For copies of the sentence (30 September/10 October 1631) of the episcopal court at Ghent, see AAW, A XXIV, no. 185; XXVI, no. 2. For William Worthington's account of the way he was dealt with by the court, see AAW, A XXVI, no. 3.

Gant>.[205] The partyes who did prosecute this busines against your brother Worthington were one Gibbins and M[r] Winter, the same ~~that~~ <who> prosecuted against D[octor] Champney and his. Now M[r] Worthington, being com[me]d home with many foule aspersions and affronts, was inwardlie much trubled in soe much that hearing Gibbins was returned he preferred a petition to the king and desired that he might have a warrant for some of the lords of the counsell to apprehend Gibbins and to imprisonne him untill such tyme as his wife might be restored (and you must knowe that a relation was made unto the king of all his busines).[206] The king granted unto his petition and gave order to my lord of Dorsett to give a warrant which he did and sent his owne officers with M[r] Worthington and they apprehended Gibbins and brought him before my lord of Dorse[t] who committed him prisonner to the Gatehouse.[207] The Jesuists peradventure will informe ther that M[r] Worthington haith done this by counsell from the

---

[205] According to Richard Worthington, in his letter to Biddulph of 13/23 August 1632, William Worthington had come over to Ghent 'for a frendlie examining of his pretences having before sent over the narration of all things that had passed between the gentlewoman and him to the bishop of Gant under his oath'. In Ghent he claimed 'his tytle before the abbes, the bishop (offering his oath to him), the officiall, F[ather] Edward Silisdon and others. Yet they professed her to hudle up the busines, and put him out of hope of recovering his rights and moreover sought to disgrace <him> with arresting him in the streets by 3 base fellowes and, because the mariage was clandestine, easilie denyed and hardlie proved, they cited him for a matter of slaunder, and sought all the meanes to terrifye him, to have <him> desist from prosecuting his pretences'; AAW, A XXVI, no. 11, p. 43. For Worthington's own account of his imprisonment, see AAW, A XXVI, no. 3, p. 21; no. 4, p. 25.

[206] An undated letter by William Worthington relates that 'on Fryday last the Ladie Parkins' and Wakeman 'were before the lords of the councell, where I was with them, and the controversie betwixt us discussed, not concerning the contract which was not proper for that place, but only concerning the unlawfull conveying of Penelope beyond the seas to Gant'. The privy council referred the case 'to the statutes and lawes of the kingdome', and Lady Parkins and Wakeman were indicted in King's Bench 'upon the statute for transporting of a subject to a nunnerie'. Worthington claimed he did not want to see his adversaries suffer the full penalty of the law, but he professed to believe that in fact Penelope Parkins had been secretly in England for two months, and that this was the only way to make them produce her; AAW, A XXVI, no. 9, p. 39.

[207] Dorset, however, did not see the matter quite as Southcot and Leyburn reported it at this time. As an embarrassed Worthington noted in mid-June 1634, the case between the crown and Lady Parkins came in front of King's Bench on 8 June 'where by the juries vardict the lady was acquitted for sending her daughter, which I conceive was contrarie to the expectation of most of the auditorie'. Worthington appeared in order to give evidence for the crown, but Dorset 'was there in person as a witnes on the ladie's syde'. The earl deposed that he imprisoned Wakeman upon Worthington's 'suggestion that hee was a preiste'; Worthington claimed that Dorset was 'soe noble and soe honorable that I can not but conceive hee might have understood it soe, but sure I am, upon the faith of a Christian, that I never sayd it'; AAW, A XXVII, no. 147, p. 449. (Furthermore, Worthington's opponents 'pleaded against my testimonie that I was a convicted recusant, and withall informed the court that I had 2 sisters in Lovan monasterie'; ibid.) See also CSPD, 1633–1634, p. 52.

clergie,[208] which is most false, for he is non[e] of ours, but ever was thers, and he haith these who take his part although others doe soe.

12. [John Southcot] to Gibbons [John Wakeman], 20 April 1632

[*AAW, A XXVI, no. 58, pp. 169–170*]

Sir,

I delivered your letter to Mr Muscot[209] and I expected his answer before this but that it seemes other urgent occasions have caused him to deferr it. You write to me that it is commonly bruicted that some of the clergy do warrant Mr Worth[ington's] proceeding, and particulerly his act[ion] [?] uppon you. To which, if I should answer that it is more commonly thought and saied that he, being no dependant of the clergy neither in spiritualibus nor temporalibus, but of others was much likelier [to] have his advise from them than from the clergy, I should say but a truth. But I see that these termes commonly bruted and credibly reported are often misapplied, and consequently mis-understood, wherfor in this present subject I will forbeare to use them and only tell you that for my part I know neither clergy man nor regular that had any hand in the buissenesse. And, although I have good cause to think that you understood me to be included in the number of those, some of the clergy, hearing what you had written to my father[210] concerning this matter before you wrote to me, yet I will not expostulat with you uppon that point but only wish you to be more sparing in your judgments and speaches least you make this common bruict to fall particulerly uppon me, who never expected nor deserved to be driven to apology for my self in a buissenesse of this nature to which I was as much a stranger till it was past and donn as your own neerest and best trusted freinds, and I have indeavoured both for Gods sake and yours aswell before the receipt of your letter as since by the best persuasions I could to draw of[f] the gentleman[211] from [*p. 170*] this course, but as I have no particuler interest in him so ame I able to prevaile nothing with him.

As for testifying your true obedience to my lord of Chalced[on][212] I shall not be wanting to do you that right which you expect at my

---

[208] i.e. the secular clergy.
[209] George Fisher.
[210] John Southcot snr. See *Letter 92*.
[211] William Worthington.
[212] Richard Smith.

hands, but you must remember that I can plead nothing but words, and how far bare words and protestations without deeds will gaine creditt in these tumultuous and suspicious times, especially if it be objected that words are not only not supported but contradicted by deeds, I need not tell you. Truly I am sory for your trouble and for the generall scandall that is like to come of it but ~~being~~, seeing it is no way in my power to remedy it as I desire, I pray accept of my poor praiers for your pacience and spiritual comfort therin which are most willingly offered by your [*two words illegible*] to serve you et[c].

20 Aprill 1632.

No address.

[*on p. 169*]

Endorsed: To Mr Gibbons.

13. Antonino [John Southcot] to [an English secular priest at Paris],[213] 1 May 1632

[*AAW, A XXVI, no. 64, pp. 183–184*]

Most hon[oured] sir,

I have yours of the 26th Aprill and Mr Laborne receaved this week two from Mr Fitton[214] of the 4th and 10th of Aprill wherin he writes that 18 noblemen[215] have sente a letter from hence to his Hol[iness] to

---

[213] See *Letter 43*; Allison, RSGB, I, p. 396.

[214] Peter Biddulph.

[215] A petition against Richard Smith ('Protestatio Declaratoria Procerum aliorum*que* Nobilium Angliae Catholicorum praetensam R*everendissi*mi Episcopi Chalcedonensis authoritatem impugnantium'; AAW, A XXIV, no. 75) had been drawn up and despatched to Rome in October 1631 with additional documentation. (See the Introduction to this volume.) In April 1632, Biddulph had reported that 'the Jesuitts have gotten 18 of the noble men in England to write against haveing a bishop in England, whereof 11 have written a com*m*on letter, and putt their names to it, and sent it to his Holiness; the other 7 would not subscribe their names butt they give their consent to the letter, vivae vocis oraculo, which was done before a notarye whom the Jesuitts caused to come out of the Low Countryes'; AAW, A XXVI, no. 49, p. 149. In fact, twelve nobles (rather than eleven) had signed the protestation itself. Five others (rather than seven) had said that they agreed with it but did not actually put their signatures to it. (The nobles who signed were John Talbot, earl of Shrewsbury; Henry Somerset, earl of Worcester; Thomas Darcy, Earl Rivers; James Touchet, earl of Castlehaven and Baron Audley; Lord William Howard of Naworth; Thomas Somerset, Viscount Cashel; Edward Somerset, Lord Herbert; Sir Henry Neville, Baron Abergavenny; Thomas Windsor, Baron Windsor; William Petre, Baron Petre; Thomas Brudenell, Baron Brudenell; and Sir George Calvert, Baron Baltimore. Those who gave their assent, without

disclaime from my lords[216] ordinariship, eleven wherof putt their names to the letter, and the other seaven gave onlie their consents before a notary whom (he saies) the Jes[uits] brought from beiond seas for that purpose, but he wisheth no notice to be taken of this as written from him, bycause the party that tould it him will come to be knowen, which were very inconvenient, and therfor we use the matter so here as if it had bin discovered here and not written from abroad. If this be true, I assure my self there hath bin much jugling and foule play, and many a o[ne] doubtlesse hath bin given without ~~their~~ <his> consent,[217] at least without ~~their~~ <his> [*ms torn*: true (?)] meaning, which I do beleeve the rather bycause my Lord Brudnel sought [to] draw in my Lord Morley by <meer> misinformation telling him of chimeras of tribunals, and undoinges etcetera, which is a pretty story to tell, and I have desired M[r] Lab[orne] (to whom my Lord Morly discovered the matter afterward) to sett it down particulerly, and I wish he would do it also ~~to~~ in his letter to you that the nonce[218] there may have a scantling of their dealings, and know in what manner they have (probably) wrought with the rest,[219] and I feare they have not been ashamed to use my lord marquis[220] his name in this kind, bycause

signing, were Richard Burke, earl of St Albans; Thomas Savage, Viscount Savage; Ulick Burke, Viscount Tunbridge; Henry Parker, Baron Morley and Monteagle; and Edward Vaux, Baron Vaux.) Of the other Catholic nobles, two (John Paulet, marquis of Winchester and Thomas Arundell, Baron Arundell) were generally favourable to the bishop, though they were said to think that it was not now the right time to restore Catholic episcopal jurisdiction in England. Two others (Francis Manners, earl of Rutland and Francis Browne, Viscount Montague) were uncommitted, and only one (Sir Henry Constable, Viscount Dunbar) supported the bishop wholeheartedly. The views of the remaining Catholic nobles were not stated. See *Letter 20*; Hughes, *HSJ*, pp. 224–227. 300 gentlemen were supposed to have signed the document. Even more, it was declared, had assented to it. See Allison, Q J, p. 139; AAW, A XXIV, no. 73 (an English translation of the text of the 'Protestatio Declaratoria' with a different series of signatures).

[216] Richard Smith.

[217] On 19/29 March 1632 Richard Smith had written to Biddulph that Smith's cousin William Rayner 'yesterday told me that my adversaries say that none of the noble men but onely my l[ord] of Dunbar is for me but herein they use ther doctrine of mental reservation [...] for it is certain that most of the noble men are for me, though in truth divers are les zealous by my absence becaus they are told I shal never come agayne'; AAW, B 27, no. 107.

[218] Cardinal Alessandro Bichi.

[219] i.e. of the Catholic aristocracy.

[220] John Paulet, 5th marquis of Winchester. In the secular clergy's January 1635 survey of the Catholic nobility, he was described thus: 'vita et famae semper intactae. Ingenio collet nec deest illi doctrina praesertim in rebus fidei controversis in quibus non mediocriter versatus est. Gallicae et Italicae linguae peritus. Est regi et reginae omnibusque proceribus et curialibus gratissimus et charissmus, nec non toti patriae ac reipublicae observandus, licet notus sit pro Catholico'. Apart from his other good personal characteristics, 'pietate ac studio devotionis praecellit singulis diebus una cum familia in oratorio honorificentissime ornato, devotissime sacrum audit officium B.M. Virginis cum rosario eiusdem quotidie recitat,

I know he was sett uppon particulerly at his last being in town by my Lord Baltimore, Sir Basil[221] and M[r] G[eorge] Gage[222] in my Lord Rivers[223] his house, and therfor we intend to acquaint him with the buissenesse this terme, and will cause Doctor Flud[224] to ask my lords of Abergaveny[225] and Vaux[226] what they have donn in the same kind.

litanias sanctorum vel audit publice in oratorio, vel privatim legit semper ante cubitum'. He was 'zelator animarum ardentissimus', and 'exemplo suo omnes passim aedificat, et eius cura ac zelo plusquam viginti animae in illa vicinia ad Ecclesiae gremium nuper reductae sunt'. He was so in favour with the king that when the order to disarm leading Catholics was issued in 1625 'curavit rex armaturam marchionis (quam habebat insignem et copiosam) ei restitui ita ut singularem regis favorem in eo genere mirarentur multi Protestantes, direcerentque esse rem sine exemplo', and Charles was pleased to visit the marquis when he was on progress; AAW, A XXVIII, no. 3, p. 13. In February 1633, Richard East reported that the Tuscan agent Amerigo Salvetti 'was the only man who lately began the persuasion with the lord marquis not to be married [to Honora, daughter of Richard Burke, 4th earl of Clanricard and 1st earl of St Albans] with his owne priests but by a Jesuit, which was soe done to the great discreditt of the [secular] clergy'; AAW, A XXVI, no. 24, p. 78. However, the secular priest William Case served as a chaplain to the marquis and his wife. See also AAW, A XXVI, no. 103 (an attestation, dated 1 August 1632, testifying that both Winchester and the Earl Rivers believed their names had been wrongly cited in support of the 'Protestatio Declaratoria' against Smith); AAW, A XXVI, no. 121, p. 335.

[221] Sir Basil Brooke.

[222] See P. Revill and F.W. Steer, 'George Gage I and George Gage II', *Bulletin of the Institute of Historical Research*, 31 (1958), pp. 141–158. See also AAW, A XXVIII, no. 58 (1635?), an account of the principal Catholic enemies of Richard Smith, among whom was George Gage, 'filius Eduardi Gage filii junioris familia Gageorum de Furle' in Sussex; *ibid.*, p. 233. He was sent to Rome by James I to negotiate over the proposed dynastic marriage between Prince Charles and the infanta, Maria Anna. He was wholly Hispanophile and a patron of the Jesuits.

[223] Thomas Darcy, Viscount Colchester, created Earl Rivers on 4 November 1626. The secular clergy's account of the English nobility, compiled in January 1635, described him thus: 'habetur pro viro prudente, est etiam non vulgariter eruditus, praesertim quoad res historicas et politicas. Sed quoad pietatis et religionis Catholicae professionem et exercitia, tepidus et timidus, numerat supra sex millia librarum anglicarum de reditibus annuis, et vivit splendide quoad hospitalitatem, more patriae. Fuit attractus falsis informationibus baronis de Baltimor defuncti, in partes eorum qui oppugnabant episcopum; sed ex se, est indifferens, et potius propendet in Clerum, nam confitetur plerumque sacerdoti seculari. Non cohabitat jam a multis annis cum uxore, quae est Protestans, ob nescio quod dissidium conjugale'; AAW, A XXVIII, no. 3, p. 14.

[224] Dr Robert Floyd. See *Letter 3*.

[225] The secular clergy remarked that Sir Henry Neville, 2nd Baron Abergavenny, was not only addicted to worldly recreations but also, since 'pro secundis nuptiis duxit in uxorem sororem Baronis Vauxii' (Catherine Vaux), he tended to favour the Society, 'quamvis alioquin ex se fit satis neutralis et moderatus'; AAW, A XXVIII, no. 3, p. 15; Anstruther, *Vaux*, p. 485. In May 1635, via Sir John Simeon, Baron Abergavenny made representations to Gregorio Panzani against the restoration of a Catholic bishop in England; VA, PD, fo. 93r.

[226] Edward Vaux, 4th Baron Vaux. See Anstruther, *Vaux*, p. 458; GEC, XII/ii, pp. 224–226. Vaux was noted for the scandal he caused in 1632 by marrying Elizabeth Knollys (daughter of Thomas Howard, earl of Suffolk), countess of Banbury: 'duxit male etiam

But I hope his Hol[iness] will not suffer him self to be abused by such tricks, nor differ what he intended to do a whitt the longer for this. Yet Mr Fitton wisheth us to gett somewhat from our freinds <here> to the contrary in writing which we shall never be able to doe, and if our [ms torn] petition commended by the qu[een] be ~~never~~ <not> sufficient to counterpoise this [ms torn] of our adversaries, it argues that in Ro[me] they have no list to do any thing for us, or els the matter is not well followed and putt home as it might be. I can say no more for that matter.[227]

audiebat dum viveret Comes Banburiensis senex octogenarius ob notoriam familiaritatem quam habuit cum eius uxore, susceptis ex ea duobus liberis de quibus publice constat. Verum quidem est, quod comitissa dictum baronem amabat, praetendebatque se ei desponsatam fuisse, antequam comiti nupta esset cum quo contraxit invita, et non nisi rogente eam sua matre. Unde post obitum comitis, statim nupsit baroni, eiusque cognomen induit, facta ex comitissa baronissa, exemplo inusitato.' He was, with his brothers, a patron of the Society, as his mother had been. He was more moderate now that she was dead, and 'a clero [i.e. the secular clergy] haud aversus'; AAW, A XXVIII, no. 3, p. 16. See also *Letter 94*. (In 1628, however, the countess of Banbury had been listed as a patron to Richard Smith's secretary, William Harewell; PRO, SP 16/529/94, fo. 146v.)

[227] The 'Protestatio Declaratoria' was shown to Gregorio Panzani in 1635 by Sir Basil Brooke. See Joseph Berington, *The Memoirs of Gregorio Panzani*, T.A. Birrell (ed.) (London, 1970), p. 178. Panzani's 'Relazione' records his opinions, based in part on information given to him by the seculars, about how far the alleged signatories had in fact subscribed to the document. Panzani claimed that John Talbot, earl of Shrewsbury, was persuaded to sign by Sir Basil Brooke's false information, and subsequently told his brother, George Talbot, that 'he did not mean to impugn the spiritual authority of the bishop'. Henry Somerset, earl of Worcester, though a patron of the Society, told Baron Arundell that he had not, in fact, subscribed the document at all. Nor, allegedly, had the Earl Rivers. The young earl of Castlehaven believed that he had subscribed a document in Smith's favour, not against him. Lord William Howard had signed only because he was told that Smith intended to proceed against him for defending the oath of allegiance. Thomas Somerset, Viscount Cashel, was such a bitter enemy of the seculars that he probably had signed, thought Panzani, but Edward Somerset, Lord Herbert of Raglan, had, in front of one of the queen's chamberlains, denied that he had done so. Baron Windsor had confessed to Baron Arundell that he would never again plot against the bishop. Baron Petre had spoken in such a way to the marquis of Winchester that it was doubtful whether he had subscribed. (Actually, Panzani elicited a confession from him that he had added his signature to the document only in 1634. Panzani visited him at the Earl Rivers's house and elicited a retraction from him.) Baron Brudenell's son was 'a great friend of the bishop'. The earl of St Albans (who was said to have acceded verbally to the 'Protestatio'; see *Letter 14*) and his son denied signing 'and are suprised that a bishop has not been granted'. Baron Morley had 'twice confessed' to Panzani 'that he was many times urged by the Jesuits and their adherents' to sign, or at least to consent, but he refused (though he too had been listed as a verbal supporter of the document). Viscount Savage repented signing 'and sent an archdeacon to testify to this to the bishop'. Baron Vaux had probably subscribed, but this was because he was infuriated when he was admonished by his confessor, a secular priest. It was ridiculous, said Panzani, that the marquis of Winchester and even Baron Arundell should be named at all in the 'Protestatio' as doubtful in any way about Smith's authority since they were both patrons of the bishop; and the same was true of the (now deceased) earl of Rutland and Viscount Montague. Panzani claimed that Baron Eure, who was not named in the 'Protestatio',

I forgott the last week to tell you that Fa[ther] Blunt[228] tould M[r]
Spiller[229] lately he had receaved a letter from his generall[230] wherin he
signifieth that the k[ing] of France his confessor[231] wrote unto him that
he had heard a complaint of our English Jes[uits] here, as if the most
part of them kept concubines in the houses where they live. What
may be the ground of this report I know not, but [*p. 184*] I beleeve
F[ather] Blunt hath either some of the clergy or els my lord[232] him self
in suspicion for it.

Doctor Bossevile[233] and M[r] Williamson[234] write out of the country that
they heare there that the superiours of the Dominicans[235] and Jesuitts[236]
have geven commaund to theirs not to oppose my lord but to speak
well of him as having donn nothing unbefitting.[237] Moreover the doctor
saieth that every man now flieth from publishing the breve,[238] and say
that it bindeth not. But here in London we hear e nonn of these things
any other way [*ms torn*]. Therfor I hardly beleeve them to be true.
He addeth also a clause concerning M[ris] Hanfords br[other], which I
send you in his own hand here enclosed.

I have spoken to M[r] Lab[orne] to send for the holy oiles to Monsieur
Flie, but your letter makes no mention what he is, nor wherabouts he
dwelleth in Calais.

---

was now a supporter of Smith, and so was the young Baron Stafford (whose 'mother and
grandmother are great friends of the bishop'). Baron Teynham, however, was under the
dominion of the Society; VA, Barberini MS LVI, 136, fos 34v–7v (transcript and translation
at ABSJ).

[228] Richard Blount SJ.

[229] Robert Spiller.

[230] Muzio Vitelleschi SJ.

[231] Charles Mailland SJ, confessor to Louis XIII. See Allison, RSGB, III, p. 168.

[232] Richard Smith.

[233] For John Bosvile, see Anstr., I, pp. 44–45; *NAGB*, pp. 86, 96, 101, 176.

[234] Richard Button.

[235] Thomas Middleton OP. In March 1633 Smith understood that a Benedictine had
abused Middleton for 'making peace' with the seculars; AAW, A XXVII, no. 22, p. 59.

[236] Richard Blount SJ.

[237] In January 1633 Smith had dinner with the general of the Dominicans in Paris. The
general was very courteous and assured him that he was 'wholy for to have bishops and hath
written to his brethren in England that, unles they have [...] privileges to the contrarie,
they shall shew me their letters of their mission and their faculties and ask my leave for
the parochials' (i.e. permission to administer the three parochial sacraments of baptism,
matrimony and extreme unction), and none of them would be permitted to oppose Smith's
episcopal authority; AAW, B 27, no. 112.

[238] This may be a reference to the papal breve of April 1631, *Super Professionibus per Regulares
emissis non facto in locos designatis Novitiatu*; AAW, A XXIV, no. 89; CRS, I, p. 108. On 9 April
1632 Richard East, in London, wrote to Smith that 'there is noe esteeme made heere of that
breve Super Professionibus'; AAW, A XXVI, no. 52, p. 158.

This day I heard of 17^l ~~give~~ sent up to London to pay for my cosen Everards^{239} soule wherof 10^l [is] for the prisons, and the rest to the poor out of prisons and <to> particuler frends wherof 40^s is [*word deleted*] <only given> for my lord, which shalbe given to M^{ris} Salsbury. Mr Francis Everard the <now heire>^{240} brought the mony <up> and the note for the distribution of it in this manner.

Haillers book^{241} is <u>not yet come</u>, neither do we know how to inquire for it intelligibly enough, bycause we know not the title of the book.^{242}

I heare <u>Mr Cunstable</u>, father in law to S^{ir} William Roopers daughter,^{243} died without help although he had a priest at the same time in his house, and desir<u>ed help at that</u> time; but the pr[iest] could not be found although he were much sought for, ~~yet~~ and never departed out <u>of his chamber</u> (as he saied him self afterwards) which is imputed to miracle, <u>seeing they</u> opened his chamber door and yet neither saw him nor heard him, nor ~~they~~ he them. This deserves to be further <u>inquired</u> of for an example of Gods judgments against the furtherers of their conversion such as this man was knowen to be from time to time, and against those that presume to[o] much of Gods will.

Thus with woonted duty, I humbly rest. 1° Maii 1632.

Antonino

No address or endorsement.

[*in margin of p. 184*]

I heare [*ms torn*] should say my lord is fallen [*ms torn*] Philip and is [j]oined herewith.

The epito[me] [*ms torn*] the Jes[uits'] faculties, I sent to Mr Fitton a fortn[ight ago] or more.

---

^{239} William Everard of Linstead, co. Suffolk, whose nuncupative will was made on 20 March 1632; PRO, PROB 11/162, fo. 334v. See also Anstr., II, pp. 96–97. One or both of the priests James and William Everard may have been his sons. The will leaves William Snr's property in trust to his brother Francis for William Snr's (unnamed) wife and children. In late 1635 Gregorio Panzani recorded a visit from James Everard 'per il vescovo', i.e. on behalf of Richard Smith; VA, PD, fo. 120r.

^{240} See PRO, PROB 11/162, fo. 334v.

^{241} Hallier, *Defensio Ecclesiasticae Hierarchiae [. . .]*. See *Letter 9*.

^{242} On 19/29 March 1632 Smith noted to Biddulph that 'D. Halliers book is now published but it is so big as there is no sending of it but by some that goeth thither'; AAW, B 27, no. 107.

^{243} Sir William Roper's daughter Anne had married Sir Philip Constable of Everingham, son of Sir Marmaduke Constable.

14. Clerk [John Southcot] to Fitton [Peter Biddulph], 11 May 1632

[*AAW, A XXVI, no. 72, pp. 203–206*]

Sir,

The last week I wrote unto you according to custome in answer to yours of the 10ᵗʰ Aprill which was the last we receaved from you. I understand that our adversaries seek to disgrace you there all they can, and to make you unwelcome to the great on[e]s of that court, but I hope your own good comportment and the commendations you have from so many both here and in France will take away creditt from all their endeavours in that kind. I understand also that his Hol[iness] inclines <rather> to settle 3 bishops here²⁴⁴ than one, which we also desire so that they may be all clergymen,²⁴⁵ and therfor if you find any overture made there of any such motion I pray follow it closely for, with that, all differences would be ended.²⁴⁶ Our adversaries seek to hinder my lord²⁴⁷ from rettourning all they can but it would be infinitly to the Churches dishonor if they should prevaile therin, and I hope in God they shall not. So many letters which have bin written from hence and from Paris in favour of his person (not only of his authority), togeather with the common petition commended by the queen, do shew that it is the common desire he should rettourne and, were it not that he him self had shewed a desire of the contrary in that unfortunat letter he wrote to his Hol[iness] before Christmasse,²⁴⁸ I assure my self there would not have bin any thought of disposing of him otherwise [*three words deleted*] than to send him back to his flock againe with sufficient authority. If nothing be donn between this and August, it will then be necessary for my lord [to] go up²⁴⁹ him self though it be like to proove

---

²⁴⁴ See *Letter 5*.

²⁴⁵ i.e. secular clergy.

²⁴⁶ On 10/20 May 1632 Smith informed Biddulph that Cardinal Bichi 'hath plainly told me that his Hol[iness] hath granted my request and saieth that he inclineth to give us twoe bishops', though Smith had made it clear that he 'tooke it ill to be discharged til an other were apointed', and went off to tell Richelieu about it. Richelieu 'semed much offended', and said more than once 'ne vous mette en peine; nous firons vostre affaire'; AAW, B 27, no. 109.

²⁴⁷ Richard Smith.

²⁴⁸ See AAW, A XXIV, no. 214 (an autograph duplicate letter, dated 8/18 December 1631, from Richard Smith to Urban VIII, explaining that in his previous letter to the pope he had not intended absolutely to resign his jurisdiction as bishop of Chalcedon). See *Letter 2*.

²⁴⁹ i.e. to go to Rome.

a very troublesome and chargeable journy to a man of his yeares and quality.²⁵⁰

For occurrences lett me tell you first that <it> is observed much of late that many here do make them selves away, and most by hanging. I heard ~~ther~~ of 3 or 4 within this fortnight²⁵¹ <besides others before and since Easter> but I know not their names.²⁵² It was much debated at [*p. 204*] councell table lately whether the k[ing] should call a parlament or noe. My lord keeper²⁵³ and Secretary Cook²⁵⁴ did plead earnestly for it. Others did mainly oppose it and these were the stronger and more in number, being, as here they call them, of the Spannish faction.

²⁵⁰ On 7/17 June 1633 Smith notified Biddulph that 'the Jes[uits] give out in England that I am cited' to Rome 'and if I shold go they wold then brag the more, *partely* becaus when I was there last', in 1609–1610, 'the Jes[uits] sought to cast me into the Inquisicion and de facto cast a booke of mine, *which* yet came out with honor' (see *NAGB*, pp. 85, 87, 129, 182). Although the nuncio in Paris assured Smith that the pope would assist him financially with his journey to Rome, Smith doubted whether he would ever be allowed back to Paris again; AAW, A XXVII, no. 61, p. 177.

²⁵¹ John Pory noted on 21 April 1632 that, on 17 April, 'a divine (and, they say, an excellent preacher) at a drapers house in Watling Street strangled himself with a garter, and the like did another minister lately at Manchester', while 'a third minister [...] of Warwickshire [...] fell upon his owne sword'; JPN, p. 250. Subsequently, Pory related that the last of these suicidal clerics, beneficed in Worcestershire rather than Warwickshire, 'payd out of his benefice 4 skore pound a year to his simoniacal patron'; *ibid.*, p. 253.

²⁵² For a survey of contemporary opinions of what had caused Henry Butts, vice-chancellor of Cambridge, to commit suicide, see M. McCrum, 'Doctor Henry Butts', *Corpus*, 73 (1994), pp. 42–53 (for which reference I am very grateful to Kenneth Fincham). On 7 April 1632, John Pory, who had heard that Butts had 'on Easter daye in the morning hanged himselfe with a three corner kercher', reported to Viscount Scudamore the speculation that Butts had despaired principally because he had been reproved for allowing, in fact encouraging, an 'obscene [...] and tedious comedy' (Peter Hausted's *The Rivall Friends*) to be performed before the king and queen during their recent visit to Cambridge, and because of the criticism he had received for 'promoting', on the occasion of the royal visit, 'so many ignoble graduates, as 21 doctors of divinity, 8 masters of arte, and 3 or 4 batchelours of lawe'; JPN, p. 241; McCrum, 'Doctor Henry Butts', pp. 49–51. Walter Yonge, who also ascribed Butts's suicide to the public criticism of him for promoting 'unworthy persons' 'contrary to the approbation of the university', described Butts as 'a greate Arminian'; BL, Additional MS 35331, fo. 47r. Cf. B.C., *Puritanisme the Mother, Sinne the Daugther [...]. Heerunto is added [...] a Funerall Discourse touching the late different Deathes of [...] Doctour Price Deane of Hereford, and Doctour Butts Vice-Chancellour of Cambridge* (St Omer, 1633). This Catholic tract, which notes that 'divers [...] ministers' of Butts's 'own coate and profession', 'by offering violence to themselves, have made like shipwracke of their soules, within the compasse of this very yeare, and some few last past', contrasts Butts's suicide with the alleged conversion to Catholicism of Theodore Price; *ibid.*, pp. 143, 139. The tract deals, *inter alia*, with the tendency of Protestant doctrine to drive men to desperation, and comments that 'whether the vice-chancellour had such secret disputes with his soule, God only knowes, though in regard of this fatall heresy of predestination, it may well be conjectured he had'; *ibid.*, p. 150.

²⁵³ Sir Thomas Coventry, 1st Baron Coventry.

²⁵⁴ Sir John Coke.

I heard of an odd prodigy that happened uppon the River Twede neer Scotland on Friday in Easter week. This it was. While some country folkes were at plough they saw a black cloud coming down the river and as it approached it appeared blacker and blacker. When it was beside them they saw a great black dogg ~~hangd~~ <hang[e]d> in chaines uppon a gibbett and crowes feeding uppon it, but presently after there came a great bird like an eagle w*hi*ch drave them all away and with that the cloud vanisht having dried up a great deale of water so that men might passe dry foot over the river. How true this is I know not nor what it betokens, but he that related it saied there were a thousand people that saw it. I can enlarge no more at this time being in great hast.

Adieu. 11 Maii 1632.

We intend shortly to write againe to the Inquisit[ion].

I heare my lo*r*d of St Albans[255] gave his voice against my lo*r*ds ordinariship not in writing but by word of mouth, but it was by importuning of Lo*r*d Baltimor misinforming him about tribunals etc*eter*a. The like importunity he used with others, being the Jesuitts chief instrument in this buissenesse, but God rewarded him soon after with an untimely death, and his memory is and wilbe hatefull for this action, as it is ridiculous [*p. 205*] for his other impertinences of mariage.[256]

In this last jubily[257] a priest directing his penitent how to gaine it, and ~~the party~~ willing the party to pray for the popes intention, the party replied that they thought it not so secure to pray for his intention having heard that his intentions were not good for the Church and religion.[258] I can not name the parties but this the pr[iest] him self tould me.

---

[255] Richard Burke, 4th earl of Clanricard and 1st earl of St Albans. The seculars described him as 'prudens, sed timidus'. 'Omnes bonos sacerdotes ex aequo fere complectitur, et olim consuevit sacerdotem secularem et Jesuitam alternis vicibus in domu*m* suam admittere, sed jam a paucis annis Jesuitae sibi residentiam illam penitus appropriarunt excluso clero'; AAW, A XXVIII, no. 3, p. 14. In April 1632 Biddulph had been scandalized to heare that 'the earle of St Albans is one of [...] [the Jesuits'] noble men'; AAW, A XXVI, no. 49, p. 149.
[256] See *Letters 4, 5, 6.*
[257] See *Letter 5.*
[258] See *Letter 3.* In mid-May 1632 John Pory picked up the news in London that 'some Roman Catholiques here in towne [...] wishe the popes head were in the king of Swedens belly'; JPN, p. 266. On 30 September 1632 Edmund Dutton certified Biddulph that 'a <Catholike> ladie a penitent of the Jes[uits] said yesterday att court before the earle of Suffolke and the l[ord] marquis of Winchester th*a*t the pope and cardinall of France had done much hurt to the Christian world and th*a*t the pope had bred quarrels amongst the Catholikes of England'; AAW, A XXVI, no. 155, p. 439. See also *Letter 44.*

Hereafter direct your letters for me thus, A Mons*ieur* le Clerc, bycause Antonino[259] is a little to[o] much knowen.

[*on p. 206*]

Addressed: Pour Mons*ieur* Fitton a Rome.

Endorsed: 11th May. M[r] Clerk.

About one who would not pray for the pope his intention.

15. Clerk [John Southcot] to Fitton [Peter Biddulph], 1 June 1632

[*AAW, B 47, no. 58*]

Sir,

We have yours of the 1 of May wherin you signify that yours of the 6 of March and ours of the 17 of February miscaried. As for ours I do not remember anything of moment which (according to custome) was not iterated the next week, and bycause with yours was lost the ambassadors answer to the qu[een's] second letter[260] we suppose that you have procured a duplicat of the same by this time, or els a second letter in supply of that which was lost, which would be to great good purpose for us, bycause therby the qu[een] should have a fitt occasion to write againe, and more earnestly than before; wherfor if you have not procured this duplicat I pray gett it as soon as you can. The last week we sent a common letter[261] to his Hol[iness] in conformity of those points which you touched in your memorialls, but some things therof we wish had bin omitted, as that of my lords ability to live of him self <abundantly> and that nonn of the clergy besides him can do the like, which indeed is not soe, bycause there are divers that have more to live on than my lord hath, as M[r] Bennet,[262] M[r] Bossevile, M[r] William Shelley and others.[263] Likewise that clause is disliked, tota

---

[259] One of Southcot's aliases.

[260] See *Letter 16*.

[261] This may be a reference to a letter to Urban VIII of 20 May 1632 (AAW, A XXVI, no. 75) signed by John Colleton and George Leyburn. The copy in AAW is marked 'duplicatum'. The words and phrases cited here do not occur in it, and it may have been altered in Rome.

[262] For Edward Bennett's will of 27 March 1635, demonstrating the considerable extent of his financial resources, see AAW, A XXVIII, no. 11.

[263] Antony Allison has discovered evidence of the episcopal chapter's financial position which confirms Southcot's statement here. In 1630 the chapter started a fund, the signatories to which pledged at least £200 each. This money was to be invested to support the donor during his life. Then, after death, the whole sum was to be put at the disposal of the chapter.

ferme Anglorum Catholicorum spes in gallica natione et*cetera*, and that also dubium est an rex tam aequo erga alterum animo etc. But take all togeather, and the memorialls are very good and to the purpose, and I hope our former letters to the pope and Inquisition, which were sent on the 2 and 9 of March,[264] will help to that good successe which is expected by these memorialls for the speedy obtaining of our cause.

I desire only the 2 last chapters of Barclaies paraenesis[265] which can not be had here, which, if you can procure there, I shall hartely thank you for them, as I do for your offer of Bentivoglios Relations of England,[266] which I shalbe ready to accept in case I cannot gett any other coppy from Paris where they were printed.

My lord is much bound to Card[inal] Balneo[267] for that kind offer he maketh of house, coach and diett but I would not wish my lord to accept it although he went up, for that were the way to loose his freindship, which he may be more assured of, so long as he is not burdensom unto him. If the acceptation hould, I do not see, as you say, what good my lords presence in France can do our cause, and I should rather wish his abode in Rome, supposing his Hol[iness] will give him some preferment there, as in reason, methinkes, he should, even with relation to England by way of some superintendancy of English

By 1637 Edward Bennett had paid in £900. John Bosvile's contributions between 1636 and 1639 came to £937, and William Shelley donated £400 between 1634 and 1638; Allison, RSGB, II, pp. 246–247. In mid-February 1635 a secular priest told Gregorio Panzani that the secular clergy were led 'de facto, non de jure' by John Colleton, George Fisher, John Southcot, George Leyburn, and John Jackson because they were the richest of the secular priests; VA, PD, fos 76r–7r.

[264] Cf. AAW, A XXVI, no. 34 (a letter of 2 March 1632 to the cardinals of the Congregation for the Propagation of the Faith, signed by Colleton and Leyburn, asking for the restoration of Richard Smith as bishop of Chalcedon).

[265] John Barclay, *Ioannis Barclaii Paraenesis ad Sectarios* (Rome, 1617); ARCR, I, nos 46–51. This book repudiated Barclay's earlier gallican opinions as set out in his *Ioannis Barclaii Pietas* (Paris, 1612). In January 1638 Smith was paying John Barclay's son, Robert, to act as his agent at Rome, in place of Biddulph; Allison, RSGB, II, p. 252.

[266] Guido Bentivoglio, *Relationi delle Provincie Unite di Fiandra [...]* (Paris, 1631), part II, ch. 3 ('Dello stato della Religione in Inghilterra', which contains a passage on the discord between secular priests and Jesuits).

[267] Cardinal Giovanni Francesco Guido del Bagno. See AAW, A XXIV, no. 4, p. 11; XXVIII, no. 131, p. 448. Until recently, he had been the nuncio in Paris. He also advised Urban VIII on British matters. See Hibbard, *CI*, p. 44. According to Gregorio Panzani, Cardinal del Bagno tended to be pessimistic about Catholicism's prospects in England. He told Panzani in September 1634 that, 'in quanto alla conversione del re' (Charles), he did not expect it, 'poichè il re non è dotto, anzi è ottuso, et però non puo restar convinto da ragioni, et poi è anche timidissimo', while the queen was essentially frivolous and little concerned with promoting Catholics' interests. He opposed the appointment of an English cardinal, but thought that the English should be granted at least one bishop to reside in the country, and perhaps as many as three; VA, PD, fos 23r–4r.

affaires, els the world will hould him disgraced, and be ready to cast undeserved aspersions uppon him, which were a thing intolerable.

That clause of the Dominicans faculties touching parochialia[268] sheweth his Hol[iness's] intention to restraine reg[ulars'] faculties hereafter and to make them more subordinat than they have bin, which is a thing necessary.[269] I ame sory you expresse not all particulers concerning your audience from [*sic for* with] his Hol[iness], as what his Hol[iness] saied in particuler, and what countenance he shewed you, and what particuler points you touched in your speach to him, and in what manner. We desire to be particulerly informed hereafter of all such points, the rather bycause we understand that your adversaries have sought to give an ill impression of you to his Hol[iness] and to the cardinals. Neither did you expresse in a former letter you writt hither the manner how your adversaries sought to entrap you about the bookes forbidden by the last breve,[270] which we would gladly know.

If you can get our matter to be remitted to those 3 card[inals] you name,[271] it ~~were~~ wilbe well, but I doubt you will never gett it to be remitted to the nonce of France[272] and 4 French bishops as Philippensis[273] was to those of Flanders, bycause our cause is much more universal than his was, and will have greater opposition.

---

[268] See *Letters 1, 13*.

[269] Cf. *Letter 13*. In a letter of 22 March 1632 [or 1633] John Jackson reported to Biddulph that a 'very vertuous and learned preist, who dare not let his name be knowne for fear the Jes[uits] wold make him loose his place, writeth' that 'since the talke of asking leave for the parochialia', members of religious orders 'have maried and christned under my lo[rd's] [i.e. Richard Smith's] officers noses, more than ever they did before, nay made most strange and unequall matches, taken upon them to decide most strange matrimoniall cases only proper for my lords court to decide of those which promised ech other and upon that were bedded togither, and yet upon the femalls saing she gave not consent, for a peice of money given to the man, the case was declared not contract'; AAW, A XXVI, no. 43, p. 133.

[270] i.e. Urban VIII's breve *Britannia* (29 April/9 May 1631) which, *inter alia*, forbade English Catholics to publish or even write again on the issues disputed between Richard Smith and his opponents. It also ordered that all the books already published on this topic should be destroyed; Allison, RSGB, I, p. 388. See also AAW, A XXV, no. 52 (a paper lamenting the 'great hurt and damage' which would result from this act of censorship).

[271] Cf. AAW, A XXV, no. 89 (a paper advancing reasons for removing the cause of the bishop of Chalcedon from the Holy Office and appointing four cardinals to decide it); AAW, A XXVI, nos 44, 45, 47. One of the cardinals appointed to consider Richard Smith's case was Martio Ginetti; AAW, A XXVI, no. 63, p. 179.

[272] Cardinal Alessandro Bichi.

[273] Philip Rovenius, archbishop of Philippi. The papacy had installed Rovenius as a titular prelate in Holland where he became locked in conflict with the Jesuits. His struggle seemed to be analogous to the pro-episcopal secular clergy's difficulties in England. They had followed his case at Rome very carefully; AAW, A XVI, no. 151, p. 590; no. 175, p. 675. See also J. Israel, *The Dutch Republic* (Oxford, 1995), pp. 377–378, 391; Duffy, 'The English secular clergy', p. 218.

What Jesuitt is he that wrote against oracula vivae vocis, English or Italian and whether is he in the Inquisition or noe for it?[274]

You do well to advertise of Signor Georgio[275] his kinsman coming towards us, from [the] Scottish college there. We will be cautious, as you desire, in trusting him.

I understand that the 6 you specified in your former letter are arrived in England long since, and have spoken with divers of the Jes[uits'] freinds in London, but as yet not one of them hath presented him self to my lords vicar nor spoken with any of his officers, which is a thing worthy to be complained of, as shewing the preposterousnesse of their b[r]eeding in that college, which, it seems, tends wholy to make them selves freinds <only> and not true clergy men. In my time the rule was that as soon as any pr[iest] should come over he should present him self to his superiour here and, before he came from thence, he should promise obedience to the archpriest which you may do well to procure to be putt in practise there and cause every pr[iest] that comes from thence to promise obedience to the bishop. This is a point very necessary to be donn. If Fa[ther] Oliver[276] come we will comply with him aswell as we can, and seek to gaine his order by him, as you advise us.[277]

The next week I hope to send you an Italian letter from an Italian pr[iest][278] that lives here to the congreg[ation] of the Holy Office to

---

[274] On 19/29 March 1632 Smith wrote to Biddulph that the Paris nuncio 'wil print here the bul of revoking oracula vivae vocis', i.e. a spoken papal utterance (with less authority than a papal bull), 'and one said that the Jes[uits] wold give a million of gold that that bul had never bene made, and added that the Sea Apostolik intendeth to restraine the faculties of reg[ulars]'; AAW, B 27, no. 107. (Southcot's diary for 1632 noted the 'revocatio oraculorum vivae vocis made in December last'; CRS, 1, p. 107.) On 7/17 April 1632 Smith reassured Biddulph that the 'bul oracula doth not take away the faculties' of the secular clergy's college of Douai, 'becaus it mentioneth [not] seminaria or collegia when it taketh away faculties, but onely ordines, congregationes, instituta, societates, which signifie such companies as intend to live continually in some course, as seminaries doe not'; AAW, B 27, no. 108. In March 1632 the Jesuit general, Muzio Vitelleschi, warned Richard Blount not to let any English Jesuit write anything which suggested disobedience 'to the brief shown in France or by the bishop of Chalcedon'; ARSJ, Anglia MS 1/ii, fo. 345v. I am grateful to Thomas McCoog for assistance with this point.

[275] George Con.

[276] Oliver Burke OP. See T.S. Flynn, *The Irish Dominicans 1536–1641* (Dublin, 1993), pp. 110, 225–227. (Biddulph wrote to Southcot on 5/15 August 1636 mentioning one Hugh Burke (of the family of the earl of Clanricard and St Albans) who was a brother of the Dominican 'Fa[ther] Oliverius'; AAW, A XXVIII, no. 150, p. 505.)

[277] At the end of August 1632 Smith remarked that 'F[ather] Oliver is now going for England'. He had promised that his order would not oppose Smith's authority; AAW, B 27, no. 127. In September 1632 Smith noted that 'F[ather] Oliver gave me some memorials' written by the Jesuits in France 'against our cause'; AAW, B 27, no. 129.

[278] Giulio Antonelli. See *Letter 16*.

informe them of the state of things here, but he desires not to be named.

I can write little newes. It is doubtfull whether the qu[een] be with child againe or noe. My Lord Marquis Hammilton (as I heare) is come home againe having lost all the men he carried over with him.[279] The single combat which should have bin <fought> between the two Scotts, [the] lord of Machee[280] and Ramsy,[281] is come to nought, yet both are still prisoners in the Tower, and the great martiall court which was erected for that purpose, wherin the earle of Linsie[282] was high cunstable, is now dissolved.[283]

When the French k[ing] was at Calais he sent over Monsieur Chaumont[284] as ambassador extraordinary to passe a complement with the k[ing] and qu[een] and (as some think) to endeavour to bring the present ambass[ador] Monsieur de Fontany[285] into grace with the queen and consequently to gett the Capucins to be in Fa[ther] Philips place. But what he hath attempted or effected therin I know not. I heare only that he took his leave of the king privatly, which sheweth that he was not so welcome. With him Fa[ther] Leonard[286] and 3 other Capucins are gonn back into France and 4 others came over with him to remaine here in their places.[287] I imagin if he dealt in any such buissinesse that he was not gratefull to the qu[een] bycause she loves Fa[ther] Philip extraordinarily, and will not part with him by any meanes, and by this occasion she is much averted from the Capucins, and it is likely she will never be gained to them in that manner as they desire, for, if Fa[ther] Phil[ip] should dye, she would rather gett others of the Oratory to supply his place than take in Capucins, which makes the Capucins weary and desirous to be gonn, but the French king will not permitt them.[288]

---

[279] See *CSPV, 1632–1636*, p. 19.

[280] Donald McKay, Lord Reay.

[281] David Ramsay.

[282] Robert Bertie, 1st earl of Lindsey.

[283] See *Letter 5*.

[284] Melchior Mitte de Miolans, marquis de St Chaumont. See *CSPV, 1629–1632*, pp. 623, 624.

[285] François Duval, marquis de Fontenay Mareuil. See *ibid.*, p. 627.

[286] Provincial of the French Capuchins. See Hibbard, *CI*, p. 44; P. Hughes, 'The conversion of Charles I', *Clergy Review*, 8 (1934), pp. 113–125, at p. 115; Birch, *CT*, II, pp. 298, 307.

[287] As the text implies, the Capuchins who returned to France had quarrelled with the queen because they wanted to provide her confessor, but she would not dismiss Robert Philip. I am grateful to Caroline Hibbard for assistance with this point.

[288] Later, in September 1634, Cardinal del Bagno told Gregorio Panzani that some of Henrietta Maria's chaplains claimed to be much in her favour, and this had caused differences with Robert Philip, on whom she principally relied. The Father General of the

The drum*m*e beateth daily up and down the streets to gett soldiars for Sweden, but I do not heare of many that goe. I heard of some that were going to serve the infanta[289] in Flanders, who by order from the counsell were cessed on and shipped for Sweden.

The Muscovits also have gotten leave from the king to leavy two thousand soldiars here under the com*m*and of a Scottish captaine to assist them in their wars against the Polonian,[290] notwithstanding the promise w*h*ich (as S*ir* Tho[mas] Roe[291] saieth) was made the last summer to the Polonian ambassador[292] here that we would not assist the Muscovit in these warrs. So that, upon S*ir* Tho[mas] Roe his remonstrance, it may be this order (w*h*ich it seemes was gott by surreption) wilbe staied.

I can no more, but all woonted remembrances. 1 June 1632.

Is M^ris Ward a prisoner or at full liberty there?[293]

Yours

Clerk

Addressed: For Mr Fitton.
        Rome.

Endorsed: 1 Jun[e]. Clerk.
        Points to be corrected in my memoriall for the b*isho*p his continuing.
        About the priests that goe from this colledg to England, who never come to their superiors.

Congregation of the Oratory had offered to recall Philip, but the cardinal had dissuaded him; VA, PD, fo. 24r.

[289] Isabella Clara Eugenia.

[290] See *CSPV, 1629–1632*, p. 646.

[291] For Sir Thomas Roe, see Hibbard, *CI*, p. 31.

[292] For the embassy of the Polish envoy John Albert Rakowsky in September 1631, see *CSPV, 1629–1632*, pp. 540, 545, 551; CRS, 1, p. 107; A.J. Loomie (ed.), *Ceremonies of Charles I: The Note Books of John Finet 1628–1641* (New York, 1987), p. 107; JPN, pp. 167–168, 172.

[293] The secular clergy opponents of Mary Ward and her institute believed that the form of religious life which she prescribed was analogous to aspects of the Jesuits' institute. (Her brother was a Jesuit (see *Letter 26*), and the Wright brothers who took part in the gunpowder plot were her uncles.) Her opponents branded her and her followers as a force for disorder in the Church. Her institute had been suppressed by papal decree in January 1631. In April 1632, Richard East wrote to Smith to advise him that Ward had gone to Rome 'with a certaynty of having her order confirmed, revelationibus animata divinitus, but as I heere los padres advise her to lay downe her imaginary pretended mission'. East asked Smith to relay this to Biddulph 'for heere they give it out with great confidence that her order is presently to bee confirmed'; AAW, A XXVI, no. 52, p. 157.

16. John Clerk [Southcot] to Fitton [Peter Biddulph], 8 June 1632

[*AAW, B 47, no. 57*]

Sir,

I was sory to understand by your last of the 10 of May of your indisposition, which I hope hath left you long since. I have not much to add this week to what I wrote the last week, only I send you Signor Giulio Antonelli[294] his letter to the pope enclosed in one to Cardinal Bagni which was promised the last week. It is written under the name of Francesco Bonzotti bycause Antonelli is not willing to have his name discovered in that court, least the reg[ulars] come to know it, which might be prejudiciall to him. And writing ~~by letter~~ as he doth, he thinkes it will do <the> more good and seem to be ~~the~~ lesse partiall, as coming from a straunger interested on neither side.[295] Yet, if you deliver the letter to the cardinall your self, you may tell him the authors true name, desiring him to keep it secrett. There are many good points touched in his letter to his Hol[iness], but they are not sett down so well as <I> would have them, and therfor I purpose to deale with the author to alter the stile a little in some places adding also some other points that are omitted, and to write it faire over againe against Wednesday next that I may send it to my lord[296] at Paris to be sent unto you that way. Wherfor I should advise you to keep this coppy by you till that come, though perhaps it wilbe a fortnight later, unlesse you see some urgent occasion of delivering it presently wherby to do us the more good, or to prevent some ~~harme~~ imminent harme.

I am sory Monsieur Brissacs[297] letter to the qu[een] miscaried. In any case gett him to write againe, for it would minister an excellent occasion to the qu[een] of writing ~~againe~~ more effectually than before, which is the best and only way for us to prevaile in our cause, and without some such occasion we shall hardly desire the qu[een] to write againe for us or for my lord. If you can gett the cause to be taken out of the Holy Office and referred to three or 4 of our freinds there, I shall have some hope, otherwise I feare our adversaries will have a stronger party than we, and will hinder all good resolutions for us. My lord writes that he hath no mind to go up, and here we do generally

---

[294] Giulio Antonelli was a Paduan priest who sent reports to the Roman curia (particularly to Cardinals Barberini and Spada, and to Monsignor Boccabella) in favour of the English secular clergy; VA, PD, fo. 70r; VA, Barberini MS 8633, fo. 246r.

[295] See *Letters 26, 28, 29, 30*.

[296] Richard Smith.

[297] Jean de Gallard, baron de la Rochebeaucourt et de Brassach, French ambassador in Rome. See *Letter 5*.

think that my lords presence there would not <do> so much good
as it doth where he is, unlesse he were a more practicall man and a
better solicitor than he is, and would follow his buissinesse closely and
dexterously when he is there, as Philippenses[298] did, which I think is
not in my lord to doe.

If his Hol[iness] intend seriously to accept of my lords supposed
resignation, all your endeavour must be 1. That it may be donn without
prejudice to us <here> who never consented to it and therfor expect
that an other (at least one, if not 3) be installed before his resignation
be either published or formally accepted. 2. That it may be donn
with his honor by making him an archbishop and giving him some
superintendency in matters of the English mission, and with that
condition it were not amisse my lord were resident in Rome continually,
and had some office in the Congregation de Propaganda Fide, as it
were, by way of reward for his labours in the common cause. 3. That
we may be provided in this kind before winter, and as much sooner as
you can, bycause if it be once knowen that my lord is to be no more
the superior here all collections which are made only in his name, and
to his use, will cease, as also all authority, even that by which pr[iests]
should be kept in order, which will cause an utter confusion, and the
ruine of our body, not being able to mantaine an agent there, or to
furnish other necessary charges either at home or abroad. This point
must be much inculcated bycause it concerns us mainly.

I send you here an abstract of the k[ing's] graunt by patent under the
broad seale to such recusants as do compound, as also such priviledges
which are promised but not yet graunted, [and] not comprehended in
the generall graunt. The patent it self is of a great length and not fitt
to be sent up, as containing a lawiers book of 30 sheets of paper. But
as yet there are no patents sealed, and it is doubtfull when any wilbe.
I think my fathers wilbe the first if any be at all, wherof many make a
question, seeing so many delaies used in the buissenesse. Some think
the proceeding depends of [sic] the successe of German affaires, which
is not unlikly. The pursevants are nothing so buissy as they were, yet
they are not without commission still.

The Jes[uits] (as I heare) have printed at St Omers a libell against
the French which is intitled Gesta Gallorum per impios, sive Gesta
Impiorum per Gallos,[299] coppies wherof are convaied from hand to
hand here amongst their freinds. Therin they bring in all their leagues
with Turkes and heretickes, and invaigh bitterly against the Cardinall
Richelieu, as one told me that saw it, though I have not seen it my

---

[298] Philip Rovenius, archbishop of Philippi.
[299] Ludovicus de Cruzamonte (pseud.?), *Gesta Impiorum per Francos, sive Gesta Francorum per Impios, ex variis auctoribus [. . .] Collecta* (Rhenopoli, 1632).

self. Perhaps the Fr[ench] ambass[ador] there, if you tell him of it, can find meanes to gett a coppy. The same man spred not long before a certaine supposed (or suppositious rather) declaration of the duke of Bavaria[300] in English pretended to be translated out of the French coppy, which I have seen and read over. Therin many glaunces are given also against the French, and <it> seemes to have bin made chiefly to disgrace them.

My lord treasurer[301] and my Lord Wentworth[302] (who is to be <lord> debitee for Ireland) are to be made earles very shortly as I heard yesterday.

That letter which Card[inal] Barberino[303] wrote to the grand aulmonier[304] was only half a dozen lines of complement in answer to his. M[r] Lab[orne] was at the reading of it. My lord and he are well againe. Thus in hast I committ you to God. 8 June 1632.

I will do what I can to procure you those brevets of the presid[ent] of [the] North and Wales.[305]

Yours,

Johne Clerk

The last week I sent you an attestation from M[r] Case,[306] a notary, touching two noblemens discourse about my lord bishop and the 18 supposed noblemen.

The substance of the graunt, the rent resolved being duly payed.

1. That no summons nor seizures go out of the exchequer.
2. That the recusant have power to sett and lett the lands graunted.
3. That the clerks of assize and peace send not processe against him for his wife.
4. That he be freed from spirituall courts and messengers nisi per regem et consilium.
5. That he and his wife be free from informers.

---

[300] Maximilian of Bavaria.

[301] Sir Richard Weston, 1st Baron Weston, created earl of Portland in February 1633.

[302] Sir Thomas Wentworth, 1st Viscount Wentworth.

[303] Francesco Barberini, cardinal protector of the English nation.

[304] Jacques le Noël Du Perron. He had arrived in England in May 1631; *CSPV, 1629–1632*, p. 503. He was a cousin of Cardinal Jacques Davy Du Perron. Smith noted in March 1632 that 'the grand almoner hath complained of me' to Richelieu 'that I sent him not a copy of the jubile[e]', though Smith thought that to have sent it would have made it appear 'that I took him for my official or minister'. The bishop of Mende (Daniel La Motte-Houdancourt), who had been in England in 1625, 'would not receive a jubile[e] from me which I sent to him'; AAW, B 27, no. 107.

[305] See *Letter 5*.

[306] See *Letter 13*; AAW, A XXVI, no. 103.

6. That he be bound once for all to the good behaviour in his own county.

7. That he be not indicted de novo.

The intended priviledges by decree.

That paying his rent duly, he be not forced to xii^d a Sunday.

That he be not prosecuted for keeping meniall and ordinary servants.

That he be freed of such servants as compound for them selves.

That conviction be not pleaded in barr to any such recusant.

Addressed: For Mr Fitton. Rome.

Endorsed: Clerk. 8 Jun[e].
The conditions of the composition with Catholikes.

17. Clerk [John Southcot] to [Peter Biddulph], 22 June 1632

[AAW, A XXVI, no. 86, pp. 235–238]

Sir,

The last week Antonin[o][307] wrote not unto you bycause he heard of no letter that came from you after that of the 8 of May wherin you certified *your* sicknesse, fearing least his letters might miscary in the meane time. But now having seen yours of the 22 of the same month, and understanding therby that you wrote not the week before to any body by reason of *your* absence from town, he entreated me to write these in his name and to certify you of the receyt of the last breve, Declaratio quod Constitutiones Ap*ost*olicae[308] etc., by w*h*ich it seemes the reg[ulars] are restrained more and more in their pretended exemptions and priviledges. How cometh it to passe that being dated in Novemb[er] 1631 it was sent up no sooner? Neither is it authenticated, as all breves should be before you send them, although they concerne the reg[ulars] only, and indeed much more when they concerne them, bycause they do oftentimes deny them unlesse they come authenticated as they did <that> of Revocatio Omnium

---

[307] i.e. John Southcot. See *Letter 14*.

[308] For a printed copy of Urban VIII's breve of 26 October/5 November 1631, *Declaratio quod Constitutiones Apostolicae in concernentibus Fidem Catholicam, & Sanctae Inquisitionis Officium hactenus editae, & in posterum etiam super quacumque alia re edendae, omnes Regulares quomodolibet privilegiatos compraehendant, nisi illi in edendis specialiter excipiantur* (Rome, 1632), see AAW, A XXIV, no. 201.

Indultorum etc,[309] and oracula vivae vocis[310] which the Jes[uits] here
say includeth not them, though it ~~be~~ <were> a true breve as they are
assured from their own superiour. This one Altam, a Jes[uit],[311] tould
one Mr Jennings,[312] a lay gentleman, within this fortnight, and therfor
notwithstanding this breve they proceed as before which deserves to be
certified there in the court among your other complaints of them and
their proceedings. Antonin[o] is glad that you have all Mr Blacklos[313]
papers, and wisheth you to look carefully to them and <to> all others,
especially in time of absence, sicknesse or any other such occasion and
to provide that they may be safe and forthcoming. It is feared that our
adversaries have gotten a coppy of one thing which was sent from hence
to Paris the 28 February to be sent afterwards to you. The title of it, as
I take it, was Humillima Narratio[314] etc., made by some pr[iests] in the
West and other parts of England uppon the grief they had of my lords[315]
departure, expressing many greevances of the clergy, and in the end
desiring his Hol[iness] either to call the Jes[uits] out of Engl[and] or
to subject them to ordinary authority. The whole narration consisted
of some 4 sheets of paper, and as yet we never heard that you receaved
it, which makes us feare that it was intercepted, or that they bribed
some of your scribes (as it is usuall there) to gett a coppy of it, for
certainly they have gotten some such thing, as one tould me that saw
it and read it (as he saied) in a lay mans hand, and came to one of
the clergy afterward, to know whether any such supplication had bin
given up to his Hol[iness] in the clergies name, and in the name of
some of the laity also, for so he saied was the tenor of it. This was one
Haughton[316] <a young> pr[iest] that came from Valiodolid[317] about
some two or 3 yeares agoe. Here he goes by the name of Pinninton,
and in Lancashire by the name of Traver, ~~but~~ and he seemed to be

---

[309] For a printed copy of Urban VIII's breve of 2/12 September 1628, *Revocatio Omnium
Indultorum Quibusvis Religionibus Societatibus, &c Quomodolibet Concessorum Audien. Secularium
Confessiones Absque Ordinarii Examine & Approbatione* (Rome, 1629), see AAW, A XXII, no.
135 (now catalogued as AAW, SEC 16/1/6).

[310] See *Letter 15*.

[311] John Grosvenor SJ. In November 1633 he sailed from the Isle of Wight, with Andrew
White SJ and Thomas Gervase SJ, for Maryland, in order to found a mission there;
Codignola, *CHL*, p. 188; Hughes, *HSJ*, pp. 244–347.

[312] Identity uncertain, but possibly Anthony Jennings of Great Dunmow, Essex, who was
named in a list of complaints, drawn up by Thomas Green, against the Jesuits; AAW, A
XXVIII, no. 15, p. 67; Anstr., II, pp. 170–171, 172. Jennings had married Elizabeth, daughter
of Sir Robert Brooke of Barkway, Hertfordshire, who was cited as a victim of the Jesuit John
Grosvenor's meddling. See *Letter 44*.

[313] Thomas White. See Anstr., II, pp. 349–354.

[314] See *Letters 6, 7, 29*.

[315] Richard Smith.

[316] Edward Haughton. See Anstr., II, p. 151.

[317] The English college (St Alban's) at Valladolid.

much troubled at the matter, and professed him self to be a sec[ular] pr[iest] though I beleeve he be a concealed Jes[uit] for he hath little or no acquaintance with any of the clergy. I pray therfor certify by your next letter whether you ~~have~~ receaved this Narratio or [*p. 236*] noe and whether you made any coppye be taken of it by any scribe, and what use you made of it there. For it was sent you not to be presented whole as it lay but to give you matter <of information> to use as you should see cause.

I ame glad to understand by your letter that the Congregacion[318] will never leave England without some bishop and that you perceave they intend to make 2 or 3 which indeed were the best and only way, though it be fitt also that my lord be not quite discharged but have some superintendancy at least over the rest whether he reside at Paris or at Ro[me], and I wish he were at Ro[me], in case he come no more hither, to assist in the Congregacion de Propaganda as I wrote to you before. The persons that ~~have ben~~ <cheefly> are in election have bin formerly proposed at Rome, namely D[octor] Kellison, Champney, Ed[ward] Bennet, Jo[hn] Bossevile, ~~D[octor] Maylard that had~~. You may propose also if you think good those two you named in your former letter: Maylard;[319] Stratford.[320] I have bin labouring long to gett those patents you desired of the two presidents, North and Walles, but I understand they are very longe and therfor I desire only to have an abstract of their power and the names of the shires of their district, which when I have gotten I will send you.[321]

I have used also diligence to gett the beginnings and endings of those bookes you wrote for long since from Oxford and Cambridg, but as yet I cannot effect it.

There was an Oxford scholler of great name, an Arminian in sect, held <to be> the best preacher there, who desired his grace to passe doctor, and having demaunded it once, twice, thrice, as the fashion is, and still opposed by the puritans, in the end having a thousand pounds in his purse and 80^l per annum he went away secretly from

---

[318] The Congregation for the Propagation of the Faith.

[319] Henry Mayler. See Anstr., I, pp. 223–224; Allison, RSGB, I, pp. 361–362. In Smith's list of 10/20 May 1632 of those he thought suitable to be made a bishop he also listed Mayler, but Smith thought that 'the Jes[uits] will oppose the fighting which was betwene him and an other in Spayne', i.e. presumably in 1623 when Mayler took part in the negotiations for the proposed Anglo-Spanish dynastic treaty. But 'otherwise he were most fit becaus he is knowne to the king' (Charles I) and 'was loved of him'; AAW, B 27, no. 109.

[320] Edmund Lechmere, who was one of Richard Smith's propagandists. See Anstr., II, p. 187. See Edmund Lechmere, *The Conference mentioned by Doctour Featly [. . .]* (Douai, 1632); ARCR, II, no. 489 [incorporated in L.I., *The Relection of a Conference [. . .]* (Douai, 1635); ARCR II, no. 461], a work which demonstrates Smith's willingness and ability to dispute with Protestants.

[321] See *Letter 5*.

the university, and what is become of him we do not yet heare, but it is thought he is gonn over and wilbecome a Catholick as one Mr Chillingworth[322] did before, wherof I certified you some two months since.

A grave and prudent priest[323] who is placed with the prime nobleman[324] [*in margin*: Morgan – marquis] of England wrote lately hither that there are two Benedictins in Hantshire who give leave to Catholickes to have their children christned at the Protestant churches by ministers wherat (as he writes) his patron is greatly scandalized seeing that in his own case it was not permitted. This is worth the information there.

There was an Arminian minister in Hantshire who going the procession in Rogation week (as the custome yet is amongst Protestants) and, coming to a crosse way where he found no crosse, would not go forward till he caused a crosse of bowes to be putt up, and then kneeling down before it he saied his praiers and so went on the procession. This the puritants there storm at mightily.

Sir Will[iam] Tresham who is coronell of an English regiment under the infanta[325] [*p. 237*] was commaunded not long since to go with his men into the Palatinat but he rather chose to give up his patent to the infanta than he would goe thither, fearing to displease the king as he saied, contrary to whose liking he came not thither to serve. He did it in a good fashion and with many good speaches, so that the Spanniards were content to excuse him from that service, and the king here took it very gratiously, and gave him thankes for it.[326]

The Arminians here do multiply a pace, and the bishop of London[327] who is very gratious with the king, and dispacheth all things belonging to matters of religion, intendeth to do his best for the suppressing of the new separists (as here we call them) who will not conforme them selves to the religion of England, saying it is altogeather papisticall,

[322] William Chillingworth. See R.R. Orr, *Reason and Authority* (London, 1964).

[323] William Case, alias Morgan.

[324] John Paulet, 5th marquis of Winchester. On 3 January 1632 William Case put Richard Smith 'in minde of your most true frend my patron' who 'dailie wisheth, endevoreth and enquireth after your good succease in your affayres'. When the marquis was 'last tearme in London the whole crew of Coreists sett uppon him; and he like an other Phineus, stood up most stoutlie amongst them, resisted them with great zeale and remaines confident of their confusion'; AAW, A XXVI, no. 17, p. 57. In October 1631 the marquis had declared that even if there were 'speciall lawes made against ordinary jurisdiction in a bishop (as there are not) he would bee burnt in the fire and chopt in peeces before he would resist it or speake against it'; AAW, A XXV, no. 194, p. 709.

[325] Isabella Clara Eugenia.

[326] Sir William Tresham was a friend of the English secular clergy leadership, and had, on 24 August 1632, signed an affidavit (AAW, A XXVI, no. 125) against the 'Protestatio Declaratoria' (see *Letter 13*).

[327] William Laud.

but runn in a new straine of most damnable pride and presumption thinking nonn but them selves shalbe saved and that no minister that is not elect hath any power to preach or can do any good by his preaching. Shortly we expect to have that new sect also to passe over to us from Holland, whom there they stile the Assurers, going to sick men (especially the richer sort) to assure them of their salvation by such and such markes. O tempora, O mores!

The fishing goeth on mainly, and, the better to assure it hereafter, all the nobility shalbe engaged in it and the king will depute ten of his great shipps to preserve it and to keep of[f] the Hollander from hindring us,[328] and now, hearing of their so happy progresse in the Low Countries and their straight union with the French, we beginn to feare them more than heretofore, and this wilbe the cause to make us joine the more firmely with Spaine, which doubtlesse my lord treasurer[329] will further all he can, and my Lord Cottington with him, who are the duumviri of this state and [those] that beare most up in the kings favour. The treasurer is to be made earle of Sussex after the death of the ould earle[330] yet living, there being no more left of his name and race to enjoy the earldom. It was reported that he was to be created earle of Chenceford[331] uppon the late mariage of his sonn[332] by this wife[333] (who is le Clercks[334] cosen german) with the dutchesse of Lennox second daughter.[335] But that report ~~was~~ prooved not true for the mariage was solemnized on Munday last, being the 18 of this month, at Rohampton, his house in Surrey within 5 miles of London, the k[ing] and queen being presente and the king giving the bride him self.[336] It is also saied (but how truly I know not) that the first man [p. 238] child shalbe a marquis as being of the kings blood. The marquis of Hamilton is not yet come home though most of his men that were left alive are come away.[337]

There are two waies much spoken of to gett the k[ing] mony without a parlament and yet legally, videlicet by taking the forfeiture of the statute made against eating flesh on forbidden daies, or els

---

[328] See *CSPV, 1629–1632*, p. 612.

[329] Sir Richard Weston, 1st Baron Weston, created earl of Portland in February 1633.

[330] Edward Radcliffe, 6th earl of Sussex.

[331] Chelmsford. See *CSPV, 1629–1632*, p. 633.

[332] Jerome Weston.

[333] Frances Waldegrave of Borley, Essex, who was Sir Richard Weston's second wife. See Alexander, *CLT*, pp. 29–30.

[334] John Southcot. Southcot's mother was Magdalen Waldegrave, daughter of Sir Edward Waldegrave.

[335] Lady Frances Stuart, a sister of the 4th duke of Lennox.

[336] See Alexander, *CLT*, pp. 170–171.

[337] For the marquis of Hamilton's attempt to render military assistance to Gustavus Adolphus, see *CSPV, 1629–1632, passim*; Sharpe, *PR*, p. 166.

compounding with such as will eat, for licences, and by taking
the forfeiture lickwise of cottages which by the statute are ~~lickwise~~
forbidden to be made but where they may have 4 acres of land
belonging to them, and yet are infinitly multiplied throuought [*sic*]
England.[338] These two forfeitures if they be pursued will raise the king
a mighty summe of mony.

There is a new secretary lately sworne in Dorchesters[339] place, whose
name is Winnebanke.[340] He was clark of the signett before, and is held
a temperat man. His promotion to this place came chiefly by my lord of
Londons[341] meanes togeather with the lord treasurer and Cottington.
This is all the newes I have to write.

And so with my own kind remembr[ances] added to Antoninos, whose
command I thinke I have hereby sufficiently discharged, I rest as ever.

22 June 1632.

I could not get the relation which was sent you from hence, with a
letter to Card[inal] Bagni a fortnight agoe by Signor Bonzotti,[342] to be
mended, and therfor you may deliver that coppy if you think good.

It were good to learne the speciall cause that mooved his Hol[iness]
to sett out this last Declaratio which now you sent us, and so of other
breves also hereafter which, if you can learne, I pray informe us.

No address.

Endorsed: Clerk. 22 Jun[e].
     About my l[ord] to have some authoryty etc.
     About the Jesuitts neglecting the breve of oracula.
     About the 2 monkes who give leave to be baptized by
     hereticks.

18. Clerk [John Southcot] to [Peter Biddulph], 6 July 1632

[*AAW, A XXVI, no. 92, pp. 253–254*]

Sir,

The last week I wrote not to you, being otherwaies hindered, leaving
to M[r] Lab[orne] the answering of your last of May the 29th, and

---

[338] See JPN, p. 332; Birch, *CT*, II, p. 170.
[339] Sir Dudley Carleton, 1st Baron Dorchester.
[340] Sir Francis Windebanck.
[341] William Laud.
[342] See *Letter 16*.

the certifying of all other occurrences from hence. Your brother Worthington[343] saieth that his uncle John,[344] who liveth with your father, standeth for him, and is ready to shew him self if occasion be offered, but hitherto he hath not donn it openly. The pr[iest][345] whom M[r] Worthington caused to be apprehended [*word deleted*] hath bin sett at liberty againe uppon baile long since with Worthingtons consent but, if he bring not the gentlewoman back by Bartlemetide or ~~thereabouts~~ Michelmas, he is to rettourne back to his prison as M[r] Worthington saieth.

Our brethren here are much discomforted bycause they heare no good newes from you concerning my lords[346] buissenesse, and wonder that neither their attestations nor the qu[een's] two letters, nor so many other helps which we have had, are able to effect any thing. My lord writes that it is necessary for two or 3 of the gravest to go to Rome as some did in time of the appeale,[347] but how this will be effected I know not, partly for waunt of meanes, and partly for waunt of disposition in the men, for every man is out of hart uppon the newes of my lords resignation, and think that ~~they~~ we are now in worse case by much than we were before we had a bishop. You may do well to inculcat there that[348] if it be knowen once here that his Hol[iness] is resolved to have my lord discharged, the whole clergy is in a manner overthrown, all offices and orders,[349] and collections of monies and whatsoever els hath relation to the subsistence of my lords authority will cease, and so we shall not be able to maintaine <any> agents neither in Rome nor else where. The Fr[ench] ambass[ador's][350] answer to our qu[een's] letter is now come hither, but not yet delivered to her Majesty. I am sory you gott not a coppy of it to send us, that we might know how

[343] William Worthington.

[344] John Worthington SJ. See CRS, 75, pp. 338–339.

[345] John Wakeman. See *Letters 9, 10, 11*.

[346] Richard Smith.

[347] i.e. the appellant (or archpriest) dispute of 1598–1602. On 13/23 September 1632 Smith advised Biddulph that he should write to the secular clergy in England advising them that 'twoe or three of the gravest of them' should 'goe to Rome', and that he wished he had done so himself when he left England in 1631; AAW, B 27, no. 129. On 7/17 June 1633 Smith emphasized to Biddulph that he himself had 'written to our brethren in England that unles 3 or 4 of the gravest of them goe to Rome as there did in time of [the] appellants they will get litle'; AAW, A XXVII, no. 61, p. 178. In December 1631 Smith and his friends had made a conscious effort to revive the memory of the appellants at Rome; *Letter 1*.

[348] The following words are interlined here: 'ut alias [*two words illegible*] ille confirmatus declaratus, capiat [?] [*word illegible*] per Angliam divulgari re itum est, [word illegible] sacerdotes incipiunt [*word illegible*] si durem [*or* ducem ?] [*word illegible*], etc'.

[349] The following words are interlined: 'dignitatus quibus conservunt disciplina inter sacerdotes seculares, deinde omnia subsidia et collectionis pecunia, etc'.

[350] Jean de Gallard, baron de la Rochebeaucourt et de Brassach, French ambassador in Rome. See *Letters 5, 24*.

to proceed uppon it here. You may do well to write sometimes to Mr Hammond^{351} bycause it will give him occasion to write back to you againe, and informe you of many particulers which he knoweth and observeth here of divers things. You know he is a man that must be complied withall punctually in his owne way.

I pray certify us how D. Hallier and Aurelius bookes are liked there in that court.^{352} Here all indifferent men that read them like them passing well but the Jes[uits'] followers will not read them, pretending that it is not lawfull to do it by reason of the breve of prohibition.^{353} All our brethren here do wonder that the <clergies> supplication in reply to the breve was not delivered there by you,^{354} and still they presse to have it delivered up. What newes of [*word deleted*] Mary Ward there?^{355} And of Fa[ther] Fitzherbert and the English college? In your letters you make no mention of them. We desire you would write more at large and more particulers of all such things as may concerne us to know and especially we desire to know what card[inals] and prelates be our freinds in every congregacion and who be those with whom you are most confident [*p. 254*] there and the like. When you write to

^{351} John Jackson.

^{352} The tracts referred to here are: Hallier, *Defensio Ecclesiasticae Hierarchiae [...]* (see *Letter 9*), and Jean Duvergier de Hauranne (the Abbé de Saint-Cyran, who published under the name of Petrus Aurelius), *Vindiciae Censurae Facultatis Theologiae Parisiensis seu, Responsio Dispunctoria ad Libellum cui Titulus Hermanii Loemelii [...] Spongia [...] Auctore Petro Aurelio Theologia* (Paris, 1632); ARCR, I, no. 498. See Allison, RSGB, II, pp. 166–169. These works, which came out in March/April 1632, were replies to John Floyd SJ's tract, published under the pseudonym of Hermannus Loemelius, entitled *Hermanni Loemelii [...] Spongia, qua Diluuntur Calumniae Nomine Facultatis Parisiensis Impositae Libro qui Inscribitur, Apologia Sanctae Sedis Apostolicae* (St Omer, 1631); ARCR, I, no. 489. The seculars saw in Hallier's and Duvergier's work essential support for their case against their opponents in England. On 2/12 December 1636 Smith enthused that 'Mr Hallier told me he wold write about confirmation', a crucial element of a bishop's sacramental duties, and that 'he hath a great booke readie to come forth after Christmas, and secondly Aurelius wil replie to Sirmond' (the French Jesuit Jacques Sirmond, who entered into dispute with Duvergier over the issue of the sacrament of confirmation); AAW, A XXVIII, no. 206, p. 643; Allison, RSGB, III, pp. 191–198. Hallier took the line, as did Matthew Kellison in his *Treatise of the Hierarchie* of 1629, that the pope should not trespass on the 'rights of particular churches and their bishops'. He argued the case, which was particularly apposite to the English secular clergy, that 'as universal pastor' the pope 'is bound to provide particular churches with local pastors at all times and he cannot limit the powers inherent in their charge'. Also, religious orders should not be exempt from episcopal discipline; Allison, RSGB, II, p. 166. Antony Allison points out that, following the death of the seculars' friend, Pierre de Bérulle, Duvergier was 'the acknowledged leader of the *parti dévot* with its ideal of a spiritual renewal centred upon the priesthood and the sacraments'; *ibid.*, p. 167.

^{353} Urban VIII's breve *Britannia* (29 April/9 May 1631).

^{354} On 1 March 1632, John Jackson wrote to Biddulph that 'we can not hear that you have given upp [i.e. in Rome] our Humilima Supplicatio', i.e. against the breve *Britannia*; AAW, A XXVI, no. 33, p. 107.

^{355} See *Letter 15*.

M^r Ed[ward] Skinner, send his letters to me open (unlesse there be any secrett not fitt to be knowen by me) bycause he hath wished me to peruse them before I send them down to him in the country where he liveth altogeather now for his health, being deep [*word deleted*] in a consumption.

With these I send you coppies of the districts of the two presidents, taken out of the rowles. My lord writes that the Jes[uits] now labour to have a b*isho*p of their own, but in any case you must seek to hinder that.[356] He writes also that the nonce there[357] tould a freind of his that the pope feared a schisme in case ep*iscopa*l authority were setled here, but that is so great a paradox that on the contrary side a schisme and utter confusion may justly be feared unlesse that authority be quickly setled, and surely there is no better way than to make 3 b*isho*ps according to the three districts of the south parts of England, North and Walles.[358]

We have litle newes here stirring. The k[ing] by his proclamation hath com*m*aunded all the gentry that have houses in the country to repaire thither, and to keep their families there resident hereafter, and not to ly in London as ~~they~~ many have used to doe, therby to avoide much riott and excesse both in apparell and otherwise as you will see by the proclamation it self w*h*ich here I send you.[359] There are other proclamations also to keep fasting daies and Lent according to the statutes, and to avoide the excesses in coaches etc.[360] And it is thought the king will have them strictly observed, or els take forfeitures, and make starr ~~cases~~ chamber cases of them to his own profitt.[361] The fishing is like to go on.

---

[356] On 3/13 September 1632, Smith wrote to Biddulph that the Jesuits in England 'brag that they shal have a b*isho*p', which would 'make matters worse', since 'Jes[uits] make a vow that if they be called to anie ecc*lesiastica*l dignitie they shal take the advise of their gen*er*al so that we shal be subject to the gen*er*al of [the] Jesuits'. The Jesuits would then oppress the secular clergy, for 'already they seek to put us out of the best residences'. Secular priests would 'be forced to leave England'. Smith recited Clement VIII's ruling in October 1602 that the archpriest should not consult with the Society about the regulation of the secular clergy, and Paul V's confirmation of that decision in 1609 when Smith was the secular clergy's agent in Rome. Should this be rescinded, 'the clergy will plainly refuse to obey'; AAW, B 27, no. 128.

[357] Cardinal Alessandro Bichi.

[358] See *Letter 5*.

[359] Larkin, *SRP*, no. 159 (20 June 1632).

[360] *Ibid.*, no. 160 (24 June 1632); JPN, p. 332. See also F. Heal, 'The crown, the gentry and London: the enforcement of proclamation, 1596–1640', in C. Cross, D. Loades, and J.J. Scarisbrick (eds), *Law and Government under the Tudors* (Cambridge, 1988), pp. 211–226.

[361] In November 1632 Walter Yonge recorded in his diary that many had been fined in the star chamber for not leaving London as the proclamation required; BL, Additional MS 35331, fo. 51r. See also Heal, 'The crown, the gentry and London', pp. 221–223.

Thus with my woonted salutes and good wishes, 6 July 1632.

Yours,

Clerk

I pray inquire diligently whether the breve which was directed to my lord and the pr[iests] and Catholickes of England forbidding all bookes and writings on both sides etc. were ever published there in Rome.[362] For I understand that Fa[ther] Knott[363] tould a gentlem[an] here that it was published there and affixed ad [*two words illegible*] in acie campi Florae.

No address.

Endorsed: 6 Julye. Clerk.
    About the clergye undone, if my lord be deposed.
    About feare of schisme by reg[ulars].

19. Clerk [John Southcot] to [Peter Biddulph], 13 July 1632

[*AAW, B 47, no. 65*]

Sir,

This week we receaved two of yours togeather of the 5 and 12 of June. Concerning the first, Mr Hammon[364] will deale with your brother Worth[ington][365] and see if he can draw him to write such a letter as you desire to the congregation.[366] Those seaven Jes[uits] putt out of their order here in England within the space of 3 yeares my lord[367] can best name unto you; three or 4 I remember, videlicet Rob[ert] Rookhood,[368] Anthony Smith, John Dukes,[369] Ferdinando Pulton.[370] I

---

[362] See *Letter 15*.

[363] Matthew Wilson SJ.

[364] John Jackson. Endorsed in margin in Biddulph's hand: 'To write to Mr Hamon'.

[365] William Worthington.

[366] The Congregation for the Propagation of the Faith.

[367] Richard Smith.

[368] Robert Rookwood, brother of the gunpowder plotter Ambrose Rookwood, was dismissed from the Society in 1622; CRS, 75, p. 284.

[369] John Jukes (dismissed from the Society in 1625); CRS, 75, p. 219.

[370] There is no record of either of the two contemporary Jesuits named Ferdinand Poulton having been permanently excluded from the Society. However, Thomas Poulton (formerly a steward to the Vaux family) who had entered the Society in 1617, was dismissed in 1630 only to be readmitted in September 1632; CRS, 74, p. 127; CRS, 75, pp. 257–258, 271; Anstr., II, p. 251. On 13/23 September 1632 Smith remarked in a letter to Biddulph that, 'for anie thing that I know', their mutual friend Thomas White 'exceded in the number of

thank you for sending me those two chapters of Barklay.[371] I suppose they are come safe to Paris, but as yet I have not receaved them from thence. Card[inal] Bentivoglios Relation I have caused to be bought at Paris.[372] The bookes which were written in [the] time of the Appeale you may have from Doway as I suppose. If not, we will procure coppies of them to be sent from hence, and you may do well to write a particuler letter about them to Mr Bennet who hath all such papers in his custody, desiring him to take order that they may be sent up to you for B[a]ronius, as also any other paper that he hath concerning our history, and therfor I pray write such a letter to him by the next opportunity.

Your second letter did not a little trouble us with the newes of those ill offices donn to us there by the Cap[uchins] and we are thinking of a course how to strengthen our selves against them by the qu[een's] meanes wherof you shall heare more when it is donn. The grand aulmner[373] was mooved to write to Rome in my lords behalf and he seemed not unwilling at the first, but after he had considered of it and (as we imagin) consulted with the Capucins he excused him self, yet he had a coppy of the qu[een's] second letter, which <the sight wherof> we thought would have encouraged him to write in conformity therunto; but seeing he drawes back I ame sory he had that letter, and I pray God he make no ill use of it, or procure us the qu[een's] or the ambassadors displeasure by it. My lord writes that it is necessary for us to send two or 3 of the gravest of the clergy <to Rome> els we shall never obtaine our desires.[374] But we find so much difficulty both in procuring the meanes, and in disposing mens minds to it, that I feare we shall never bring it to passe. There is a common letter,[375] written from us to the Congregation de Propaganda, which we intend to send to you on Wednesday next by the way of Paris. I suppose you have written to my lord what you writt to us concerning the Capucins opposition, that and advised him what to do in it. Here we are of opinion that he should complaine of them to the French bishops and see what help he can have by their meanes

seven Jes[uits] for I remember no more than five'. Smith could not recollect all their names; but he recalled, in addition to those listed by Southcot, James Hargrave, ordained in 1609. Hargrave entered the Society in 1612 and was dismissed in c.1622, but was regarded with suspicion by the seculars, who believed he still supported the Jesuits against Smith; AAW, B 27, no. 129; Anstr., II, pp. 145–146; CRS, 75, p. 201; AAW, B 48, no. 4.

[371] See *Letter 15.*

[372] See *Letter 15.*

[373] Jacques le Noël Du Perron.

[374] See *Letter 18.*

[375] This may be a reference to John Colleton's letter of 1 July 1632 written in the name of the English secular clergy to the Congregation for the Propagation of the Faith; AAW, A XXVI, no. 90.

either to withstand them, or to gaine them, though I presume they
will not easily be gained, for they have combined them selves (as we
understand) with the Jesuitts here, who to engage them the more
to them, and by them to strengthen their party against my lord and
the clergy, have made divers offers and promises unto them already
of procuring them here some residences in gentlemens houses for
their young novices, where, when they have learnt the language,
they shall rettourne and ~~take the br~~ make their profession in France,
and being made priests shall afterward be sent hither in mission.
With these conceipts [*word deleted*] the Jes[uits] feed the Capucins
here, and oblige them to them and sooth them mightily making all
the shewes of love and kindnesse unto them they can desire. Yea,
they are thought to animat them also in that course of opposition
they are in against Fa[ther] Philip, which in the end doubtlesse will
breake their neckes, and <doth> avert the qu[een] from them more
and more.[376] Wherof the Jes[uits] cannot be ignorant, but therby
perhaps they think to serve their own turns in the end and to putt
both out. The Italian Capucin Pad[re] Alessandro,[377] who hath bin
here almost this twelmonth, approoveth not the violent proceeding
of these French Capucins, and I think hath written to Rome already.
We intend to complaine to him, as having understood of the [*word
deleted*] <saied> Capucins opposing us at Rome, and will desire him
to write for us to Card[inal] St Onophrio.[378] In our last consult[379] we
resolved to write a common letter to my lord both in our own names
and of our lay freinds, to entreat him to rettourne unto us speedily,
and therin to expresse the interest we think our selves to have in his
not resighning the place without our consents. We intend also to
send <severall> coppies to every archdeacon of a certaine negative
forme of a disclaime to which it can be no daunger for any Cath[olic]
to subscribe, desiring them to procure either by them selves or by
some fitt person the subscription of every nobleman within their
district. The forme shalbe thus. Ego infra*scrip*tus rogatus ab amico an
suffragium <meum> dederim adversus Chalcedonensem episcopum
vel episcopalem authoritatem in Anglia stabiliendam, testor me nunquam eiusmodi suffragium dedisse. To this if we can gett but a dozen
or 15 noblemens hands in severall papers, I think it will counterpoise
the 18 supposed writers against my lords authority.[380] Mr Plantin[381]

---

[376] See *Letter 15*.

[377] Alessandro d'Ales.

[378] Cardinal Antonio Barberini, a Capuchin and brother of Urban VIII.

[379] William Bishop, bishop of Chalcedon, had set up a 'consult', i.e. an inner circle of
advisers.

[380] See *Letter 13*.

[381] Lawrence Platt.

is come over about some buissenesse of his own and will rettourne shortly. Also Mr Blacklo[382] is come hither to settle all agreements for Lisboa college. We expect also Doctor Maylard[383] very shortly, whom perhaps we will entreat to go to Rome for us as agent extraordinary for a yeare ~~or soe~~ <at least> to hasten the dispach of our maine buissenesse.

The proclamation[384] I sent you last week is much resented by the gentry of England, in so much that the k[ing], as it is thought, will remitt the intended rigor of putting it in execution bycause it is generally so displeasing to all. The k[ing] and qu[een] are gon to Otelands. My lord treasurer his sonn[385] is still preparing to go ambassador into Savoy. Some say M^r G[eorge] Gage intendeth to go with him, who, you know, is no freind to us. The mention of cardinals in our common letter hath reference to him and Sir Toby[386] and, if you will, to Sir Griph[in] Markam and Signor Giorgio.[387] Particuler newes I have nonn.

Adieu. 13 July 1632.

No address.

Endorsed: Clerk. 13 Julye.
      About the Jesuitts ejects.
      About getting bookes from Mr Bennet.
      About those who are excepted for cardinalls.

20. Clerk [John Southcot] to Fitton [Peter Biddulph], 20 July 1632

[*AAW, A XXVI, no. 98, pp. 273–274*]

Sir,

The last week I wrote unto you in answer to yours of the 5 and ~~the~~ 12 of June[388] since which time we have an other short one of the 19 of the same month from you, wherin you write little saving only that

---

[382] Thomas White. See Anstr., II, p. 350; *Letter 20*. White was President of the college of Saints Peter and Paul at Lisbon. He resigned in 1633.

[383] Henry Mayler.

[384] See *Letter 18*.

[385] Jerome Weston. See *Letter 20*.

[386] Sir Tobie Mathew.

[387] George Con.

[388] Endorsed in margin in Biddulph's hand: 'to duplicat mine of the 10th of July'.

the Jes[uits] have gott [the] qu[een] mother[389] to write for them and against my lord[390] to Borghese,[391] which I wonder at considering that my lord is that qu[een's] aulmner.[392] Perhaps D[octor] Champney can gett a countermaund from her, if he be solicited by you to do it, and that you judg it needfull.

We are now in hand to present a memoriall to our qu[een] to complaine of the aggreevances donn us by the Capucins here,[393] and to request her Majesties new letters in behalf of my lord, which I hope we shall obtaine shortly, but we do this with as much secresy as we can, least we be prevented. M[r] Lab[orne] mooved the grand aulmner[394] to write for my lord which at first he seemed willing to do, but after he had thought on it, and perhaps consulted with the Capucins (contrary to whose good liking he adventures to do nothing, fearing perhaps to offend Pere Joseph[395] and Monsieur Bouttelier the secretary[396]), he excused the matter.

This day we receaved letters from my lord with which he sent us a coppy of the Protestatio Declaratoria,[397] subscribed and consented unto by 17 of the nobility, which I imagin my lord had from you, and therfor I send you no coppy of it, not doubting but he him self will send one to you if he had it any other way, whereof he saieth nothing in his letter to us. This Protest[atio] is the very same verbatim in English which I sent long since to my lord and I think to you also. It was composed, as it seemes we understood then, by M[r] Ploydon[398] and by Sir Basil[399] and other their complices as also by the Jesuitts them selves carried up and down all England and obtruded to all Catholickes they could meet withall, whose consents sometimes by persuasions, by sometimes by threatnings, and alwaies by deceipt and cosenage, they extorted from divers as some have <of> them have and witnessed, and as hath bin formerly written unto you from hence.

[389] Marie de Médicis.
[390] Richard Smith.
[391] Cardinal Gasparo Borgia, archbishop of Seville and Toledo.
[392] There had been a parting of the ways between Marie de Médicis and former friends, such as Richard Smith, after she moved into opposition to Cardinal Richelieu.
[393] For Southcot's views on the Capuchins, see also *Letter 38*. For the activities of the Capuchins in London and at the court, see Albion, *CI*, pp. 106–107, 108; 'Memoirs of the mission in England of the Capuchin friars of the province of Paris, from the year 1630 to 1669. By Father Cyprien of Gamache, one of the Capuchins belonging to the household of Henrietta Maria [...]', in Birch, *CT*, II, pp. 289–501.
[394] Jacques le Noël Du Perron. See *Letter 19*.
[395] François Joseph le Clerc du Tremblay.
[396] Léon Bouthillier, comte de Chavigny, French secretary of State.
[397] See *Letter 13*. Endorsed in margin in Biddulph's hand: 'I have not received the Protest[atio]'.
[398] Francis Plowden.
[399] Sir Basil Brooke.

The impostures in this protestation are many and great, as shalbe made manifest, God willing, shortly, wherof you shall heare more by the next.

M[r] Blaclo[400] (who is now here to treat of making up all matters about Lisboa college),[401] M[r] Lab[orne] and my self went a week agoe to P[adre] Alessandro[402] to desire his letter in behalf of episcopall authority to Card[inal] S[t] Onofrio,[403] which he promised to ~~give~~ write this week at least to the Capucin, one P[adre] Negro[404] (as I take it) their procurator generale in Rome, by whose advise that card[inal] doth wholy governe him self, as Alessandro tould us, and you may do well to acquaint your self with that Capucin, as also with P[adre] Valeriano[405] that came out of Bohemia thither this last spring.

Your brother Worthington[406] had once written a <Lattin> letter to the Congreg[ation] de Propaganda to informe them of his proceeding in the buissenesse between him and M[r] Gibbons,[407] but, his lawier telling him that it was daungerous in regard of premunire, he will advise further before he send it, yet I wished him to write unto you particulerly about the buissenesse and to send the letter open to you to be kept or delivered as you should see cause. But I know not what he will do. I wish you had written to him your self to know the matter for that would have [p. 274] given him occasion to write to you back againe. But, when you write, take no notice of any <usuall> correspondence with Antonino,[408] nor of knowing much by him in this matter, but by M[r] Laborne only or M[r] Hammond.[409]

There is no newes currant here at this time. The court is at Otelands there to remaine yet these 5 or 6 weekes. The lord treasurers sonn is not yet gonn from hence towards Savoy as ambassador extraordinary, but it is sayed that he goeth very shortly.[410] Compositions for recusants are at a stay during this vacation. I heard that two judges were dead of late going their circuitt, but I know not how true it is, nor who they were nor how they died.

---

[400] Thomas White. Endorsed in margin in Biddulph's hand: 'to send ~~the~~ [*word illegible*] letters to me'.

[401] See Anstr., II, p. 350.

[402] Alessandro d'Ales.

[403] Cardinal Antonio Barberini, a Capuchin and brother of Urban VIII.

[404] See Pastor, *HP*, XXVIII, p. 400.

[405] For Valeriano Magno, see Father Cuthbert, *The Capuchins*, 2 vols (London, 1928), II, pp. 312–320; Pastor, *HP*, XXVIII, pp. 346, 348.

[406] William Worthington.

[407] John Wakeman. See *Letters 9, 10, 11*.

[408] i.e. John Southcot.

[409] John Jackson.

[410] For Jerome Weston's appointment and instructions as ambassador extraordinary, see *CSPV, 1629–1632*, p. 613; PRO, SP 78/91, fos 382r–9r, 390r–405r.

More I have not to say now and so in hast I end. 20 July 1632.

We have written a round letter to my lord to which we will gett as many hands of pr[iests] as we can, and the consent also of our lay freindes, testified by a notary. It is to request him, or rather conjure him, to rettourne. The next weeke you shall have a coppy of it.[411] It is not yet subscribed, and goeth not till next Wednesday.

On Wednesday last we sent a common letter to the Congregacion de Propaganda open to Mr Wake[412] to be sent to you that way, and we send no duplicat of it by Bruxelles.[413]

We have sett our freindes in work in the country to procure the hands of as many of the nobility as they can in severall papers to this negative disclaime wherin there is no daunger. Ego infrascriptus rogatus an suffragium dederim adversus Chalcedonensem episcopum vel authoritatem episcopalem in Anglia stabiliendam testor me eiusmodi suffragium nunquam dedisse. Yet I feare we shalbe able to procure few or nonn to subscribe bycause every one is wary to give his hand, even our best and surest freinds.

Addressed: Pour Monsieur Fitton a Rome.

Endorsed: July. Clerk.
           About the Protestatio Declaratoria.

21. Clerk [John Southcot] to Fitton [Peter Biddulph], 27 July 1632

[*AAW, A XXVI, no. 100, pp. 277–278*]

Sir,

This week we receaved a short letter from you of June the 26 but we expect a longer by the next, and some further resolution about our buissenesse.

My lord[414] hath sent the coppies of divers memorialls and writings unto us which were given up at Rome and to the nonce[415] (as I suppose) by his adversaries, and particulerly that Protestatio Declaratoria of the nobility and gentry,[416] wherof I certified you by my last letters as also

---

[411] See AAW, A XXVI, no. 96, p. 265, for the letter of 19 July 1632 from the English secular clergy to Richard Smith, urging him to return to England, and arguing that he ought not to have resigned without their consent.

[412] Michael Merriman, who was then at Paris. See Anstr., II, p. 217.

[413] See *Letter 19*.

[414] Richard Smith.

[415] Cardinal Alessandro Bichi.

[416] See *Letter 13*, and *passim*.

this quaestio: an regulares sine gravi praejudicio dependere possint a Chalcedonensi vel alio quovis delegato in Anglia pro administratione parochialium? etc., with 3 or 4 other memorialls in Italian, all shewing the difficulty of regulars asking approbation, or coming to my lord or his vicars to present them selves, which in my opinion deserved no better answer, to satisfy any indifferent man, than this, that none of these difficulties would be pretended by Jesuitts, if a Jesuitt were made bishop, nor by Benedictines if he were a Benedictine, and the practise of presenting them selves to the bishop or his officialls would soon appeare to be easy enough to any regular, if in lieu of asking approbation it were ordered that the bishop or his vicars should give every regular, at his first coming in, five pounds, but <should> deliver it to nonne but <to> him self in person. And I wish that you would but mention such an answer as this is to some of the congregacion[417] there. Yet it will not be amisse to give a further answer also to all particulers of difficulty objected, and of other pretended reasons, which will not be hard to do, if the true state of things here be once made well knowen, and those mists and exaggerations taken away and qualified which our adversaries seek to cast before strangers eies, by the example of other practises here.

We have gotten the prime nobleman of England[418] and my Lord Morly[419] to subscribe their names to that forme of a disclaime[420] which I sent you last week, and we will labour to gett the like from others. I hope also we shall obtaine the qu[een's] letter shortly in behalf of my lord which will much availe us.

We wrote a common letter this week to my lord inviting him to come back, the coppy whereof I send you here enclosed.[421]

I can no more at this time but refer other occurrences to Mr Lab[orne]. 27 July 1632.

I have not yet receaved Barclaies 2 chapters.[422]

[on p. 278]

Addressed: Pour Monsieur Fitton. Rome.
                Avec un autre papier.

Endorsed: Clerk. July 27.
                An answeare to the regulars objection against bishops.
                About the Jesuitts memorialls.

---

[417] The Congregation for the Propagation of the Faith.
[418] John Paulet, 5th marquis of Winchester. See *Letter 13*.
[419] See *Letters 13, 22, 23*.
[420] See *Letters 19, 20*.
[421] AAW, A XXVI, no. 96 (dated 19 July 1632). See *Letter 20*.
[422] See *Letters 15, 19*.

22. Fountyne [George Leyburn][423] to [Richard Smith], 1 August 1632

[*AAW, A XXVI, no. 104, pp. 289–292*]

Most honored sir,

Since I commended unto you my last I have not receaved any from you, but I now heare that the post is arrived soe that I expect yours this afternoone. All the daye yesterdaye I was at Otlands <u>with good Fa[ther] Ph[ilip]</u> who now assisteth us with <u>all his forces</u>. I have drone a petition for her Majesty and I hope that I shall obtayne from <u>her two letters,</u> one in answere to Mons*ieur* Brissac,[424] the other to his Holynes. I hope alsoe that many <u>of our nobility</u> will be wonne to exclame from the late protestation.[425] I have my lord marquis[426] hand and my Lord Morlys alreadie and I have write[n] unto Mr Martyn[427] for my Lord Sturtons,[428] unto my cosen Broughton[429] for his

---

[423] The AAW, A series catalogue erroneously cites John Southcot as the author of this letter.

[424] Jean de Gallard, baron de la Rochebeaucourt et de Brassach, French ambassador in Rome.

[425] See *Letter 13*, and *passim*.

[426] John Paulet, 5th marquis of Winchester.

[427] This may be a reference to the secular priest Thomas Martin; Anstr., I, pp. 221–222; *NAGB*, pp. 4, 125. In September 1631 he was in the diocese of Bath and Wells, i.e. where he may have served as Lord Stourton's chaplain; AAW, A XXIV, no. 161, p. 621. Subsequently, in 1635, we find him listed as chaplain to Roger Widdrington in Northumberland; AAW, A XXVI, no. 68, p. 285.

[428] Edward Stourton, 10th Baron Stourton. The secular clergy noted that Stourton's heir, Sir William, 'favet monachis Benedictinis' but 'est etiam amicus cleri', and he had had his eldest son educated at the secular clergy's college at Douai; AAW, A XXVIII, no. 3, p. 16. On 20 March 1632 Thomas Longueville reported to Biddulph that 'divers, as you knoe, have theare been given up by our adversaries as to have subscribed against our maister my l[ord] b[ishop] [Richard Smith], wherof one <was> my Lord Stourtons eldest sonne and heyre Sir William Stourton. As for my Lord Stourton himself I conceive you knoe how they urged him hard yet could not prevaile, whome they knoe farwel to be a Catholicke, [and] as for Sir William Stourton his sonne and heire, true it is he did subscribe, but you must knoe that now he hath cast of[f] the monke whoe then lived in his house, by name Don David [Codner], whose continual table talk was against my lord bis[hop], and now he hath taken a sec[ular] pr[iest] wholy depending upon him. And by manie discourses which I have had with Sir William Stourton concerning this busines he hath sufficiently manifested how he wisheth he had never subscribed, and divers and sundrie times he hath told me how with all his hart he desireth a bishop in England, yea both Sir William and his brother in law Sir Edward Suilliard, whoe alsoe subscribed against our bishop, have told me that the regulars their ghostly fathers, whereof the formers was a monke, the others was and yet is a Jesuit, secur*ed* their conscience in the busines, otherwise they never would have done what they did'; AAW, A XXVI, no. 41, p. 129.

[429] Richard Broughton. See Anstr., I, pp. 54–56.

lord,[430] unto M[r] Rogers[431] for his lord, unto M[r] Trolop[432] for the Lord Euers,[433] and here we shall have my Lord Arundells[434] assuredly and my Lord Mountegues,[435] and M[r] Muskett[436] undertaketh for Casle Haven.[437] Here is noe danger to subscribe to such a forme as here I doe send unto you. And giving hands in this nature will doe as much as if they had soe given to desire episcopall authority. We

[430] i.e. Francis Manners, 6th earl of Rutland, at Belvoir, where Broughton was chaplain to the countess of Rutland. (The earl died in December 1632.)

[431] Identity uncertain. This man may be the 'Rogers' named in *Letter 34* as a priest in Sussex.

[432] Cuthbert Trollop. See Anstr., I, pp. 363–364. He was Richard Smith's vicar-general in the North from 1 June 1625.

[433] William Eure, 4th Baron Eure. In January 1635 the leading secular clergy noted of him that 'ob debita quae contraxit cum Barone Arundellio (cuius filiam primogenitus illius duxerat in uxorem) est hodie magna lis inter utrumque, sed vicit causam Arundellius; et quia Eure non obedit judicum decreto, detinetur in turre Londinensi'. (See also *CSPD, 1631–1633*, pp. 425, 441.) Although it was distressing to see the secular clergy's patrons, Eure and Arundell, locked in conflict in this way, nevertheless Eure 'favet clero seculari prae ceteris ordinibus'; AAW, A XXVIII, no. 3, p. 16.

[434] Thomas Arundell, 1st Baron Arundell. The secular clergy's January 1635 survey of the Catholic nobility described him, in admiration, as 'vir ingeniosus, prudens et magnanimus, versatissimus, si quis alius laicus, in controversiis fidei saepeque rationando cum Protestantibus, eorum errores aperte redarguit. Est amicissimus clero prae reliquis ordinibus, quamvis etiam aliorum ordinum sacerdotes humaniter excipiat'. He led a virtuous life, had been active on behalf of English Catholics, and had co-operated closely with the count of Gondomar while the Spanish match was in negotiation in the early 1620s. And 'quare cum primum coepit oppositio contra episcopum Chalcedonens*em* nihil magis solicitos habuit ep*iscop*i adversarios quam ut illu*m* in suas partes attraherent, quod nunquam facere potuerunt, nec p*er*suasionibus nec minis, na*m* fortiter se semp*er* opposuit, et per celebrem epistolam quam ad Vicecomitem Montis Acuti [Montague] scripsit, clare ostendit, oppositionem adversus ep*iscop*um ex intra factione procedere'; AAW, A XXVIII, no. 3, p. 17. See Allison, Q J, p. 124. A note in the state papers, conjecturally dated to December 1632, records that the secular priest, George Fisher, was resident with Arundell; *CSPD, 1631–1633*, p. 470. Arundell informed Gregorio Panzani in December 1634 that the return of Richard Smith was essential for the restoration of order in the Catholic community. Arundell said he would advise Smith to come back to London and present himself to the king; and Arundell personally guaranteed that he would stand surety for him; VA, PD, fo. 43r.

[435] Francis Browne, 3rd Viscount Montague. He was the son of the secular clergy's great patron, Anthony Maria Browne, 2nd Viscount Montague (d. 1629). Although the 3rd viscount never enjoyed his father's influence in the Catholic community, the secular clergy's January 1635 survey of Catholic nobles said that, after a pleasure-filled youth, Francis Browne 'nunc a nonnullis annis studet parsimoniae et pecunias modis omnibus accumulare nititur'. Though he was 'ingenioisus et callidus', nevertheless he was 'in religionis exercitiis tepidus', but, all the same, 'favet clero saeculari prae aliis omnibus ordinibus'; AAW, A XXVIII, no. 3, p. 15.

[436] George Fisher.

[437] James Touchet, Baron Audley, 3rd earl of Castlehaven. The leading secular clergy claimed that 'nulli ordini partialiter addictus quin potius favet clero prae reliquis et sacerdotem secularem alit domi', but he was dedicated to the pursuit of pleasure; AAW, A XXVIII, no. 3, p. 14.

may now thanke our adversaryes for th*a*t they have (through ther late protestation) put us into this waye, into w*hi*ch we could never have putt our selves. Agayne I have writte to all places to obtayne the cheef gentrys hands to this forme.[438] And by Fa[ther] Ph[ilip's] meanes I have imployed a very powerfull friend to my Lord Harbert[439] to see if it be possible to make him disclame. I shall be able to signifye more unto you by the next. This art[icle] [?] practised by the Jesuists I did droe my selfe and I thinke it convenient th*a*t it should be sent presently unto Ro[me] and Mr Fitton[440] may translate it and showe [it] unto the cardinalls or [*sic for* of] [*p. 290*] Propaganda Fide and assure them th*a*t ther is coming after this a generall disclame w*i*th the true handes of nobility and gentry.[441] I was yesterdaye alsoe a great while w*i*th the grand almynier.[442] I doe assure you faithfully th*a*t he is a true clergie man and truly loveth you. And if herafter a good ambassador come who is not too partial as this, he will showe him selfe more. He did imparte unto me some pasages in w*hi*ch he did tye me to secrecy w*hi*ch you will knowe hereafter. He desired me to remember unto you his kinde respects. Speaking yesterdaye w*i*th Fa[ther] Ph[ilip] about Mother Magdalyne of the Carmalytes[443] he wisheth th*a*t you will visit her often. She haith great friends in France by w*hi*ch she may doe you much good. Agayne she writeth often to our queen and if in some letter she give a toutch of you it will be to good purpose. I have wished Fa[ther] Ph[ilip] to desire her Ma*jes*ty when she writeth unto her to thanke her for her love towards English pr[i]ests. You may tell her th*a*t her last letter Monsi*eur* le grand alminier did deliver yesterdaye unto her Majesty. There are not many occurrences. And I am in great hast

---

[438] See e.g. AAW, A XXVI, nos 122, 123; *Letter 24*.

[439] Edward Somerset, Lord Herbert of Raglan, heir to the 5th earl of Worcester. He was mentioned in Edward Bennett's will of 27 March 1635; AAW, A XXVIII, no. 11. Although the Somersets were patrons of the Jesuits, Edward had married, in c.1628, Elizabeth, the sister of Robert Dormer, 1st earl of Caernarvon, and granddaughter of Elizabeth (Browne), Baroness Dormer (d. 1631), to whom Edward Bennett had been chaplain. (See *NAGB*, pp. 35, 41, 66, 114, 152.) This may explain why the seculars thought it was worth approaching him, even though he was believed to be among the ranks of Richard Smith's opponents. (On 1 March 1632 John Jackson had written to Biddulph that 'I am told th*a*t 2 noblemen, which I think are the Lo[rd] Somerset [Edward Somerset, Lord Herbert of Raglan] and the L[ord] Baltimore', were among those who had 'written some months since to th*e* p[ope] against th*e* b[ishop] and his authority and protested that thowgh his Hol[iness] shold give it to him they cold not admit him'; AAW, A XXVI, no. 33, p. 107.)

[440] Peter Biddulph.

[441] See AAW, B 27, no. 127, for Smith's assurance of 20/30 August 1632 to Southcot that Leyburn was organizing the dispatch of the 'disclame of the nobilitie and gentrie from that infamous prot*estati*on made in their names against my authoritie'.

[442] Jacques le Noël Du Perron.

[443] Magdalen Palmes, who was professed in 1630 in the Carmelite convent at Antwerp. I am grateful to Caroline Bowden for this reference.

readie to returne againe to the court about our busines. They remove to morrowe to Nonesuch.

Sweet Jesus blesse all your endevours.

Your obedient servant,

Fontyne

Excuse my hastie writing.

Aug[ust] 1th 1632.

[in margin of p. 290]

All friends are in the country. M^{ris} Gage, your nece,[444] Mr Lovell[445] alsoe, he and his lady[446] are at Chelsey.[447]

[on p. 292]

Addressed: For my maister.

Endorsed: Lords agains[t] the Protestat[i]on.

23. [John Southcot] to [an English secular priest at Paris],[448] 7 August 1632

[AAW, A XXVI, no. 107, pp. 299–300]

Most hon[oured] sir,

The last week I wrote not to you being newly gonn to Chelsey[449] from whence I had then no commodity to send. But now being there better

---

[444] Mary Gildon. See *Letter 66*.

[445] John Southcot.

[446] From Southcot's diary it would appear that the patroness referred to here was Lady Mary Aston, with whom he 'came to dwell [...] at Whitewebb's the 23 of September 1626', and with whom he lived at 'London, Greenwich &c'. She 'began to dwell [...] in Drury Lane the first day of February 1628', and had been 'confirmed by the bishop of Chalcedon the first of April 1627', CRS, I, p. 98. She was the wife of Sir Arthur Aston of Enfield (d. 1627), a friend of Lord Baltimore, who had gone out to Newfoundland as governor of the colony of Avalon; Codignola, *CHL*, pp. 17–18, 163 and *passim*; *CSPD, 1627–1628*, p. 525.

[447] The location in Chelsea is not certain, but, as Luca Codignola notes, the Roper family of Canterbury and Eltham had a house in Chelsea inherited from Sir Thomas More, and Thomas Dawson ODC (whose name in religion was Simon Stock), the Ropers' chaplain, resided there from time to time; Codignola, *CHL*, pp. 89, 180. Southcot and his friends would have been welcome there as well.

[448] See *Letter 43*; Allison, RSGB, I, p. 396.

[449] See *Letter 22*.

setled I must not omit my custome of writing, being to acknowledg the receipt of two of yours, videlicet of the 26 July and 2 of August the former wherof was in answer to my sorrowfull letter of June the 26 which sorrow hath bin ~~more~~ <somwhat> allaied since by the hopefull newes of Mr Fittons[450] last to you which was very gratefull to us to read, and the rather bycause we have receaved nonn from him this fortnight and more, which makes us doubt that some of his <to us> miscarry. And for that reason we dare not send the enclosed by the way of Flanders but desire you to send it by Lions and, to the end it may go the more securely, it were not amisse to send your next packett for Mr Fitton with this enclosed in it by Mons*ieur* Chateauneuf[451] his meanes or els by the nonce[452] or some other <such> sure way as you think best. And it will not be amisse also to shew a coppy of the queens letter to the pope both to the nonce there and to the French b*isho*ps also <in confidence and secretly> the more to encourage them and to hasten the sending away of their com*m*on letter in my l*or*ds[453] behalf wherof we will desire here to have a coppy. I assure my self this of the qu[een] to the pope (God send it may go safe) will do more good than anything that hath bin donn yet and therfor it is wished to be sent away with all speed but I pray lett John[454] write out coppies of both letters for Mr Fitton that he may know what the qu[een] ~~letter~~ writes both to the pope and the ambass[ador] and that he may shew a coppy of the qu[een's] letter to the pope to the ambassador in case the popes come sealed to his hands from the queen.[455] We are much behoulding to o*ur* freind at court here <and> my l*or*d can do no lesse than write here a thankfull letter for his paines and care herein.

I ame glad you sent us coppies of those memorialls given up at Rome. I suppose they came to you from Rome though you write not so much to me. But, if they do not, it is Mr Fitton [who] should have coppies of them all, who hath instructions enough to answer them. Yet we will do o*ur* best to assist him further therin from hence also hereafter. But for the present we can do little bycause we are now so dispersed. Mr Hare is gonn into the country, I know not whither, not

---

[450] Peter Biddulph.

[451] Charles de l'Aubespine, marquis de Chateauneuf, former French ambassador in England.

[452] Cardinal Alessandro Bichi.

[453] Richard Smith.

[454] Presumably either John Galmarch or John Legat, both of whom are mentioned in *Letters 81, 82.*

[455] See AAW, A XXVI, no. 115 (a copy of the letters, dated 17 August 1632, from Henrietta Maria to Urban VIII and to Jean de Gallard, baron de la Rochebeaucourt et de Brassach, the French ambassador in Rome). See also *Letter 24*; and, for the originals, VA, Barberini MS CVII/2 (for transcripts of which see PRO, 31/3/126, p. 250). Robert Philip informed Gregorio Panzani in December 1634 that the queen believed that the absence of an English Catholic bishop in the realm injured her reputation; VA, PD, fo. 41r.

to rettourne till Michelmas. M[r] Hammon[456] is also abroad, and others. But his best help and instruction for answer to all the saied memorialls wilbe from my lord him self who can best and most readily do it. The last week Mr Fountaine[457] certified you, as [*p. 300*] I suppose, of my Lord Morleis disclaime[458] and of the motives used to him to incense him against my lords authority and person, wherof it were good the nonce were informed and M[r] Fitton also. The motives were these. 1. That the bishop would tyrannize. 2. Excommunicat lightly. 3. Exact tythes. 4. Place and displace pr[iests] ad libitum. 5. Erect a publick tribunall etcetera. And this art they used with the rest also, as may probably be presumed and as some do also witnesse, [*word deleted*] whose testimonies we will seeke to gett. My lord marquis is netled, and so is my Lord Arundell also. And I hope they will both do somwhat to vindicat them selves.[459] M[r] Dorington[460] tould Fa[ther] Philip that my Lord Herbert[461] assured him he gave not his hand to any paper, but only that he went to the Fr[ench] ambassador to tell him of the difficulties of the practise of the authority here in these times etcetera. There is a forme also of a disclaime framed which is sent into all parts to gett hands and voices to it. M[r] Lab[orne] sent it also to you the last week as he tells me, who is now out of town.

We have another <common> letter ready for his Hol[iness] to be subscribed by M[r] Colleton and those of his district, which shalbe sent when hands are gotten to it.[462] I rather wish than hope that the <vicars> will do the like, yet they shalbe admonished of it.

The Jes[uits] and their adherents were afraid when M[r] Plantin[463] came hither that he had brought some ill newes [*word deleted*] for them of subjection to the bishop and still they feare some order will come, which they will seek to prevent if they can, and, the better to prepare Cath[olic] minds, Rob[ert] Winter[464] goeth up and down as I

---

[456] John Jackson.

[457] George Leyburn.

[458] See *Letters 21, 22*.

[459] See *Letter 13*.

[460] Identity uncertain. A Francis Dorrington and a Robert Dorrington were both ordained as Catholic priests in 1638 but there is no evidence that either were in England at this time; Anstr., II, pp. 86–87.

[461] Edward Somerset, Lord Herbert of Raglan. See *Letter 13*.

[462] See AAW, A XXVI, no. 109, for the letter of 13 August 1632 to Urban VIII, subscribed by John Colleton and thirty secular priests. It states that for nearly five years, but especially since Smith's exile, the secular clergy have petitioned the pope to reform the English Church. And the clergy of the eastern shires and London now add their voices. Scandals abound, and the sacraments, particularly of marriage, are profaned. The only remedy is the return of the bishop.

[463] Lawrence Platt.

[464] Brother of Sir John Winter. See H. Peters, *Mary Ward* (Leominster, 1994), pp. 56, 62–65.

heare and speaketh openly ag*a*inst obaying. Mr Longvile⁴⁶⁵ tould Mr Lane⁴⁶⁶ that, being at S*i*r William Sturtons table in Surrey (where Mr Longvile is now placed), he saied <openly> the Catholickes might be secure in conscience not <u>to obay the b*i*shop th</u>ough the pope should give sentence for him.

Aurelius⁴⁶⁷ <u>is come, but wit</u>hout a preface and yet Mr Plantin did putt us in hope that the preface would also be out before this <time>. My packett is not yet come, neither doth John <u>certify <what or> to whom</u> I must pay the mony I ow[e] <u>for those bookes.</u>

<u>I heare Mr Charnock</u>⁴⁶⁸ is dead, but know not the particulers, how or when, only that he died in London in a Protestantes house.

By Mr Cheekes⁴⁶⁹ <u>note wh*i*ch I here send</u> you, it appeares that they dispens their bookes still under hand. Don David⁴⁷⁰ is sworne the qu[een's] servant.

I have no more newes now but, duty remembred, rest. 7 August 1632.

No address or endorsement.

24. Clerk [John Southcot] to [Peter Biddulph], 10 August 1632

[*AAW, A XXVI, no. 108, pp. 301–302*]

Sir,

The last week I wrote not to you being newly gonn out of town and being not yet rettourned I cannot write much now <out of the country> but only thought good to advertise you that we sent two letters from the qu[een] by the last post to my l*o*rd,⁴⁷¹ the one to the ambassador⁴⁷² and the other within it to the pope, the coppies wherof we will venture to send <now> by this way, though we thought it more

---

⁴⁶⁵ Thomas Longueville, who had been expelled, with Biddulph, from the English college in Rome in 1623. See Anstr., II, pp. 202–203. He accompanied Lord Baltimore to Newfoundland in June 1627; Codignola, *CHL*, pp. 43–5, 47, 163, 184. When he returned he showed himself thoroughly hostile to the Jesuits and Benedictines. See *Letter 22*.

⁴⁶⁶ Richard Lane. See Anstr., II, p. 183.

⁴⁶⁷ i.e. Duvergier de Hauranne, *Vindiciae Censurae Facultatis Theologiae Parisiensis [. . .]*.

⁴⁶⁸ Robert Charnock. See Anstr., I, pp. 73–74.

⁴⁶⁹ Anthony Whitehair. See Anstr., II, p. 354. Whitehair's father, Christopher, had been a retainer of the 2nd Viscount Montague; BL, Harleian MS 7042, fo. 153r, and Montague had paid for Anthony to be educated at St Omers.

⁴⁷⁰ David Codner OSB.

⁴⁷¹ Richard Smith.

⁴⁷² Jean de Gallard, baron de la Rochebeaucourt et de Brassach, French ambassador in Rome. See *Letters 22, 23*.

secure to send the letters them selves by the way of France. I hope these letters (God send them to come safe) will do more good than anything hath yet donn, and we hope shortly after to send you some discoveries of the imposture used in getting hands to the Protes*tatio* Declaratoria,[473] having gotten already the lord marquis of Winchester, my Lord Morley, and my Lord Arundell also (as I think by this time) to disclaime under their handes in that forme w*hic*h I sent you a fortnight since.[474] My Lord Morley confesseth that the motives w*hic*h were used with him to incense him ag*ain*st the b*isho*p (but not ~~as he intended~~ to give his hand or consent to any writing <which he never intended>) were these. 1. that the b*isho*p would tyrannize. 2. Excommunicat uppon small occasions. 3. Exact tythes. 4. Chang[e] priests pro arbitrio. 5. Erect a publick tribunall ~~etcetera~~ and the like.[475] Now how honest men these were that dealt in this manner, notwithstanding they knew the b*isho*p neither had, nor would, nor could do any of these things as [*word deleted*] they had bin severall waies assured before, even under the b*isho*ps own hand and by many protestations of word of mouth, and by an expresse writinge called ~~manifestatio~~ <u>A generall manifestation for the establishing of ep*isco*pall authority over the Catholickes</u>[476] etc*etera*, wherof I suppose you have a coppy to shew there, if need be, the better to convince these men of willfull malice ag*ain*st the b*isho*p bycause this manifestation was tendered to my Lord Baltimor and others with

---

[473] See *Letters 13, 17, 20, 21, 22*. See also AAW, A XXVI, no. 114, for the declaration, of 15 August 1632, of the sons of Baron Brudenell and Baron Morley and Monteagle (Robert Brudenell and William Parker) that they never agreed to the 'Protestatio'. (In 1632, Robert Brudenell had married Mary, daughter of Henry Constable, 1st Viscount Dunbar, who was one of Richard Smith's leading aristocratic supporters. In January 1635 Brudenell came with George Leyburn to visit Gregorio Panzani and offer support for Smith; VA, PD, fo. 68r.) See also AAW, A XXVI, no. 125 (a similar declaration by Sir William Tresham); *ibid.*, no. 122 (an attestation dated 22 August 1632 from the Catholics of Norfolk against the 'Protestatio Declaratoria'); *ibid.*, no. 123 (a list, dated 22 August 1632, from East Anglia, of gentlemen who allege that they never consented that their names should be appended to the 'Protestatio Declaratoria', and deny that they consented to the impugning of Richard Smith's authority).

[474] See *Letter 22*.

[475] For an account in Southcot's hand of the 'the motives used by the Jesuitts and their chief instruments to incense the lay Catholicks of England against the b*isho*p of Chalcedon, and to enforce divers of the nobility to give their hands ~~and~~ <or> voices against his ordinary authority', see AAW, A XXV, no. 14, pp. 25–26. Here Southcot gives more detail about Lord Morley's 'disclaim'.

[476] See AAW, A XXV, no. 94 ('A Generall Manifestation for establishing of episcopall authoritie over the Catholikes of this kingdome of England allowed and approoved b[y] all Catholikes of the sayde kingdome, aswell by those who doe adhere unto regulars as by those who doe serve them selfes of secular priestes').

assurance that the b*isho*p would exact no more ~~than~~ nor pretended any other ordinariship than was therin expressed, and yet neither he nor his associats would desist from their seditious practises, or take any satisfaction therby, although they had nothing to except ag*ain*st that forme, how honest men, I say, these were ~~may~~ lett others judg. Now as touching those particular noblemen that subscribed, or consented, besides the ~~deceipt~~ imposture that was used to persuade them, by w*hi*ch a man may directly say (and some have saied it them selves) that they were directly circumvented and cheated, this may be added to abase the creditt of this foule protestation with strangers, first touching the eearle [*sic*] of Shrewsbury[477] that he was particulerly laboured by S*i*r Basil Brook and M[r] Foster[478] to go to the French ambass[ador][479] to joine him self with the declarers, these two men being his interpreters, w*hi*ch <as> it seemes he did by their importunity, but when he was chalenged of it by a freind, who rectified [*two words deleted*] his judgment with a true information touching my l*or*d b*isho*p, he sent his brother presently to the ambassador (him self being then out of town) to tell him that he no waies was ag*ain*st my l*or*ds spirituall authority, but only temporall, if any were pretended. Againe this earle gives an yearly exhibition to my l*or*d, by w*hi*ch it appeares that he is no way averse from my l*or*ds person or authority. The 3 Som*m*ersetts are

---

[477] In the secular clergy's survey (dated January 1635) of the Catholic nobility, it was noted that John Talbot, 10th earl of Shrewsbury 'ex se non magis propendet in regulares quam in clerum secularem, sed pari fere affectu omnes amplectitur'. Also 'ab ep*iscop*o adeo non abhorret, ut pensionem annuam adhuc hodie illi secreto largiatur. Attamen ob conjugis suae propensionem in Jesuitas, reputatur ex eorum numero, qui stant a partibus Jesuitar*um* contra ep*iscop*um. Nihil in eo deprehenditur singulare vel quoad pietatem et zelum, vel quoad prudentiam aut literaturam imo literas nequaquam callet', and in fact he was addicted to pleasure; AAW, A XXVIII, no. 3, pp. 13–14. Gregorio Panzani's 'Relazione' claimed that Shrewsbury had probably not subscribed willingly to the 'Protestatio Declaratoria' against Richard Smith; VA, Barberini MS LVI, 136, fo. 35v (transcript and translation at ABSJ).

[478] Richard Forster (knighted in September 1649). According to the secular clergy (AAW, A XXVIII, no. 58, p. 225) Forster (aged about fifty and 'vocatur com*m*uniter Fosterus Gallicus') had, soon after Henrietta Maria's arrival in England, moved from Yorkshire to avoid harassment for recusancy. He came with his wife and children to London, and 'coepit in agendo Catholicorum Angliae causam apud Gallos', and 'ab eisque dictus est agens Catholicorum Angliae'. Furthermore, 'paulatim vero ita se insinuavit in gratiam Card*in*alis de Richelieu, ut pensione annua eius mediatione, donatus sit a rege Galliae'. At the same time 'se addixit obsequio magni Angliae thesaurii [Sir Richard Weston]'. Neither the queen nor Robert Philip liked or trusted him. Despite his attachment to Richelieu, Forster was also one of Smith's leading opponents. See M. Foster, 'Sir Richard Forster (?1585–1661)', *RH*, 14 (1978), pp. 163–174.

[479] François Duval, marquis de Fontenay Mareuil. See *Letter 3*.

the father,[480] the sonn[481] and a brother,[482] to whom you may add the Lord Peter[483] a brother in law, all but one family, wholy and blindly lead by the Jes[uits]; Lord William Howard,[484] a worldly man, and in respect of the world afraide of his own shadow; Baltimor (now dead), contracted to an other meane woman, his daughters maide, not being sure of his former wifes death, and having gotten her with child as now is commonly knowen[485] (a fitt man to have his voice in these buissenesses); as also my Lord Vaux who kept an other mans wife so publickly even to the scandall of our religion.[486] These two last had reason to oppose a bishop, for surely if his authority had bin setled they had reason to feare a publick excommunication against them. For the earle of St Albans[487] and his sonn,[488] Dr Bosvile can and will depose that the earle, in his discourse with him, did much condemne our neglect of bishops so long time. [*p. 302*] The like exceptions might be taken to [*word deleted*] <the> rest of the subscribers, but this perhaps will be sufficient to shew that it was a forced thing, and donn uppon designhe and by instigation only of others.

Mr Plantin[489] came lately over from Paris and the Jes[uits] and their adherents were much afraide that he brought some order from the pope or popes nonce in favor of my lord. But, to prevent the fruict of any such order when it shall come, Mr Rob[ert] Winter, the nunns

---

[480] Henry Somerset, 5th earl of Worcester, was said by the seculars to be 'timidus et cautus in profitenda fide Catholica'; but this may in part have been because they knew him to be 'Jesuitis unice addictus, quamvis non nisi occulte cum eis agat, et plerumque sive omni teste. Alterius generis sacerdotes nunquam admittit in suam domum'; AAW, A XXVIII, no. 3, p. 14. His sister, Blanche, had married Thomas Arundell, the future 2nd Baron Arundell, and stepson of Smith's patron, Anne Arundell; and his brother, Sir John, married Mary, Anne Arundell's daughter; J.L. Vivian (ed.), *The Visitations of Cornwall* (Exeter, 1887), p. 7; *NAGB*, pp. 164, 210.

[481] Edward Somerset, Lord Herbert of Raglan.

[482] Probably Sir Charles Somerset. In July 1629 Sir John Coke noted that George Fisher, who had recently been released from prison, was going to reside in London with Sir Charles (who gave him a pension of £40 p.a.); PRO, SP 16/147/12, fo. 22r. In late December 1634 Gregorio Panzani visited Sir Charles to consult him on the controversy among Catholics over Richard Smith, and Sir Charles alleged that he was in favour of the restoration of a bishop, but one whose power was essentially spiritual; VA, PD, fos 47r–8r. In May 1636, however, Panzani described Sir Charles as 'amicissimo del vescovo'; PRO, 31/9/17B (transcript of Panzani's letter to Cardinal Francesco Barberini of 4/14 May 1636).

[483] See *Letter 9*. William Petre, 2nd Baron Petre, had married Catherine, daughter of Edward Somerset, 4th earl of Worcester.

[484] Lord William Howard of Naworth.

[485] See *Letters 4, 5, 6*.

[486] See *Letter 13*.

[487] Richard Burke, 4th earl of Clanricard, 1st earl of St Albans.

[488] Ulick Burke.

[489] Lawrence Platt.

champion[490] and the Jesuitts broker, and as some say a Jesuitt him self, goeth up and down to Cath[olic] houses, and there assureth them that, although the pope should confirme the bishop in his authority, yet they were not bound to obay him. To this effect he spoke at Sir William Sturtons ~~table~~ <house> in Surrey before much compaghny at the table openly, Mr Tho[mas] Longvile being then present and hearing it.[491]

By occasion of this protestation Dr Bossevile sent ~~me~~ up out of [*word deleted*] his district the subscriptions of divers gentlemen[492] <there> which were made when the declaration came forth and amongst others there is one from my Lord Vicount Mountgaret,[493] who dwells in Warwickshire, which here I send you.

We have receaved no letters from you [for] a long time, and the last ~~of~~ was a short one of June the 26 wherin you make no mention of the receipt of mine of 11 May,[494] notwithstanding you say the post was then come. I pray God some of ours have not miscaried. But, if you find that the way of Flanders be dangerous, I pray write ordinarily hereafter by France.

The last time I wrote to you which was the 27 of July[495] I sent you a coppy of our common letter to my lord desiring his rettourne,[496] and at the same time you were to receave a letter also from Mr Worthington[497] to informe you truly of his buissenesse.[498] God send all come safe.

Thus with my woonted love and respects I rest. 10 August 1632.

We are now in hand to write severall letters from the vicars generalls ~~<to his Hol[iness]>~~ and the pr[iests] in their districts <to his Hol[iness]>. That from Mr Colleton and the <pr[iests] of the> easterne parts is already made but not yet subscribed.[499]

No address.

Endorsed: Clerk. 10 Aug[ust].
     About the imposture in getting the Catholikes subscriptions.
     About those noble men in particular who subscribed.

[490] See Peters, *Mary Ward*, pp. 56, 62–5; Lunn, *EB*, p. 200; *CSPD, 1631–1633*, p. 537 (a note, dated 14 February 1633, that Robert Winter had made two journeys to Rome concerning the schism in the convent of the Glorious Assumption at Brussels).
[491] See *Letter 23*.
[492] See *Letter 38* for John Bosvile's letter of 20 August 1632 to Urban VIII, denouncing the 'Protestatio Declaratoria'.
[493] Richard Butler, 3rd Viscount Mountgarret.
[494] *Letter 14*.
[495] *Letter 21*.
[496] See *Letter 19*.
[497] William Worthington.
[498] See *Letters 9, 10, 11* (for details of Worthington's suit concerning Penelope Parkins).
[499] See *Letter 23*; AAW, A XXVI, no. 109.

25. [John] Southcot to [an English secular priest at Paris],[500] 21 August 1632

[*AAW, A XXVI, no. 120, pp. 333–334*]

[Sir,]

The post of these parts not being yet come, by reason of the contrary winds which have held these ten daies and more, we have nonn from you since that of the 9 of August, <to> which I briefly answered the last week, and sent you one at the same time from M[r] East with a little note from M[r] Morgan[501] to whom I sent yours for his patron,[502] which wilbe very welcome to him when he rettourneth out of Suffolk and Essex where it is saied that he is to meet with the dutchesse of Buckingham[503] and her freinds, <and> to treat of a match between them two. M[r] East is gonn with him this journey, and purposeth also to rettourne with him about the end of this month.

I expect this day to have M[r] Colletons Latin letter[504] to his Hol[iness] subscribed with the names of his pr[iests] which, if it come in time, I will send to you by this post. I have advertised the other vicar generals of this course, but I know not what effect my advertisement will take with some of them, who will do little unlesse my lord[505] him self write to them, as I signified in my last. Mons*ieur* Fontaine[506] is out of town. He went this day sennight to Wardour to see what he can gett that lord[507] to do in the disclaime.

With these I send you the coppies of what I sent a month agoe and more to M[r] Fitton[508] about the two districts of Walles and the North.[509]

Even now I have receaved M[r] Colletons letter with the names of 30 pr[iests] which here I send enclosed with an open seale to be read by your self and M[r] F[i]tton, to whom you may please to send it by some safe way with as much speed as may be.

---

[500] See *Letter 43*; Allison, RSGB, I, p. 396. This letter, however, appears to have been endorsed in Richard Smith's hand.

[501] William Case.

[502] John Paulet, 5th marquis of Winchester.

[503] Katherine (Manners), widow of George Villiers, 1st duke of Buckingham.

[504] AAW, A XXVI, no. 109. See *Letters 23, 24*.

[505] Richard Smith.

[506] George Leyburn.

[507] Thomas Arundell, 1st Baron Arundell.

[508] Peter Biddulph.

[509] See *Letter 5*.

M[r] Hill[510] hath bought 20 coppies of Aurelius,[511] and sent them into divers parts of England to our brethren, hoping to recover his money from them againe.

Thus nothing els occurring for the present I humbly rest as ever. 21 Aug[ust] 1632.

You may please to send an ~~other~~ coppy of the two districts to M[r] Fitton for feare the other first coppy miscaried.

M[r] Chambers the Scottish pr[iest] hath had 40[li] as other pr[iests] use to have. Fa[ther] Oliver[512] is not yet come that I can heare.

The packett of bookes which John[513] sent by Fetherstons[514] factor is not yet come.

No address.

[on p. 334]

Endorsed: D[octor] Southcote.

26. Clerk [John Southcot] to [Peter Biddulph], 23 August 1632

[*AAW, A XXVI, no. 124, pp. 343–344*]

Sir,

I wrote nothing to you the last week, nor M[r] Fountaine[515] being out of town. Since I wrote last, we have receaved 3 of yours, videlicet of the 3, 17 and 24 of July. But nonn of the 10th and yet you do not say that you omitted to write that week, which we should be ever glad to know. M[r] Webster[516] writes that ours of the 8 of June is miscaried, and it should seem to be so by what you write in your last of the 24th of July, where you say that you have nothing by that weekes post either from M[r] Webster or us, notwithstanding the post brought divers letters the

---

[510] Identity uncertain. If a priest, this man could be either Thomas Hill OSB, a friend of the secular clergy (Anstr., I, pp. 167–168), or William Hill, a secular priest who was a supporter of Richard Smith (Anstr., II, p. 372).

[511] Duvergier de Hauranne, *Vindiciae Censurae Facultatis Theologiae Parisiensis [. . .]*.

[512] Oliver Burke OP.

[513] Presumably either John Galmarch or John Legat, both of whom are mentioned in *Letters 81, 82*.

[514] This may be a reference to the priest John Featherstone; Anstr., II, p. 372.

[515] George Leyburn.

[516] Anthony Champney.

same week to others. Yet we sent a great packett that week <which was receaved by Mr Webster> wherin there was a long narration in Italian written with a letter to Card[inal] Bagni from Sig*nor* Giulio Antonelli by the name of Francesco Bonzotti[517] wherof I advertised you also in my next letters of the 22 of the same month[518] (for I wrote nothing on the 15). This ~~letter~~ <writing> was to informe his Hol[iness] by Card[inal] Bagni his meanes of the state of things here, which perhaps would have don <us> good if it had come safe. I feare there is some foule play, and that some of your adversaries do intercept your letters there, which you may do well to prevent by changing the addresse. This is the third packett which hath bin missing this yeare, of those which we sent <to you> from hence. The first was of the 17 of Febr[uary], the second of the 11 of May, and now this of the 8 of June. Hereafter what is of moment we will send by the way of Paris, as we did a fortnight since the qu[een's] two letters to his Hol[iness] and the French ambass[ador][519] there which I pray God may come safe in the end. Perhaps also some of these packetts which we think to be lost will come in the end to your hands, if you make some enquiry after them. Howsoever, to be sure, good it were that you chaunged the addresse, and advertised Mr Webster and Mr Strong[520] therof.

Now for answer to these three, there is not much to be saied, seeing your later destroies those hopes which you gave in your former about the assessor, who you say is changed, and an other putt in his place whom you know not. My lord[521] writes unto us that there he is tould, by such as best know his Hol[iness's] mind, that we shall have 3 bishops and not with titles in partibus infidelium, but he thinkes withall that one if not two of the 3 are intended to be regulars. Mr Samford[522] writes also ~~that~~ <from thence> in secrett to us that the nonce[523] there tould a French bishop (who is our special freind) that his Hol[iness] would rather give 3 or 4 bishops yea ordinaries for England than him[524] whom we have already. Yet our chief care must be to preserve him we have at least till more be made, and no lesse must we stand for our own priests to be made when new on[e]s are graunted, and to exclude all regulars, but especially the Jes[uits], both bycause, as my lord noteth well, they are suspect to the State, and ennemies to the clergy, and bycause they

[517] See *Letter 16*.
[518] *Letter 17*.
[519] Jean de Gallard, baron de la Rochebeaucourt et de Brassach, French ambassador in Rome. See *Letter 24*.
[520] Matthew Kellison.
[521] Richard Smith.
[522] Robert Ducket, alias Francis Samford. See Anstr., II, pp. 90–91.
[523] Cardinal Alessandro Bichi.
[524] Richard Smith.

have a vow after they are chosen to be advised by their own order in all things, which you know was directly forbidden to our superiour [*p. 344*] by Pope Clement the 8 in his breve which beginns Venerunt nuper ad nos.[525] I sent you up coppies of the ~~two~~ districts of the two presidents of the North and Walles[526] uppon the 6 of July, and I sent the same againe the last week to my lord in case the former should have miscaried. If 3 bishops be made according to that division, perhaps his Hol[iness] will not be so much against my lord that now is, who may be made the chief of those three ~~and jud[ge]~~ and of the southerne parts, and judg in appeales to the other two. At least we must be sure to provide, whensoever 3 bishops are made, if we can not hinder one or two of them from being regulars, that the chief (who is to be of the southerne parts) be of ~~secular~~ the clergy. As for the subjects that are now chiefly in election, although I can determine nothing without the consent of the rest, yet these are the persons of greater note amongst us: M[r] Ed[ward] Bennett (who would do well to be bishop in Walles and the westerne parts), M[r] D[octor] Bossevile, M[r] D[octor] Champney and D[octor] Kellison, [and] <D[octor] Southcoat>.[527] These are all primae classis. Secundae classis may be these: D[octor] Maylard,[528] M[r] Stratford,[529] M[r] Blackloe,[530] [and] M[r] Will[iam] Shelley.

We are now in hand to gett every vicar generall to write a distinct letter to his Hol[iness] subscribed with the names of most of the priests of his district. M[r] Colleton hath sent his[531] already this week to my lord, which you shall receave open, God send it come safe. These distinct letters, togeather with the qu[een's] letter and the bishops of France, will do somwhat no doubt in the end. I send you now a coppy of M[r] Colletons saied letter by the way of Bruxelles; and the next week I will send you also a coppy of D[octor] Bosseviles[532] which is not yett subscribed.

You desire to heare more particulers of such inconveniences as happen here for waunt of authority. But I have little to say more than what I have saied already. Concerning matrimony two things occurr which I know not whether you have heard: the one is that of Fa[ther]

[525] See *NAGB*, pp. 5, 16, 46, 47, 76, 81.

[526] See *Letter 5*.

[527] Inserted in Peter Biddulph's hand.

[528] Henry Mayler.

[529] Edmund Lechmere.

[530] Thomas White.

[531] See AAW, A XXVI, no. 109; *Letters 23, 24*.

[532] See AAW, A XXVI, no. 117, p. 327; *Letter 24*. This letter, like Colleton's, was forwarded via Richard Smith in Paris; AAW, B 27, no. 132.

Blunt, who gave my cosen Kircham[533] counsaile ~~to~~ (as she her self tould my lord bishop and others) to speake the words of mariage between Mr Francis Ploydon the younger and her self, and yet to reserve her intention not to marry.[534] The other is ~~of~~ that of my cosen White[535] (Mr Blacklows brother) his daughter[536] and young Brett[537] whom one Ward[538] (Mary Wards brother), a young Jesuitt, (as I was tould) married by joyning their hands togeather and saying, even thus, <u>be married</u>. More I have not at this time to write. Only I thought good to lett you know that I heare nothing yet of Barklaies two chapters, which you saied you sent to Paris but not by whom nor when.[539] I pray advertise me of both by your next.

Adieu. 23 August 1632.

No address.

[on p. 343]

Endorsed: Clerk. 23 Aug[ust].
About those who are to be bishops.
About Ward that married two together saying only, be married.

---

[533] According to AAW, A XXVII, no. 111, p. 321 ('Scandalous cases', 1633), Mrs Kirkham was 'then [a] widdow'. See *Letter 44*.

[534] Francis Plowden married, first, Elizabeth, daughter of Alban Butler of Aston-le-Walls, Northamptonshire, and, secondly, Katherine, the widow of Richard Butler of Callan, co. Kilkenny; Foley, IV (pedigree of Plowden of Plowden, Shropshire, and Shiplake, Oxfordshire); Allison, Q J, p. 142. On 22 March 1632 John Jackson notified Biddulph that 'I thincke [in] Mrs Kirkhams case and Mr Ploydens that a monke and Fa[ther] Blunt was [*sic*] to decide', and that this kind of decision 'was proper for my lords court and as clear a contract de praesenti as any can be made, yet now it is reported she is maried to an other. (Fa[ther] Blunt gave her such advise therin as he can not justifie, if it were urged against him, and surely it is scandalous.) I make noe dowbt but many such cases are strangely shuffled up in this kind'; AAW, A XXVI, no. 43, p. 133.

[535] Richard White of Hutton, Essex. See Metcalfe, *The Visitations of Essex*, I, p. 521. Richard was a brother of the priests Jerome and Thomas White. Their mother, Mary, was a daughter of the lawyer Edmund Plowden. The White brothers were thus cousins of Smith's leading opponent, Francis Plowden. See Anstr., II, pp. 348–349, 349–354; G. de C. Parmiter, *Edmund Plowden* (London, 1987), p. 145. Richard's second wife was Katherine, a daughter of Sir Richard Weston, the lord treasurer; Alexander, *CLT*, pp. 32, 171. In the second week of January 1635 Richard White (accompanied by David Codner OSB) visited Gregorio Panzani and intimated that he was favourable to a restored episcopal authority in England 'ma con giurisdittione limitata'; VA, PD, fo. 64r.

[536] Mary, daughter of Richard White by his first marriage to Anne, daughter of Andrew Gray of Hinxworth; Metcalfe, *The Visitations of Essex*, I, p. 521; J.B. Calnan, 'County society and local government in the county of Hertfordshire, c.1580–c.1630, with special reference to the commission of the peace' (Ph.D. thesis, University of Cambridge, 1979), p. 52.

[537] Robert Brett of Whitestaunton, Somerset.

[538] George Ward SJ. See Peters, *Mary Ward*, pp. 40, 355.

[539] See *Letter 15*.

27. Laborn [George Leyburn] to Fitton [Peter Biddulph], 31 August 1632

[*AAW, A XXVI, no. 129, pp. 355–356*]

Worthie deare sir,

My absence hath caused my silence, for since I procured her Majestyes letters[540] I have not been in the towne, notwithstanding M[r] Lovell[541] haith signifyed unto you all our affayres to whom I doe referre you now for I am onely newly arrived. Concerning bishops, if divers will be granted I could wish with many more that they may be chosen out of thes vid[elicet] D[octor] Kellison, D[octor] Champney, M[r] Bennett, M[r] Lovell, M[r] William Shelley [and] M[r] Stratford.[542] Many others here deserveth the dignity but they are very old.[543] I protest unto you that I doe not thinke that our State is soe much against episcopall authority as the Jesuists. In that Protestatio Declaratoria the Jesuists did abuse many of our Catholike nobility as will herafter appeare.[544] Divers alreadie have subscribed against it, and one of the queens gentlemen told me and Fa[ther] Ph[ilip], being wish[e]d of me to speake unto my Lord Herbert,[545] that he never did subscribe to any writing whatsoever, and the Lord Vaux protesteth as much as for my Lord Arundell of Wardor, my Lord Viscount Mountegue, my Lord Morley,[546] [the] earle of Rutland,[547] my Lord Viscount Dunbar,[548] [and] the marquis of Winchester. They desire nothing more than the

[540] See *Letter 24*.

[541] John Southcot.

[542] Edmund Lechmere.

[543] See *Letter 26* for John Southcot's own nominations. In March 1633 Richard Smith wrote to Biddulph that he had given to the Paris nuncio the names of five men he thought suitable, 'as M[r] Southcot [...] and M[r] Musket [George Fisher] for the Southe, D[octor] Champney and M[r] Trolop for the Northe, and M[r] Benett for Wales'; AAW, A XXVII, no. 22, p. 59.

[544] See *Letter 13*, and *passim*.

[545] Edward Somerset, Lord Herbert of Raglan.

[546] See *Letters 21, 22*.

[547] Francis Manners, 6th earl of Rutland.

[548] Henry Constable, 1st Viscount Dunbar. The secular clergy's 1635 survey of the Catholic peers noted that he was 'prudens et intrepidus, necnon mediocriter doctus. In clerum secularem singulariter afficitur'; AAW, A XXVIII, no. 3, p. 15. See also AAW, A XXVIII, no. 24, pp. 109–110 (May 1635?), which contains (p. 109) a declaration in favour of the bishop by Viscount Dunbar. He asserts that the king is disposed to tolerate the presence of a bishop in England for the Catholics, exercising spiritual not temporal power, just as the king tolerates priests and Jesuits. For a declaration, written in Southcot's hand, by the marquis of Winchester which endorses the bishop's claims and denies that any serious temporal inconvenience might arise for Catholics from them, see *ibid.*, p. 110.

returne of our bish[op],[549] and my Lord Rivers Viscount Colchester is much offended that it should be sayd that he did subscribe. I cannot furnish you with any occurrences. This is a barran tyme of newes here unlesse I would imparte foraine occurrences which doth not a litle afflict us, they are soe unpleasing. I beseech you to remember my humble service unto Signor Georgio.[550] His brother[551] now is to be sworne her Majestyes servant. I was with him yesterdaye and with his nephew. And tell him that I wish from my hart that it were in my power to serve him. This is all, onely my best wishes for your happie successe in your affayres.

Yours ever.

Aug[ust] 31 1632.

[on p. 356]

Addressed: A Monsieur Monsieur [*sic*] Fitton. Rome.

Endorsed: Laborn. 31 Aug[ust].
          About the lords that refused to subscrib[e] to the Protestatio.

28. Clerk [John Southcot] to [Peter Biddulph], 31 August 1632

[*AAW, A XXVI, no. 130, pp. 357–358*]

Sir,

We heare by M[r] Webster[552] that you have bin lately sick and therfor have omitted to write to us. The last we receaved from you was of the 24 July. But he wrote withall that you were uppon recovery, which did comfort us exceedingly, and we expect every day to heare the same confirmed by new letters.

My lord[553] writes that his Hol[iness] is inclined to make 3 bishops wherof one at least (if not two) [are] to be regulars. No doubt this

---

[549] In July 1633 Smith passed on a story he had received from William Case, the Paulet family chaplain, that Winchester, 'the chefest noble man that is Catholik in England, hearing of the smal assistance I have of his Hol[iness] brooke into thes words': 'wil not the p[ope] mainteyne the authoritie which he hath given? Wil he suffer him self to be thus constrained and limited? Beleve it, this wil prove the most pernitious president that hath bene in the Church of God, and let him looke unto it, for men hereafter wil reject whome and what they please which shal come from that [...] sea'; AAW, B 27, no. 122.

[550] George Con.

[551] Francis Con. See Hibbard, *CI*, pp. 200, 201.

[552] Anthony Champney.

[553] Richard Smith.

would stopp the present tumults in some sort by giving ~~contempt~~
content to the regulars hindring them from joyning any way with the
State against episcopall authority. But God knowes what inconveniences
it might draw herafter uppon the clergy by opening such a gapp to the
promotion of regulars who would look perhaps to have it a custom
ever after to have nonn of the clergy made bishops unlesse some of
theirs also be made togeather and so bread a stronger emulation than
before. Yet the inconveniences that may be feared this way will in some
sort be prevented if the chief of these three bishops be a secular and
made judg in appeales from the reg[ular] bishops, and that all their
vicars and officers be of the clergy only. Yet we must do what we can
to withstand the making of any regular and seek only to have seculars,
and for that end you may do well to give up particuler memorialls
with such reasons as occurr unto you for the present, and we will here
also think of the like reasons and send them up to you as soon as we
can conclude anything by common consent. But in case you see his
Hol[iness] resolved to make a reg[ular] bishop ~~first~~ let us endeavour
that only one regular be made, and that the other two be seculars.
And if he will make two regulars then lett us, as I saied before, be
sure to gett the chief to be a seculer and the other two subordinat to
him. Then you must procure that the clergy may have an exclusive
voice to any particular regular order man that nonn be made against
the good liking of the clergy, or without their consents. Thirdly we
must wholy except against the Jes[uits] bycause they are suspected
to the State, ennemies to the clergy, and tyed by vow to do nothing
without their generalls approbation, after their promotion, which are
three strong reasons to exclude them. The last week by the way of
Paris we sent you the first vic[ar] generalls letter subscribed with 30
pr[iests'] names, and a coppy of the same by the way of Bruxelles.
Shortly you shall have other two [*sic for* two other] vicars letters to the
same purpose, videlicet D[octor] Bosseviles and Mr Nortons, and I
hope the rest will do the like from other parts of the kingdom.[554] And
we cannot but hope well if these and all other letters which have bin
lately written in my lords behalf come safe to Ro[me]. I heard that our
ambassador,[555] my lord treasurers sonn, was wished by the king to take
no Catholick in his compaghny ~~yet~~ and yet that Sir Tob[ie] Mat[hew]
and Mr Gage[556] have wrought under hand to gett Sir Kenelm Digbyes
younger brother, John Digby, to be one of his followers in this journy,
and that he hath order (when the ambassador is at Florence) to go
from thence to Rome, where it is likely they intend to make use of

[554] For Benjamin Norton, see Anstr., I, pp. 257–258. See *Letters 24, 25, 26, 27*.

[555] Jerome Weston. For his embassy, see *CSPV, 1632–1636, passim*.

[556] George Gage. See *Letter 19*.

him for their own ends, which therfor you must endeavor to prevent
what you can both by informing his Hol[iness] and the card[inals]
privatly before he cometh and by meeting <him> and talking with
him when he comes to Ro[me] ~~and~~ to try what you can learne of
his intentions, and to make <what> use you can there of him to
our advantage. It is probable that he will serve the Jes[uits] all he
can, bycause he hopeth by their meanes to gett all his mothers lands
setled uppon him, who is wholy their creature.[557] In any case visitt the
generall of the Dominicans[558] and M[r] Barklay, the popes cameriero,
at their rettourne to Rome from Paris. For my lord writes that they
are both desirous to see you, and promise to do good offices for my
lord when they come thither, and particulerly M[r] Barcklay tould my
lord that he would procure you audience of his Hol[iness] when you
would. The same man, as my lord writes, would have M[r] Rob[ert]
Duckett (whom I think you know) come to Rome and live there with
him, which would be honorable for him and good for our clergy, if you
think he intend it really, and that M[r] Duckett be a fitt man for such a
purpose. My lord saieth he hath left mony for him at Paris to defray
his journy when he cometh. But I would gladly heare your opinion
before he adventure uppon this course, for he is in a good residence,
and being very sound and true to the clergy he doeth us good offices
where he is. [p. 358] I hope you will remember also to visit Fa[ther]
Valeriano the Capuchin <as> I wrote to you long since.[559] He is a
great man in Bohemia with Card[inal] Pazzamen[560] and powerfull also
in the court of Ro[me] and a freind to the clergy, as his compaghnion
here, Fa[ther] Alessandro,[561] tells me. If a reg[ular] bishop be made for
the present we can think of no fitter man amongst the reg[ulars] of
England than Fa[ther] Simon Stock.[562] I heare many of ours except

---

[557] Smith's letter to Biddulph of 13/23 September 1632 recited this information about
'Digbie sonne to the powder traitor', and stated that Digby's estates were currently held by
his 'elder brother'; AAW, B 27, no. 129.

[558] Nicholas Ridolfi OP. See Flynn, *The Irish Dominicans 1536–1641*, p. 174.

[559] See *Letter 20*.

[560] For Cardinal Peter Pázmány, a supporter of Habsburg political interests, see Pastor,
HP, XXVIII, pp. 156–159, 294–304, 306–308.

[561] Alessandro d'Ales.

[562] For Thomas Dawson (Simon Stock) ODC, see *NAGB*, pp. 37, 133, 156; Codignola, *CHL*,
passim; Hughes, *HSJ*, pp. 181–191. Ironically, Dawson had been closely involved with the
colonial project, in Newfoundland, of Richard Smith's enemy Sir George Calvert, 1st Baron
Baltimore. Codignola suggests that the association of Calvert with Dawson (and indeed the
secular priest Thomas Longueville and the ex-Jesuit Anthony Smith) indicates that until
Baltimore returned from Newfoundland he did not 'take a clear stand in the quarrel between
Bishop Smith and the regulars'; *ibid.*, pp. 44, 54. On 25 October/4 November 1632 Smith
wrote to Biddulph that 'I send not the names of such regulars as I think fittest to be bishops
becaus I know not manie of them, and I feare if I shold name anie that my brethren like not

by name ag*ain*st Fa[ther] Rudesind,[563] Fa[ther] Leander,[564] Fa[ther] Price[565] and some other Benedictines. The next week we intend to send you an instrument under a notaries hand of my lo*r*d marquis[566] his protestation both concerning him self and the earle of Rivers to shew how much they hould them selves abused by the Protestatio Declaratoria to w*h*ich there were 18 noble mens subscriptions. My lo*r*d marquis is very zealous for my lo*r*d and you may do well to give him that com*m*endation in that court w*h*ich his vertue and good parts deserve, and the rather bycause the Jes[uits], seeing him so constant to my lo*r*d, go about to take from him all they can, according to their custom. This enclosed note will shew you how stoutly he carried him self in the parlament court heretofore. We are in a course to gett as many <as we can> of our chief freinds of the laity here to disclaime from the Protestation. Some have donn it already, who are of no small note, as you may see by these papers enclosed.

I heare now from M[r] Webster that you have receaved that letter and information to Card[inal] Bagni from Bonzotto here w*h*ich I mencioned in my former,[567] and w*h*ich you intimated to be lost by yo*u*r last letters to M[r] Lab[orne]. I shalbe glad to know what good it doth. We have no newes here stirring. Recusants compositions stay ~~at~~ <in> the lo*r*d keepers hands. They have passed my lo*r*d treasurer and the attorney with the privy signett but have not yet the great seale.

Yesterday M[r] Tho[mas] Taylor, brother to the infantas agent[568] and his chaplaine, was arrested by seargeants for certaine monies <that were in his hand of one deceased> by the instigation of one who lived heretofore in S[t] Omers and is saied to be a Catholick. You may putt this into the number of other abuses for waunt of authority here. The Spanish resident[569] took up the matter presently as I heare.

---

it wold displease the*m*. Yet the fittest I can think on are F[ather] Simon Stock a Carmelite discalced, and F[ather] Bonaventura Jac[k]son a cord[e]l[i]er and Dom Mauro Tailer a Benedictin of Italie'; AAW, B 27, no. 133. Bonaventure Jackson was the secular priest John Jackson's brother; Dockery, *CD*, pp. 22, 26, 27, 29, 41, 117. For Taylor, see *NAGB*, pp. 95, 160. The list of those suitable for episcopal office, presented by Southcot to Panzani in March 1635, included Jackson, Taylor and Dawson; VA, PD, fo. 83r.

[563] William (Rudesind) Barlow OSB.

[564] John (Leander) Jones OSB.

[565] William (Benedict) Jones OSB.

[566] John Paulet, 5th marquis of Winchester.

[567] See *Letter 26*.

[568] Henry Taylor, agent in London for the infanta, Isabella Clara Eugenia. See A.J. Loomie, 'Olivares, the English Catholics and the peace of 1630', *Revue Belge de Philologie d'Histoire*, 47 (1969), pp. 1154–1166, at p. 1165. See also Anstr., II, pp. 314–315; A.J. Loomie, 'Sir Robert Cecil and the Spanish Embassy', *BIHR*, 42 (1969), pp. 30–57, at pp. 35–36, 38–42, 44.

[569] Juan de Necolalde.

Thus with all wonted good wishes I rest. 31 August 1632.

I heare nothing yet of those two chapters of Barklay.[570]

Perhaps if we made a peace with the Benedictines and Dominicans before any order were taken for more bishops we might obtaine by their help (notwithstanding the Jes[uits'] opposition) to have more bishops of clergy men, especially if such were proposed as are pleasing to them, as Mr Bennet for one.

Out of the North Mr Cuthbert Trollop vicar generall of those parts writeth thus 16th August. Urbans [*word obscured*: deniall ?] and our catching of nothing all this time but labor and expences terrifieth and weakneth some of ours.

No address.

Endorsed: Clerk. 31 Aug[ust].
          About haveing no regular bishops.
          About Mr Digbye with my lord treasurers sonn.

29. [John Southcot] to [an English secular priest at Paris],[571] 5 September 1632

[*AAW, A XXVI, no. 132, pp. 361–362*]

[Sir,]

I acknowledged the last week the receipt of your two last letters of the 16th and 30 of August since which time we have receaved nonn from you, the post not being as yet come, as I suppose. I forgott to tell you in my last that I heare nothing in particuler of Mr Charnocks death.[572] Mr Warmington[573] assisted him, but I feare he never mooved him to recant his opinion concerning that point wherin you desire to be informed, and Mr Colleton saieth [*word deleted*] that he feareth he died in that opinion without any shew of recantation.[574] I ame

---

[570] See *Letter 21.*

[571] See *Letter 43*; Allison, RSGB, I, p. 396.

[572] See *Letter 23.*

[573] William Warmington. See Anstr., I, pp. 370–371. A series of notes (dated 1635) on clergy who allowed the oath of allegiance and/or led loose lives cites Warmington (now aged seventy) as 'capellanus ordinarius legatorum Venetum' in London. Noting his book on the oath of allegiance (*A Moderate Defence of the Oath of Allegiance* (London, 1612)), it is claimed 'quamvis coram episcopo Chalcedonensi postea revocaverit suam sententiam tamen adhuc eam tueri dicitur suisque paenitentibus instillare'; AAW, A XXVIII, no. 68, p. 285.

[574] For Robert Charnock's opinions concerning the Jacobean oath of allegiance, see *NAGB, passim.*

now 3 or 4 miles out of London, where I remaine for a time to take the aier. Before I came last from thence one tould me that he heard the Venetian ambassador[575] had putt away his chaplaine,[576] but I had no time to inquire whether it were true or noe, and uppon what cause, wherof by the next rettourne I hope to informe you. My lords[577] letter was delivered unto him, wherat he was not a little netled; and saied that he would not make an answer till he were gone from the ambassador. What he meant therby I do not know. He stormed mightily against Signor Giulio,[578] saying that he had betraied him bycause he spake those words (as he saieth) no where but in the ambass[ador's] chamber in the presence of Giulio. He that procured the qu[een's] letters desires to be secret, and would not have you make knowen his name to any there, and when I tould him that his generall was made acquainted with it he seemed to me to be somwhat troubled at first, though afterward he ~~was~~ passed it over againe, and would seem only to have bin troubled for feare that <the> bishop should also have knowen it, to whom (<as> you wrote to me) you shewed the saied letters of the qu[een] which I also tould this party. I have an attestation[579] made by Mr Hare of some passages ~~between~~ concerning Mr Morgans patron[580] and his <ladies> grandfather[581] which I propose to send you by this post. I expect such an other concerning the other lord of whom I wrote to you before to whom Mr Lab[orne] is of kinn.[582] Two daies agoe Mr Lab[orne] and the French ambass[ador][583] had a long and hoat expostulation togeather, wherof he tould me that he would advertise you him self at large, as I suppose he doth by this post. Mr Lab[orne] tells me that he is resolved to go over for a while, partly to satisfy the lady our great friend, and partly to avoide <for a time> the displeasure of the Theatines[584] <from> whom he feareth, as he saieth, some mischief ~~another~~ if he stay and follow buissenesse as he hath donn, but I answer him to that, that Mr Lov[ell][585] ~~as~~ hath as much cause and perhaps more to fly than he hath. Yet he saieth he wilbe advised, and do as my lord and <other> freinds shall advise

---

[575] Vicenzo Gussoni.

[576] i.e. Warmington.

[577] Richard Smith.

[578] Giulio Antonelli. See *Letter 16*.

[579] Endorsed in margin: 'Of this instrument good use may be made there before it be sent to Rome, and therfor a coppy should be taken of it'.

[580] John Paulet, 5th marquis of Winchester, patron of William Case, alias Morgan.

[581] Thomas Darcy, Earl Rivers, the grandfather of Jane Savage, the marquis of Winchester's recently deceased first wife; GEC, XII/ii, p. 768.

[582] For Leyburn, and his relationship to various peerage families, see Anstr., II, p. 192.

[583] François Duval, marquis de Fontenay Mareuil.

[584] The Jesuits.

[585] i.e. John Southcot.

him, and therfor I would wish my lord to write particulerly unto him for that purpose. I tould him what I heard one say, videlicet that the lady, uppon whose entreaty he goeth, hath bin wrought by our adversaries to take him of[f] in this manner from following the the common buissenesse.[586] Fa[ther] Phil[ip] tells me that Fa[ther] Bertin[587] hath written unto him to know how matters may be accommodated between the bishop and the regulars, as also between him and the lay Cath[olics] and he saied to me that in case my lord would not exact approbation of the regulars he <u>did not see why he</u> and they might not agree, and, if he would not claime <u>to prove wills and</u> displace priests in Cath[olic] houses, why he and the lay Cath[olics] might not also well agree togeather. And he intended to write thus to Fa[ther] Bertin. I tould him that my lord was willing to remit approbation so <he> might have the 3 parochialls,[588] and that for wills and displacing of priests he had severall times given it under his hand that he would practise neither of them, and that the latter belonged not to him as [p. 362] bishop but as archpriest <yet not to be practised> and that the former he never yet claimed, or intended to claime. He would gladly have seen somwhat under my lords hand to this effect that he might write back <u>with more assurance</u>, and, bycause I have nothing to shew in this kind, I desire that you will procure some certificat of this nature from my lord under his hand and seale that Fa[ther] Phil[ip] may shew it either at home or abroad as occasion shall serve. And I think he were a fitt man to make a peace between my lord and the monkes which, if it were once made, and the Dominicans also taken of[f], we should have no difficulty to have more bishops of our own, especially if <u>Mr Bennet</u> were to be one, whom the monkes would not oppose. I heare Mr Richard Foster is gonn with our ambassador, and it is feared the Jes[uits] have some project by him when he cometh into Italy, wherof I wish Mr Fitton were betimes advertised. I heare also John Digby, brother to Sir Kellam,[589] is gonn with the ambass[ador].[590] By him also the Jes[uits] are likely to desighne some things in Rome. I could also tell you somwhat <u>more of the ambass[ador]</u> him self, but I ame tied to secresy yet a while.[591] And perhaps you may heare the same ~~els where~~ <by other meanes>. But I pray you lett not <u>this clause of my</u> letter be

<hr>

[586] A letter to Biddulph of 26 October 1632, from Edward Ireland, informed him that, since Leyburn had 'gone over', 'wee want one to labour amongst the nobles here'; AAW, A XXVI, no. 142, p. 385.

[587] Claude Bertin, superior of the French branch of the Congregation of the Oratory.

[588] See *Letter 13*.

[589] Sir Kenelm Digby.

[590] See *Letter 28*.

[591] Against this passage in this paragraph, and against the next paragraph, Southcot has written in the margin, 'Soli, Soli'.

seen to [*sic*] any. And I feare it would displease the party from whome I had the secrett to know that I had written thus much, although he <u>be one that</u> wisheth well to o*u*r cause, but he feareth to be blamed if the matter should come forth. Yet I will see if I can gett his leave to communicat it to you to the end you may informe the nonce[592] of it privatly, if perhaps he should not know it already, as like enough he doth.

You may do well also, if you please, to inquire of the noncio whether his Ho[liness] had no intention to make the grand <u>aulmner</u>[593] <u>superiour or superin</u>tendent of the mission here. But I pray do this as seeming rather to heare it from Rome than from hence, bycause it is a matter of great secresy, and must not seem to have come from any here, if it be any way taken notice of <at> all. Yet I think the aulmner hath refused to undertake it, chiefly for feare of offending the king who is better pleased, as he thinketh, with o*u*r divisions.

M[r] Nortons com*m*on letter, as also D[octor] Bosseviles,[594] wilbe shortly ready for to send and they expect nothing but subscription of hands.

Thus with all woonted duty. 5 September 1632.

M[r] Fitton[595] writes thus: 'the Humillima Narratio[596] w*h*ich was framed by some priests in the West and sent to my lo*r*d to Paris in February last was sent unto him by one Allen a priest,[597] who came to Rome in compaghny of an English Jesuitt and, as he thinketh, com*m*unicated that writing unto him, by w*h*ich meanes it comes to be knowen here to the Jes[uits]. For, he saieth, he never shewed it to any there. But I wonder that M[r] Plantin[598] would venture to send such a thing by no surer messenger, and (as it seemes) send it open also by him, a Jesuitt being his compaghnion all the way. This may do us here a great displeasure.'

The pack of books is not yet come, and therfor I have not yet paied Johns[599] wife the mony.

No address or endorsement.

[592] Cardinal Alessandro Bichi.
[593] Jacques le Noël Du Perron.
[594] See *Letters 24, 26, 28*.
[595] Peter Biddulph.
[596] See *Letters 6, 17*.
[597] Gilbert Leek, alias Francis Allen, who was living in Cornwall in 1631; Anstr., II, p. 189.
[598] Lawrence Platt.
[599] Presumably either John Galmarch or John Legat, both of whom are mentioned in *Letters 81, 82*.

30. Clerk [John Southcot] to Fitton [Peter Biddulph], 7 September 1632

[*AAW, A XXVI, no. 134, pp. 365–366*][600]

Sir,

I was glad to understand by yours of the 14th of August of your recovery againe, as also of the receipt of that packett of the 8 of June, which we feared ~~was~~ <to have bin> lost. I hope Bonzottos information[601] will do good, although it be not couched so well as I could have wished, and you did very well to entreat C[ardinal] Bagni to send it to Ginetti. It was a great oversight to send Humillima Narratio by such a messenger[602] unto you, and a much greater if it were sent <by him> open and unsealed, as it seemes by your letter it was, else I hardly think either he or his compaghnion would have bin so bould as to have opened it, and then send it [to] you.

With what face can any urge to have Hallier forbidden,[603] and not the Spongia[604] which gave the occasion of writing it? Though Hallier be more prolix in dilating him self uppon matters, yet Aurelius[605] is solid and judicious also, and answers very aptly ad hominem though briefly.

You doe much comfort us with that assurance which you say was given you by Card[inal] Ginetti, and we hope, uppon the arrival of the qu[eens] letters and the bishops of France, it will not be long ere that be donn which they intend to do, whatsoever it be. I hope also those common letters[606] which my lords vicars generall intend to write (Mr Colleton having begunn and sent his already subscribed by 30 priests) will make some impression as also our common letter to my lord, which he saieth he hath sent unto you to shew unto his Hol[iness] and to know of him what answer he shall make unto it.[607]

---

[600] This letter consists of four pages, the second and third of which are numbered '378' and '379', i.e. as they were numbered before they were bound in this present volume.
[601] See *Letter 16*.
[602] Gilbert Leek. See *Letter 29*.
[603] Hallier, *Defensio Ecclesiasticae Hierarchiae [. . .]*.
[604] Floyd, *Hermanni Loemelii [. . .] Spongia [. . .]*.
[605] Duvergier de Hauranne, *Vindiciae Censurae Facultatis Theologiae Parisiensis [. . .]*.
[606] See *Letter 23*; AAW, A XXVI, no. 109.
[607] See e.g. AAW, A XXVI, no. 146 (a memorandum of 1 October 1632 by Edward Bennett and the clergy of Wales to pope Urban VIII, claiming that in Wales and neighbouring areas there were at least forty priests and 2,000 Catholics, and declaring that the bishop should return with a grant of ordinary jurisdiction); AAW, A XXVI, no. 139 (John Colleton's and the Midlands priests' letter of 12 September 1632 to Urban VIII); AAW, A XXVI, no. 140 (another letter, of 18 September 1632, from Colleton to the pope); AAW, A XXVI, no. 143 (a letter of September 1632 from the clergy of the southern shires to Urban VIII, but without

Wheras you wish us to write a common letter to Propaganda we have done so on the 18th of July, and we sent a duplicat of the same by Mr Websters[608] meanes.

Thus much to your letter of the 14th of August which is as much as I can well do at this time, having bin much distempered all the last night and this morning with a fitt of the stonn. Yet I must add one thing, which is a secrett, videlicet, that it was mooved not long since from thence by order from his Hol[iness] to the grand aulmner[609] <here> to take uppon him the superintendency over pr[iests] and Catholickes,[610] but I understand that he refused it chiefly uppon a temporall feare of loosing the kings ~~faith~~ favour, whom he thinkes to be better pleased with our divisions. He that dealt with him about [p. 378 sic] this matter is one that was Card[inal] Peron his secretary, and liveth now in Rome. His name I have forgotten. ~~But~~ It were not amisse that you sought him out, and made acquaintance with him, but in no case take notice of this matter either to him or any other French there, bycause it is a great secrett. Only you may please dexterously to make use of the knowledg of it there with the p[ope] and card[inals] in seeking to prevent any such thing hereafter. I should have advertised you of this a month agoe but I forgott it. Another secrett I will also impart unto you which one tould me since I wrote ~~last~~ unto you the last week with condition to impart it to nonn but your self, not so much as to my lord at Paris, fearing to be blamed (if it should come abroad) by a great person who tould it him. It is that my lord treasurers sonn,[611] who is gonn ambass[ador] to France, Savoy, Venice <and> Florence, hath a privat instruction ~~to either~~ to go to Rome also, which though it seemes a hard matter to be beleeved, yet the party who tould it me did assure me that it was soe. Of this you may do well in some dexterous manner to make that use as may gaine you creditt with his Hol[iness] and with some <one> speciall card[inal] your freind, not avouching it directly to be true (least perhaps it prove otherwize) but insinuating the matter handsomly as a thing either resolved uppon, or at least deliberated here, and not unlikely to proove soe. But I pray write back of this to nonn but my self alone. I have not a particuler list of his followers names, but I heare that Mr Rich[ard] Foster, alias

signatures, requesting the pope to send Smith back not just with ordinary authority but with metropolitan jurisdiction over other appointed bishops); AAW, A XXVI, no. 144 (a similar petition, also of September 1632, from the clergy of the northern shires); AAW, A XXVI, no. 160 (a copy of a letter of December 1632, from the priests of the Midlands shires to the pope).

608 Anthony Champney.
609 Jacques le Noël Du Perron.
610 See *Letters 28, 29.*
611 Jerome Weston.

French Foster, whom you knew in Paris, is one of them, and John Digby an other, as I wrote to you the last week,[612] by whom no doubt the Theatines[613] have some desighne which you may prepare as well as you can before hand to prevent.

This day I was tould by a pr[iest] <a grave priest> of ours, of two notable apostatas, or rather one apostata, and another counterfeit lately discovered here. [*p. 379 sic*] The apostata was a Franciscan friar that came out of Holland almost two yeares since, and brought a trull with him, with whom he was found to have bin in bed all night by a Dutch Duch mans wife a Catholick and an [En]glish pr[iest] that went with her one morning to his lodging to speake with him uppon some buissenesse, and thinking him to have before to have bin a good religious man as he bore shew outwardly to them, having preached also once before the queen in French. But when he saw him self discovered he presently fled from London, and whither he is gonn I do not heare. The counterfeict is a French man discovered not passing ten daies or a fortnight agoe, who pretended to be a priest and an abbot of the Camaldulenses,[614] and as such was enterteined by a certaine priest that is in the New prison who procured some almes for him and for the compaghny with whom he came over which (as I heare) are two women, the mother and the daughter, the mother being English, but married to one Monsieur Subize (as I take it) in France, and a notorious strumpet. They pretended to this priest, who mett them in their way from Canterbury to London, that they had bin robbed and had lost above 300[li] and the abbot shewed him a Latin book of written in forme of a history of the Camaldulensian order, wherof he pretended to be the author. And for a time the good priest beleeved him, and so procured him some almes, but now, uppon further inquiry, he is found to be a counterfeict.[615] This you may add to your information of abuses which are like to grow here for waunt of authority. But if I cann I will gett the pr[iest] [*p. 368*] to sett down the whole story under his hand.

---

[612] See *Letter 29*.

[613] Jesuits.

[614] The Camaldolese were hermits living within the framework of the Benedictine Rule. See Bellenger, *EWP*, p. 12.

[615] For Richard Smith's account of these events, see AAW, B 27, no. 132. See also AAW, A XXV, no. 99 (Biddulph's memorandum to Cardinal Spada concerning these two individuals, though he does not name them). In early 1636 Gregorio Panzani mentioned in his diary, and in correspondence with Cardinal Barberini, a French Franciscan apostate called Jacomo Salvadori, and an impostor, 'il falsar[io]', 'Antonio della Valle', who had been arrested; VA, PD, fos 120r, 126r; PRO, 31/9/17B (transcript of Panzani's letter to Cardinal Francesco Barberini of 2/12 March 1636).

And now I ame weary indeed of writing and so I rest as ever.

7 Septemb[er] 1632.

Addressed: Pour Mons*ieur* Fitton a Rome.

Endorsed: Clerk. 7 Sept[ember].
        About Peron his secretary. About 2 apostats lately discovered.

31. Lab[orn] [George Leyburn] to [an English secular priest at Paris], 9 September 1632

[*AAW, A XXVI, no. 137, pp. 371–372*]

Honored sir,

At Otlands I did commend unto Fa[ther] Ph[ilip] a remembrance of yo*u*r respects. I perceave by him th*a*t a cheef man of the Society haith been w*i*th him. He did not tell me his name, and I would not be inquisitive. Howsoever I doe imagine th*a*t it was Fa[ther] Blunt. I doe assure my selfe th*a*t he haith had notice from R[ome] and some litle tinkling here th*a*t her Majesty is much for the bishop and his authority; wherfore the reason of his comming to Fa[ther] Ph[ilip] was to manifest unto him th*a*t he and his did much honour the bishop <(yea desireth two or three more)> and did greatlie desire the establishing of his authority, in soe much th*a*t he and the rest are most willing to embrace an accord uppon any indifferent conditions and haith wish[e]d Fa[ther] Ph[ilip] to deale in the busines; imparting unto him in what poynts he and the rest would yeeld unto the bishop, and in what poynts he and the rest ~~rest~~ did expect th*a*t the bishop should condescend unto them. And when Fa[ther] Ph[ilip] told him th*a*t the bishop did not desire to erect a <publik> tribunall, place and displace priests et[c]., or to exercise his authoritie any waye to [the] prejudice of the flock committed unto his charge, to w*h*ich [*sic for* this] he replyed saying, then an accord may easilie be obtayned. For my part I told Fa[ther] Ph[ilip] th*a*t this was but a florish to persuade him th*a*t they did not sticke at episcopall authority but certaynely they did intend noe thing lesse than an accord. Howsoever it behouveth us to showe a willingnes to make peace. Wherfore I thought good to signifie thus much unto you th*a*t you may advise w*i*th our friends and droe some articles and deliver them unto Fa[ther] Ph[ilip]. I am sorrie th*a*t I am not furnish[e]d w*i*th leasure to be soe exact in this relation as I could wish. Howsoever raptim[616] I have form[e]d some

---

[616] i.e. hastily.

conditions which I doe assure my selfe Fa[ther] Ph[ilip] will judge
most reasonable. You may change and adde as you please. These are
they.

9° Septemb[e]r 1632.

I have not read[617] a word of what I have written.

Quantum ad regulares

Episcopus non aegre feret si summus pontifex velit eximire regulares
ab eius approbatione. Nihilominus ut bono [*word obscured*: regularium
(?)] debitum expedire existimat, ut missionarii ac non missionariis
apostol[ic]e ac non apostatis dignoscantur. Quare ut justum petit
superiores regularium episcopum admoveant [*word illegible*] om[nes]
et singulis missionariis tum [*word illegible*] illis qui jam in hac vinea animarum lucrandarum gratia operacitur tum etiam de aliis quoti-
escumque visum suerit superioribus aliis ad tum jam tum messem
transmittere. Si aliquis regularium <grave> scandalum aut alium
errorem apprehensione dignum perpetret, a superiore sue non depre-
hendatur, poenis erit episcopum procedere contra dictum regularium
juxta ordinationes sacrorum canonorum.

Quantum ad laicos

Episcopus habebit potestatem in laicos quam habent ordinarii in
suis diaraesibus, utpote laici omnes episcopum debita reverentia
et obedientia prosequentur eumque suum pastorem superiorem et
judicem [*word illegible*] et quandoquidem episcopi officium est regere
et pascere gregem non abesse vel perdere. Curabit episcopus evitare
omnem potestatis suis executionem per quam dicti laici in [*word
illegible*] aliquod eis [*word illegible*] possint adduci. Quare [*two words
illegible*] temporum difficultatibus [n]on eriget publicum tribunal,
non exiget deremas non collocabit non dimovebit pro suo arbitrio
prostitores e domibus [*word illegible*] aliorumque et[c].

See that regulars in this proposition of peace doe not [*word obscured*]
them selves nor the laity ther penitents which I have reason to suspect.

No address.

[*on p. 372*]

Endorsed: Lab[orn]. 9 Sep[tember]. Conditions of peace.

---

[617] i.e. read through.

32. Clerk [John Southcot] to [Peter Biddulph], 18 January 1633

[AAW, A XXVII, no. 3, pp. 9–10][618]

Sir,

The last week I wrote not to you bycause I had nothing from you to answer, and little from hence to informe. I have receaved, since, yours of the 18 December wherein you mention an other written the week before, which we have not yet receaved, for the last I had from you before this of the 18 was dated the 4th December, and was the first which we receaved from you since the 16 of October. If you remember any particuler worthy [of] our knowledge written in that middle letter between the 4 and 18th December, which I feare hath miscaried, I pray advertise us by your next, as also what particuler papers you sent with it; and you may do well even to specify in the succeeding letter ~~what~~ the summe of what you wrote in the former when it is matter of importance, and all particuler writings sent therwith.

With these of the 18th I receaved Fa[ther] Phil[ip's] discourse touching our divisions here, which I like very well and hope that it will do good there. I shalbe glad also to see that compendium in Italian which you sent to my lord[619] (to whom I have written for a coppy of it) and much more the whole relation it self in Latin partly for my own and others information here, and partly for posterity intending to keep a register therof as we do of all common letters, supplications, informations and the like for future history. You write nothing in this letter of the effect of her Majesties letter to his Hol[iness] which we greedily ~~here~~ expect to heare. You sent also a letter for Mr Duckett, which I have sent unto him, but I feare it wilbe to[o] hard a task for him to bring with him an Irish grayhound or English masty[f] as you desire to present to Card[inal] Antonio;[620] but if any marchant that traficks from hence to Civita Vecchia will undertake to carry one with him in his shipp, I know no better way, and I have already sent to inquire. I hope Mr Duckett will write a few lines to Mr Barklay him self, for so I have entreated him to doe, and to prepare him self for his journy with as much speed as he can. But, bycause he must needs visitt his freinds first in Yorkshire, I beleeve it wilbe after midsomer

---

[618] This letter consists of four pages. The second and third are numbered '386' and '387', i.e. as they were numbered before they were bound in this present volume.

[619] Richard Smith.

[620] A reference, perhaps, to Urban VIII's brother, the Capuchin cardinal Antonio Barberini. But, since the secular clergy tended to refer to him by his title of St Onophrio, it is more likely to denote Urban VIII's nephew of the same name.

ere he can stirr from hence. Your letter to M[r] Skinner I can find no man willing to carry to him. You will know the reason therof ere this by what [I] wrote to you formerly. The good man is gonn to an other world, having left you a legacy of 50[8621] which you may take up there as you do your other monies, and what extraordinary charge your sicknesse hath putt you to I pray advertise by your next, and I will cause it to be satisfied, togeather with your accustomed half yeares pencion. [*p. 386 sic*] I was very glad to be partaker of those particuler newses of the court there which you wrote unto him weekly, and were it not to put you to too much trouble I would entreat that curtesy of you my self, in a paper apart, when there is any thing worth the knowing. It seems by what you write to him that Card[inal] Ludovisio is dead,[622] which we [*word deleted*] heard <not> of before.

My lord wrote lately hither that the nonce[623] there desired to have an information of the present state of religion here, and by the last post I sent him one of some 5 sheets of paper which is to[o] long now to write out for you but the next week I purpose to send you a coppy of it.[624]

I ame glad those two letters you mention from the clergy were so well liked of. They were penned by severall hands, and both of them now out of town. Indeed the former to the congre*gacio*n was penned by M[r] East, that to my lord by M[r] Blacklo,[625] and we are faine to make use of many bycause we have not meanes yet to maintaine one setled and certaine man for a secretary, and unlesse his Hol[iness] determine somwhat quickly concerning my lord we shall not be able to do that which is more necessary, for many of my lords freinds fell from him by reason of his absence and will contribute nothing towards his maintenance. I pray informe this point there amongst the rest for it is most true I assure you, and will be our undoing quickly, if his Hol[iness] do not help the sooner.

I imagin there will be great complaint made there of a certaine <English> comedy supposed to be made by M[r] Drury,[626] called the Antibishop,[627] wherin some Benedictins, Dominicans and Jesuitts as also the 3 first opposers[628] and Sir Toby Mathew and M[r] G[eorge]

[621] See *Letter 46*.

[622] Luigi Ludovisi, archbishop of Boulogne, and nephew of Cardinal Alessandro Ludovisi. He died at Boulogne.

[623] Cardinal Alessandro Bichi.

[624] This may be AAW, A XXVI, no. 167 ('The cause of the downefall of religion').

[625] Thomas White.

[626] William Drury. See Anstr., II, pp. 87–89.

[627] See S. Gossett (ed.), *Hierarchomachia or the Anti-Bishop* (London, 1982).

[628] Francis Plowden, Sir Basil Brooke, and Sir Thomas Brudenell, authors of the 'letter of the three gentlemen'. See *Letter 3*.

Gage are brought in uppon the stage, being full of scoffs and taunts against them. I was tould lately that Mr Ploydon hath gotten a coppy of it and that he and his complices that are toucht in it have had much consultation about it this Christmasse. If any such complaint be made there, you may answer that the clergy in generall doth not avow any such work, nor hath any knowledg of it, nor that Mr Drury is the author but rather [*word deleted*] are persuaded that he could not be the author by reason of his sore arme (his right arme) which hath held him these <u>6</u> or <u>7</u> yeares, wherby he is altogeather unable to write with that hand.[629] Neither doth my lord bishop know either the work or the author for certaine, but only by hearsay. Nor is it in his power as things stand with him to take any order for the hindering or suppressing of any such writing by reason of the opposition made against him.[630] Nor in fine did any of those who are touched therin ever yet [*p. 387 sic*] complaine to him to that purpose, so that my lord and the clergy must needs be blamelesse herein, whosoever the author were.[631] Besides it was penned and finished above two yeares agoe, and few coppies are to be found, so little common or publick it is.[632] Finally the plaintiffs (if any shew them selves) have little cause to except against this, considering their own shamfull actions, which were fitter to be derided uppon a stage than answered with reasons, and so they may thank their own folly by which they have made them selves so ridiculous to the world. If you desire a coppy of it, lett me know your mind, and I will gett Mr Duckett to carry up one with him.

My lord martiall[633] went over in [the] Christmasse holidaies to the Hague in Holland with commission, as here is commonly reported, to invite the Lady Elizabeth[634] into England with her children. But as yet we do not heare what certainty there is of her coming, fearing least the Hollanders hinder her, or some other adverse councells by which she hath hitherto bin though[t] to have bin too much guided.[635]

---

[629] See Anstr., II, p. 89.

[630] Smith argued to Cardinal Bichi in February 1633 that if the Jesuits 'had not rejected my authoritie over the laitie I had commanded them to suppresse it. Now I can do no more but request them'; AAW, B 27, no. 117.

[631] For a discussion of the authorship of the play, see Gossett, *Hierarchomachia*, introduction, esp. pp. 21–25. Gossett argues that one possible candidate is Biddulph himself, but says that the attribution cannot be made with certainty.

[632] On 18/28 May 1633 Smith responded to Cardinal Bichi's request for a printed copy of the play by telling him that 'it was never printed nor yet made of the author to be either plaied or published, but onely for his owne exercise, and a scrivener getting a copie hath written divers for to get money'; AAW, B 27, no. 118.

[633] Thomas Howard, 2nd earl of Arundel.

[634] Princess Elizabeth, daughter of James I and widow of Frederick V, Elector Palatine.

[635] See *CSPV, 1632–1636*, pp. 49–70, *passim*.

The queen [*word deleted*] with divers of her ladies acted a certaine pastorall[636] at her own house in the Strand on Tewsday last was sennight,[637] which was 8 howers long. Of this many speak diversly, and the most do rather wish it had not bin donn, chiefly in regard of the majesty and state which a queen should keep, and some think the k[ing] did not altogeather approve it, and do report also that he caused the book afterward to be burnt, as not willing to have it remembred any more, or acted againe. Yet in fine it is very tolerable in a young queen, whose chief ayme was no doubt to please the king.

Concerning recusants compositions I can say little, only this that it is expected this terme some will have the broad seale, which hitherto hath bin graunted to none, or but to one or two at the most. It is also reported that M[r] Attorney hath a list of 60 persons and more of quality that are supposed to have broken the proclamation about their residing in London longer than the time appointed.[638] The pursevants have not searched any house, that I heare of, all this Christmasse, [*p. 10*] only they watch to catch such as they know in the streets, and lett them goe againe for a little mony.[639] This is all I have now to write.

One thing I forgott, which is this, that Fa[ther] Simon[640] understands that the court there inclineth to make a stranger bishop here, no French nor Spanniard but an Italian. To this you know what answer to make, for the thing hath many inconveniences with it, besides the impossibility of finding a fitt person truly apostolicall and indifferent. The State will be jealouse of it, the clergy disgraced by it, the laity unsatisfied, and no other good but confirmation etc*etera*.

So with hast adieu, for one staies for my letter. 18 Januar[y] 1633.

No address.

Endorsed: Clerk. 18 Jan[uary] 1633.
>   About the clergye forsaken by the laity.
>   About M[r] Druryes comedye.
>   About an externe to be made bishop.

---

[636] Walter Montagu, *The Shepheard's Paradise. A Comedy* (1629 [i.e. 1659]). See Birch, *CT*, II, pp. 214, 216; cf. *CSPV, 1632–1636*, p. 28; JPN, p. 292; K. Sharpe, *Criticism and Compliment* (Cambridge, 1987), pp. 29–31, 39–44. See also M. Foster, 'Walter Montague, courtier, diplomat and abbot, 1603–77 – I', *Downside Review*, 69 (1978), pp. 85–102, at pp. 93–94.

[637] 10 January 1633.

[638] See Birch, *CT*, II, pp. 189, 195.

[639] On 25 October/4 November 1632 Smith had reported to Rome that Southcot had written to him that 'pursuivants were busie in the streets but entered not much into houses'. The notorious James Wadsworth had 'accosted a priest' and yet the priest 'was not so much as arreigned' at the next sessions; AAW, B 27, no. 133.

[640] Thomas Dawson (Simon Stock) ODC.

33. R. E. [Richard East] to [Richard Smith], 6 February 1633

[*AAW, A XXVII, no. 6, pp. 15–16*]

My best lord,

I joy much when I heere of your lordship and of your good health, but the compleat joy would be to ly at your feet heere and injoy your holy blessing, soe much desired by your obedient flock which now groweth dayly st[r]onger by the apparent and impudent impiety of your adversaryes. Bitowattus[641] is even cried downe by his owne side and such lords as heer to fore upheald him, they now saying that hee is a bold and impudent fellow, and withall confesse that hee is a Jes[uit] as they verely thinke.[642]

Foster, soe busy there with you, is comming home, his wife having obtayned leave of the threasurour[643] for his returne, by reason of setling his owne meanes in the North, which are sett upon the tenterhookes as shee sayth by the president.[644] Whether this bee a trick or noe I know not, but shee pretends that unlesse shee could have gotten leave for her husband to have come over shee would have gon to him. This I understand by a servant of hers who came to Mr Hill to aske his advise whether shee should goe with her if she went. I beseech you lett Mr Fitton[645] know that ~~the~~ <a> comedy called the Antibishop[646] is now much in the mouth of your adversaryes. Hee must know that hee [*sic for* the] auctor, who soe ever it was, is but gessed at by them, that it nameth noe man, that it was written in the heat of theire bookes and when the Spongia[647] called the bishops of France assembled [*p. 16*] crocitantes ranunculas lacus Lemanuque. Besides, the coppyes which they now disperse are very much corrupted and made to speake many absurdityes which the first manuscript hath not. And they have done this of purpose to procure a censure agaynst it at Rome, which they say they will doe, which will sound heere very ridiculous.

More over hee must know there is a pamphlett going through hands here called Meditations upon the Jesuits which compares them and their actions to the Pharasies, and to the present puritans.

---

[641] Sir Tobie Mathew. See Gossett, *Hierarchomachia*, p. 17.

[642] Mathew was not, in fact, a Jesuit. He was a secular priest who was sympathetic towards the Society of Jesus.

[643] Sir Richard Weston, 1st Baron Weston, created earl of Portland on 17 February 1633.

[644] Sir Thomas Wentworth, 1st Viscount Wentworth, lord president of the council in the North. For Richard Forster's journey to, and return from, France, see *CSPV, 1632–1636*, pp. 99, 102.

[645] Peter Biddulph.

[646] *Hierarchomachia*. See *Letter 32*.

[647] Floyd, *Hermanni Loemelii [...] Spongia [...]*.

It is generally thought this is theire owne doing and sett forth by some follower of theires, and now to make envy they cast it upon the clergy, and some say Mr East made it, which is a most notorious ly invented by them agaynst that servant of yours, whom they hate. Cave et angue peius.

This last weeke a body was found in the Churche of Canterbury. It was wrapped in lead. Being opened there was a bishop in his pontificalibus, mighter, crosier, coape, upon his breast a fayre chalis of gold with the paten upon it. In the chalis was the bishops hart, intier, but the body was consumed to the boanes. The inscription was Richardus Cantuariensis.⁶⁴⁸ This holy bishop is sayd to bee the immediat successor to St Thomas. The king hath the chalis and the hart in it.

I have tired your lord shipp. Therfore I only aske a blessing and rest, this 6 of Feb[ruary].

Your ever most obedient child,

R.E.

No address.

[*on p. 15*]

Endorsed: East. 6 Feb[ruary].
    About the Antiepiscopus.⁶⁴⁹

34. Clerk [John Southcot] to [Peter Biddulph], 8 February 1633

[*AAW, A XXVII, no. 7, pp. 17–20*]

Sir,

The last week I sent you the later part of the summarium⁶⁵⁰ and a note⁶⁵¹ of such priests regular and secular as live in <or about> London to which you may add these: 1. Bonham⁶⁵² 2. Altham⁶⁵³ 3. Holland⁶⁵⁴

---

⁶⁴⁸ Richard of Dover, who died on 16 February 1184.

⁶⁴⁹ Although this letter is clearly addressed to Richard Smith, this endorsement appears to be in Biddulph's hand.

⁶⁵⁰ AAW, A XXVI, no. 161 ('Summarium de Rebus Religionis in Anglia 1632' – in five sections: 'De Persecutione'; 'De Regina aliisque Catholicis'; 'De Rege et Ministris regiis'; 'De Missionariis'; and, as an appendix, 'Quid sentiendum de necessitate Episcopi in Anglia?').

⁶⁵¹ AAW, A XXVI, no. 164.

⁶⁵² John Alexander Evison SJ.

⁶⁵³ John Grosvenor SJ.

⁶⁵⁴ Presumably Guy Holland SJ, who was based in London; CRS, 75, p. 209.

4. Jennison[655] <5. Wood>,[656] Jesuits; Peter Wilford,[657] Chaundler,[658] Benedictines; Ed[ward] Manning[659] a sec[ular] pr[iest] but suspected to be a Jes[uit], and one Crisp a fallen young priest that came 3 yeares since from Sevile ~~and fell~~ and married <here> within the first yeare he came over.[660] Nowe I send you notes of Sussex and Lincolnshire, having receaved them first, and I shall send you the like of other shires as soon as they are sent to me, having written for them.

I was yesterday with Fa[ther] Phil[ip] and shewed him the summarium, who hath advised us to shew the king that which toucheth him therin, not doubting but it will do the clergy good, and so we intend to do by a meanes that wilbe found if fitt for that purpose. Mr Colleton was tould within these two daies that my lord of London[661] saied openly ~~at his table~~ <to some freinds of his> not long since, that if he were as the king he would rather have the Catholickes governed by a bishop than otherwise, or than by the Jesuitts (for I heard it both waies reported), and he gave this reason, bycause, saieth he, if the bishop be a quiett man and a lover of his country, the king may be the securer by his government of all his Catholick subjects. This is a good point to be informed there with the first. You shall receave with these a letter from a good priest[662] that is placed with the best Catholick noble man of England,[663] which you may do well to shew to his Hollinesse or the Congregacion. The next week perhaps you shall have the same in Latin, if the party have so much leasure, yet I cannot promise it certainly.

This daie a certaine lawier[664] that brake the church windowes at Salisbury in contempt of images is to be censured in the star chamber. Not long since, there was a minister of Essex[665] that, preaching at Cambridg, in the prayer of his sermon praied God either to convert the queen or confound her, for which he hath bin deeply censured in the high commission court and degraded.[666] The king is so much offended with him for it that he threatneth to hang him. There is also a plea

---

[655] Presumably Robert Jenison SJ. See CRS, 74, p. 178.

[656] Not identified.

[657] Peter (Boniface) Wilford OSB. Wilford was a prominent opponent of Richard Smith; AAW, A XX, no. 159, p. 602.

[658] Boniface Chandler OSB.

[659] See Anstr., II, p. 373.

[660] See ibid., pp. 75–76; Letter 7.

[661] William Laud.

[662] William Case.

[663] John Paulet, 5th marquis of Winchester.

[664] Henry Sherfield. See Sharpe, PR, pp. 345–348.

[665] Nathaniel Bernard, 'late lecturer at St Sepulchre's Church', Birch, CT, II, p. 225.

[666] For Bernard's sermon, see also ibid.; Milton, CR, p. 171; PRO, 31/9/127, p. 42. In February 1633 Smith noted that 'from England they write that a minister', i.e. Bernard,

commenced in the exchequer court against twelve men, 4 ministers, 4 lawiers, and 4 marchants, who had a plott to keep up certaine impropriations of benefices in many places of the land, and therby to sett up the silenced ministers againe, but the plott being discovered all wilbe forfeited to the king, and perhaps the parties also censured in the star chamber.[667] The Lady Wootton, a Catholick baronesse of Kent,[668] is censured in 500[li] fine by the high commission, through the malice of some, for putting the word Catholick uppon her husbands tombe and not consenting to take it away againe <her self>, with order to have that word blotted out by the officers.[669] My lord martiall[670] is [p. 18] come home without the Lady Elizabeth,[671] and is commended by the king for the [word deleted] good service which he did in Holland in discovering something which the king knew not before. He was but couldly entertained there, his person not being gratefull to that State, nor some of the compaghny that were with him, particulerly Sir William Monson, sometimes viceadmirall of the narrow seas of England.[672] Many lords and others of quality both Protestants and Catholickes are to be sued in the starr chamber for breaking the proclamation about not residing in London out of terme time, and it is thought the king will gett much mony therby, as also by the other proclamation about fasting daies, especially the Lent.[673] Two daies agoe the Polonian ambassador (sonn to Duke Rochevile a Protestant, and the greatest subject in Poland),[674] had audience of the king and made a Latin oration of half an hower long, which was well liked.[675]

'was convented before the high commission for calling the pope knave in a sermon'; AAW, B 27, no. 116.

[667] For the case brought by the crown against the Feoffees for Impropriations, see R. Ashton, *The City and the Court, 1603–1643* (Cambridge, 1979), pp. 193–194; I.M. Calder (ed.), *The Activities of the Puritan Faction of the Church of England* (London, 1957).

[668] Margaret (Wharton), wife of Edward Wotton, 1st Baron Wotton.

[669] See A.J. Loomie, 'A Jacobean Crypto-Catholic: Lord Wotton', *Catholic Historical Review*, 53 (1967), pp. 328–345, at p. 344; William Laud, *The Works of William Laud*, J. Bliss and W. Scott (eds), 7 vols (Oxford, 1847–1860), V, p. 311.

[670] Thomas Howard, 2nd earl of Arundel. See Birch, *CT*, II, p. 212.

[671] Princess Elizabeth, widow of the Elector Palatine, Frederick V. See *CSPV, 1632–1636*, pp. 75–76, 77.

[672] For Sir William Monson's hostility to the Dutch, see BL, Harleian MS 4113 ('A Discoverie of the Hollanders Trade of Fishinge, and the circumventing us therein [...]. Written by Sir William Munson knt, sometyme vice admiral of England, and now in agitation togeather with his Majest[ie]s Letters Pattents for the Execution of the same, An[no] Domini 1632').

[673] See *Letter 18*.

[674] Janusz Radziwill, son of Krzysztof Radziwill. See *CSPV, 1632–1636*, pp. 74, 77, 78; Birch, *CT*, II, pp. 167, 168, 226; Loomie, *Ceremonies of Charles I*, pp. 134–137.

[675] The ambassador's principal purpose was to report the demise of King Sigismund III, and the election of his son Vladislaus in his place; *CSPV, 1632–1636*, p. 77; Loomie, *Ceremonies of Charles I*, pp. 134–137.

I heare that in his privat discourse afterward with the king he complained of the Jesuitts of Poland that would have hindered this kings election, wherat the king was much mooved.

The Jesuits followers invaigh much against two writings that goe about here under hand. The one is a certaine comedy[676] wherin the opposers of the bishop are made ridiculous. The other is called a <u>Meditation of the Jes[uits] proceedings in England to the greate glory of God</u>,[677] wherin they are paralelled with the Pharisees and puritans, plainly but wittily enough. Of the peace between the clergy and the Benedictines I can write noe more bycause I have not heard from the monkes since I wrote therof last unto you.

Thus with all wonted salutes, I rest. 8 February 1633.

M[r] Laborne is here in office againe, and will correspond weekly with you hereafter.

Since Christmasse at Canterbury there was found an ould tombe of 400 yeares standing wherin an archbishop of Canterbury was buried in his pontificall attire and a silver chali[c]e and paten in his hand (not <of> gould as I was first informed). The chalice is yet extant, but the body and attire went to dust presently being touched. His name was Richard, the second of that name.[678]

I pray do me the kindnesse to procure me the 2[d] part of Cardinal Bentivoglios Relationi, which I heare is not to be gotten in Paris.[679] [p. 19]

<u>Sussex</u>

Benjamin Norton	
N Rogers[681]	
Edw[ard] Kenion	secul[ar] pr[iests]
N Brough[682]	
N Smith[684]	

<u>Sussex</u>

N. Smith[680]	
Andr[ew] White	Jesuits
N Johnson[683]	Benedictine
N. Perott[685]	Franciscan

[676] *Hierarchomachia.* See *Letter 32*.

[677] See *Letter 33*.

[678] See *Letter 33*.

[679] See *Letter 15*.

[680] Not identified.

[681] Not identified.

[682] Identity uncertain. This is probably a reference to the priest Richard Burgh who signed AAW, A XXIV, no. 167. See Anstr., II, p. 370. See also *NAGB*, p. 41 (where this priest may be wrongly identified as Richard Broughton).

[683] William Johnson OSB.

[684] This is probably the priest John Smith who, with Richard Burgh, signed AAW, A XXIV, no. 167. See Anstr., II, p. 374.

[685] George Perrott (George of St William) OFM. See Dockery, *CD*, pp. 29, 41.

N Williams[686]
N Anderton[687]
Geo[rge] Gage[688]
Peter Warnford
Richard Lane   } secul[ar] pr[iests]
Thomas Fathers
Anto[ny] Shelley
N Hanson[689]
Will[iam] Shelley

Lincolnshire

Henry Green
Will[iam] Hedlame[690]   } sec[ular] pr[iests]

N Man[691]   Benedictine

Christoph[er] Cancefield[692]
N. Thompson[693]
N. Neale[694]   } Jesuitts
Joh[n] Albin[695]
N Wentworth[696]

No address.

[*on p. 20*]

Endorsed: Clerk. 8 Feb[ruary] 1633.
              About the Jesuitts that live in London.
              About the bishop of London his speach concerning haveing
              bishops.
              A catalogue of priests in Sussex and Lincolnshire.

---

[686] Not identified.
[687] George Gorsuch.
[688] See Anstr., II, pp. 121–124. Gage joined Henrietta Maria's entourage at the same time as George Leyburn was taken into her service.
[689] Thomas Smith, alias Hansom.
[690] John (or William) Headlam. See Anstr., II, p. 154.
[691] Not identified.
[692] Brian Cansfield, alias Christopher Benson. See CRS, 74, pp. 134–135.
[693] Richard Thompson SJ. See CRS, 75, p. 312.
[694] Robert Neale SJ. See *ibid.*, p. 250.
[695] 'Albin' is an alias. This individual cannot be identified with certainty.
[696] No contemporary Jesuit is known to have had either the name or alias of Wentworth. John (Dunstan) Pettinger OSB used the alias of Wentworth.

35. Clerk [John Southcot] to [Peter Biddulph], 15 February 1633

[*AAW, A XXVII, no. 14, pp. 43-44*]

Sir,

This week I receaved yours of the last of December and I shall be glad to receave that relation from my lord[697] of Sign*or* Ingoli w*h*ich you mention, although as yet I have not received from <him> the compendium of that information mentioned in y*our* former letters. Concerning an English card[inal], if it could be obtained by the [*six words obliterated*]. We will try that way w*h*ich you advise as soon [as] we can by the qu[een] and Card[inal] Richel[ieu]. The last week I sent you [a] lett[er], from a priest that live[s] in the country,[698] w*h*ich you may do well to translate and shew there for it may do much good, we being to heare what is resolved by his Hol[iness] upo*n* the qu[een's] letter.

This day sennight there was a fam[ou]s star chamber cause heard and adjudged ag*ain*st one Charfield,[699] recorder of Salisbury and a justice of peace there, who brake down the painted glasse window of a church in that citty. He was condemned by the court in a fine of 500[li] and injoined to cry peccavi at the same place <where he offended> and putt from his recordership and justiceship. Many of the l*or*ds and especially the two b*isho*ps of York and London spake much in behalf of images w*h*ich was much admired at especially by the puritans.

There was a minister of Essex[700] also fined in the high com*m*ission court a little before, and degraded for praying in his sermon publickly either to convert or confound the queen, and the king, as I heare, was so offended at it that he threatneth to hang him.[701]

The other buissenesse of the 12 men putt in trust w*i*th 40 thousand pounds to be employed for the releef and setting up of lecturers and silenced ministers is also ended in the exchequer court, but not w*i*th that rigor w*h*ich was expected. They are only injoyned to ~~spend~~ employ the mony in a legall way to the use of the Church and w*i*th approbation of the b*isho*p or ordinary of the place.[702]

---

[697] Richard Smith.
[698] See *Letter 34*.
[699] Henry Sherfield. See *Letter 34*.
[700] Nathaniel Bernard.
[701] See *Letter 34*.
[702] For the Feoffees for Impropriations, see *Letter 34*.

It is expected that my lord treasurer, uppon the rettourne of his sonn home, shall be made an earle. The Jes[uits'] followers give it out that we shall shortly have a persecution, perhaps to terrify only and to hinder his Hol[iness's] resolution about our bishop whose rettourne they feare. Duke Rachevile his sonn that was a student [*p. 44*] at Leyden in Holland is come over hither from thence as ambassador from the king of Poland, and is not yet gonn.[703] We heare of no other certaine buissenesse he hath but only to advertise the kings election which (as some say) he tould our king that the Jes[uits] would have hindered [*six lines illegible*] number be known there, and therfor use your discretion therin.

Thus referring the rest to M[r] Lab[orne], I end. 15 Febr[uary] 1633.

<u>Essex</u>

Th[omas] Gooch Tho[mas] Barker Rob[ert] Ducket James Everard Alban East[704] Thomas Green James Thoro[u]ghgood	secul[ars]
Henry More Henry Coppinger Nicholas Shepeard N. Palmer George Ward Thomas Keel[705] N. Morly[706]	Jesu[its]
George Bacon	Bened[ictine]

---

[703] See *Letter 34*.
[704] Brother of Richard East. See Anstr., II, p. 92.
[705] See *Letter 78*.
[706] George Morley. See CRS, 75, p. 246.

Hantshire

D[octor] Tempest[707]
Onuphrius Hide[708]
N. Cole senior[709]
N. Cole junior
Will[iam] Morgan[710]   } secul[ars]
N. Brown[711]
N. Clinch[712]
Will[iam] Nelstrop[713]
Dr Will[iam] Wright[714]

Will[iam] Palmer
Georg Gore   } Benedict[ines]

Edward Walpole
Thomas Burton[715]
Jo[hn] Bamfield[716]   } Jesuit[s]
Tho[mas] Shelley
N Bentley[717]
N. Man[718]

---

[707] This may be a reference to Robert Tempest SJ, who died in Hampshire in July 1640. See Anstr., I, pp. 349–350. Tempest is listed here as a secular priest, although he had entered the Society in 1624. He was the only English priest named Tempest at this time who is definitely known to have held a doctorate. However, a letter from the Jesuit general, Muzio Vitelleschi, in December 1623 referred to Dr Edward Tempest, apparently the secular priest who had been involved in the anti-Jesuit disturbances in the English college in Rome in 1595–1596 (*ibid.*, pp. 348–349). The man listed here may, in fact, be him; ARSJ, Anglia MS 1/i, fo. 187r.

[708] Humphrey Hyde. See Anstr., II, p. 166.

[709] See *ibid.*, p. 67; Anstr., I, p. 82. At this time there were three priests named Cole (Edward, Edmund, and Thomas).

[710] William Case.

[711] This is probably the priest John Browne who signed AAW, A XXIV, no. 163. See Anstr., II, p. 370.

[712] Presumably either Henry or John Clinch. See Anstr., I, p. 81.

[713] See Anstr., II, pp. 230, 373.

[714] Richard Wright. See *ibid.*, p. 367.

[715] John Baron. He had been ordained in 1630 and had left the English college in Rome in September 1632. He entered the Society in 1633 at Watten; CRS, 74, p. 132; Anstr., II, p. 17; *Letter 40*.

[716] John (or Thomas) Rogers. See CRS, 75, pp. 283–284; Anstr., II, p. 269.

[717] Edward Bentley. See CRS, 74, pp. 117–118.

[718] Not identified.

The only charge which was given my lord keeper at the end of the terme to the judges was to look to the execution of the two late proclamations about fasting daies and restraint from London.[719] Nothing about recusants at all. Another proclamation is expected to forbid all soldiers to serve forrain princes without speciall leave.

No address.

Endorsed: Clerk. 15 Feb[ruary].
          The catalogue [*three words obliterated*].
          Essex [*two or three words obliterated*].

36. Clerk [John Southcot] to [Peter Biddulph], 1 March 1633

[*AAW, A XXVII, no. 18, pp. 51–52*]

Sir,

I receaved one this weeke from you of the 15th of January wherin you mention not that you omitted to write the week before, and yet we receaved none of that weekes date, the last we had bearing date the 31 of December, so that I feare one of yours of the 7th or 8 of January is miscaried. We are all glad to heare that the qu[een's] letter hath wrought so good [an] effect in his Hol[iness] and we will do our best to see whether we can procure an other from her Majesty to the same purpose that may be written with the same hand, which was not her own, but an others, yet the subscription was written with her own hand. I ame sory St Onophrio[720] is one of the 3 for he is much directed by his order, and they are not our freinds. It falleth out unhappely that Balneo[721] is out of Rome at this time. We shalbe glad to heare the good successe of that information which you gave up, the compendium wherof I have not yet seen, and I feare my lord[722] hath lost it. That letter from the nonce[723] to Ingoli will add much creditt to it. I like well that his Hol[iness] did insinuat a desire of having my lord to come up to assist there with his advise and counsaile touching English affaires, and I wish he were there indeed, if it be only to that end, and not spoken in policy to draw him away from the place where he is. But the chief difficulty wilbe waunt of meanes unlesse the cardinal[724]

---

[719] See *Letter 18*.
[720] Cardinal Antonio Barberini, a Capuchin and brother of Urban VIII.
[721] Cardinal Giovanni Francesco Guido del Bagno.
[722] Richard Smith.
[723] Cardinal Alessandro Bichi.
[724] Cardinal Richelieu.

provide some priory or abby for him in France, for I would not have him expect anything in that kind from his Hol[iness] least it be a tye to him and make him the lesse welcome.[725]

I can advertise you of little newes from hence more than what I wrote the last week. My lord martiall[726] hath pleased the king well with the service he did him lately in Holland, and so he is <in> good grace and favour with his Majesty and shalbe presently made lord steward of the k[ing's] househould. I wrote to you last week that my lord treasurer[727] was made earle of Portland upon the 17 of the last month.[728] Some say that Sir Toby Mathew is sworne of the k[ing's] privy chamber, but I do not beleeve it, bycause by the ordinary course he must first take the oath of supremacy and alleageance.[729] The fishing buissenesse goeth on amaine.[730] But the <new> sopeboilers are like to break againe as I heare.[731] The Lord Baltimor goeth on lickwise with a new plantation in Virginia, and most that goe I think are Catholicks and freinds to the Jes[uits] who send two of theirs to be their ghostly fathers, Fa[ther] Andrew White and Fa[ther] Alexander Baker. I understand for certaine by one that hath many times privat conference with the k[ing] that he is well persuaded of all the Cath[olic] tenets, but when he talketh with any Protest[ant] minister or other [p. 52] he is presently drawn of[f] againe, but yet the same party saieth that he is not against bishops and might be soon persuaded to admitt of them, and to think them convenient for the government of his Cath[olic] subjects. He read also lately that part of the summarium[732] which concerns persecution and his own person, and was well pleased with it, as the party tould me. We have had no searching of houses by pursevants of late, so that we think their commissions are taken from them or els some restraint is made. True it is they catch now and then some pr[iests] in the street and lett them goe againe for mony. It is reported that my lord keeper,[733] who is a great favorer of the puritans, is like to loose his place shortly, and some think that my lord of London shall

---

[725] For Richelieu's financial patronage of Smith, see Allison, RSGB, II, pp. 248–251; J. Bergin, *Cardinal Richelieu: Power and the Pursuit of Wealth* (London, 1985), p. 213.

[726] Thomas Howard, 2nd earl of Arundel.

[727] Sir Richard Weston, 1st earl of Portland.

[728] *CSPV, 1632–1636*, p. 80; Alexander, *CLT*, pp. 33, 39, 105, 119.

[729] There seems to be no evidence that Mathew received any such appointment. But Walter Yonge noted on 30 March 1633 that 'Mathewe who was thought to bee a Jesuite or priest was sworne of the k[ing's] bedchamber'; BL, Additional MS 35331, fo. 51v. See also *Letter 37*.

[730] For rivalry with the Dutch over fishing, see Loomie, 'The Spanish faction at the court of Charles I, 1630–8', pp. 38–39; Sharpe, *PR*, pp. 101–102, 250–251.

[731] See *ibid.*, pp. 121–123, for soap manufacture and patents.

[732] See *Letter 34*.

[733] Sir Thomas Coventry, 1st Baron Coventry.

succeed him therin.[734] The kings journy to Scotland still houlds, and there is much preparation made for it.

I wrote to you before that a third part of London Bridge to the number of 60 houses was burnt by accident on the 12 day of February last.[735]

Touching the burgesses of the parlament I can not informe you of the certaine number, but those towns that have the priviledge to elect burgesses do commonly elect two. The lower house commonly consists of 400 persons in all or thereabouts. I sent to buy a table wherin were the names of those that were elected throughout England in the last parlament, but my man could not find any coppy left but in lieu therof I send you a table of those of the upper house with their titles and armes. This is what now occurreth to me. The rest you shall have from Monsieur Fountaine[736] who is in office againe, and intends to write weekly to you.

1 March 1632.

The dutchesse of Buckingham commenceth a suite against her uncle the now earle of Rutland to recover he[r] fathers land to which she pretends to be heire, being his only daughter and child, and it is thought she will prevaile bycause the king and councell doe favour her.[737]

The Jes[uits] do give out here that <one> Anthony Smith a fallen pr[iest] divulgeth copies of the comedy called the Antibishop,[738] but the truth is he <was> no secular pr[iest] but a Jesuitt and while he was Jes[uit], as I heare, he had children for which cause they putt him out and, since, he hath taken a wench or two, and hath had, I heare, ten children. He was priested among the Jes[uits] and read figures at St Omers.

---

[734] The Venetian ambassador, Vicenzo Gussoni, on 15/25 March 1633 observed that William Laud, bishop of London, was seeking to 'obtain the charge of the great seal, to the exclusion and ruin of the lord keeper, who is manoeuvring in opposition'. Gussoni believed his 'fall is near', but Coventry retained his post; *CSPV, 1632–1636*, p. 86. By contrast, Walter Yonge noted that Coventry was 'putt out of his place upon some difference betweene him and Sir Rich[ard] Weston [...] but [is] restored againe'; BL, Additional MS 35331, fo. 51r. Subsequently, in July 1633, Yonge wrote in his diary that Coventry was 'like to be putt from his place', apparently because of his support for Henry Sherfield; *ibid.*, fo. 54r.

[735] See *CSPV, 1632–1636*, p. 81; Birch, *CT*, II, p. 167; BL, Additional MS 35331, fo. 51r.

[736] George Leyburn.

[737] George Garrard informed Viscount Wentworth on 3 June 1634 that 'the dutchess of Buckingham and the earl of Rutland are come to an agreement: he hath for his life 7000l. a year to live on, legacies and annuities are parted betwixt them: Belvoir and 2000l. goes to the heir, Mr. John Manners [...] all the rest falls upon the dutchess and her children after her'; Knowler, *ESLD*, I, p. 261.

[738] *Hierarchomachia*. See *Letter 32*.

No address.

Endorsed: Clerk. 1° Mart[ii].
About one Smith who divulgeth the Antibishop.

37. Fountayne [George Leyburn] to [Peter Biddulph], 1 March 1633

[*AAW, A XXVII, no. 19, pp. 53–54*]

Respected sir,

This inclosed will answere unto yours written the 15 of Jan[uary] which was full of comfort and good hopes. This daye I have imparted unto Monsieur Ph[ilip] the cheef contents, who will acquainte her Majesty with as much as concerneth her. And I am confident that I shall procure new commendations of the affayre both to his Holynes and to Monsieur Chrichey[739] who is to goe extraordinarie from the king of France.[740] If episcopall authority were once established, this country I doe assure my selfe would be most happie. In my former I did signifie such occurrences as the tymes did yeeld and, since, ther is noe great variety. I was informed by a person of great worth that Sir Tobie[741] was admitted of the kings bed <privie> chamber wherupon I did repaire unto our two good friends at the court who had not heard any such newes. Moreover they did assure me that neither the king nor queen maketh any esteeme of him and as often as ther is any speech of him they gyre and mocke at him. They did alsoe relate unto me a very strang[e] conversion of one Mr Godbolt, brother unto Mr Godbolt whos wife is rocker to our prince, both good Catholikes. This Godbolt was newly arrived from a sea voiage wher he had been rob[be]d pillaged and becom[e]d so w[e]ake with miserie that ther were smale hopes of his recovery, which his brother perceaving delt very earnestly with him about his conversion, but he, an obstinate heretick, would give no eare, and cheefly in regarde he could never persuade him selfe that the body of our saviour Christ could be truly and really in the sacrament (which he knew to be a

---

[739] Charles de Blanchefort de Créquy, duke of Créquy. See *CSPV, 1632–1636*, p. 126; Pastor, *HP*, XXVIII, p. 327.

[740] On 1/11 February 1633 Richard Smith reported to Peter Biddulph that Cardinal Richelieu would give instructions to Créquy 'who is shortly to goe extraordinarie embass[ador] to R[ome] to deale for me'; AAW, B 27, no. 116.

[741] Sir Tobie Mathew. See *Letter 36*.

cheef poynt of the Catho[lic] religion). He could not imagine how
soe great a body could be contayned in soe litle a space. His brother
seeing his perversnes [and] dispearing of his conversion did leave
him and he was noe sooner gone but that the woman who did tend
upon him, a peevish heretick, did in her fashion encourage him to
remayne constant and, the better to confirme him, she gott one of
the 2 ministers of the chappell at St James to come unto him, and he
was [p. 54] noe sooner entered into his chamber but that he beganne
to relate unto him how his brother had delt with him and how he
would have persuaded him that the body of Christ was really in
the sacrament, to which the minister replyed that it was very true
doctrine and that he was bound to believe it, and withall he added that
the Catholike religion was a good religion in soe much that he presently
sent for his brother, desired a priest, was reconsiled and immediately
after departed this life. The great goodnes of God towards this poore
creature [sic]. I doe assure you unfainedly that I am of opinion that
we shall see shortly an other face of religion in this country. And
abstracting from some private reasons to move therunto which I dare
not committ to writing I doo see evidently that the byshop of London[742]
and of Yorke[743] and divers others who run with them (which are many
because London haith very great power with our king) doth finde that
ther predecessours have been much defective in 3 poynts. The first is
that they did abandon confessions,[744] the second that they did reject
all ceremonyes without which ther Church is without majesty, and the
third is that they did take away all kinde of worship and honour to
pictures.

The Jesuists keep a great doe about the comedy[745] and I heare that
they have translated it into Italyen but very untruely as many doe
imagine. My maister[746] formerly haith instructed you how you are to
make your answere and therfor it is not needfull that I saye any more.
Onely signifie the tyme when it was composed, in the very heat of the
controversie and by an unknowne author, how my lord did suppresse
it untill now that the Jesuists gott a copie of it and did divulge it; and
you may justly accept [sic] against the translation. Here is one Smith[747]

[742] William Laud.
[743] Richard Neile.
[744] For the significance to English 'Arminians' of the practice of confession, see Tyacke,
AC, pp. 221–222.
[745] Hierarchomachia. See Letter 32.
[746] Richard Smith.
[747] Anthony Smith.

a falne Jesuit. Besyds the scandale is like to doe much hurt.[748] This is all, onely my best wishes for your happie successe in all your affayres.

Your obedient servant, Fountayne.

London. March 1th 1632.

No address.

Endorsed: Lab[orne]. 1 March.
About the Antib*ish*op.

38. Clerk [John Southcot] to [Peter Biddulph], 6 March 1633

[AAW, A XXVII, no. 21, pp. 57–58]

Sir,

This week I receaved two togeather from you, videlicet of the 8 of January w*hich* was missing the last week, as I then wrote unto you, and of the 22 of the same month. Y*our* advise touching a French agent there for the qu[een] is very well liked of here, and I hope good use wilbe made of it to hinder any such desighne, by F[ather] Phil[ip's] meanes, who saieth that the qu[een] never wrote yet for Sig*nor* Georgio[749] to that purpose you speake of in y*our* letter. Yet I cannot but think that there is some such intention and that the Jes[uit] faction here ~~do~~ have some such practise in hand. The French ambass[ador][750] here and the grand aulmner[751] runn an other course different from Fa[ther] Philips, by occasion of the Capucins whom this ambassador thought to have putt in Fa[ther] Philips place, but Fa[ther] Phil[ip] stands upon to[o] good grounds to be putt out by him, for the king and queen both love him, and so do all the courtiers, and therfor I make account he is sure of the place as long as he liveth, unlesse he come to some other preferment w*hich* is likely enough he may ere long, and for my part I could wish he were a cardinall and lived in Rome, where he might do his king and contry and us all much good service. How to deale in this matter about an English card[inall] I do not well know, bycause it is a buissenesse of a high nature, and things are not handsomly prepared

---

[748] Richard Smith rather shamelessly took up and pursued the story spread by the ex-Jesuit Anthony Smith that John Gerard SJ had been directly involved in the gunpowder plot, digging the, in the end unused, mine under the palace of Westminster. See Allison, JG.

[749] George Con.

[750] François Duval, marquis de Fontenay Mareuil.

[751] Jacques le Noël Du Perron.

for it. What clergy men to propose, and by what meanes, we cannot resolve without some help and advise. And indeed it is a matter that requires consultation from the chiefest of the clergy, who are not now assembled togeather, nor are like to be till Easter terme at the soonest, and yet the buissenesse requires that secresy that it were better to do it without any great consultation, I meane without communicating the matter to many, if it were possible. The likeliest way in my opinion is to gett the queen mooved by some letter from the French king to that purpose in behalf of one of those that shalbe named and then leave it to Fa[ther] Phil[ip's] solicitation with her Majesty. The fittest man in all respects (if we leave out my lord[752] by reason of his age) is in my opinion M[r] Blacklo,[753] who hath eminent parts for it, and is like to live long, having a healthy and strong body. Only I feare the Spaniards wilbe drawen to oppose him, unlesse it be donn sodainly, by reason of an exception taken here lately by the Spanish resident[754] to some speach of his (falsely related unto him) in behalf of France against Spaine, for which he threatneth to write against him into Spaine, to have him putt from his residentship and although the relation be false, and both M[r] Blacklo and we have sought to satisfy him, he will take no satisfaction. He is wholy for the Jes[uits] and this is supposed to be donn by their instigation.

I pray God Signor Georgio be not offended with you for getting his card[inal][755] to ~~name~~ appoint you an othe to receave your informations of England. If he be [word illegible] by this, [p. 58] or by any other disgust taken, I feare he will do us much harme there in that court. Lett us therfor seek to preserve him at least from being our enemy.

We have drawen a French letter from my lord to the queen to entreat her favour for an other letter to Rome in his behalf, and I feare our buissenesse will not be ended before we gett [two words deleted] an other letter from her Majesty. Yet I pray solicit what you can to gett a dispatch speedily, and if any new delay grow upon the expectation either of a new letter from the qu[een] or of any agreement with the monkes, seek what you can to putt it of[f], for although the monkes, as I heare, were lately with M[r] Strong[756] at Do[uai] to offer peace, yet it is feared they do this in policy to stay the sentence at Rome, wherfor lett them be assured there that we shall never have peace here without a sentence there.

[752] Richard Smith.
[753] Thomas White.
[754] Juan de Necolalde.
[755] Cardinal Francesco Barberini, cardinal protector of the English nation, to whom George Con had served as secretary; Hibbard, CI, p. 46.
[756] Matthew Kellison.

I make account the reg[ulars] will know what is determined sooner than we shall, by St Onophrios[757] meanes, who doth nothing without the Capucins advise. It is like Fa[ther] Leonard[758] is by this time come to Rome, who is no freind of ours, no more are the rest of his brethren here.[759] There are some complaints of priests here in London against the Capucins for drawing their penitents from them and for bringing in new customes about confessing (as they do in Italy) by a cathalogue of sinns which the ghostly father readeth to the penitent. This is here much misliked as also the admitting any to come to their house, and <sometimes> into their cells (even women) under colour to be instructed, or the like, and their often marrieng <Catholickes>, and someti[m]es Cath[olics] and heret[ics] togeather, without giving no-tice or taking any advise from the superiors of the clergy.[760] When you have a fitt opportunity perhaps it were not amisse to lett these things be knowen to the congregacion that some order may be taken here.

Doctor Bossevile desires to know whether his <privat> letter to Urban were delivered or no.[761] I pray let us heare from you of that by the next, as also whether the bishop of Bellay[762] be come to Rome, and what he doeth there, <and> when he rettourneth. The names of <the> missionaries in Warwickshire I send you in a note here enclosed. Other occurrences I referr to Mr Laborne.

Adieu.

6 March 1633.

---

[757] Cardinal Antonio Barberini, a Capuchin and brother of Urban VIII.

[758] Provincial of the French Capuchins. See Hibbard, CI, p. 44.

[759] On 9 November 1632, however, Richard Worthington had suggested to Biddulph that Father Leonard should be petitioned to intervene in the Worthington–Parkins marriage case on William Worthington's behalf, and against the regulars; AAW, A XXVI, no. 13, p. 49.

[760] Gregorio Panzani recorded that Richard Smith had prohibited mixed marriages but 'li Capuccini congiungevano tutti et vennero scandali'. Charles, by Henrietta Maria's means, had now prohibited the Capuchins from marrying Catholics to Protestants; VA, PD, fo. 56r.

[761] See AAW, A XXVI, no. 117 (John Bosvile's letter of 20 August 1632 to Urban VIII, claiming that Rome had failed to sort out the troubles of the Catholics in England, and that the 'Protestatio Declaratoria' against Smith was a calumny).

[762] This is a reference to Jean-Pierre Camus, bishop of Belley (who had resigned in 1629), rather than to the current holder of that see, Jean de Passelaigue, a Cluniac monk. See Bergin, *The Making of the French Episcopate*, pp. 591, 680. Miles Pinckney had translated a work by Camus, his *Crayon de l'Eternité* (Douai, 1631) as *A Draught of Eternitie* (Douai, 1632), ARCR, II, no. 644. The translation was dedicated to Anne Arundell (wife of Thomas Arundell, 1st Baron Arundell), Smith's patroness. On 19/29 March 1632 Smith reported that 'the mendicants urge much to suppresse a booke of [the] bishop [of] Belley which toucheth their mendicity'; AAW, B 27, no. 107. Pinckney translated and published another book by Camus, his *Lutte Spirituelle*, as *A Spirituall Combat* (Douai, 1632), ARCR, II, no. 645, which he dedicated to Mary Percy, abbess of the English Benedictine convent at Brussels. Another work by Camus, his *Le Directeur Spirituel Désinteressé*, was translated by Lawrence Platt. See *Letter 9*.

I pray lett us know by your next wherfor the generall of the Dominicans[763] is in disgrace there.

I will cause those knives to be bought which you desire, and, if Mr Duckett go up, I will entreat him to bring them with him. But I doubt he can not bring a dogg.[764]

No address.

Endorsed: Clerk. 8 March.[765]
      Complaints against the Capucines.

39. Clerk [John Southcot] to Fitton [Peter Biddulph], 22 March 1633

[*AAW, B 47, no. 63*]

Sir,

This week we have had no letters from you. The last we had was of the 5 of February which I answered the last week. I have little newes to informe you this week. My lord ambassador Weston[766] is rettourned togeather with the duke of Lennox[767] his brother in law. Between Dover and Calais they, being in one of the k[ing's] ships, mett with a fleet of ten ships of the Hollanders who, not vailing bonett to the ki[ng's] ship, as they were bound by the custome of those seas, the k[ing's] ship [*word deleted*] shott of[f] a peec[e] of ordinance to give them warning, but they still went on their course without taking notice of any thing and, being againe warned with an other peece of ordinance, they sent up one of their ships and shot of[f] 4 peeces of ordinance against the k[ing's] ship and 30 muskets, wherupon the k[ing's] ship stered towards them and passing through the middest of them shot of[f] 36 peeces of ordinance, 18 on a side, on both sides of the Hollanders, and made some of their heads ake. The king is much offended with the Hollanders ~~with~~ <for> this affront, and purposeth to be revenged [*word deleted*] shortly.[768] Out of Yorkshire they certify that there are in all 40 missionaries or therabouts wherof 24 are secular, 6 Jes[uits], 6 Benedict[ines], and 2 newtralls that go for seculars. The next week

[763] Nicholas Ridolfi OP.
[764] See *Letters 32, 41, 46*.
[765] This letter was dated 6 March by Southcot but endorsed 8 March by Biddulph.
[766] Jerome Weston. *CSPV, 1632–1636*; p. 91; Birch, *CT*, II, p. 175.
[767] James Stuart, 4th duke of Lennox.
[768] For this incident, see *CSPV, 1632–1636*, pp. 92–93; Birch, *CT*, II, p. 175.

I purpose to send you some notes of such things as we desire here touching regulars.

Thus in hast I rest.

22 March 1633.

Addressed: Pour Mons*ieur* Fitton a Rome.

Endorsed: Clerk. 22 Mar[ch].
    The number of missionaries in Yorkshire.

40. Clerk [John Southcot] to [Peter Biddulph], 29 March 1633

[*AAW, B 47, no. 64*]

Sir,

I have yours this week of the 19th of February, and ame sory to heare that nothing wilbe donn in our buissenesse. Our brethren wilbe quite dishartned with this newes. What can we do more from hence than hath bin donn already? If neither the queens letter nor so many com*m*on letters from the clergy can prevaile, I see no other remedy but either my lo*r*d[769] must go up him self, or two or 3 of the auncient priests, w*h*ich will require a better purse than we have, or can make, unlesse my lo*r*d can procure something to be settled upon him in France before he goe. We will do our best notwithstanding to procure an other letter from the qu[een] if not to his Hol[iness] at least to Mons*ieur* Crequy the extraordinary ambassador who, I heare, is on his way already.[770] In the meane time I pray solicit and importune them all you can and make all the freinds you can to that end. For my part, unlesse my lo*r*d have health and meanes to go up, I should advise him, with leave of the nonce,[771] to come back againe hither, and possesse him self of his authority via facti, and beginn in things favorable, as for example by declaring the fasts and feasts of the country, and such like. No doubt he would be obaied, and then his Hol[iness] would also confirme him in it. Only I feare my lo*r*ds disposition, which is a little to[o] stiff and not so pliable and condescending as were fitting in such a case. And if this can not be donn, we must com*m*end our selves to the mercy of God and give over all <negotiation> and fall to writing bookes to make our cause knowen to the Christian world,

---

[769] Richard Smith.
[770] See *Letter 37*.
[771] Cardinal Alessandro Bichi.

as D[octor] Bossevile saied well in his letter to the pope,[772] which he would gladly know whether ever it were ~~receaved~~ <delivered> or noe. I receaved a letter lately from him where he writeth thus: 'I could wish my lord would urge much that the Jesuitts should not send any of ours[773] into England till we send for them, for if so many regulars come in as do, and may have power to send in such a number of ours at their pleasures (be they sufficient or insufficient), many must needs waunt places, and consequently will fall into waunts. If any oppose his motion upon pretence of waunt of priests in the country, or the like, answer may be made that the clergy wilbe content upon this condition, that regulars may take all such places as are voide for waunt of clergy men. I could wish also that regulars might be stinted to a certaine number. But I feare that would be harder to gett, and subject to more opposition, and, were it graunted, yet it would not free us so well as the other, nor make ours beyond the seas to stick to their body, and respect superiours here so well as when they shall know that their coming in depends upon the will of their superiours here. Againe, the reserving the administration of mariage to the clergy is of great importance, and hath great colour of reason for it, aswell bycause reg[ulars] do not do it in any country as also bycause being exempted from the bishop if they committ any abuse therin, the bishop can take no order.'[774] So he. Which are good points to be proposed togeather with those which I send you in an other Latin paper here enclosed, where you shall have the number of pr[iests] in Suffolk, Norfolk, Bedfordshire, Buckinghamshire and Hartfordshire.

Touching that matter wherof Mr Burton[775] wrote to Fa[ther] Fitzherbert, I suppose you have given a good answer already. The rector should ever advertise the bishop or his vicar either by letter or letters patents of the number, names and quality of those he sends, or at least he should be bound a month or two before to advertise this to the agent in Rome, wherfor I pray you stand hard for this, bycause it is a thing most reasonable. I ame tould that Burton and two more that came with him intend to be Jesuitts, and they keep no correspondence at all with the clergy. Only they came for their 40^s a peece and took the oath of their obedience to my lord, with what reservation God knoweth. It seemeth that the Jes[uits] do all they can to devide the clergy by sending in such priests, hoping in time to make them the greater number and so to keep the clergy at

---

[772] See AAW, A XXVI, no. 117; *Letter 38*.

[773] Secular priests.

[774] 'I could wish my lord [. . .] take no order' is underlined in the text.

[775] Presumably John Baron, alias Thomas Burton, cited in the list of Hampshire clergy in *Letter 35*.

their devotion. This must be in time lookt unto, and prevented by all meanes possible, either by that way D[octor] Bossevile suggested or by getting the seminaries into our hands. And I make no question but they are such striplings as these that give this information to Rome of persecution, upon the instigation perhaps of the Jes[uits] that are their freinds, and for their ends. As for Signor Giorgio[776] we know not what to say. The clergy will hardly be persuaded to commend him unlesse they see some reall cause of desert on his part towards them. Yet I will speak with Fa[ther] Phil[ip] about him and we will do our best in that which Fa[ther] Phil[ip] shall advise us.

For newes I can say little. The king would have borrowed mony of the citty, but they refused to lend him any, pretending waunt, especially since the restraint made by proclamation of resort <to London> ~~of compaghny~~. Now I heare it reported that the king will gett mony of the citizens as he did lately of the gentlemen in the country for their knighthoods, which will much trouble the citty. The lords of the councell have mooved all noblemen to a contribution for mending of Paules church, and every one offereth something: some 90ˡ, some more, some lesse.[777] The kings going to Scotland this summer holdeth still good. The fishing buissenesse goeth on apace.[778] One Coronell Hebron,[779] a Scottish man and a Catholik that served the k[ing] of Sweden at Lipsick,[780] is newly come over out of France to levy a Scottish regiment to serve in France where he hath a great pension.[781] Sir Morris Drummon[782] <a Catholick and> one of the qu[een's] gentlemen ushers is committed to the Tower for jusling my lord of Carlile, a privy counsellor, in the presence chamber. The king is much offended with the Hollanders for the affront they did our ambassador at sea, as I wrote to you the last week,[783] and I heare some souldiars are

[776] George Con.

[777] For the restoration of St Paul's, see Sharpe, *PR*, pp. 322–328. On 30 September 1632 Edmund Dutton had informed Biddulph that 'the lords are to give 40ˡⁱ or 50ˡⁱ a peece' towards the rebuilding. Charles asked Henrietta Maria 'what shee would bestow', and 'shee answered ten thowsand powndes', whereupon Charles 'gave her great thankes and commendacions for her bountie and said he would cause it to be proclaymed all the kingdome over'. But 'shee replyed that then he must graunt her the next suyt, which was that shee might dayly have two Masses celebrated in it, otherwise shee would not give a peny'; AAW, A XXVI, no. 155, p. 439.

[778] See *Letter 36*.

[779] Sir John Hepburn. See Birch, *CT*, II, p. 175; *CSPV, 1632–1636*, p. 92; *Letter 44*; PRO, C 115/105/8207.

[780] Leipzig.

[781] See PRO, C 115/105/8207.

[782] Sir Morice Drummond, gentleman usher of Henrietta Maria's privy chamber. See PRO, LR5/57, fo. 3r (for which reference I am grateful to Simon Healy).

[783] See *CSPV, 1632–1636*, pp. 92–93; *Letter 39*.

stayed upon it that were going from hence into Holland, and others permitted to go into Flanders with Coronell Thressam.[784] I can no more at this present but, with woonted respects, rest.

29 March 1633.

No address.

Endorsed: Clerk. 29 March.
          The points propounded by D[octor] Bossevile.

41. Clerk [John Southcot] to Fitton [Peter Biddulph], 13 April 1633

[*AAW, A XXVII, no. 38, pp. 105–108*]

Sir,

I have yours of the 12 of March, by which we were glad to understand that the first point at least is determined which is to maintaine episcopall authority, and we hope, this being resolved, it will not be long ere the rest do follow concerning titles, number, persons, etc. But be sure above all things that you stand stiff for ordinary authority, else we shall never be free from brubbles.

As for that report which the Jes[uits] do there give out of persecution, it is false in all particulers, excepting only compositions; which, although they be high racked, yet are not so intolerable as they make them, and Catholickes had rather have them at any rate than loose their lives and liberties, as there they report. And I wish you could find meanes to have Welspoken informed of those reports from thence and of their authors, by some meanes or other. Perhaps it would putt him quite out with them hereafter. Neither is it true that all prisoners or any were delivered upon the k[ing's] recovery from the small pox, only some prisoners that were to be executed at Tyburne were reprived for that time.[785] They do his Majesty a great deale of hurt in that court with these reports, and no doubt great wrong withall, and it were pitty but the good and just should know of it and the innocent also.

---

[784] Sir William Tresham. See *Letter 17*.

[785] For the king's brief (and minor) illness in early December 1632, and for this incident of the reprieve, see *CSPV, 1632–1636*, pp. 47, 49; Birch, *CT*, II, pp. 205, 211–212; Laud, *Works*, III, p. 216; JPN, pp. 337, 340. One rumour had it that the reprieve was granted on news that Gustavus Adolphus was still alive.

Our friends here are wholly ag*ai*nst the making any but an English man the cardinall of our nation, and think that the making of either Scottish or Irish would in time draw great prejudice upon us. If matters be determined there before the end of sum*m*er, it wilbe needlesse for my lord[786] to go up, else we are all here of opinion that he should go up at the beginning of next autumne. We are now in hand with Mr Anthony Smith a fallen [*p. 106*] priest and Jesuit, that hath lived divers yeares with a Protestant woman, and hath had divers children by her, two wherof do yet live, to go over to do pennance, and reconcile him self againe to God and his Church. He never fell directly from his faith, but only lived in this scandalous manner. What help we shall have from the Jes[uits] or their freinds God knowes, but all the burthen therof to help this poor soule both spiritually and temporally lighteth upon the clergy, and it is a thing worthy to be complained of that we must receave all their outcasts and provide for them, w*h*ich is both a dishonor and an intolerable burden to the poor clergy, who have not meanes to provide sufficiently for their own, and to maintaine their necessary agents at home and abroad, especially since they have so much decried my lords authority <here> in whose name we were woont to make our collections, many of his freinds and ours now refusing to contribute bycause they are tould, as they say, that my lord is not their superiour.

Mr Duckett purposeth to be with you, God willing, before the end of autumne, and I purpose to send by him those knives w*h*ich you desire, but there is no meanes possible to send the greyhounds or mastives. I referr all domesticall newses to Mr Lab[orne]. The earle of Holland[787] is served as I heare with a letter from the lord keeper[788] to answer in the star chamber, and so are the two you*n*g lords, my Lord Fielding[789] and my Lord Goring his sonn,[790] who fought the last week by occasion of some words touching the same buissenesse, [*p. 107*] my Lord Fielding, as you know, having maried my lord treasurers daughter,[791] and the other taking part with Holland. The king would faine have the qu[een] runn with my lord treasurer in his courses, w*h*ich doubtlesse are most for the kings profitt and for the good of the English nation, seeking to keep out both the Scotts and the French as much as he can, yet the qu[een] will hardly be drawn to joine in that course.[792]

[786] Richard Smith.

[787] Henry Rich, 1st earl of Holland.

[788] Sir Thomas Coventry, 1st Baron Coventry.

[789] Lord Basil Fielding, heir apparent of the earl of Denbigh.

[790] George Goring, son of George Goring, 1st Baron Goring of Hurstpierpoint. See *CSPD, 1633–1634*, pp. 3, 11, 12, 14–15.

[791] Fielding married Anne Weston. See Alexander, *CLT*, p. 171.

[792] Cf. *ibid.*, p. 190.

We are in good hope the next week to send you the qu[een's] letter in my lords behalf to Monsieur Crequy, who by this time I suppose is come to Rome. He hath charge also from the ki[ng][793] and cardinal[794] to solicit my lords buissenesse, wherfor I ~~pray~~ pray see him as soon as he cometh.

Thus in hast I committ you to God and rest.

13 Aprill 1633.

[on p. 108]

Addressed: Pour Monsieur Fitton a Rome.

Endorsed: Clerk. 13 April.
             About Smith the Jesuitt.

42. Clerk [John Southcot] to [Peter Biddulph], 19 April 1633

[AAW, A XXVII, no. 41, pp. 117–118]

Sir,

I have yours of the 26 of March with the enclosed occurrences of that court which were very welcome, and although I would not putt you to the paine of writing them weekly yet I should be glad to heare sometimes what passeth in that kind, and if you be at any extraordinary charge for them it shalbe defraied you againe uppon notice given by you what the particulers are. The last I receaved from you was of the 12 of March which I answered the last week, and this bearing date the 26 of March sheweth that there is one weekes letters waunting of the 19 of March, which as yet we have not receaved.

With these you shall receave the qu[een's] letter sealed to Monsieur Crequy who, being a duke, the qu[een] calls him cosen. You shall have also a coppy of the letter sent a part, that you may see the contents.[795] I conceave the best way to deliver the letter wilbe by M[r] Barklay his meanes, as if he had receaved it immediatly from France, for so perhaps the ambassador wilbe sooner mooved to solicit the effect of it, and be the farther of[f] from thinking it to be procured by any importunity of ours. Yet being delivered you may lett the ambass[ador] know that

[793] Louis XIII.

[794] Cardinal Richelieu.

[795] See Letter 37; AAW, A XXVII, no. 43 (Southcot's copy of Henrietta Maria's letter of 25 April 1633 to the duke of Créquy).

you are advertized from hence that the qu[een] hath written unto him, and solicit him for an answer. This is my conceipt, but you will best know what is to be donn that are there, and therfor I leave it to your discretion.

At length my lord[796] hath sent us a coppy of the compendium of your long information, written in Italian, which I like exceeding well, and I doubt not but all may be verified from hence by such instances and examples as I suppose have bin formerly writt unto you, and do here daily occurr. At this present there are divers examples of disorders concerning mariage and particulerly that between M\ Henry Wilford and my Lady Suliards daughter,[797] [*p. 118*] wherof my lord will advertise you more at large.[798] Concerning disorderly pr[iests] there are at this

---

[796] Richard Smith.

[797] Mary Suliard, daughter of Sir John Suliard (d. 9 February 1627), and sister of Sir Edward Suliard. See PRO, PROB 11/151, fo. 146r; *Letter 49*. Sir John Suliard's son, William, married Elizabeth Wilford; Metcalfe, *The Visitations of Essex*, I, p. 523.

[798] An undated memorandum in Peter Biddulph's papers recorded that 'Edward Suliard eques in publico theatro aggressus est nuper D. Henricum Wilford [...] et, nisi populus impedivisset, sese invicem vel occidissent vel vulnerassent ob negotium praetensi matrimonii inter dictum Wilfordum et sororem dicti Suliard'; AAW, A XXVII, no. 110, p. 319. A letter sent to Biddulph from London related that 'Wilfordus post aliquot menses longioris [...] impatiens [...] videret nihil Romae determinari, alium faeminam in uxorem duxit illamque haereticam; et pars adversa litem contra ipsum instituit in curia archiepiscopi Cantuariensis, unde procul [...] gravia scandala orientur, non sine periculo, ne altera pars et fortassis utraque a fide deficiat'; AAW, A XXVII, no. 112, p. 323. Since an account of the Wilford–Suliard case appears in a separate list of scandals sent to Rome in April 1635 by the priest and rural dean, Thomas Green, it may be that this information came originally from him; AAW, A XXVIII, no. 15, p. 70. Yet another account of the case alleges that 'Robertus Rookwood eques, Thomas Ruckwood frater, et Gulielmus Syliard frater Edwardi [Rookwood] eques, cum aliis invitant, sollicitant, impellunt Wilfordum ad tabernam, ubi post longam commessationem, tantum vini infunditur Wilfordo, ut plane inebriaretur; tunc ebrio inducitur soror Edwardi Syliard, variis inter illam et Wilfordum commutatis blandimentis, cubile affertur (quid verbis opus est rem sordidam depingere) ibi (ut Robertus Ruckwood eques literis sua manu conscriptis testatus est) illo inspectante concubuere (ut solent conjuges) Wilfordus et soror Edwardi Syliard. Taedis hisce peractis supercalibus, a somno, et crapula rediit ad mentem Wilfordus, quem faemina (ad id docta satis) maritum vocat, respuit ille illam, una et mariti nomen, negat contractum ullum maritalem; immo cum affirmatur illam ab eo cognitam, negat Wilfordus, affirmans se ut res erat, ebrium fuisse, aut si cognovisset, cognovisse tantum aut meritricem'. As a result, 'currit hoc scandalum per ora vulgi, in questionem res ducitur' and two Jesuits (John Alexander Evison and Christopher Greenwood), a Benedictine (David Codner), and one other regular convened an ad hoc tribunal, cited the parties before them, interviewed witnesses and so on. But they could not reach a decision. And in the meantime 'Wilfordus [...] matrimonium molitur cum alia faemina, quod Syliard pro sorore sua prohibere contendit, publica obtenta inhibitione ex curia archiepiscopatus Cantuariensis; sed veritus publicam sororis suae infamiam, confugit nunc tandem ad officialis reverendissimi episcopi Chalcedonensis, ut authoritate sua litem dirimans [...] hoc flagrans scandalum'; AAW, A XXVII, no. 113, pp. 325–326.

present in Hantshire two Irish pr[iests] (whether sec[ular] or regular none can tell, or whether pr[iests] at all) who go up and down the country there to all Cath[olic] houses to begg, and what they gett they spend in drink, at least one of them, who saieth no other Mass but of requiem even upon the greatest holidaies. Many other great disorders there be, but I have neither time nor health at this present to write them down, and I think you have bin informed already of most of them.

For newes I must refer you to Mr Lab[orne]. The earle of Holland is come to court againe, and is made freinds with the treasurer[799] and my Lord Weston.[800] The king houldeth his journy for Scotland, and beginneth it on the 11 of the next month, being the 4th day of the terme and, with us, Saterday. The queen is quick with child. I pray God blesse her and graunt her a good delivery. It is saied that Mr Foster[801] is gonn over againe into France, though his freinds here give it out he is gonn into the North.

There is a great correspondence between Card[inal] Richelieu and the lord treasurer, which the Spanniards here do not like. Some doubt whether the card[inal] be fallen or falling of[f] from my lord bishop, perhaps to comply with the Capucins and Jesuites. Otherwise methinkes my lord might gett the card[inal] to write effectually for him to the treasurer which would do him good with the king.

Thus in hast I bid you hartely adieu being our Good Friday and the 19 of Aprill 1633.

To the little cipher I sent you a fortnight since, add these:
  (Jesuitts. The afflicted.)
  (Clergy. The rising.)

No address.

[*on p. 117*]

Endorsed: Clerk. 19 April.
        About the 2 Irish priests.

---

[799] Sir Richard Weston, 1st earl of Portland.

[800] Jerome Weston. For the Venetian ambassador Gussoni's report of the quarrel between and reconciliation of the earl of Holland and the Westons, see *CSPV, 1632–1636*, p. 100.

[801] See Foster, 'Sir Richard Forster', p. 165.

43. [John Southcot] to [an English secular priest at Paris],[802] 24 April 1633

[*AAW, OB I/ii, no. 129, fo. 245r–v*]

[Sir,]

The last week I had a short letter from you of the 19th of this month togeather with the <u>two printed papers</u>[803] in French w*hic*h we will cause to be divulged here <u>as well and as soon</u> as we can. But how to gett direct proofs to convince them to be the true authors of the bookes, we do not know more than the com*m*on voice and opinion w*hic*h is generally here such that all that read this declaration presently <u>cry out against</u> the untruth thereof. M[r] Homes[804] the Bened[ictine] tould me that <u>Fa[ther] Knott</u>[805] gave him one of his bookes[806] and he saieth that <u>he composed it in</u> the Clink. Fa[ther] Faulkener[807] tould M[r] Beckett,[808] if I be not deceaved, that Fa[ther] Flud[809] ~~was~~ had <u>answered the</u> Sorbon censures, and was the author of the Spongia.[810] That he was the author also of the Apologia[811] both the anagram of his name sheweth, and <was> acknowledged by them selves in divers

---

[802] R. Stanfield suggests that this letter may have been intended for Richard Smith's secretary; CRS, 22, p. 178. The letter (printed in *ibid.*, pp. 178–179) was originally addressed 'pour Monsieur Antoine Penon à Paris'; *ibid.*, p. 179. See also Allison, RSGB, I, p. 396.

[803] AAW, A XXVI, no. 148 (*Arrest de la Cour de Parlement de Roüen* (Paris, 1632); cf. ARCR, I, no. 501; a judgement, dated 28 September/8 October 1632, by the parlement of Rouen concerning 150 copies of Floyd, *Hermanni Loemelii [...] Spongia* which had been illegally brought to Rouen); AAW, A XXVII, no. 28 (*Declaration et Desadveu des Peres Jesuites* (Paris, 1633)); ARCR I, no. 1408; a statement, dated (in the text) 13/23 March 1633, by the Society of Jesus that various books (ARCR, I, nos 1400, 481, 489, 496) were not written 'par aucuns religieux de nostre compagnie'; to which is added a declaration (of 9/19 February 1633) by representatives of several religious orders acknowledging episcopal rights of approbation). These papers are bound and catalogued in AAW as SEC 16/1/8 and SEC 16/1/9 respectively.

[804] This individual cannot be identified with certainty; Allison, RSGB, I, p. 396. It may conceivably be Hugh (Bede) Helme OSB.

[805] Matthew Wilson SJ.

[806] Antony Allison identifies the book as either Matthew Wilson SJ, *A Modest Briefe Discussion [...]*, or idem, *A Defence of Nicholas Smith against a Reply to his Discussion of some Pointes taught by Mr. Doctour Kellison in his Treatise of the Ecclesiasticall Hierarchy* (Rouen, 1631); ARCR, II, no. 819; Allison, RSGB, I, p. 345.

[807] John Faulkner SJ. See Anstr., II, p. 99.

[808] Not identified. The priest Thomas Becket, ordained at Seville by 1631, did not receive his viaticum until 1634; *ibid.*, p. 20.

[809] John Floyd SJ.

[810] Floyd, *Hermanni Loemelii [...] Spongia*.

[811] Idem, *Apologia Sanctae Sedis Apostolicae quoad Modum Procedendi circa Regimen Catholicorum Angliae Tempore Persecutionis cum Defensione Religiosi Status* (Rouen, 1631); ARCR, I, nos 481–483, a reference to Floyd's translation of his own *An Apolagy*.

parts of the kingdom, though I know not their names in particuler, and Mr Gray[812] the Jes[uit] sould them up and down, from whom I procured two or three coppies by Peter Windors meanes.[813] Besides, all their penitents and followers ~~that~~ of the better sort had these bookes in their houses, and carried them sometimes in their pocketts, and they were read generally by them all, who notwithstan[d]ing refused to read any book written ~~of~~ <on> the other side. Moreover they w[ere] read publickly at the table (as I heare) at St Omers[814] to the s[cho]llars there, and my young nephew[815] that came lately from thence tould me that he had read the Apology him self, being at Gaunt or at Liege as I take it. I beseech you lett us not faile to have some few coppies at least of Aurelius answer to all their exceptions against his bookes, which we will keep secrett, or divulge, as you shall direct us.[816] It is great pitty that there was nothing added in this declaration in dislike of the doctrin. Methinkes <that> should have bin stood uppon much. I cannot yet learne who that Bagadry is mentioned in your letter. Mr Laborne will inquire. The holy oiles are not yet come. I heare no more of Anth[ony] Smith. God send him to be constant in his purpose.

Mr Fitton[817] wrote to us the same which he wrote to my lord[818] and it were good those reports of the Molin[ists][819] <touching persecution> were knowen to the k[ing] and treasurer,[820] but we know not well how to do it, for our friend at court is fearfull to speak. We sent you the last week a coppy of the qu[een's] letter to Crequy, but desire you not to shew it to the nonce, who will the sooner conceave it was not gotten by importunity, and think there is more in it than perhaps there is, [fo. 245v] which it were not amisse he should, that he may informe to Rome according to his own conceipt of it. We all wish there could be a letter procured from the card[inal][821] to the treasurer here in my

---

[812] Lawrence Anderton SJ.

[813] For Winder, see *Letter 56*; Anstr., II, p. 220. In 1631 Winder had supplied information against some of the leading pursuivants who harassed Catholics; PRO, SP 16/533/74, fo. 137r.

[814] The English Jesuit school founded at St Omer.

[815] John Southcot, aged twenty-one in 1633. See Metcalfe, *The Visitations of Essex*, I, p. 491.

[816] In January 1633 Richard Smith had noted the appearance of Jean Duvergier de Hauranne's *Assertio Epistolae Illustrissimorum ac Reverendissimorum Galliae Antistitum* (Paris, 1632); ARCR, I, no. 496; (a follow-up work to the *Vindiciae Censurae Facultatis Theologiae Parisiensis*). Smith remarked that 'the 2 parte of Aurelius is not permitted to be sold publikly by the printer but is sold by Monsieur [Jean] Filsac [see *Letter 65*] who hath al the copies'; AAW, B 27, no. 115; Allison, RSGB, III, pp. 165, 169. On 1/11 February he recorded that 'the 2 part of Aurelius is sold by the deane of Sorbon [i.e. Filesac]' and that the Jesuits were unsuccessfully trying to hinder the sale of it; AAW, B 27, no. 116.

[817] Peter Biddulph.

[818] Richard Smith.

[819] i.e. Jesuits.

[820] Sir Richard Weston, 1st earl of Portland.

[821] Cardinal Richelieu.

lords behalf. Surely it would do much good, and it is wished that the cardinal would write more than once to him about that matter and employ the French ambass[ador] or some other here to [*word deleted*] treat about it with the treasurer, and to seek to allay and answer all difficulties. If he be my lords freind indeed, and a freind to the cause, he cannot refuse to do this, being desired.

The king beginns his journy towards Scotland upon the 11 day of May. There <u>are 4000</u> and 500 persons registred to accompaghny his Majesty in this journy and the jests are so layed that he intendeth to be here at London back againe by St James tide the 24 of July.

This is what occurreth and so, with duty remembred to my lord, I rest.

24 Aprill 1633.

We here some flying repor<u>ts that Fa[ther] J</u>oseph[822] there is in disgrace, but we do not beleeve it.

No address or endorsement.

44. [John Southcot] to [Peter Biddulph], 26 April 1633

[*AAW, A XXVII, no. 44, pp. 121–125*]

Sir,

I answered yours of the 26 of March the last week with many thankes for the avisi that came with it, wherof I hope to make good use and therfor desire you to continew the same now and then, leaving out those things that are not of much moment that your paines may be the lesse. The dispensation of the duke of Mantuas mariage[823] is much wondered at here, and disliked ~~by~~ generally by all Protestants and by the k[ing] him self, wherfor signify so much there, that it may not be graunted. As for that report which the Jes[uits] give out there of persecution, it is more than they dare avouch openly, and <the truth is> far otherwise in all respects, having only the compositions, which although they be high in many, yet in others they are reasonable, and in none, that I heare of, so great as to undo them utterly. The king is nothing inclined to use severity, but rather clemency, as all the world knoweth, and the times are now very calme which maketh more freedom than hath bin seen a great while. The k[ing] and currant of the State is wholy now antipuritan, and tends to a moderation both in opinions and practise. I was tould that a certaine preacher in Bredstreet here in London preached much to his paritioners the

---

[822] François Joseph le Clerc du Tremblay.
[823] See *CSPV, 1632–1636*, pp. 154, 160.

necessity of satisfaction, and that one of them came to him a little after and brought him a bag of mony of 22^l sterling desiring him to give it to the maister of the Horne tavern in Fleetstreet, whom he saied he had defrauded of so much heretofore, but wished him to conceale his name, and the minister went presently with the mony and delivered it to the taverner, who wondering much at it took it thankfully [*p. 122*] and gave the bearer a couple of peeces, one for himself and an other to give to the poor of his parish. Upon this there is a talk as if they intended to bring in auricular confession againe, but I know not how true that is. I was tould also that the k[ing] him self, before some of his own domesticall servants, spake very Catholickly both of the use of the Inquisition and of the popes pardons by occasion of a book that was read unto him by a bedchamber man while he ~~was~~ had his picture drawen, wherin were taunts ag*ain*st both. The k[ing] replied <thus>: '<u>you mistake</u> that matter for the papists do not hould that pardons take away sinn, but the temporall paine dew to sinn, and say that there is such a power in the Church, w*hi*ch the pope assumes to him self'. And of the Inquisition he saied thus: '<u>it is a go</u>od thing, and it were to be wished that it were in all places of Christendom to bridle mens tongues', and then turning to the reader he saied 'you and I might be long enough in Spaine without feare of the Inquisition if we held our peaces and spake nothing in matters of religion etc'. This was related to Mr Lab[orne] by a Catholick gentleman, ~~the~~ servant to the qu[een] in ordinary, that saieth he was by, and heard the king say thus much.[824] By this it appeareth that the k[ing] hath ben prettily well informed in these matters, and is better disposed to speake well of his Hol[iness] than some buissy Catholickes are. Even now one writt unto me to give you notice of a certaine [*p. 123*] penitent of the Jes[uits] who within these few daies saied in a great assembly that, if it were lawfull to wish any mans death, he would wish the popes as a turbulent spiritt and partaker with heretickes, to the scandall of the hearers. The same frend of mine wished me also to tell you that Sig*n*or Amarigo,[825] secretary here for the duke of Florence, giveth out speeches here very unworthy about th*e* pope as the bringer in of the Swedes.[826] I think it were good to lett this be knowen bycause this man

[824] For Richard Smith's account, in May 1633, of Charles's words, and in particular of his opinion that 'the Inqui*sicio*n was good to keep an uniformitie of religion', see AAW, B 27, no. 117. Smith argued that the king's words showed that this 'was the fittest time to send in a b*isho*p'.

[825] Amerigo Salvetti, ambassador in England of the grand duke of Tuscany.

[826] A letter from Richard East to Biddulph of 6 February 1633 [misdated in the AAW, A series catalogue to 1632] said that he had heard these remarks made by Salvetti in summer 1632, and that Salvetti blamed him for his remarks being reported to Rome. According to East, 'this Americo [...] is the very fierbrand to kendle the coals of faction heere, the

is saied to to [*sic*] do as much hurt many waies by the creditt he hath abroad, being much addicted to Tob[ie] Math[ew] and his complices. Here is one Fath[er] Francis,[827] a Franciscan friar held in great esteem by those of his order for a great scholler and preacher. I ame tould for certaine that he hath written a book in Latin wherin he undertakes to make a kind of reconciliation between the Roman and Protestant religion of England, perhaps to comply with the State and gett favour. But it is <a> most dangerous subject and like to do much harme if it be published, and to hinder manies conversion to the Cath[olic] religion, wherfor it is here by the best much disliked. I heare he hath shewed it to Mr Preston[828] and others to have their allowance of it but I do not heare what their judgment is of it as yet. These friars do multiply here apace and grow almost as politike in some kinds as the Jes[uits] do, in appropriating residences and penitents wholy to them selves by meanes of their gurdles. I heare there came in lately 8 or 9 at a clapp, but [*p. 124*] some of them as I heare were Irish, who perhaps when they find the sweetnesse of this pasture wilbe loath to leave it for Ireland, and there be to[o] many here already, both Irish and Scottish, who might better be spared.

The last St George his day the Count Palatin[829] was made k*nigh*t of the garter, as also the duke of Lennox,[830] and I think the <yong> earle of Northumberland,[831] earle of Southampton,[832] and earle of Newcastle,[833] but they are not installed till the king come back from Scotland who intendeth to be not passing 6 weekes away, having appointed to be back at London the 24 of July, and he beginns his journy from hence the 11 of May. 4000 and 500 are registred to go with him, some before and some after, to waite upon him this journy, among whom is my lord treasurer,[834] lord chamberlain,[835] duke of Lennox, marquis [of] Hamilton,[836] lord martiall[837] and others. The qu[een] remaines at Greenwich till he come back. Sweet Jesu blesse

cheefe way the Jes[uits] make use of heere [...] to wright abroad what they would have him agaynst the bishop and clergy and to sollicite great personages to discard the clergy, and take Jesuits'; AAW, A XXVI, no. 24, p. 78.

[827] Christopher Davenport OFM, whose name in religion was Francis a Sancta Clara.

[828] Roland (Thomas) Preston OSB. The book was Davenport's *Deus, Natura, Gratia* (Lyons, 1634).

[829] Charles Louis, Elector Palatine of the Rhine. See Hibbard, *CI*, pp. 25–27.

[830] James Stuart, 4th duke of Lennox. See *CSPV, 1632–1636*, p. 102.

[831] Algernon Percy, 10th earl of Northumberland.

[832] Thomas Wriothesley, 4th earl of Southampton.

[833] William Cavendish, 1st earl of Newcastle.

[834] Sir Richard Weston, 1st earl of Portland.

[835] Philip Herbert, 4th earl of Pembroke.

[836] James Hamilton, 3rd marquis of Hamilton.

[837] Thomas Howard, 2nd earl of Arundel.

him and send him safe both going and coming. The earle of Holland[838] although he be come to court againe yet it is thought he is nothing so much as he was in the k[ing's] favour. Newcastle, who is a Candish,[839] being a very proper man and very moderate, is like to be in good grace, and no doubt my lord treasurer will help it on to oppose Holl[and] the more. Coronel Heburne,[840] a Scott and a Catholik, ~~went~~ is gonn into Scotland to leavy a regiment of 2000, and he saied he would gett as many Catholickes as he could. Perhaps there was some intention hereby to provide for the k[ing's] security this journy, though the souldiars be for France, which the Spanniards <here> are displeased with. [*word deleted*] I heare that our English monkes who had an abby given them in Westfalia by the emperor are driven out by the [*p. 125*] Swedish forces,[841] and have lost all their moveables. They made 500 per annum every yeare, and in time would have doubled the rent. They were in good credit there, and the superior was abbot of the place, and they read divinity there publickly with applause. God knowes whether this be not a punnishment to them for their opposition here.

The duke of Lennox doth give it out that he will not marry these 7 yeares, yet there are good grounds ~~that he~~ to think that ~~he~~ there is a mariage in store for him by the k[ing's] appointment, videlicet one of the Lady Eliz[abeth's] daughters, the k[ing's] neece. But this is a great secrett, and therfor use it soe there.

No more but all woonted good wishes.

26 Aprill 1633.

Herewith you shall receave certaine scandalous cases lately happened.[842]

---

[838] Henry Rich, 1st earl of Holland.

[839] i.e. Cavendish.

[840] Sir John Hepburn.

[841] The Abbey of Rintelin, tenanted by English monks (Clement Reyner OSB and fifteen others) in 1632, was taken by Gustavus Adolphus. See Lunn, *EB*, p. 171.

[842] This is a reference to AAW, A XXVII, no. 111 (1633), which cites various alleged instances of scandal caused by members of the religious orders:

'1. Between F[ather] Alexander Baker al*ias* Saunders and Mr Ed[ward] Courtney about jewells and plate imbezeled away from his father Sir William Courtney [of Powderham; see F.T. Colby (ed.), *The Visitation of the County of Devon in the Year 1620* (Harleian Society 6, 1872), p. 247] 5 or 6 yeares agoe.

2. Between F[ather] Andrew White and Mr Jo[hn] March, Sir Will[iam] Courtneys man about mooving his maister to give ~~all to the~~ <himself wholy to> the Jesuitts direction spiritually and temporally by means of the spir[itual] exercise.

3. Between F[ather] Rich[ard] Blunt and M*ist*ris Kirkame then [a] widdow about speaking the words of matrimony to yong Francis Ploydon, reserving her intention, about two yeares agoe.

No address.

[on p. 121]

Endorsed: 26 Aprill 1633.

45. Clerk [John Southcot] to Fitton [Peter Biddulph], 7 June 1633

[*AAW, B 27, no. 120*][843]

Sir,

The last week we wrote unto you, and sent you a letter enclosed for his Holinesse from the clergy, which we desire may come safe. This week we received yours of the 14 of May to M[r] Lab[orne] wherin you write that it is determined my lord[844] shall have a successor, but you know not who it is nor what his power shalbe. Here the reg[ulars] do give out that we shall have 3 bishops and an archbishop,[845] and they seem indeed

4. Between F[ather] Knott and Mary Winn about consenting to ly with the Lord Baltimor, a yeare and a half agoe, etc.

5. Between F[ather] Faulkener and <M[r] Darcy with> divers poor people whose monies he took up, and to the valew in all of 2000[l], not paying either rent or capital, to the undoing of some of them, 5 or 6 yeares agoe.

6. Between F[ather] Gray alias Anderton and Mr Will[iam] Worthington about marrieing M[ris] Penelope Perkins two yeares since.

7. Between M[ris] Clopton and her Jes[uit] ghostly father [Charles Thursby SJ] permitting her to place her daughter with heretickes and to suffer her to be so bread, in hope of preferment against the childes desire.

8. Between F[ather] Altham [i.e. John Grosvenor SJ] and Sir Robert Brook about his denieing him absolution for not disposing some thinges as he advised, three yeares agoe and more. [See Hughes, *HSJ*, pp. 230–231.]

9. Between Doctor Mettam and ould M[ris] Parrham about the setling of 20[l] per annum upon him during her life for which his heires do now sue in the courts of justice, M[r] [Humphrey (Placid)] Peto, a Benedictine, supporting the sute which yet depends.

10. Between M[r] Peto the monk and Sir William Sturtons man about a summe of mony for which he caused the man to be arrested 3 yeares since.

11. Between F[ather] Alexander Fairclough and the Lady Mordan[t]s steward about monies dew to the saied steward for which he sued Fairclough in the open court 2 yeares since.

12. Between M[r] Christopher Barrowes and M[ris] Hanfords sonn who arrested him and charged him with fellony within this twel[ve]month. [See Anstr., II, p. 18.]'

[843] AAW, B 27 is unpaginated.

[844] Richard Smith.

[845] See *Letters 5, 14, 18, 26, 28*. On 7/17 June 1633 Smith notified Biddulph that the Jesuits in England were spreading rumours both that Rome would appoint Smith as an archbishop over the English Catholics (causing the Jesuit general to threaten the withdrawal of all Jesuits from the country), and that shortly Smith would return 'with ful authoritie', but they did

to beleeve it, but I do not think that so many wilbe made togeather. Perhaps in time and by degrees we shall come to have them, and no doubt it were needfull for the good government of this Church that so many were made, bycause neither the reg[ulars] nor the State would then have any hope to suppresse ep*iscop*all authority, being setled in so many, and, the faculties of missionaries being once well ordered, they would quickly bring all things here to a good passe, and <the laity> to some conformity and unity of minds who are now pittifully divided amongst them selves by reason of their ghostly fathers differences. Yow write that you have given up a forme of faculties to be approved for all missionaries, and a particuler forme besides ~~for so~~ of such as are to be reserved to the b*isho*p. We desire to see these formes, and therfor pray you to send us a coppy by the next as also ~~of~~ coppies of any other memoriall or paper w*hi*ch you give to the pope or congreg*acion*[846] at any time, partly for o*ur* own better instruction here, and partly for future memory to be registred in the com*m*on booke. Particulerly we desire to see the Benedictins memoriall, and your answer touching the taking away of cords, scapulars, com*m*unicacion of meritts, etc*etera*. You write nothing [*word deleted*] concerning my lo*r*ds advancement in case he be sent back hither with sufficient authority, w*hi*ch is a matter much to be stood upon both for his honour and the generall interest of all b*isho*ps, seeing there hath bin nothing prooved ag*ains*t him that deserves deprivation, and indeed hath donn nothing for w*hi*ch he doth not rather deserve to be rewarded. And you may assure them there that it wilbe a great scandall here both to Catholicks and hereticks if the Sea Apostolick do abandon him without reward or advancement only for the clamors and violences of his adversaries, and wilbe an ill example in the Church, and of dangerous consequence for future times. We wrote a com*m*on letter not long since to Card[inal] Richelieu to desire his intercession and the French kings for my lo*r*ds advancement to be cardinall, but we heare not what impression it makes in him. It was sent by Mons*ieu*r Roch[847] his meanes to the cardinall. Here o*ur* adversaries do consult amongst them selves and with their lay freinds about their businesse, w*hi*ch we imagin to be chiefly to keep of[f] bishops or at least to hinder their authority as much as they can. Fa[ther] John Worthington no doubt shall carry with him some instructions to this purpose who is not yet gonn from hence. He tould

this only to 'annoye o*ur* brethren' and to ensure that they 'write not to Rome but think them selves sure'; AAW, A XXVII, no. 61, p. 179. For the Jesuit general's worries, aired in a letter of December 1633 to Richard Blount, about the appointment of new bishops in England, see ARSJ, Anglia MS 1/iii, fo. 384r.

[846] The Congregation for the Propagation of the Faith.

[847] Michel Masle, prieur des Roches, who served as Richelieu's secretary. See Allison, RSGB, II, pp. 247, 280.

one also (as I wrote to you before) that he bringeth a command to you from your father to come away; but I do not see what power he hath to command any such thing, for you were long time emancipatus and extra patriam potestatem for such matters.

What hath been written formerly to you of the calme we enjoy from the violence of persecution, and of the good disposition that is in many principall statesmen, is most true, and the Jes[uits] cannot contradict it without wronging them and us, and abusing the cardinalls and his Hol[iness]. And that you may beleeve this the rather, we shall answer to any particuler that shalbe objected to the contrary, and if need be shew particuler examples to confirme that which we have written touching this point, wherin for the present I remitt you to the summarium de rebus religionis[848] which I sent you in February. A westerne gentleman tould me no longer agoe than yesterday that a Protestant of his acquaintance assured him that in all Devonshire and Cornwall (which were woont to be the most puritannicall countries of England), of so many hundred lecturers and puritan preachers that have bin formerly knowen there, there are not passing two or three now left in all the country, and that the country is notoriously changed within these two yeares, and become quite of an other spiritt.[849] The like may be saied of other shires, and no doubt generally the whole realme is much altered to the better in point of moderation, and never were there known more temperat and well disposed ministers than now, in so much that, with a little diligence and good order, many conversions are likely to be made. But these men that cannot endure to heare this reported of the state of our country are such as are averted also from our Catholike queen and from his Hol[iness] him self, of whom they speake most irreligiously and disloyally (not only untruly) and spread false and foule reports of them to the scandall of the hearers. M[r] Longvile heard a Jes[uit] in Kent, one Henry Hawkins,[850] say openly in compagny that our Catholick queen did us no more good than if she were an heretick. An other concealed

---

[848] See *Letter 34*.

[849] For an assessment of the religious temper of pre-Civil-War Devonshire, see M. Stoyle, *Loyalty and Locality: Popular Allegiance in Devon during the English Civil War* (Exeter, 1994), chs 10, 11. Stoyle notes in particular the Exeter Cathedral establishment's reputation for Arminianism (*ibid.*, pp. 205–206), but he argues that Joseph Hall's tenure of power as bishop of Exeter from 1627 to 1642 'enabled Devon puritanism to emerge from the Personal Rule largely intact', although, in 1634, even Hall could be found taking action against radicals; *ibid.*, pp. 186, 194. On Hall's rule in Exeter, see K. Fincham and P. Lake, 'Popularity, prelacy and puritanism in the 1630s: Joseph Hall explains himself', *English Historical Review*, 111 (1996), pp. 856–881, at pp. 869–877.

[850] See Anstr., II, p. 152.

Jes[uit], who calls him self William Walgrave,[851] tould M[r] Farrar[852] his fellow prisoner[853] that the queen refused to ask any favour of the king for Catholicks at his going now into Scotland, and particularly she refused to gett the pursevants warrants taken from them.[854] Other particulers there are divers in this kind to[o] long to be related. In confirmation also of what I saied before, touching the goodnesse of the times, I may add that, since the king went for Scotland, no search hath bin made either in citty or country, that I heare of, in so much that some say all commissions for searchings are taken away. All publick chappells are mightily frequented without disturbance. Prisoners goe freely abroad without restraint. M[r] Dade,[855] superior of the Dominicans, is particulerly warranted to go freely where he will, and Secretary Windebank charged his keeper to give him this freedom. It is a shame we should be so ungratefull to his Majesty and the State when the favours are so manifest. Neither are compositions so intolerable as they seem to make them. For wheras they report that the king taketh a full third part, it is nowhere true, but ~~of~~ at the most of some few a forth [*two words deleted*] <and generally> a fift part, who by the law might take two parts from all convicted recusants.

I refer particuler newes if there be any to M[r] Lab[orne]. Many tales have bin reported since the k[ing's] departure of deaths and daungers, but they are all fictions. The king, God be thanked, is well, being yet in the skirts of England. The queen is also well and with child. The prince hath bin ill of late, but I hope on the mending hand. There are two <~~brothers~~> noble men of Flanders lately come hither, the one is the Prince of Chemey and the other his brother, to see the country.[856] They have bin feasted by divers and by the queen also and now they are gonn to overtake the king and to see his coronation in Scotland. W. Johnes is <their conducter>.

I forgott to tell you that a certaine Jes[uit] pr[iest] demanded of an other pr[iest] that had bin a Jes[uit] (hearing that we were to have

---

[851] William Waldegrave was a secular priest who was known to be hostile to Richard Smith. He had been released from the New prison in January 1633; *ibid.*, p. 332; VA, PD, fo. 79r.

[852] William Harewell. He had served as Bishop William Bishop's secretary in 1623, and continued in the same office under Richard Smith. He had been arrested in 1628; Anstr., II, p. 145; CRS, 22, p. 173. Up to this point he had been resident with the countess of Banbury, who was now the wife of Lord Vaux; PRO, SP 16/529/94, fo. 146v.

[853] See Anstr., II, pp. 145, 332; PRO, SP 16/118/25; AAW, A XXVI, no. 164, p. 495.

[854] Some Jesuits, notably Robert Jenison, made statements of this kind to Gregorio Panzani about Henrietta Maria; VA, PD, fo. 51r.

[855] Thomas Middleton OP.

[856] For Albert d'Arenberg, prince of Chimey, and Philippe d'Arenberg, count of Beaumont, see *CSPV, 1632–1636*, pp. 111, 117, 141, 148; Loomie, *Ceremonies of Charles I*, pp. 141, 317.

more b*ishop*s) whether it were a mortall sinn to seek to hinder it by meanes of the State, by w*hich* it appeares how these men are minded and how strang[e]ly they are bent ag*ainst* ep*iscop*all power. Sed durum est contra stimulum calcitrare.

I forgott also to tell you that one Alexander Baker, a Jes[uit], lieth in or near Cambridg seeking to draw the towardliest youths from thence w*hich* they can gett. The like they intend at Oxford. In this they are <to> be com*m*ended for their zeale and diligence, but the clergy, if they had government, should chiefly attend to this.

I com*m*ended the last week D[octor] Champneis buissenesse to y*our* care as a thing not only concerning him (whose creditt we ought to preserve) but the whole clergy also, and therfor I wished you to sue for his clearing and for the ending of the whole cause depending in the Congrega*c*ion of Regulars,[857] in the clergies name, as we determined in o*ur* last consult it should be donn. There are some new and some ould scandals w*hich* perhaps have not bin yet certified unto you concerning divorces and the like; but as now I have them not ready to send you.

So with all woonted remembrances I rest.

7 June 1633.

Addressed: Pour Mons*ieur* Fitton.

Endorsed: Clerk. 7 Jun[e].
About papers he would have mee to send.
About Jesuitts that speake against the q[ueen].
About one who would complain to the State against b*isho*ps.

46. Clerk [John Southcot] to [Peter Biddulph], 14 June 1633

[*AAW, A XXVII, no. 60, pp. 173–176*]

Sir,

This week I had one from you of the 21 May. I ame glad to heare that F[ather] Alessandro[858] doth so good offices there for the clergy. He hath more true understanding of o*ur* affaires than Fa[ther] Leonard[859] or any of the French Capuc[hins] and lesse interest to draw him from indifferency. I remember you wrote from Paris <long since> that the

---

[857] For the Congregation of Regulars, see Codignola, *CHL*, pp. 66, 127.
[858] Alessandro d'Ales. See Hughes, 'The conversion of Charles I', pp. 120–121. He assisted with the mission to Rome of Robert Douglas in October 1633. Douglas sought the promotion of a British cleric, George Con, to the rank of cardinal; VA, PD, fos 24r–5r.
[859] Provincial of the French Capuchins.

French Capucins proposed to them selves certaine projects here for the enlargment of their order, which it seemes they go in hand to execute by the Jes[uits'] help, who no doubt laugh at them in their sleeves, and in the end will serve them as they have donn the monkes and Dominicans, who now find them selves in the lurch. Since I wrote to you the last week the superiour of the Dominicans[860] was with me, and he complained greevously of the Jesuitts proceeding with him of late having taken some penitents from him that were very beneficiall to him. He saied also that the monkes were served by them in like manner and therfor were weary of their freindship, and he wished us to make some overture to them of a new league by occasion of their general chapter which is to be held in Doway in August next. But I find little disposition in our brethren here to any such league with the monkes, considering their violent proceeding heertofore[861] and their unsinceare dealing now, their agent[862] at Rome being still combined with the Jes[uits], as you write, against bishops here. They are so divided amongst them selves that our frendship with them would little availe us. I heare there are five severall excommunicacions come from their generall and generall chapter in Spaine to be served uppon five particuler monkes here that will not be ruled by their superiours here,[863] wherof one I heare is Peto,[864] an other Chambers,[865] the other 3 I know not, unles Wilford[866] be one, as some say he is. Neither do I know what the cause is in particuler unlesse it be for detaining certaine monies dew to the monastery by the death of one Norton,[867] a monk that had an estate in the world, which he left to the monastery of Doway. Mr Lab[orne] saies he wrote to you long since of this project which the French Capucins have with the Jesuitts about erecting a nunnery in France to be guided by the Jes[uits], but I hope therin the clergy will prevent them for they have obtained already a graunt of it in Paris and Mr Car[868] is now here to gett some gentlewomen with

---

[860] Thomas Middleton OP.

[861] See D. Lunn, 'Benedictine opposition to Bishop Richard Smith (1625–1629)', RH, 11 (1971–1972), pp. 1–20.

[862] Richard (Wilfrid) Selby OSB. See Dockery, CD, p. 78; B. Weldon, Chronological Notes containing the Rise, Growth, and Present State of the English Congregation of the Order of St. Benedict (Stanbrook, 1881), pp. 169, 182; Letters 83, 84.

[863] See Letter 52; Lunn, EB, pp. 149–150. I am grateful to Geoffrey Scott for advice on this point.

[864] Humphrey (Placid) Peto OSB.

[865] William Johnson OSB.

[866] Peter (Boniface) Wilford OSB.

[867] John Norton OSB, who had died in 1631.

[868] Miles Pinckney.

good portions.[869] God speed it well, but for my part I affect not such courses, and in my opinion the clergy hath to[o] much to do already with Lisboa college[870] and with the nunnery of Bruxelles, yet I shall be ready to concurr with the rest, and follow the major part. In our last consult we concluded that, in case Fa[ther] Fitzherbert should dye, you should sue by a particuler memoriall in the clergies name to have [*p. 174*] that college restored to the clergy, and to take it quite out of the Jes[uits'] hands, and to this end it is thought convenient that you should have such a memoriall ready drawen with such motives and reasons in writing as may moove his Holinesse therunto. If you look emongst these papers which D[octor] Bossevile carried with him, you will find particuler reasons for this purpose to which you may add what you think good. I pray consult this point with your sure freinds there and send us your opinion and theirs by the next post. If the clergy be not able to furnish men to governe it presently, lett it be depositated [*sic*] in the hands of some of the oblati[871] or of the chiesa nuova[872] priests or some such indifferent men till the clergy can provide, but the Jes[uits] were to be presently remooved and, to the end there may be lesse opposition from them, the matter must be carried with that

---

[869] Francis Barber (half-brother of Stephen Barnes, chaplain to the Augustinian convent at Louvain, and a supporter of Richard Smith; AAW, A X, no. 135, p. 387; Anstr., I, p. 24; II, p. 15) reported to Smith from Douai on 3 August 1633 that Miles Pinckney was 'like to be here this night with some gentlewomen, he having taken shipping at London the 28 of our July last'. He noted also that 'Dame Mary [Letitia (Mary) Tredway] remembers her humble service unto your lordship, and will rest [...] indifferent to tacke whom it shall please' Smith, Pinckney 'and her superiours to permitt to begine with her' for her Augustinian foundation at Paris, where she would become the first abbess; AAW, A XXVII, no. 80, p. 237. Under the influence of George Leyburn, she had decided to found her convent in the French capital rather than at Douai, the aim being to keep its spiritual direction firmly in the hands of the secular clergy and avoid the divisions which had arisen at Brussels, even though Pinckney had wanted to see it set up at Douai; A.F. Allison, 'The English Augustinian Convent of Our Lady of Syon at Paris: its foundation and struggle for survival during the first eighty years, 1634–1713', *RH*, 21 (1993), pp. 451–496, at pp. 456–458. Permission was obtained in March 1633 from Louis XIII to set up the house under English secular clergy control and under the authority of the archbishop of Paris. On 23 March/2 April 1633 she wrote to Smith from Douai thanking him for his assistance; AAW, A XXVII, no. 33, p. 93. After opposition from Archbishop Gondi of Paris was finally overridden, with Richelieu's assistance, the convent was opened in early 1634 in the Faubourg St Michel; Allison, RSGB, II, pp. 273–276. Pinckney collected Tredway from Douai (where she was a member of the Augustinian community of Notre Dame de Beaulieu), and she was instituted as abbess by Smith on 16/26 March 1634; AAW, B 27, no. 113; Allison, RSGB, II, pp. 271–277. Pinckney's *St Austin's Rule translated out of his 109. Epistle Verbatim* (Paris, 1636); ARCR, I, no. 643, is dedicated to Smith.

[870] The college of Saints Peter and Paul at Lisbon.

[871] The Oblates of St Ambrose (a congregation of secular priests founded by Charles Borromeo in 1578).

[872] The Congregation of the Oratory.

privacy, and their remoovall must be commanded so sodainly, that they can have no time to practise or resist. But, if this cannot be obtained as we desire, at least we must sue for a clergy man to be confessarius <and an other to be> procurator of the college to see the schollers well bredd to the end of the seminary, and their monies well spent to the same end.

Amongst other faculties reserved to the bishop lett one be that [no] bookes be printed in English without his leave, for in this there is a great abuse, and much trouble and scandal comes to us for waunt of good order herein.

I saw an advertisment given to a freind of mine lately touching a book of one Franciscus Mendoza Soc[ietatis] Jesu doctor theologus. The title of the book is Viridarium Sacrae et Profanae Eruditionis. He hath this question: utrum nobis utilius sit Jesu nomen sanctissimum implorare an nomen Mariae, and therin hath these words: <u>admitto virginem et Christum aequali ferme apud Deum authoritate valituros;</u> and againe, <u>dicere possem Christi et virginis intercessionem aequalis fere momenti esse apud Deum.</u>[873] I pray you look into the book, and if you find these propositions there you may do well to putt them up to the Inquisition, for here our heretiques are much scandalized with them, and indeed not without reason for they sound blasphemously.

Mr Duckett[874] is resolved to begin his jorney towards you in August. But he desires first to heare from you about the safest way, as by the enclosed from him self you may perceave. It is not possible for him to bring [p. 175] doggs with him, but knives I hope he will bring such as you desire, and I have desired Mr Lab[orne] to buy them presently to whom I delivered the 50^s for that purpose, left you by M^r Ed[ward] Skinner.[875]

We have not much newes stirring. The king is newly entered into Scotland safe and sound, God be thanked. The queen is quick with child. The prince is well recovered againe, and the princesse is well. For persecution we have as great a calme as ever we had, God continew it long. The grand aulmner[876] hath certified so much to the nonce[877] in Paris of late as I heare, which will have some authority with it.

---

[873] Francisco de Mendonça, *Viridarium Sacrae ac Profanae Eruditionis [...]. Posthuma Proles*, 2 vols (Cologne, 1633), I, book 3, pp. 67–75 (quotations at p. 70).

[874] In August 1633 Smith informed Biddulph that he had written to England to 'hasten Mr Ducket of whome as yet I hear nothing'; AAW, A XXVII, no. 87, p. 253.

[875] See *Letter 32*.

[876] Jacques le Noël Du Perron.

[877] Cardinal Alessandro Bichi.

This is what occurreth for the present. So in hast, I rest.

14 June 1633.

Our antibishopists are much terrified with the newes of 3 or 4 bishops[878] and they labour all they can to hinder it, having many consults and meetings amongst them selves and with the Jesuitts to that purpose. But I hope his Hol[iness] will not be deterred by them any more for in fine they dare do nothing, and wilbe quickly husht when they see his Hol[iness] resolute in the buissenesse. But delaies do emboulden them.[879] They make the Spanish resident[880] their instrument herein, as they did Don Carlos,[881] by way of a nationall faction.

In any case you must complaine by a particuler memoriall to the congregation[882] that the last pr[iests] <from Rome> were remitted in their faculties ad archipresbyterum Angliae which argues an intolerable pride and spleen in the superiours of that college that do not vouchsafe to give my lord his title and gett it to be effectually remedied in the next as also that the rector be obliged to certify the clergies agent some time before of the number and sufficiency of those that are sent and that the pr[iest] be bo[u]nd to come to the agent for his letters of commendation to the superior here.

No address.

[*on p. 176*]

Endorsed: Clerk. 14 Jun[e].
      About the provinciall of the Dominicans complaints against the Jesuitts.
      About 5 Benedictines excommunicated.
      About recovering this colledg.
      About the faculties of the last mission ad archipresbyterum.

---

[878] On 26 July/5 August 1633 Smith wrote to Biddulph that he was glad Biddulph's letter of 23 June/3 July was so hopeful that three bishops would be appointed 'and I writ your very words to our brethren in England'. From England, Smith had received 'the copies of the patents of the 2 presidents of York and Wales', which had also been dispatched to Biddulph; and Smith now sent a map of the proposed sees, 'marked [. . .] with read oker'; AAW, B 27, no. 125. See *Letter 5.*

[879] In fact, in March 1633, Smith had reported to Biddulph that 'by the nonce [Bichi] it seem[s] we are to have but one bishop for he told me that they who protect the Catholiks (who this should be he told not) wold that we had a bishop but no more, for this time, than one least it shold offend the estate', and said that Smith should return to England, though evidently Smith was not keen to go; AAW, A XXVIII, no. 22, p. 59.

[880] Juan de Necolalde.

[881] Carlos Coloma. See *Letter 3.*

[882] The Congregation for the Propagation of the Faith.

47. Clerk [John Southcot] to Fitton [Peter Biddulph], 5 July 1633

[*AAW, B 47, no. 60*]

Sir,

This week we have yours of the 11 of June written to M[r] Lab[orne]. For my self, I cannot write at large by reason of my remoovall to a new lodging where I am buisied in ordering my things. I was wished by your brother Worthington[883] to lett you know that he heareth nothing as yet of the breve which (as you wrote unto him) you procured to the archbishop of Mecklin[884] to examin his buissenesse, and he desireth you by your next to certify him whether the breve were sent or no, and by what meanes. All other occurrences I must refer to M[r] Lab[orne] being not at leasure my self. Only this I must add in answer to the contents of your letter touching Fa[ther] Hyacinth the Capucin[885] that it were good you dealt with their chief superiour there to hinder their missions into Cath[olics'] privat houses as they desire, as a thing which will infallibly proove prejudiciall to their order in time, and make them loose that esteem which now they have, besides that it will cause much opposition not only in the ~~Jes[uits] but~~ secul[ar] clergy but in ~~the reg[ulars]~~ all English missionaries against them, and they wilbe able to do little go[od] for the true advancement of religion.

I spake this day with Fa[ther] White[886] and Fa[ther] Price,[887] the superior and definitor of the monkes, and find them ready to embrace peace with the clergy upon assurance that they shall not be prejudiced in their mission here, and they offer to bring back at their rettourne a full commission from their generall chapter (to be held at Doway in August) to treat ~~in that~~ and conclude in that kind. I have not yet propounded this to our brethren but I intend the next consult to do it. I see by them that they are weary of the Jes[uits]. We are in hand to write a common letter to my lord[888] againe to invite him to rettourne, or else ~~to~~ <we will> threaten him that we will seek help otherwise, bycause we must needs have a bishop to be our head. No more but all

[883] William Worthington.

[884] Jacques Boonen, who had become archbishop of Mechlin in 1621; P. Arblaster, 'The infanta and the English Benedictine nuns: Mary Percy's memories in 1634', *RH*, 23 (1997), pp. 508–527, at pp. 525–526; P. Guilday, *The English Catholic Refugees on the Continent 1558–1795* (London, 1914), pp. 209, 260, 261, 263, 264.

[885] See *CSPV, 1632–1636*, p. 45; Hughes, 'The conversion of Charles I', p. 121.

[886] William (Claude) White OSB, who was president general of the English Benedictines in 1633; Bellenger, *EWP*, p. 242.

[887] William (Benedict) Jones OSB.

[888] Richard Smith.

woonted salutes. The king hath had 100^m pounds sterling given him by the Scots,[889] and hath brought their church service to the English fashion, as I heare.[890] His Ma*jes*ty will be back within this fortnight, and hath already dismissed all the nobles. The Scottish did far exceed the English in bravery.

Adieu, in hast. 5 July 1633.

Addressed: Pour Mons*ieu*r Fitton a Rome.

Endorsed: Clerk. 5 July.
Concerning the Cappucines mission.

48. Fountyne [George Leyburn] to Fitton [Peter Biddulph], 5 July 1633

[*AAW, A XXVII, no. 65, pp. 187–188*]

Worthie good sir,

This week I receaved onely one from you directed to my selfe. Mr Clerck[891] haith it, soe th*a*t I cannot expresse the date. I am sorrie th*a*t the Capucins should proceed in th*a*t nature, and they will see their owne error at last. Notwithstanding, my maister[892] writeth from Paris th*a*t he is confident th*a*t they are not against episcopall authority, seeing th*a*t Pere Joseph[893] often speaketh and defendeth the necessity of th*a*t authority in our contry. Howsoever I am certayne th*a*t they here complye w*i*th the Jesuists, and never did any one good office for us.

I doe commend unto you thes inclosed conclusions w*hi*ch were defended 3 dayes aggoe in a publick Act att Cambridge.[894] I doe imagine th*a*t the pope will be glad to read them. A minister lately did preach using this text Ave Maria gratia plena.[895] And his sermon was in the praise of the Blessed Virgine.

I beseech you in the name of all our friends th*a*t you will often inculcate the great miserie and hurt w*hi*ch doth happen unto the clergie here, in th*a*t the Jesuists have the power to make and send

---

[889] Walter Yonge noted that Charles had obtained '6 subsidies which amounte unto 600000^l in 6 yeres'; BL, Additional MS 35331, fo. 52r. See Sharpe, *PR*, pp. 781–782.

[890] For the liturgical arrangements made for Charles in Scotland, see *ibid.*, pp. 780–781, 782.

[891] John Southcot.

[892] Richard Smith.

[893] François Joseph le Clerc du Tremblay.

[894] See *Letter 49*.

[895] See *Letter 49*.

priests into England. Here is the rout of many mischeefs. For generally thes men are either factious, being in voto Jesuists, or unlearned and very ignorant. This is a poynt of as great consequence as is the busines of establishing episcopall authority.

Other occurrences are onely that our king was crown[e]d with great solemnity. The next week he feasteth the Scotch nobility at Barwick, and is exspected here the 25 of this month. Sweet Jesus make you happie in all your affayres.

Your humble servant. London, July 5 1633.

Fountyne

I doe thinke that if Mr Barklay should write unto the treasurer here and informe him of passages which concerneth our king that it would be well accepted.

[on p. 188]

Addressed: A Monsieur Monsieur [sic] Fitton a Rome.

Endorsed: Laborn. 5 July.
        Concerning the priests sent from hence into England.

49. Clerk [John Southcot] to Fitton [Peter Biddulph], 19 July 1633

[AAW, A XXVII, no. 74, pp. 221–224][896]

Sir,

I have yours of the 25th June togeather with the avisi and with the other papers which you gave up in your relation for which I hartely thank you and much commend your diligence and judgment therin being [word deleted] couched togeather in that manner which is likeliest to moove there and to be a meanes to obtaine that we seek for. But I pray God the party you trust to write such coppies be faithfull and true, for I have heard that some of our former agents have bin betraied by such men heretofore, and they have given coppies to our adversaries. I have not yet understood by any of these later letters from you whether you receaved the summarium[897] and those 4 packetts dated at the end of Januar[y] and begining of Febr[uary] which I signified unto you in my

---

[896] Passages on p. 222 of this letter are marked and numbered in the margin. Presumably it was intended that they should be translated and copied into reports shown to curial officials in Rome.

[897] See Letter 34.

former I was desirous to heare of, fearing that they were miscaried all, bycause none of your letters which I receaved ~~ever~~ made any mention therof.

When M[r] Innis[898] cometh, he shalbe acquainted as you desire with the avisi, but, being converted by a Capucin, do you think he may be trusted therwith?

They write to us from Paris that the Capucins were the authours of those reports at R[ome] against the qu[een] and Fa[ther] Phil[ip] and that they expect to have great matters from Ro[me] but wilbe deceaved, and in truth it were strang[e] that Fa[ther] Hyacinth or any other straunger should make them beleeve there that French Capucins should be fitt missionaries and usefull for England, and that a bishop or bishops should be hurtfull. We begin to feare that the shew the cardinalls made of reforming faculties was but a florish for the time to give content. But I pray solicit hard that it may go forward and that our maine buissenesse may bee ended. We intend shortly to write an other peremptory letter to my lord[899] to call him home, and to tell him that, if he wil not come, we will provide otherwise for our selves. We propose also to write to the two nonces, ordinary[900] and extraordinary,[901] by the grand aulmner[902] who hath leave for some months to go over. It is thought <by some> he shalbe made bishop ere he come back but I know not what ground [there is] for it.

I will look out an other coppy of the parlament table for you,[903] and send you the explication of it if I can learne it my self.

For newes, I can write little this week, only this, [which] M[r] Lab[orne] tould me he had from a freind at court, that there is an intention to treat with his Hol[iness] after the k[ing] rettournes hither wherby good must needs follow to Cathol[ics] here. What the particular subject of the treaty is, I do not know, but will endeavour to learne. All things here go on more and more in a moderat way, and this chiefly by my lord of Londons[904] meanes. There is now an order made [p. 222] that service shalbe saied in Latin in the universitie colleges all daies but Sundaies.[905] Altars are dressed up in [word deleted] <most> churches collegiat and cathedrals alla Catolica with candles

---

[898] Not identified. See *Letter 53*.

[899] Richard Smith.

[900] Cardinal Alessandro Bichi.

[901] François Adrien de Ceve. See PRO, SP 78/91, fo. 130r.

[902] Jacques le Noël Du Perron.

[903] See *Letter 36*.

[904] William Laud.

[905] Cf. Laud, *Works*, V, pp. 156–157.

and crucifix[es].⁹⁰⁶ The k[ing] hath discountenanced the puritans exceedingly in this his journy,⁹⁰⁷ and refused to heare puritan ministers preach in severall places. He caused also in a place in Lincolnshire certaine boies to be whipt that presented him a petition in the name of a puritan minister that durst not do it him self. He countenanced Doctor Cosens,⁹⁰⁸ prebend of Durham, and made him be sworne his chaplen for dressing up his church <and altar> after the Catholick manner contrary to the use of Morton⁹⁰⁹ the bishop there. There was a minister that preached upon the Ave Maria in praise of Our Lady at Northampton <(a puritan town)> and, being accused by his paritioners to the high commission court, he produced his sermon there and then to justify it to the court, and so was dismissed to his cure againe.

The pursivants have donn little in the country as yet (saving only in one or two houses in Norfolk) and lesse in London. And generally it is confessed that we never had a greater calme since the queene came in than now. God continew it. The compositions go on slowly. Some are strained high, but they are such as can pay well, and it is not any desire of persecution but only the kings waunt that enforceth it.⁹¹⁰

---

⁹⁰⁶ Smith had commented in February 1633 that 'some bishops set up alters, images and candels and doe confirme, and they [are] severely punished who eate flesh on Fridayes', and Southcot had recently sent 'a longe relation' to Bichi, the nuncio in Paris, 'of the like matters'; AAW, B 27, no. 116. Cardinal del Bagno ascribed the restoring of crosses in churches directly to Laud; VA, PD, fo. 25r.

For the 'Laudian' altar policy, see J. Davies, *The Caroline Captivity of the Church* (Oxford, 1992), ch. 6; Sharpe, *PR*, pp. 285, 333–345; K. Fincham, 'The restoration of altars in the 1630s', *Historical Journal*, 44 (2001), pp. 919–940; K. Fincham and N. Tyacke, *Altars Restored: the Changing Face of English Religious Worship, c. 1547–1700* (forthcoming). For an account of why 'Laudian' attitudes to the definition of holy space, and particularly to the altar, were likely to be recognized by contemporaries as innovatory, see P. Lake, 'The Laudian style: order, uniformity and the pursuit of the beauty of holiness in the 1630s', in K. Fincham (ed.), *The Early Stuart Church 1603–1642* (London, 1993), pp. 161–185, at pp. 174–178.

⁹⁰⁷ Charles's journey to Scotland.

⁹⁰⁸ John Cosin.

⁹⁰⁹ Thomas Morton, bishop of Durham.

⁹¹⁰ See AAW, A XXVIII, no. 66, p. 279 ('The Immunities graunted by his Majestie to recusants in their leases upon composition', dated, by Southcot on p. 280, to 1635):

'1. First that noe commissions or summons of pipe or other proces out of the exchequer or other courts shall issue forth against the landes or goodes of the recusant or his executours or administrators or shall trouble or molest him or his wife or his tenants during his lease for his recusancy.

2. That his landes shalbe free from all seisures.

3. That hee may lett or sett his landes or any parte thereof to any person or persons.

4. That he may receave and take the rentes thereof to his owne use notwithstanding the statute of 3° Jacobi.

5. That noe clarke of the assise or of the peace shall make out any warrant or writt for his or his wives appearance att the assizes or quarter sessions.

The king is expected here at London to morrow being the 20 of the month. He hath receaved and given all content in Scotland as I formerly wrote unto you. Some think the good successe he hath had with the parliament there will draw on a parlament here also ere long. But I beleeve the puritans must be somewhat more abated.

M[r] Henry Wilford having had an inhibition from the prerogative court not to marry, at the sute of M[ris] Mary Suliard[911] who claimed him for her husband, the time being expired and no cause brought against him by his adversary, hath since maried the <former> party[912] who is a Prot[estant]. The mariage was not made nor counselled by any clergy man,[913] tho[ugh] he belong to the clergy, but by one Cocks,[914] a Benedictine, by the appointment (as I heare) of M[r] Peter Wilford a Benedictine also, the gentlewomans uncle. Now the other party comenceth an other sute in the saied spirituall court against him, and it is like to proove very foule and scandalous.[915]

6. That hee and his wife shalbe freed from excommunicacions and all other ecclesiasticall sensures touching recusancy.

7. That he shall not be molested in his howse or goodes by any ministers of our chamber or any other of our ministers or subjectes of the same kinde unles by speciall warrant from us or our privy councell.

8. That no person or persons shall exhibit any information, bill or plaint against him or his wife, by reason of his recusancy, and, if any such be exhibited, noe officer shall receive the same.

9. That he shall not be inforced to appeare in the Kinges Bench or to putt in suerety for the good behaviour notwithstanding the statute of 35° Eliz. and 3° Jacobi unles by speciall direccion of the lordes of the councell and then but once onely.

10. That he shall not afterwardes be indited or outlawed for recusancy, but if any such thing should chance to be upon shewing of his lease he shall have a certiorari to remove the same, and that no further proceding shalbe therupon.

11. That the shewing of the letters patentes or the inrollment thereof shalbee a sufficient warrant and discharge to all his Majest[i]es officers and subjects, aswell spirituall as temporall, for all and every the premises.'

[911] Mary Suliard, daughter of Sir John Suliard (d. 9 February 1627). See PRO, PROB 11/151, fo. 146r.

[912] Susan, daughter of Sir Leventhorpe Frank. See Metcalfe, *The Visitations of Essex*, I, p. 523.

[913] i.e. a member of the secular clergy.

[914] Robert (Benedict) Cox OSB.

[915] Henry Wilford (of Quendon in Essex) was the eldest son of James Wilford of Hartridge, Kent, who had married Anne Newman of Quendon; D. Shanahan, 'Wilford of Quendon Hall', *Essex Recusant*, 8 (1966), pp. 16–22. The Wilford family was divided in its allegiances. Edward Stafford, son of the 4th Baron Stafford, had married Anne, daughter of James Wilford of Newman Hall in Quendon. (The Stafford family were regarded by Smith's friends as patrons and supporters; see *Letter 94*.) But the Benedictine Peter Wilford, a relative of Henry Wilford, is cited here as one of the instigators of the allegedly scandalous Wilford–Suliard marriage contract.

No more now, but woonted respects.

19 July 1633.

[*on p. 223*]

One thing I forgott to tell you: that, wheras the Spanish resident[916] here complaineth of my lord bishop[917] and hath written to Card[inal] Borgia against him pretending that he is an enemy to Spaine, as being a creature of Card[inal] Richelieu,[918] a Catholick baron[919] our good freind, who is both a wise and able man, hath offered to the saied resident by Mr Henry Taylor, agent for the infanta[920] here, to stand bound in ten thousand pounds bond for my lord bishop that he shall not oppose Spaine, or meddle with any State matter to the k[ing] of Spaines disadvantage. This the lord him self tould me within these two daies, and therfor you may beleeve it to be true and if you have any occasion to speake with Card[inal] Borgia, or any other Spanish card[inal] or minister of State, you may informe them hereof and complaine to them of the rash and partiall proceeding of the resident, who by these courses seekes to make a division amongst Catholickes to the disadvantage of his own kings affaires here.

We had prepared a remonstrance to give him to this effect, the coppy wherof in Italian I sent you a fortnight since, but, I know not how, it was not presented him, and, since, my lord writes to us that he thinkes it better to be donn by word of mouth.

I forgott also to tell you that in the Act at Cambridge they have defended some points of Cath[olic] religion, as that good workes are

---

[916] Juan de Necolalde.

[917] Richard Smith.

[918] On 3/13 August 1633 Smith reported to Biddulph that he had 'seene a letter of Mr [Henry] Tailor, agent of the infanta in London', written to Cardinal Borgia, 'where he giveth the reason why the Spanish agent there hath writ against me to R[ome], to wit by reason of the dayly complaintes made to him of me for the continual il[l] offices I doe against Spayne, which in truth is false'. Apparently, Taylor was not sure these stories were true, but 'he saieth that he is sure that manie priests are French', and that Smith's dependency on Richelieu meant he should not be allowed to return; AAW, B 27, no. 126.

[919] Probably Thomas Arundell, 1st Baron Arundell.

[920] Isabella Clara Eugenia.

necessary for salvation, and meritorious etc.[921] Mr Lab[orne] tells me
he sent you the conclusions them selves a fortnight since.[922]

I send you now a catalogue of pr[iests] in Lancashire, and other
northren [*sic*] shires.

[*on p. 224*]

Addressed: Pour Mons*ieu*r Fitton a Rome.

Endorsed: Clerk. 19 Julye.
About Mr Wilford who hath now married an heretick.

50. Laborn [George Leyburn] to Fitton [Peter Biddulph], 9 August 1633

[*AAW, A XXVII, no. 81, pp. 239–240*]

Worthie deare sir,

I have yours of the 16 of July, and I have acquainted yo*u*r brother
Worthingtons brother[923] w*i*th the 44^s and it will be payed according
to yo*u*r desire. Infallibly you are much mistaken concerning jus

---

[921] At the 1633 Commencement at Cambridge, one of Richard Neile's chaplains, Eleazor
Duncon, who was also a friend of William Laud and John Cosin, defended Cardinal
Bellarmine and argued in favour of a series of theses located in Bellarmine's works, among
which theses was the proposition that 'bona opera sunt efficaciter necessaria ad salutem';
Milton, *CR*, p. 76; *CSPD, 1633–1634*, p. 150. Anthony Milton points out that this appeared
as an appendix in Robert Shelford's *Five Pious and Learned Discourses* (Cambridge, 1635), itself
an extreme statement of 'Arminian/Laudian' thought, and was exploited by, for example,
the Franciscan Christopher Davenport in his book *Deus, Natura, Gratia*; Milton, *CR*, p. 76.
See also Tyacke, *AC*, p. 227; Lake, 'The Laudian style', pp. 165, 170, 171; Albion, *CI*, ch. 7.
(Davenport's book was dedicated to Charles.) For Davenport's favourable reception by
some of the Laudians, see Milton, *CR*, pp. 245, 250–251. On 3/13 August Smith sent
Biddulph 'thes printed trea*ti*ses [?] wh*i*ch were the *conclusi*ons publikly defended in the Act
at Cambridge wh*i*ch they wil be glad to see and it is a certaine signe of great inclina*ti*on to
Cath[olic] faithe'; AAW, B 27, no. 126. Gregorio Panzani was informed in late 1634 by the
Benedictine William Johnson that, at the 1633 Commencement, 'nell'addottorare li scolari
fu detto publicamente: papam esse universalem ecclesiae patrem, regem esse temporalem
patrem, sed debere utrumque regere et temporale et spiritualem statum'; VA, PD,
fo. 45r.

[922] See *Letter 48*.

[923] Richard Worthington. See *Letters 11, 38*. On 26 August 1633 Richard's brother, William,
wrote, from the Worthington family seat at Blainscow, to Biddulph about his marriage case,
and remarked that he had seen Biddulph's letter of 29 June/9 July to Richard 'wherin you
give notice of the duplicate of the breve sent to Flanders from whence I will expect a copie,
and then give order about it as cause shall requyre; the money shall be repayed to M^r
Laborne'; AAW, A XXVII, no. 88, p. 255.

patronatus in this contry; first in respect that Cardenal Allans facultyes as also the archpriests run thus: do tibi potestatem dispensandi ut vendatur jus patronatus, and I doe thinke that Fa[ther] Ph[ilip's] facultyes which he receaved lately from that city contayneth the same words. Secondlie to sell jus patronatus haith been practized ever in this contry since the first change. Thirdly it is the opinion of all our ancient priests, secular and regular. Moreover according to the ancient lawes <of this contry> in Catholique tyme jus patronatus is esteemed aliquid temporale.[924]

I am very glad that Monsieur Crequy haith imparted her Majestyes letter to his Holynes and I wish that it may effect a happie dispatch. Thos former delayes have caused great discontent and maketh Catholiques thinke that his Holynes is not much sensible of ther miseryes, and I have heard some of worth saye that, if ever good tymes come, the pope shall never have ther consent to enjoye the first fruits of benefices as formerly popes did in this contry.

I doe send unto you the conclusions of Oxforde,[925] but they are not soe good as the last which I sent unto you. Never was ther soe great a disposition in thes two universityes towards Catho[lic] religion as now ther is.

Our occurrences are that the bishop of Canterbury departed this life on Mundaye last in the morning[926] and he made a profession of his faith a litle before his death which was that he did abhorre the religion of papists in his hart and that in his conscience he did esteeme this pope to be the greatest Antichrist that ever was. It is thought that discontent di[d] hasten his death in regarde that the king, by meanes of the bishop of London,[927] did urge him to approve a booke (much contrarie to the doctrine of puretans) composed by one Doctor Potter of Oxforde,[928]

---

[924] For contemporary Catholic views on rights of presentation to Church-of-England livings, see AAW, A XIV, no. 34 (William Bishop's opinion, of February 1615); AAW, A XVI, no. 187 (Thomas Martin's opinion, of 1622). See also ARSJ, Anglia MS 36/ii, fo. 353r ('An liceat cuidam Catholico in Anglia habenti jus presentandi ad beneficium presentare aliquem haereticum ad majora mala impedienda').

[925] Leyburn may be referring to the recent confrontation, on 6 July 1633, between John Prideaux and Peter Heylyn during the Oxford Act; CSPD, 1633–1634, p. 190; A. Wood, The History and Antiquities of the University of Oxford, 2 vols (Oxford, 1792, 1796), I, p. 392; A. Milton, 'The creation of Laudianism: a new approach', in T. Cogswell, R. Cust, and P. Lake (eds), Politics, Religion and Popularity (Cambridge, 2002), pp. 162–184, at p. 170.

[926] George Abbot died on 4 August (E.B. Fryde, D.E. Greenway, S. Porter, and I. Roy (eds), Handbook of British Chronology, 3rd edition (London, 1986), p. 234), though here Leyburn gives the date as 5 August.

[927] William Laud.

[928] i.e. Christopher Potter's Want of Charitie Iustly Charged, on all such Romanists as Dare [...] Affirme, that Protestancie Destroyeth Salvation, 1st edition (Oxford, 1633). For Potter, one of Laud's vice-chancellors at Oxford, see Milton, CR, pp. 155–157; Letters 53, 55, 56.

a man much beloved of the bishop of London. Will you heare the prophesie which was written 80 yeares aggoe? It shall never merrie in England be, whilst Abbats is bishop of Canterbury; but when Abbats bishopricke is commed and gone, then priests and muncks in England shall swarme. I have noe faith in prophesies. Notwithstanding, I am confident that we shall enjoye better tymes. Our king and queen are removed to Otlands.

I commend unto you the contents of the inclosed which should have gone with a French priest.

Aug[ust] 9 1633.

[on p. 240]

Addressed: A Monsieur Monsieur [sic] Fitton a Rome.

Endorsed: Laborn. 9 Aug[ust].
          About jus patronatus.

51. Clerk [John Southcot] to [Peter Biddulph], 16 August 1633

[AAW, B 47, no. 62]

Sir,

Being newly rettourned out of the country I mett with two of yours of the 16 and 23 of July, having omitted the last week to write unto you by reason of my absence from London. I ame glad to heare that Abbote [sic for Robert] Barklay is in no disgrace there, as was formerly signified.[929] I advertised Mr Ducket therof, but now I must recall it againe, and wish him to continew his journy in case he can gett of his bonds out of the high commission court, which is not yet donn.

Your second letter is full of good newes. God send the effects to be answerable in all points, and, the more to engage Crequy in soliciting the buissenesse, lett him know that the queen expects his answer for which I pray you presse him earnestly. I thank you for the avisi which are very gratefull and wellcome here. I have little to advertise you from hence being newly come to town. Abbots, lord of Canterbury, died on the 4th of this month at Lambeth, and he professed on his death bed to dy neither papist nor Arminian. Laud, lord of London, is nominated[930]

---

929 See Letter 32; Allison, RSGB, II, p. 281.
930 William Laud was nominated archbishop of Canterbury on 6 August 1633.

and elected already (as I heare) to succeed him, and Doctor Jukes,[931] bishop of Hereford (as I take it), is to be of London, being a creature of [*three words deleted*] Lauds and promoted by him.[932] This wilbe a great strengthning of the Arminian party against the puritans, and will make a great change generally ere long to the better, the king inclining wholy that way and having left the puritanicall principles in which he was bred and brought up wholy. It is generally thought that the times will every day grow better and better for Catholickes, and that the State by degrees will bring all <all> to the same passe, as in 3° Elizabethae, before the chief penall lawes were enacted. The compositions go on slowly.[933] Pursevants do little either in London or in the country. The king and queen are at Otelands in Surrey both well in health, God be thanked, as also the prince and princesse. There was a deliberation not long since in councell here about our breaking with the Turk, and setting forthe a navy to that end, but now I heare it is dashed againe, or at least suspended till a better occasion and all those commaunded silence who were demaunded their advize therin both marchants and seamen. I heare nothing to any purpose donn by the judges in their circuitts this summer against recusants or priests, and a little before they began their circuitt one Alexander Baker, a Jesuit, being taken openly in the street and committed to Newgate, was within few daies delivered by my Lord Chief Justice Richardson[934] him self, at the queens entreaty, to whom meanes was made for it.[935] Some of the Jes[uits'] followers here do observe as a great wonder that, since the queen came in, none of the ladies at court are become Catholickes, and I heard my self a Jes[uit][936] speake this openly, as it were to the queens disgrace, in a gentlemans house in the country. But they do not observe in the meane time, or at least they do not speake much of, those good offices which the queen hath donn both for Catholickes and priests, and particulerly for the Jesuitts them selves, which are not few in number, nor of small regard being dewly

[931] William Juxon.

[932] For Richard Smith's satisfaction at Juxon's promotion to the see of London, see AAW, B 47, no. 62. See also *CSPV, 1632–1636*, p. 152. For Laud and Juxon, see Davies, *Caroline Captivity*, p. 45. When Juxon was promoted to be lord treasurer in 1636, Smith said he could not believe the rumour that it was done through the influence of the faction which was opposing Laud; AAW, A XXVIII, no. 106, p. 385. For an account of Juxon's appointment which interprets it as a partial reverse for Laud, see B. Quintrell, 'The Church triumphant? The emergence of a spiritual lord treasurer, 1635–1636', in J. Merritt (ed.), *The Political World of Thomas Wentworth, Earl of Strafford, 1621–1641* (Cambridge, 1996), pp. 81–108.

[933] For Viscount Wentworth's complaints in October 1633 that the compounding process in the North was being obstructed by the 'exchequer men', see Knowler, *ESLD*, I, p. 129.

[934] Sir Thomas Richardson, lord chief justice of King's Bench.

[935] See *CSPD, 1633–1634*, p. 557.

[936] This may be a reference to Henry Hawkins SJ. See *Letter 45*.

weighed. I heare that upon some complaint made unto the king by occasion of some mariage made by the French Capucins, the queen hath absolutely forbidden them to marry any English hereafter, which perhaps is not amisse considering how easily they admitted all sorts to marry, and sometimes Catholickes and Protestants togeather, to the hurt of religion, and never inquiring of the parties whether it were with consent of parents. I send you here a relation of my Lord Baltemors new plantation in Mary Land, which perhaps you will willingly see.[937]

Fa[ther] Francis[938] doth still prosecute his purpose of printing his book[939] and would have <the> approbation of divers priests of severall orders to it. M[r] Blacklo[940] hath in some sort approoved it (unawares) and the friar sent also to me before I went out of town for the same purpose. But I putt it of[f] with the excuse of my journy. I do not heare by them that have seen the book that it will answer expectation, especially in that point touching the reconciling of the English Protestant doctrine to the Cathol[ic] wherin he is very short and scant (although that seem[s] to be his chief scope), the work otherwise seeming to be of ostentation more than of use, the au[thor] being well conceited of him self, and the more bycause the stroke of his order conceave him to be one of the best schollers in the world. I cannot learn what that minister is who hath sent his book to the Venetian ambassador in Rome to be shewed to his Hol[iness] and I doubt there is some trick in it. Yet we heare that many ministers are growen not only very temperat but also Catholickly minded in their opinions, and all generally are so reputed in Oxford at this time. The Capucins here do say that they have converted divers ministers, but I do not heare of any in particuler.[941]

Thus with all woonted good wishes I rest.

16 August 1633.

No address.

---

[937] Not surprisingly, many of the secular clergy were unimpressed with the 1st Baron Baltimore's missionary efforts. In February 1633 Richard Smith wrote to Biddulph that the Paris nuncio, Bichi, had asked him whether Charles I sent 'any Cath[olic] nobleman to make plant*ati*on in the north of America'. Smith replied shirtily that he knew 'of no such', though he admitted to Biddulph that Bichi must have been talking about Baltimore 'who went thither some yeers agoe with 2 preists but returned without fruite'; AAW, B 27, no. 116.

[938] Christopher Davenport (Francis a Sancta Clara) OFM.

[939] Davenport, *Deus, Natura, Gratia*.

[940] Thomas White.

[941] For Cyprien de Gamache's account of Henrietta Maria's Capuchins' conversion of Protestant ministers (though in and after 1635), see Birch, *CT*, II, pp. 332f.

Endorsed: Clerk. 16 Aug[ust].
     About F[ather] Francis his booke.
     About the Capuccines forbidden to give sacram[ents].

52. Clerk [John Southcot] to Fitton [Peter Biddulph], 30 August 1633

[*AAW, B 47, no. 61*]

Sir,

I have yours of the 6 of August. The excommunications against those 5 or 6 monkes, which were sent <hither> from Spaine, were not served upon them otherwise than by way of threatning, and they (as I heare), having notice given them that way, have subscribed them selves.[942] If Fa[ther] Fitzherb[ert] dye, you may at least sue for a visitt of the college[943] by that occasion. All here are against having a straunger bishop and infallibly he would not be obaied neither by the laity, nor by the clergy,[944] but if Mr Bennet or D[octor] Champney <your other correspondent>[945] were made bishops they would governe well and give content to the far greater part.[946] Nothing makes the clergy complaine of waunt and poverty but the absence of a bishop with ordinary power, for the Jes[uits] in their bookes and speaches do commonly teach their followers that they are not bound to mantaine

---

[942] For the proceedings against those Benedictine monks professed in Spain who refused to submit to the authority of the new Benedictine congregation in England, see Lunn, *EB*, pp. 149–150; *Letter 46*.

[943] The English college in Rome.

[944] See AAW, A XXVII, no. 91, p. 263, for Anthony Champney's letter of 31 August/10 September 1633 to Smith, warning him that the appointment of a foreign bishop to rule over Catholics in England would be 'offensive to the State and not gratefull to any sort either clergy or regulers or the layty'. Champney repeated this warning on 10/20 September; AAW, A XXVII, no. 93, p. 269. On 30 September/10 October 1633 Smith wrote to Southcot that 'it may wel be that they intend to make F[ather] [Robert] Phil[ip] bishop but I can not see how he can doe both offices, both of bishop and confessor, and I think he wil not leave this last'; AAW, B 27, no. 131.

[945] George Leyburn.

[946] On 1/11 June 1633 Smith wrote that he believed that Edward Bennett would be appointed to replace him 'becaus both I and others have much commended him, and also becaus I was since asked' by Cardinal Bichi whether Bennett 'had not taken the oathe of fidelitie', i.e. the 1606 oath of allegiance. Smith had replied that Bennett never had. Smith thought that Bennett had signed the 1603 protestation of allegiance, but 'that protestacion is not the oathe'. And the protestation did not hinder 'my predecessor [William Bishop] from being bishop nor M^r [Robert] Drurie or M^r [Roger] Cadwalader from being glorious martyrs'. Smith then went off to get a copy of Thomas Preston's *A New-Yeares Gift for English Catholikes* (London, 1620), which listed the subscribers of the protestation, and found that Edward Bennett was not, in fact, among them; AAW, B 27, no. 121.

their b*isho*p unlesse he be an ordinary, so that they need not feare in Rome to give us a b*isho*p for waunt of meanes to mantaine him, but rather may justly feare to deny us a b*isho*p least we seek to his Hol[iness] for meanes to mantaine the clergy w*hi*ch must necessarily be supported, and yet without a b*isho*p or b*isho*ps cannot possibly subsist, but wilbe quickly eaten up by the regulars. This point is mainly to be urged there, and it is most certainly true.[947] This week I heare not any newes worth the writing. The k[ing] and qu[een] and prince, God be thanked, are well in health. Only the qu[een] felt some kind of numnesse in her arme while she was at Nonesuch, and therfor is come away about a month sooner to London than she had appointed. But here, God be thanked, she is prettily well againe of that numnesse. Perhaps she had fed to[o] liberally upon fruict, w*hi*ch hath bin unwholsome this yeare by reason of the wett weather and the couldnesse of the sum*m*er by w*hi*ch [the] harvest is like to come very late. The young prince of Chemey and his brother, having bin in these parts ever since before midsomer, are going back to Brusselles, and to morrow they begin their journy, having bin well entertained by the king and others here to their contentment.[948] There is one Jean Arismendes a subject of the k[ing] of France, borne upon the confines of Spaine, who made a journy last winter into Spaine, whether upon his own buissenesse, or my L*or*d Montagues[949] (whom he serveth) I know not, but, rettourning by Paris <in June last>, it seemes he dealt with my l*or*d b*isho*p[950] or his man to convay his letters safely hither from Spaine.[951] This man was sent for this day fortnight by an expresse

---

[947] On 16/26 August 1633 Smith wrote to Biddulph that he understood from him that in Rome 'resolution is taken to give England a b*isho*p' though he feared they would delay in finding 'a fit p*er*son'; AAW, A XXVII, no. 87, p. 253.

[948] See *Letter 45*.

[949] Francis Browne, 3rd Viscount Montague. See ESRO, BA 84 (a counterpart of a deed of sale of 24 January 1632 by Montague to Thomas Caporne and Christopher Bridger, witnessed *inter alia* by Jean Arismendy).

[950] Richard Smith.

[951] On 19 August 1633 Jean Arismendy, under interrogation, admitted that he had 'served Lord Montagu[e] 14 years', that he had gone to Spain to settle a financial matter with his brother, and that at Madrid he had delivered a letter from Montague to the count of Olivares. Since Arismendy returned, he understood that Lord Cottington had 'been advertised from Spain' that he, Arismendy, had 'made means for the bishop of Chalcedon to return into England', which accusation Arismendy denied. In Paris he had, however, discussed with Lord D'Aubigny and his circle the prospects for 'some good marriage in France for the duke of Lennox [James Stuart, 4th duke of Lennox, Lord D'Aubigny's brother], to fortify the queen's party' in England; *CSPD, 1633–1634*, p. 187. In the same month Arismendy wrote to William Cape, a Browne family retainer, to get him to use George Leyburn's and Père Joseph's influence with Henrietta Maria to secure his freedom; *ibid.*, p. 200. Subsequently, in February 1634, he admitted that he had been instructed to advise Chateauneuf, the former French ambassador in England, that the Spanish faction

messenger by Secretary Windebank, by whom he hath bin twice examined, and is still kept close prisoner in the messengers house. One of the points upon which he was examined was about my lord of Chalcedons agents here, who they were, wherby we ghesse that this fellow hath abused my lord, or at least his man, in putting uppon them the office of convaying his letters hither from Spaine, wherin perhaps are State matters, wholy (I dare say and sweare) unknowen unto my lord bishop who is no medler in such affaires.⁹⁵² Yet this may chaunce to

in England was 'greatly strengthened [...] to the prejudice of France' by means of the earl of Portland, Lord Cottington, and the earl of Arundel. Arundel's and Portland's eldest sons had 'married two sisters of the duke of Lennox', and threatened to 'draw the house of Lennox and the Scots towards that faction, by a marriage between him and a daughter of the house of Howard'. Chateauneuf should try to hinder this, in particular by proposing to the duke 'some good marriage in France'; *ibid.*, p. 461.

⁹⁵² Richard Smith reported to Biddulph on 13/23 September 1633 that 'this last poste from England I had no letters [...]. And the cause I suspect to be that which D[octor] Kellison writeth to me, that Aries Mendes [...] servant to my L[ord] Montague hath bene sent for by the counsel and examined what he did in Spayne and France, and what dealing he hath with Chalcedon and with his agents', which made Southcot and Leyburn 'to keep close'. Smith suspected this was a conspiracy by his Catholic opponents to 'drive Mendes from my L[ord] Mont[ague] as some of his freinds have long since desired. Yet perhaps the Jes[uits] wil make this some new persecution'; AAW, B 27, no. 130. Though the affair came to nothing (see *Letter 53*), as late as 26 October/5 November 1633 Smith was still complaining about Arismendy's imprisonment 'for writing and doing something against the l[ord] treas[urer]'. Despite Lord Treasurer Weston's reputation as a Hispanophile and, therefore, the probability that he would not be sympathetic to Smith and his supporters, Smith was determined to rectify matters. He found that some of his enemies had told 'the k[ing] that I set him [Arismendy] on and have writ a booke against the treas[urer] which hath no jot of truthe and, long since, I was told that Mendes was an apostata frier, which made me take heed of him'. Smith had written formally to Windebank to disavow the rumours. But, reflected Smith, 'perhaps it is a plot of State to aswage puritans and to make them think that the treasurer is odious to Catholiks; for there is no colour that I shold medle against him. But the Jes[uits] no doubt wil make great cries of this [...] to hinder a bishop'; AAW, B 47, no. 9. On 8 November 1633 Smith wrote directly to the lord treasurer excusing himself from blame over the affair. Smith informed Portland 'in verbo episcopi' that 'nether by my selfe, nor by Aresmendes [...] did I ever speake or write, or cause to be spoken or written any thing tending to his Majesties displeasure, or to the dishonor of any of his Majesties privy councell'. Instead, he had sought to 'extolle his Majesties most eminent parts both naturall and morall, and particularly to defend his royall clemencie towards his Catholike subjects'. Smith insisted that he himself refused to 'send any letter or message' to England via Arismendy; AAW, A XXVII, no. 102, p. 293. On 28 December/ 7 January 1634 Smith notified Biddulph that Richelieu had also written to Portland, as well as to Windebank, presumably about this affair, and that Portland 'saieth he hath nothing in particuler against me', and that the queen would deal with Charles 'to wink at episcopal authoritie, that it is for his good'; and furthermore, a 'noble man', perhaps Baron Arundell, 'hath given reasons to the secretarie to that purpose and he promised to shew them' to Laud. And a privy councillor, perhaps the earl of Dorset (see *Letter 53*), had agreed to talk to Charles and 'show him that episcopal authoritie would be useful to him'; AAW, B 27, no. 113. See also AAW, B 27, no. 114. Robert Philip told Gregorio Panzani in December 1634 that 'un signore', perhaps Dorset, 'interrogò il re per il Vescovo Calcedonense, et rispose

prejudice my lord not a little, especially if his ennemies come to heare of it, who will make the worst construction of things and do their best to stirr up the State against him, and against the clergy, and perhaps this is nothing but a trick to breed a jealousy both in our State and in the French cardinal[953] against my lord. I thought good to advertise you hereof (though I knew not of anything till yesternight, and therfor hope that all will come to nothing in the end, hearing all this while of no other bodies trouble) that you may be armed what and how to answer in that court if any thing be objected against my lords person here.

Thus with all woonted respe[cts] I end. 30 August 1633.

No address.

Endorsed: Clerk. 30 Aug[ust].
　　　　Concerning Arismendy his examination.
　　　　I pray send this to Mr Fitton.

53. Clerk [John Southcot] to Fitton [Peter Biddulph], 13 September 1633

[*AAW, B 47, no. 67*]

Sir,

I have yours this week of August the 20th with the avisi for which still I thank you, having received all since first you began to send them, saving only the last week of the 13 of August which D[octor] Champney saieth he received not, and feareth either that they are intercepted or lost by the way. I pray you therfor advertise us what you wrote that week and what papers you sent enclosed. You promised to send unto us coppies of all the memorialls that you give up there, which we should be glad to see, and to know the date in what yeare and month they were given.

I heare not yet of the Scottish courtier Mr Innis, but will inquire further of him, and shew him the avisi when we are acquainted. You need not feare the shewing of these avisi to the afflicted. I shalbe as careful therin as your hart can desire. It is strang[e] that they will make no end of our buissenesse there, after so many cries and clamors from hence. Our brethren in the country are exceedingly discontented, and so are our lay freinds, and both of them have failed in divers

che li piaceva la persona, ma non la qualità di vescovo'; VA, PD, fo. 42r. For Arismendy's activities in the late 1620s in support of Smith, see PRO, SP 16/152/34, fo. 76v; SP 16/159/5, fo. 5r–v.
953 Cardinal Richelieu.

places of their woonted contributions, wherin others are like to follow
their example, and then we shalbe quite blowen up and not able to
mantaine an agent there any longer, nor pay for letters, and you would
not beleeve what shifts we are faine to make to hould out thus long.
Although it be not good to inculcat much there *our* poverty and waunt
of meanes (which *our* adversaries wilbe apt enough to take advantage
~~of~~ <at> therby to hinder us from a b*isho*p) yet you may represent
the state we are in as caused by waunt of a b*isho*p with ordinary
power, seeing the Jes[uits] in their condemned bookes have taught
the Cath[olics] of England that they are not bound to mantaine their
b*isho*p unlesse he <be> an ordinary. And therfor, if the matter be
well propounded, this consideration ~~will~~ <must> rather help us than
hinder us in *our* sute ~~of~~ <for> b*isho*ps. And as concerning a straunger
b*isho*p I find nobody here that is not utterly against it, yet better it
were to have a straunger than none at all. Lett Crequy be remembred
to send an answer to the qu[een] that, in case the buissenesse be not
<speedily> effected according to her desire, she may have occasion
to write againe to him, or to his Hol[iness]. For without some such
occasion she will not write any more.

My l*or*d hath sent com*m*ission to treat with the Bened[ictines] of a
peace if they desire it in earnest, but as yet the treaty is not begunn, nor
will beginn, I think, till the terme. I feare the report of this in Rome will
putt a stay to their proceeding there, and therfor your best course wilbe
(as I think) not to be knowen that any such thing is really intended, and
that they are only devises sett on foot by *our* adversaries to hinder their
resolutions at Rome. And, in effect, if the treaty do proceed, nothing
shalbe concluded therin but with this clause salva determina*tione* Sedis
Ap*ost*olicae. Yet, to tell you plainly my opinion, I do not think that
the monkes will yeald to any reasonable terms when we come to
particulers. My l*or*d would have us stand uppon approbation and the
parochialls, or, if that cannot be obtained, uppon acknowledgm*en*t
of his ordinary authority over the laity, referring the rest to his
Hol[iness's] sentence. One writeth to me out of the country that, in
referring the faculties of missionaries, they had need to examine that
faculty w*hi*ch many here have of dispensing in restitutione bonorum
occultorum pertinentium ad haereticos w*hi*ch, if it come to the eares
of the world, will proove very scandalous.

S*i*r Toby Mathew wrote a <little> book some yeares past w*hi*ch he
calleth <u>Charity Mistaken</u> prooving therin that it is not ag*ain*st charity
for Cath[olics] to say that Protestants, remaining such, cannot be
saved.[954] There is an answer lately published to this book by one Doctor

[954] Sir Tobie Mathew, *Charity Mistaken, with the want whereof, Catholickes are uniustly Charged* (St Omer, 1630); ARCR, II, no. 528.

Potter, chaplaine to his Majesty, wherin (although the matter be but poor otherwise) he laies load uppon the Jesuitts, and cites Aurelius,[955] Ossat[956] and others for proofes against them in divers things.[957] The book is to[o] bigg to be sent to you, being at least 40 sheets of paper in 8[vo].

I wrote to you last week and before about one Arismenes his restraint, and of the bruict that was cast abroad as if it were concerning my lord of Chalcedons buissenesse.[958] But the secretary Windebank tould my Lord Montague[959] that the buissenesse did no way concerne my lord of Chalcedon, and the king saied as much to the earle of Dorsett. It were good to make this knowen there, bycause our adversaries (no doubt) have informed the court there to his disadvantage, as they have made it fly here over England already, seeking therby to putt frights into mens heads concerning the bishop as a man odious to the State.

We have no newes stirring here. The queen hath had a numnesse in one of her sides, for which she came to London 3 weekes before the time apointed and yesterday she went to reside at S[t] James, being within 6 weekes or a month of her time. Since her coming up she findes her self somwhat better having bathed and used other remedies by the appointment of her physitions. The times are very calme here and so have bin a great while God be thanked, and his Majesty, for it. The Irish Dominican,[960] of whom I wrote to you last week, that came from Lisboa, is still close prisoner, and so is M[r] Dade[961] also. The cause is not knowen, but it is saied that a merchant accuseth the Irish man of certaine words spoken in Spaine against the king, and Dade is called in question only for some correspondence he had with him since his arrivall here.[962] M[r] Fountaine[963] is out of town at this present, and so you must expect nothing from him this week.

Adieu. 13 September 1633.

[955] Jean Duvergier de Hauranne.
[956] Cardinal Arnaud d'Ossat (d. March 1604).
[957] Potter, *Want of Charitie Iustly Charged.*
[958] See *Letter 52.*
[959] Francis Browne, 3rd Viscount Montague.
[960] Arthur McGeoghan OP.
[961] Thomas Middleton OP.
[962] The Venetian ambassador Gussoni reported on 29 November/9 December 1633 that the Dominican, McGeoghan, 'suffered the extreme penalty two days ago'. He had returned from Spain where he had been overheard to say that he would not come into the realm 'unless it was to assassinate the king'; *CSPV, 1632–1636*, p. 172. John Flower recorded the rumours that McGeoghan had said that 'the king was an heretick and [. . .] it was lawfull to kill him', and also that he had said he would never return to England 'till he came to be revenged for the blood of the martirs spilt here'; PRO, C 115/105/8212. Richard Smith was remarkably unsympathetic and observed that 'the friers death hathe done rather good to Cath[olics] than harme'; AAW, B 27, no. 113. See Knowler, *ESLD*, I, p. 166; CRS, 1, p. 108.
[963] George Leyburn.

The lord debite of Ireland[964] carrieth him self there very haughtily as I heare, and hath, in a kind of scornfull manner, refused divers presents that were made ~~by~~ him by some of the nobility.

The lord marquis of Winchester was married last week to the Lady Honor[a], daughter to the earle of S[t] Albans and Clenrickard. 8 thousand pounds portion she is to have.

Address: Pour Mons*ieur* Fitton.

Endorsed: Clerk. 13 Sept[ember].
About Arismendy his buisiness.

54. Clerk [John Southcot] to Fitton [Peter Biddulph], 8 November 1633

[*AAW, B 47, no. 66*]

Sir,

This week I receaved yours of October the 13 with the woonted enclosed for which I thank you. But y*our* letter gives us small comfort, and [*word deleted*] <shewes> nothing but delaies, with w*h*ich our freinds here are very ill satisfied, and they wish you by all meanes to deliver that com*m*on letter of the clergies to my lord for his rettourne hither, togeather with his to the cardinals, and whatsoever other letter of the chapters you have kept back hitherto. I ame glad to heare that M[r] Con and you are become so confident <freinds>. My lord thinkes it is by M[r] Chambers meanes, that lives in Paris. God continew it. M[r] Fountaine[965] will certify you of some passages w*h*ich are fitt for you to know concerning this last borasco,[966] and so I refer you to him having no other particulers to write at this present. Lett us heare sometimes from you concerning M[ris] Mary Ward and that compaghny. Here it is confidently given out that they shall have their desire. Write also how matters stand with Fa[ther] Fitzherbert and the college, and what Fa[ther] Blunts negotiation is there.[967]

At this time there are divers controversies depending between Catholickes w*h*ich are like to be prosecuted in the open court with scandall, namely these: Suliard and Wilford <about a mariage>

---

[964] Sir Thomas Wentworth, 1st Viscount Wentworth.
[965] George Leyburn.
[966] A Mediterranean squall.
[967] On 13/23 September 1633 Richard Smith had reported to Southcot that 'F[ather] Blunt is gone up to R[ome] about the assembly of procur[at]ers; perhaps he is not to returne any more to England'; AAW, B 27, no. 130.

wherof you were certified long since;⁹⁶⁸ Mʳ Jo[hn] Arundell and his mother about his fathers last will;⁹⁶⁹ Lady Penelope Gage and Sir John Gage his executors about his last will and the wardship of his eldest sonn etc.⁹⁷⁰ And, bycause they are all (excepting Suliard) ghostly children of the clergy,⁹⁷¹ it is likely their adversaries will make some complaint a~~gai~~nst the clergy there, as they clamer here by this occasion. But howsoever particuler ~~men~~ priests may be to blame (though I know no great matter in those whom these buissenesses chiefly concerne) yet we see and feel by this the waunt of a b~~isho~~p ~~wonderfully~~ exceedingly.

Thus in hast. 8 Novemb[er] 1633.

Addressed: Pour Mons*ieu*r Fitton. Rome.

Endorsed: Clerk. 8 Nov[ember].
About controversies amongst Catholikes.

55. Clerk [John Southcot] to [Peter Biddulph], 13 December 1633

[*AAW, B 47, no. 68*]

Sir,

I have yours this week of the 19ᵗʰ November with others enclosed both for Mʳ Innes and Mʳ Orpe⁹⁷² which shalbe delivered. As touching Mʳ Orpe, although you say you advertised me of him before, yet I never receaved any such advertisment. Perhaps it was in that letter w*hich*

---

⁹⁶⁸ See *Letter 49*.

⁹⁶⁹ For the will of John Arundell of Lanhern in Cornwall and Chideock in Devon, of 15 April 1632, see PRO, PROB 11/164, fo. 326v. The will refers to a deed of January 1626 raising various fines on Arundell's property. Under the terms of the deed the testator could appoint a person to receive the funds, and Arundell's will appoints Sir Henry Compton of Brambletye, Sussex, for this purpose. It charges 'as ernestly and deeply as a father can charge his children in dutie to obey him' that each of his sons (John, Thomas, and George) should 'not [. . .] attempt practise or doe anything to alter, transport or dispose otherwise of the aforesaid mannours than the uses in the [. . .] indenture mencioned, lymitted or appoynted'. For John Arundell Snr's wife, Anne (Jernigan), see PRO, PROB 11/177, fo. 15r. For the sentence delivered in arbitration of the case, see PRO, PROB 11/164, fos 429v–30r.

⁹⁷⁰ See *Letters 85, 91*; PRO, WARD 7/85/38.

⁹⁷¹ i.e. secular clergy.

⁹⁷² Thomas Arpe. He was (by Michaelmas 1636) appointed Henrietta Maria's provider of the robes. He married Katherine, the daughter of Jean Garnier. She became one of the queen's chamberers. (I am very grateful to Caroline Hibbard for this information.) In February 1636 Biddulph 'sent some sweet oiles to Mʳ Orpe', whom Biddulph understood to have been 'reconciled to the Catholike Church'; AAW, A XXVIII, no. 93, p. 353.

miscaried, of the 5 of Novemb[er] if you writt at that time, as it seemes you did, bycause in your next of the 12 you mention no omission. I think I advertised you in some of my former that I heard nothing from you of the receipt of three of mine written since the beginning of June, videlicet of the 21 June, 2 August and 13 September, and I desire to heare by your next, in answer to this, whether those letters came to your hands or noe.

In one of my late letters I did advertise you of one Mr Francis Harris, a pr[iest] and prisoner in Newgate, according to a report which I heard then, that he had [word deleted] not carried him self so well in his last troubles towards Mr Lab[orne], Mr Ireland[973] and Mr Curtese[974] as he should have donn, and that there was therupon conceaved some suspicion of his fall. But now, having spoken with the party my self, I find that he hath bin wronged, and that <he> did nothing worthy of any such censure or suspicion, and therfor I pray you lett any information you have had to the contrary quite cease, and lett the gentleman be fully restored to his former good name. I perceave the worst that hath happened is but indiscretion <at most> but no malice.[975]

The day after I writt to you last which was being Saterday,[976] the king came from Theobalds, and upon the queens complaints to him of the second nurse, and those that preferred her, she being since prooved (either truly or counterfeitly) madd,[977] he presently delivered the young duke of York to the former Catholick nurse againe, notwithstanding she had refused to take the oath of alleageance, and he gave order withall she should have as much given her as was given to the other upon the christning of the child.[978] Some think that the finger of God

---

[973] This may be a reference to Edmund Dutton, alias Ireland, who had come to London in April 1632 as agent for Douai college; Anstr., II, pp. 91–92. Dutton became secretary to the episcopal chapter and appears to have been chaplain to Baron Arundell; Allison, RSGB, III, p. 191; AAW, A XXIV, nos 29–33; XXIX, no. 83.

[974] This may be a reference to the priest Peter Curtis, whose father was pewterer to Henrietta Maria. See Anstr., II, p. 78.

[975] For Francis Harris, see ibid., p. 148. An undated petition (PRO, SP 16/487/20) by Harris, written while he was in the Marshalsea, offered his services to the State, and indicated that he had been reconciled to the Church of England. Harris was one of those who had been expelled from the English college in Rome during the 'Fitton' rebellion, i.e. the protest, led by Biddulph, against the college's Jesuit administrators.

[976] i.e. 9 November 1633.

[977] On 14 December 1633 John Flower reported to Viscount Scudamore that the second nurse 'grew to be mad' when the child was removed from her (despite the best efforts of the physician, Sir Theodore Turquet de Mayerne), and because of the 'disdainfull and despitefull termes which the insulting papist [nurse]' gave her. The king committed the deranged nurse to 'Dr Shephard', 'a curer of mad folke'; PRO, C 115/105/8164.

[978] The Venetian ambassador Gussoni remarked in November 1633 that, 'to the astonishment [...] of many', the queen had 'persuaded the king to agree to her choice

is extraordinarily in this buissenesse. It is also reported that young S*ir* Charles Sherly, a youth of ten yeares of age, baronett, since he was taken from his mother my Lady Dorothy, and given to her brother, his uncle the earle of Essex,[979] to be bred in Protestantisme, hath never since shewed any joy, and still refuseth to go to church or to praiers with them, saiing that his father charged him upon his death bed to keep his religion.[980] Yea it is reported further that his father hath appeared severall times unto him and spoken to him to this effect, but I suspend my beleef for that matter till I heare better proof than I have donn yet.

~~Since~~ Within this fortnight I heare there are 4 prisoners released <upon bond> videlicet M*r* Henry More ~~the~~ <a> Jes[uit] out of the New prison, and M*r* Tresame, agent for the Benedictines,[981] out of the same prison, Fa[ther] Bonaventure,[982] Franciscan, out of Newgate, and a fourth whose name I know not. By this it may appeare that the report which is there given out of persecution is not so true; as also by an other instance concerning my lord of Arguile,[983] against whom an informer intended to sue the law for placing his daughter in a nunnery

of a lady who openly professes the Catholic faith to act as nurse to the baby prince'. There was a great deal of discussion as to what oath of loyalty should be put to her, but 'in the end the queen overcame everything and induced the king to agree to an ordinary oath of fealty, such as is taken by the other Catholics, including ecclesiastics, who take part in the queen's service'; *CSPV, 1632–1636*, p. 160. Walter Yonge noted that the nurse, one Mrs Eliot, refused the oaths of supremacy and allegiance; BL, Additional MS 35331, fo. 56r. Lord Cottington reported that the nurse was offered the oath of allegiance, 'and she refus'd it, whereupon there grew a great noise both in the town and court, and the queen afflicted herself with extream passion upon knowledge of a resolution to change the woman, yet after much tampering with the nurse to convert her, she was let alone to quiet the queen'; Knowler, *ESLD*, I, p. 141. Smith also relayed the story to Biddulph, and said 'it is to be noted that the Cath[olic] nurses confessor is a sec[ular] preist, for otherwise I doubt she wold not have refused the oathe'; AAW, B 27, no. 113.

[979] Robert Devereux, 3rd earl of Essex.

[980] Sir Charles Shirley was the son of Sir Henry Shirley and Dorothy Devereux (daughter of Robert Devereux, the 2nd earl of Essex). See R. Cust, 'Catholicism, antiquarianism and gentry honour: the writings of Sir Thomas Shirley', *Midland History*, 23 (1998), pp. 40–70, at pp. 45, 65, n. 20.

[981] Presumably this is the William Tresham who was arrested, by Francis Newton, on the grounds that he was a Benedictine monk (Foley, I, p. 519; PRO, SP 16/376/34. i) though no such person is identified as a Benedictine in Bellenger, *EWP*.

[982] Bonaventure Jackson OFM.

[983] Archibald Campbell, 7th earl of Argyll. Southcot, in his diary, records that he, Southcot, had come to England 'the second time in the yeare 1621 in the company of Don Carlos Coloma Spanish ambassador in May, and staied in England between 2 or 3 months only, and then retourned into Flanders and went with the earle of Argyle to the siege of Berghen'; CRS, 1, p. 97.

at Bruxelles,[984] but that the king will <have> him to desist, and to lett fall his sute. Neither are the pursevants very buissy in searching and when they do search they do it but slightly, and nothing so vigorously as heretofore.[985] My lord writes that the Jes[uits] in Paris do shew the clergies information touching the calmnesse of these times presented at Rome. I wonder how they came by it. They say that it causeth the encrease of persecution here, but how impudently and foolishly they say soe, any wise body may judg.

There is a second edition of Potters answer to Charity Mistaken lately sett forth.[986] And within these few daies I saw a book of William Alabaster (who was sometimes prisoner in the Inquisition there about the for writing about the same subject) full of cabalisticall devises, derived out of the Hebrew Bible, to proove Protest Protestantisme.[987] He presented one to the king, and an other to the new archb[ishop] of Canterb[ury][988] and to some privat freinds a few. But I heare for certaine that they are commanded to be supprest, as containing much folly and madnesse, so that he fareth no better here with those devises than he did at Rome.[989]

Here is arrived lately an <Italian> doctor of phisick, one Signor Leonardo, that was, as he saieth, sometimes phisition to Card[inal] Doria.[990] As yet he hath not kissed the kings hand nor the queens. Only he hath bin with my lord martiall,[991] who will not bring him to the king till he see wherfor he cometh, and whether he intend to chang[e] his religion, being Catholick in shew. He spent 4 months in France, and, if he can gett any preferment here, he will stay. Otherwise he will rettourne from whence he came. Some that have conferred with him say he is universally read and talkes well. Perhaps he will gett to be the kings doctor.

There is a <Cath[olic]> lord who is much our freind and zealouse in our cause that hath spoken very effectually already to some of the

[984] Barbara (Melchiora) Campbell. She was placed at the convent of the Glorious Assumption in Brussels in 1628 and was clothed there in late December 1642; Arblaster, 'The infanta and the English Benedictine nuns', pp. 523, 526, n. 28.

[985] For James Wadsworth's and Francis Newton's difficulties in harassing Catholics at this time, see e.g. *CSPD, 1633–1634*, p. 319.

[986] Christopher Potter, *Want of Charitie Iustly Charged [. . .]* (London, 1634), RSTC 20136, a revised edition produced with the encouragement of William Laud. See *CSPD, 1633–1634*, pp. 232–233; Laud, *Works*, VI, p. 326.

[987] Presumably this is a reference to William Alabaster's *Ecce Sponsus Venit* (London, 1633), though it could also denote Alabaster's *Spiraculum Tubarum [. . .]* (np, nd), which was printed by the same printer, William Jones, who produced the former work.

[988] William Laud.

[989] See also AAW, B 27, no. 113. For Alabaster, see *NAGB*, p. 87.

[990] Giovanni Doria, cardinal deacon, archbishop of Palermo, and viceroy of Sicily.

[991] Thomas Howard, 2nd earl of Arundel.

councell in behalf of the hopefull and he purposeth to speake further and to present a coppy of those reasons which I sent you the last week. Wherof we have also hope to give some coppies privatly to others of the councell, which will prepare them well against my lords rettourne, or the setling of any other bishop hereafter.

For waunt of better matter I send you here enclosed a ballat made upon the execution of the Irish frier.[992]

Thus referring all other occurrences to M[r] Roberts,[993] I rest. 13 December 1633.

If that decree De Judice should passe it would breed infinit disgust, as I suppose you have seen partly already by the Disquisitio made in France.

It is true that M[r] Innes married such a woman, and no Catholick, but now I suppose she liveth well, and he continewes a good Catholick, though he be not a man to do us any great good. Yet it is not amisse to keep his freindship, bycause he hath much acquaintance at court with the great ones, and I take him for an honest man. M[r] Duglas[994] I think [to] be our freind. M[r] Hammon[995] and M[r] Lab[orne] are well acquainted with him.

No address.

Endorsed: Clerk. 13 Dec[ember].
        That M[r] Harris is innocent.

56. [John Southcot] to Fitton [Peter Biddulph], 10 January 1634

[*AAW, B 47, no. 69*]

Sir,

I receaved yours of the 3 Decemb[er] a fortnight agoe, and purposed to have answered it sooner but that sicknesse hindred me, wherof I ame now, God be thanked, recovered. I signified in one of my former the death of that M[r] Orpes father, who you say is coming away from thence, and I delivered that letter (which you sent a little after

---

[992] Arthur McGeoghan OP. See *Letter 53*.

[993] George Leyburn.

[994] Robert Douglas, who is referred to as 'Monsieur Robert Douglas, mon cousin' in William Douglas, 11th earl of Angus's commendatory letter of January 1633 in Robert Douglas's favour to the pope; PRO, 31/3/126, p. 121.

[995] John Jackson.

the former for Mr Orpe) for the countesse of Westmerland[996] to M^r
Roberts[997] who saieth he will deliver it.

As for directing any letter for me or Mr Roberts by any freind that
comes from thence you may indorse your letter to either of us by our
names, and wish the party to inquire for us of Mr Peeter Windor,
a taylor dwelling at the upper end of Holborne next to the Feather
taverne, and by him he shall easily come to speake with either of us.

I will inquire also for that Mr Clark in Milkstreet as you desire.
This to your letter. Now for other matters. The queen spake to the
king since twelftide in behalf of my lord,[998] and would have shewed
him those reasons made by way of pararell betwixt a bishop and
provincialls, wherof I sent you a coppy a fortnight agoe, but that the
king would not read them. Yet he tould the ~~king~~ queen that he liked
the bishop well enough for his person and thought him an honest man
but liked not the authority which he claimed. We were glad to heare
that his Majesty spake so well at least of the bishops person, and hope
it wilbe a step to bring on the liking also of his authority by degrees.
It seemes the k[ing] is persuaded that the puritans would make some
sterrs if the bishop were here, for he tould the qu[een] that neither she
nor he could protect him if he came, but that they would gett him
into their hands, and therfor he wished the qu[een] not to lett him
come. And, if this be the k[ing's] chief motive for not permitting him,
I hope we shalbe able to satisfy him ere long, bycause really there is
no such daunger from the puritans, but a great deale more from the
Jesuitts party amongst the Protestants, uppon their persuasions and
misinformations.

There hath bin no searching in London all this Christmasse, nor in
the country that I heare, neither are any warrants abroad, and some
warrants are particulerly called in, as that of Grey[999] the pursivant who
also was committed to prison for misbehaving him self in a certaine
search. There was a pursevant sent from the high commission court
to one Mr Georg Brown[1000] 60 miles from London to fetch him and
his Catholick schoolmaister up to answer the statute concerning that
matter in the court,[1001] and he is now here seeking by the queens

---

[996] Grace, daughter of Sir William Thornhurst and Anne, daughter of Thomas Howard,
1st Viscount Howard of Bindon. She had married Mildmay Fane, 2nd earl of Westmorland,
in July 1626.

[997] George Leyburn.

[998] Richard Smith.

[999] John Gray. See M. Havran, *The Catholics in Caroline England* (London, 1962), pp. 124,
127; Foley, I, pp. 516–517.

[1000] Son of Sir George Browne of Great Shefford, Berkshire.

[1001] High commission records in the State Papers (for April–November 1634) record that
George Browne and Eleanor (Blount), his wife, and one John Cole were dealt with by the

meanes to have the matter taken up wherof he is in hope. This is an unusuall matter, and proceedeth not (as perhaps the afflicted will make beleeve there) from any intention to persecute, but meerly uppon an information and complaint of a malitious neighbour, (as it is thought) the minister of that parish. I heare of divers ministers that are well disposed, and there is one Lugar[1002] whoe hath noted down in a cople of sheets of paper the chief reasons for which he doubteth of the Protestant religion, wherof I intend to send a coppy to my lord and will wish him to send it you, for I think them well worth the reading and shewing there.[1003] And it is not unlikly that others will follow his example. I heare the Jesuitts are in hand to answer Doctor Potters book in answer to Charity Mistaken;[1004] which book doth much harme and confirmes many readers in Protestantisme. It hath bin twice printed.

The tediousnesse of these delaies about our matters made us resolve in our last consult to write to D[octor] Maylard[1005] at Paris (inconsulto <et inscio> Chalcedonensi) to entreat him in the clergies name to propose our case to the Sorbon, and to know of them what we may lawfully doe to help our selves in case we cannot gett a bishop from Rome. Perhaps the noise of this in Rome (when the nonce there shall heare of it and write it to Rome), though we intend to do it privatly, will awake them a little, and bring them to some resolution about our buissenesse. Use your discretion in taking or not taking notice hereof there, but I rather think it better for you to take no notice of it.

court. Browne was ordered to send up to London the popish books seized in his house (by the pursuivant John Wragge); *CSPD, 1633–1634*, p. 583; *ibid., 1634–1635*, pp. 51, 110, 118, 316, 324; *NAGB*, pp. 43, 99; W.H. Rylands (ed.), *The Four Visitations of Berkshire*, 2 vols (Harleian Society 56, 57, 1907–1908), I, p. 76.

[1002] John Lewgar. He had been converted to Catholicism allegedly by William Chillingworth's own arguments in favour of the Church of Rome. Lewgar, in 1635, resigned his Church-of-England benefice and in 1637 travelled to Maryland to serve as the 2nd Baron Baltimore's secretary there; Anstr., II, pp. 189–190; R.R. Orr, *Reason and Authority* (Oxford, 1967), pp. 28, 31, 38, 96, 101, 127, 128, 134; Hughes, *HSJ*, p. 232.

[1003] See 'A conference betwixt Mr Chillingworth, and Mr Lewgar', in *Additional Discourses of Mr. Chillingworth*, 4th edn (London, 1727), bound with William Chillingworth, *The Works of William Chillingworth*, 9th edn (London, 1727). On 20 June 1635 the Franciscan Christopher Davenport took Lewgar to visit Gregorio Panzani; VA, PD, fo. 98r. On 23 July the Benedictine John (Leander) Jones brought 'un memoriale' from Lewgar to give to the queen; Panzani referred Jones to Robert Philip; *ibid.*, fo. 104r. Lewgar himself came on 11 August with a letter from Jones, and was similarly told to see Philip; *ibid.*, fo. 107r.

[1004] Christopher Potter's *Want of Charitie [...]* was answered by Matthew Wilson SJ, *Mercy & Truth. Or Charity Maintayned by Catholiques* (St Omer, 1634); ARCR, II, no. 821. Wilson's tract provoked Chillingworth's *The Religion of Protestants a Safe Way to Salvation* (London, 1638).

[1005] Henry Mayler, who was a doctor of the Sorbonne; Anstr., I, p. 223.

There was a great councell day held since twelftide wherin the fishing buissenesse <was> fully concluded,[1006] and the last of the 24 compaghnies of London subscribed to it with the rest. There are also a dozen of the kings shipps preparing, perhaps for defence of the saied fishing, wherin now all the three kingdoms, England, Scotland and Ireland, are interested, and no lesse than a hundred thousand of the kings subjects have part, some more some lesse. It is a maine buissenesse, and, if it go well forward, it will enrich the king and kingdom exceedingly, and the king shall have then lesse need of parlaments for mony. This alone will bring in at least two hundred thousand pounds yearly to the king. The admiralty is to be disposed of very shortly (the duke of Buckinghams debts being all paied) but it is not yet knowen uppon whom it shalbe bestowed. Some think the earle of Holland, but I rather think some other.

Three daies agoe Sir Francis Nethershall,[1007] agent for the Lady Elizabeth[1008] here, was sent to the Tower, and presently after his chamber and closett were searched by order from the councell. I cannot certainly heare what the cause is.

Thus, for the other occurrents remitting you to M[r] Roberts, I end with woonted good wishes. 10 Januarii 1634.

No address.

Endorsed: For M[r] Fitton.
　　　　　London. 10 Jan[uary].
　　　　　How to direct my letters to Peeter Winder.

57. [George Leyburn] to Leuis Amaryn [Richard Smith], 14 January 1634

[*AAW, A XXVII, no. 129, pp. 401–404*]

Most honored sir,

Since I writte unto you my last I have not heard from you, the post as yett being not arrived. I have <u>now sent</u> unto you a masti[v]e dog as good I thinke as can be desired.[1009] I pray God that he come safe to your hands. I forgott to signifie in my last how much our queen haith

---

[1006] See *Letters 6, 17, 18, 36, 40.*

[1007] Sir Francis Nethersole. See *CSPV, 1632–1636*, pp. 183, 189, 202; Birch, *CT*, II, p. 233 (Nethersole's criticisms of Charles's policy on regaining the Palatinate).

[1008] Princess Elizabeth, widow of the Elector Palatine, Frederick V.

[1009] See *Letter 46.*

been offended lately with Monsieur Buttarde.[1010] I doe not knowe the occasion of her disgust, but I am certayne that she did take him up twise very roundly when he had his audience in the presence of the king and two dayes before, and the poore man was soe out of countenance that he was not able to replye one word. It is great pitty that the State ther will not send one who may be gratious unto her Majesty. But assure your selfe, whosoever shall be sent, if Foster have any doings with him, the French about the queen will be jealous of him. But now Monsieur Buttarde haith receaved a new order to continue here longer for which I am very sorrie.

Some few dayes aggoe the queen told the king that she had receaved a letter from the b[ishop] of Calcedoine[1011] and wish[e]d him to read it as also certayne reasons wherfore he should not be more molested than others. The king did not refuse either. Wherupon her Majesty tooke occasion to speake much in the commendation of the b[ishop] of Calcedoine, to which the king did replye that he did esteeme him to be a very honest good man but his autority would not be suffred here, to which the queen made answere that the b[ishop] would take an oath of fidelity.[1012] Howsoever, replyed the king, I doe not wish that he doe come over, for (sayd he) peradventure it will not be in your power nor [p. 402] myne to save him, he will be soe much sought after. The king formerly was wont to accept [sic] much against his person, now onely against his authority, which the queen as also Fa[ther] P[hilip] was glad to heare. I hope that in tyme some good will be effected. Howsoever, for my part, I am confident that if the

---

[1010] Le Sieur Boutard, the French agent to England. He had signed the *Général Désadveu des Catholiques Lais d'Angleterre [. . .]*, in which the ambassador François Duval, marquis de Fontenay Mareuil had sided with Richard Smith's supporters against Smith's critics; AAW, A XXIV, no. 99, p. 401; *Letter 3*. According to the Venetian ambassador Gussoni, Henrietta Maria took offence against Boutard because 'he spoke too warmly in defence' of Fontenay, who had recently departed the country, and who had displeased her. He 'spoke with modest zeal and defended himself very reasonably', but the queen 'would have nothing of it', and had 'chosen by special letters to make complaint' to her brother Louis XIII; *CSPV, 1632–1636*, p. 187. John Finet recorded that Henrietta Maria believed that Boutard had assisted in the theft of the papers of François de Rochechouart, who had conspired against Fontenay in a scheme which was intended to bring about the fall of Lord Treasurer Portland. See Loomie, *The Ceremonies of Charles I*, pp. 147–148; *CSPV, 1629–1632*, pp. 527–528; *ibid., 1632–1636*, pp. 83, 85.

[1011] Richard Smith.

[1012] On 28 December/7 January 1634 Smith informed Biddulph that 'a noble man', probably Baron Arundell, 'offered the counsel of England to be bound in five thousand pounds that I shall not meddle in matters of estate, and the q[ueen] said that the k[ing] wold be glad to see me offer to take any oathe which Cath[olic] bishops make to kings, but in England some have drawn a new forme of oath, which perhaps may displease in R[ome] and give the Jes[uits] occasion to calu[m]niate me, but in truthe I made it not'; AAW, B 27, no. 113.

b[ishop] were here at this present he would not be once sought after. For most of the <u>cheef lords of the</u> counsell have been truly informed of all matters concerning the b[ishop] and his clame of w*h*ich they were formerly ignorant.

F*athe*r Tobye[1013] haith been this Christmas w*i*th M*r* Southcott[1014] and now is newly returned to this towne and he was noe sooner arrived than th*a*t he writte a letter unto the Lady Carlile[1015] in thes words: 'Madame I was noe sooner com*me*d out of the country to this but th*a*t I went to White-hall w*i*th intention to see yo*u*r ladyship but, you being not to be found, I did not see in Whit-hall any thing more than Whit-hall, you being the onely creature th*a*t doth beautifie and adorne th*a*t place, and the sole object w*h*ich I adore. Wherfore returne, Madame, for w*i*thout you Whit-hall is nothing.' Certaynely he is soe extravagant growne th*a*t thos who formerly did adore him doe now laugh at him.[1016]

I writte unto you in my last concerning a noble knight. I praye God that you may effect what is desired. It will be to good purpose. Our miserie is want of friends in the court. I praye, if you doe procure such a letter as is desired, lett it be sent unto Madame Nurse.[1017] For other matters I doe referre you unto Monsi*eu*r Clerk[1018] who will send unto you <u>the commission</u> to be sente by this post. I receaved yesterdaye a

[1013] Sir Tobie Mathew.

[1014] i.e. John Southcot Snr, the Jesuit-favouring father of the priest John Southcot.

[1015] Lucy, wife of James Hay, 1st earl of Carlisle, and daughter of Henry Percy, 9th earl of Northumberland.

[1016] For contemporary comment about Mathew's relationship with the countess of Carlisle, see A.H. Mathew, *The Life of Sir Tobie Matthew* (London, 1907), pp. 303, 304; *CSPD, 1631–1633*, p. 437. In May 1632, William Case had related how Mathew had 'conducted my patron', the marquis of Winchester, 'into the chamber of a most gallant lady and a principall courtier', evidently a reference to the countess. 'As soone as hee had espied the lady a farr of, hee falls into a wonderfull admiration, crying out and turning towards my patron, was there ever such a creature seene? Behold my lo[rd] this admirable bewtie etc.' Winchester told Case that 'it was in such an extravagant manner that hee thought hee would have bawded for him', and then, 'comming to her', Mathew 'tooke her by the hand, saying, how doe you Madam? Shee answering not very well, hee replied you are not dead sure. If you bee, that soule of yours must needs bee in h[e]aven. And this fayer flesh of yours can not bee corrupted.' Case added that afterwards, at dinner, Mathew had 'discoursed about dispensations for mariage, viz. that my lo[rd] migh[t] gett a dispensation to marrie w*i*th an other of the sisters'. (Winchester's wife, Jane (Savage), had died in April 1631.) His audience 'generally saying that it was unlawfull', Mathew replied that the pope could dispense in any thing that was not against the 'law of nature', and called them all 'dunces'; AAW, A XXVI, no. 69, p. 194.

[1017] Françoise de Monbodiac, wife of Jean Garnier. She had been Henrietta Maria's childhood nurse. I am grateful to Caroline Hibbard for this point.

[1018] John Southcot.

letter from your best lady and an other from her husband,[1019] which
I intend to send unto you that you may see his zeale. My lady
wishes her service may be presented unto you and she is myndfull
of you as she will shortly manifest.

Sweet Jesus make you happie in all your affayres. 14 Jan[uary] 1634.

[on p. 404]

Addressed: A Monsieur Monsieur [*sic*] Leuis Amaryn demeurant dans
       la Place Maubert a Paris.

Endorsed: King of the bishop.

58. William Morgan [Case] to [an English secular priest], 4 February 1634

[*AAW, A XXVII, no. 131, pp. 407–410*]

Very reverend sir,

Were it possible to make his Holines understand the misery of our
cuntry doubtles wee should have releife, especially the remedie lying in
his hands. It is most evident that if the authority given to our pastor[1020]
by that holy Sea had been speedily declared to be the same which
other bishops have in their dioceses, there would never have been this
lamentable scisme, which wee now see, to the schandall of many, both
within and without. For, at the first, all lay Catholiks, excepting 3 or
4 sturdy statesmen (as they would seeme), were willing to obey, and
most free from the spirit of rebellion; which the Jesuits and some other
regulers perceiving right well, and not being able to skarr them with
their clamors of odious jurisdiction, they made most of their penitents
beleeve that the bishop had no jurisdiction at all in foro externo over the
laytie. And though in process of tyme (his Holines declaring nothing in
confirmation of the authority given) they have brought some more to
a desperate rebellion against authority, yet the most and best of theirs
are still upon this point that, if his Holines would declare my lo[rd]
bishop to have the authority by him chalenged over the laytie, they
would readily obey, prostrating them selves at his feet with all religious
humility. This hath been lately and seriously expressed by Earle Rivers,

----

[1019] John Jackson identifies Smith's 'best lady', i.e. patroness, as Anne (daughter of Miles
Philipson of Crook, Westmorland), wife of Thomas, 1st Baron Arundell; AAW, A XXVI,
no. 32, p. 105.
[1020] Richard Smith.

my Lo[rd] Savage, and the earle of Northumberlands unckle,[1021] who doubt not but that a good attonement would quickly ~~would quie~~ bee made, considering the disposition of the farr greater part of the laytie is to submitt [*p. 408*] in case the pope should plainly declare. For, as for such as Ployden,[1022] Rob[ert] Wintor and some ten hirelings of the Jesuits, they would easily be either reduced to better termes, or disgraced so that none would follow them. His Holines may consider into what absurd temerity some of these sectaries are fallen as to say the pope cannot oblige us to ~~such~~ admitt of such authority etc., and to question the power of his Holines in many things, and soe to censure the actions of the pope, as if hee were to bee judged and condemned by every one. The Florentine agent[1023] (as hee calls himself) in my hearing condemned him of being guilty of the warrs in Germany by assisting the French for the bringing in of <the> Swed[es] and (as I was most credibly informed) hee sayd, in the presence of some noble persons, that the cardinalls had called the pope coram nobis. A lady alsoe of principall rank, and a maine piller of the Jesuitts faction, sayd in the presence of two very great lords that <u>the pope went not well nor never would till God tooke him out of the world</u>, and <u>that hee is cause of dissention betweene preistes</u> here <u>in England</u>. That which may most deterr his Holines from giving a remedy to these mischeifs is the disposition of the State, as it is, perhaps, portraited to him. But lett it bee considered that our gratious soveraine is of a most mild and mercifull spirit, howsoever he may bee disposed in religion. And our most vertuous and Catholike queene beeing soe deere unto him, in so much that <the> reciprocall love betweene them is ad-mired by all, it cannot bee imagined that hee will bee ~~crewell~~ cruell [*p. 409*] to any of her religion, especially to those who jumpe with her in religious obedience to God and king. And howsoever the opposers of authority goe (as one of them sayd within these few dayes) the way of the State, yet are they noted to bee such as the State will never esteeme them nor trust them. It is credible ynough that our king hath the same dictamen with Constantius, and will never beleve they can bee true to their king who are false to their God.[1024] But lett it bee graunted that the State will not permitt episcopall authority over Catholiks, must not God be obeyed rather than man? And will

---

[1021] Sir William Herbert, 1st Baron Powis, husband of the 9th earl of Northumberland's youngest sister, Eleanor. I am very grateful to Mark Nicholls for his assistance with this point.

[1022] Francis Plowden Snr.

[1023] Amerigo Salvetti, ambassador in England of the grand duke of Tuscany.

[1024] The Emperor Constantius justified the employment of Christians in his service on the grounds that their open dissent from the imperial religion guaranteed that their professions of loyalty to himself must be true and not deceitful.

their want men willing to spend their bloud in this cause? No, no,
I dare say they will gladly suffer for the same furias atque ferocia etc. It
is most lamentable to see the contentions, disorders, enormities, and
ou[t]rages committed by many Catholiks for want of authority. In so
much that a good preist, prisoner in London, told mee within these
24 howers that the Catholiks are noted to bee [the] most litigeous,
most exorbitant, and most deboist of all other people here in London.
And when hee hath laboured the conversion of some Protestants, they
object these disorders and that there is not menes to remedy them.
I protest before God and his angells that, if his Holines permitt the
soveraigne authority to bee thus resisted, that [sic] every one may
according to his humor reject what hee list. It will be the utter ruin
of religion. In the name of Jesus Christ, whose vicar hee is, lett him
performe his duty, et ruat caelum. Here you have a rude scantling of
our misery.

Endevour to help us, and God bee your reward, Hantshire, 4°
Februar[y] 1633.

Yours,

Will[iam] Morgan

No address.

[on p. 410]

Endorsed: Of the libertinage of Catholicks for want of goverment.
          Of contemptible speaches of somme Catholicks against the
          pope.
          Of the necessity of a bishop.

59. Roberts [George Leyburn] to Louis Amarine [Richard Smith], 29 April 1634

[AAW, A XXVII, no. 144, pp. 441–444]

Most honored sir,

Since I writte myne by the last weekes post I have received yours
of the 26 of Apr[il]. Mr Car[1025] is arrived here and within 15 dayes
intendeth to returne agayne. He will have the best assistance that our
friends can afforde, and I am confident that within a short tyme that.

[1025] Miles Pinckney.

house[1026] will be prittely furnished. M[r] Chamberlayne[1027] is returned
into thes partes. He is a man wedded to the fathers,[1028] and therfore noe
wonder to be made of his reportes. The number of priests in prison
are <u>some 10, most</u> of w*h*ich I thinke would not enjoye ther freedome
if they might, in regarde some charities are sent to the prison w*h*ich
would not be sent unto them in particuler, as Captayne <u>Stuckley</u>,[1029]
<u>Goodman</u>,[1030] <u>Rivers</u>,[1031] M[r] <u>Harris</u>,[1032] <u>Canon</u>[1033] et[c]. I have <u>spoke for
a</u> masti[v]e bitch to present unto Mons*ieu*r de Roche[1034] and I will end-
evour to send [it] by Humfry,[1035] but I desire to have a very good one.

I cannot tell what to say of Fa[ther] Francis his booke.[1036] Infallibly
the State here will make great advantage of it, and I am told from

---

[1026] The new Augustinian convent at Paris. See *Letter 46*.

[1027] John Varder, alias Robert Chamberlain and Jones. See Anstr., II, pp. 326–327. He had
been a chaplain in the French embassy in London.

[1028] Jesuits.

[1029] John Stukeley. See Anstr., II, p. 375. He had been imprisoned in Newgate in 1632.

[1030] John Goodman, first cousin of Godfrey Goodman, bishop of Gloucester. He was
cited in a 1635 list of disreputable priests; AAW, A XXVIII, no. 68, p. 287. Although he
had been converted to Catholicism by the secular priest Richard Ireland and entered the
secular clergy's college at Douai in 1621, he joined the Jesuit novitiate at Watten in May
1624, though he did not stay; Anstr., II, p. 133.

[1031] John Abbot. He was a nephew of George Abbot. See *ibid.*, p. 1. He was released from
Newgate on 13 April 1635.

[1032] Francis Harris. He had been sent to Newgate in December 1633; *ibid.*, p. 148.

[1033] Edmund Canon. See Anstr., I, p. 62. In 1635 he was described as 'ex praecipuis P.
Prestoni alumnis. Male audit ob nimiam consuetudinem quam a multis annis habere dicitur
cum uxore custodis carceris qui vocatur Clink, in quo longe tempore non tam detinetur
quam sponte commoratur'; AAW, A XXVIII, no. 68, p. 285.

[1034] Michel Masle, prieur des Roches.

[1035] This individual served as a letter-carrier for Richard Smith between France and
England. In September 1636 Smith gave him Jacques Sirmond's *Antirrheticus II. De Canone
Arausicano* (Paris, 1636) to take to England; AAW, A XXVIII, no. 161, p. 535; no. 163, p. 541.

[1036] Davenport, *Deus, Natura, Gratia*. When John Southcot and John Jackson met Gregorio
Panzani in December 1634, they assured him that the book 'non haveva partorito bono
effetto'. Davenport, with two other Franciscans, came to see Panzani shortly afterwards and
promised to send him a copy of the book; VA, PD, fos 41r, 43r. On 3 January 1635 Robert
Philip urged Panzani to find out from Sir Francis Windebank what the regime's opinion of
Davenport's work was, and to reassure them that, if they approved it, he, Panzani, would
try to ensure that it was not censured at Rome; *ibid.*, fo. 58r. William Howard came to
Panzani on 11 January to convey a message from Windebank that the king was greatly
displeased at news that a Scottish priest in Rome had claimed that the book was distasteful
'al re et al Stato'; *ibid.*, fo. 65r. On 14 January Windebank impressed on Panzani that the
regime was anxious that Davenport's work should not be condemned at Rome, and Panzani
informed Barberini of this in a letter of 16 January; *ibid.*, fo. 66r; VA, Barberini MS 8633,
fo. 107r (transcript and translation at ABSJ). On 17 January, however, Robert Jenison SJ told
Panzani that both Davenport's book and Roland (Thomas) Preston's *A Patterne of Christian
Loyaltie* (London, 1634) (see *Letter 60*) were prohibited there; VA, PD, fo. 67r. On 10 March
Davenport visited Panzani 'a dire molti buoni frutti del suo libre'; *ibid.*, fo. 84r; VA, Barberini
MS 8633, fo. 137r (transcript and translation at ABSJ). Panzani advised Barberini that he
had managed to delay the publication of a second edition; *ibid.*

This is all, onely I wish you all happines who am your obedient servant.

Fa[ther] Leander[1065] is com[me]d over.

Roberts

July 1 1634.

[*on p. 454*]

Addressed: A Monsieur Monsieur [*sic*] Louys Amarine marchant de-
meurant dans la Place Maubert a Paris.

Endorsed: Lord Dorset of regulars.

62. Roberts [George Leyburn] to Fitton [Peter Biddulph], 5 July 1634

[*AAW, A XXVII, no. 149, pp. 455–456*]

Worthie sir,

Yesterdaye I receaved yours of the 7 of June with one inclosed unto
Monsieur Philip, and that to her Majesty will this daye be delivered and
I hope that it will doe great good. Howsoever we are infinitely obliged
unto that noble gentleman whose friends here are all in perfect health.
His <man> parted many dayes aggoe and from Dover he writte unto
me. You feed us constantly with hopes, but when shall ther be a
wish[e]d resolution? If his Holynes were truly acquainted with the
proceedings of the regulars in this country he would be much more
sensible of our affayres. Onely 5 dayes aggoe a deare friend[1066] of myne
did dyne with a great privie counceller[1067] whom I could nominate, and
he told him that the puretans did not persecute the bishop soe much
as the regulars, and that it was a regular and (says he) I doe knowe
him very well, who first of all did propose unto the State a forme how
to persecute the bishop. This is soe certayne that my friend will take
his oath uppon it.

The French ambassadeur is newly arrived. The grand ausmonier
arrived 5 dayes before.[1068] The queen is now at Somersett house to
gayne the jubile[e]s. On Mundaye the court doth remove to Tybuls,
and, on Mundaye after, the progresse dothe beginne. The witches,

---

[1065] John (Leander) Jones OSB. For his mission to England in 1634, see Hibbard, *CI*,
pp. 45–46; G. Sitwell, 'Leander Jones's mission to England, 1634–1635', *RH*, 5 (1960),
pp. 132–182.

[1066] John Colleton. See *Letter 61*.

[1067] Edward Sackville, 4th earl of Dorset.

[1068] Jacques le Noël Du Perron. For the ambassador, see *Letter 63*.

which in a former[1069] I did [men]tion, will not <be> believed to be witches, notwithstanding that one doth con[fess]e her selfe a witch, and therfore shall returne into Lancheshire agayne.

Sweet Jesus be with you. July 5 1634.

[on p. 456]

Addressed: A Monsieur Monsieur [sic] Fitton a R[ome].

Endorsed: Roberts. 4 [sic] July.
    Concerning the regulars causing the persecution against my lord.

63. [John Southcot][1070] to Louys Amerin [Richard Smith], 9 July 1634[1071]

[AAW, A XXVII, no. 152, pp. 461–464]

[Most honoured master,]

The last weeke, bycause I was not well disposed, I entreated John[1072] to excuse me to you. Since I wrote last I must acknowledg the receipt of two of yours of the 28 June and 5ᵗ July.

I entreated John to inquire diligently among the stationers about the printing of Aurelius,[1073] but he saieth none will undertake it, especially to ~~sell~~ <take> the coppies <to> them selves, not houlding it a book sailable. Besides they all doubt of having leave to print it, without which none will venture uppon it. And surely it were better [three words deleted] and easier to send it into some part of Germany and to have it donn there.

Our meeting had the less successe in regard we waunt a head without which nothing can be donn to any purpose either out of meetings or in meetings. Neither can parish priests be made without a bishop. In fine all our miseries are attributed to my lords[1074] absence, by whose example others are animated also to fly and leave all. Our brethren were all of opinion that it was necessary for my lord either to come back speedily or else to go to Rome and there to negotiat

---

[1069] Letter 61.

[1070] The AAW, A series catalogue erroneously attributes this letter to John Bosvile.

[1071] Misdated in the AAW, A series catalogue to 7 July 1634.

[1072] Presumably either John Galmarch or John Legat, both of whom are mentioned in Letters 81, 82.

[1073] i.e. a revised version of Jean Duvergier de Hauranne, Anaereticus adversus Errores & Hereses (Paris, 1633). See Allison, RSGB, III, pp. 194–195.

[1074] Richard Smith.

his own cause, or, if neither would be donn, <u>they expect he</u> should procure an other to be sent hither in his place to governe, for as the case is now they hould them selves in worse state than when they had no b*isho*p at <u>all</u>. <u>I make bould</u> to signify plainly thus much to my l*or*d that somwhat may be donn if it be possible for the satisfaction of o*ur* brethren who are all generally discontented. As for my self I can but pitty o*ur* case and pray for amendment, having laboured the best I [*p. 462*] could hitherto, though to little purpose, seeing all the fruicts we [*ms torn*] nothing but discontent [and] confusion. I ame now <u>in[vi]ted by my fa</u>ther and some other freinds into the country, where I know not how long I shall stay, whether a month or six weekes, and therfor wish that <u>no letters be addressed to me</u> till my rettorne from this time, as this wilbe also th*e* last th*at* I write to you. Mr Fountaine[1075] hath bin with the new ambassador[1076] and I hope will <u>take possession of</u> the two chambers promised. Fa[ther] Leander[1077] <u>is come hither and</u> hath bin with my l*or*d of Canterb[ury].[1078] I visited him once or twice, and spake in generall termes of peace to w*hi*ch he seemes very inclinable, and when he sees Mr Bennet [he] will treat further therof.

Thus referring all occurrences to Mr Fountaine I humbly rest. 9 July 1634.

[*on p. 464*]

Addressed: Pour Mons*ieur* Louys Amerin a Paris.

No endorsement.

64. Roberts [George Leyburn] to Fitton [Peter Biddulph], 12 July 1634

[*AAW, A XXVII, no. 153, pp. 465–466*]

Worthie sir,

I have yours this week of the 7 of June, wherin you mention letters of Mr Mountegues[1079] sent by the way of Paris w*hi*ch as yett I have not receaved. His to her Ma*je*sty was delivered on Saterdaye last and she sayd to the party who did deliver it th*at* she did much wonder how he

<hr>

[1075] George Leyburn.
[1076] Jean d'Angennes, marquis de Pougny, who had arrived in England on 6 July. See *CSPV, 1632–1636*, p. 243.
[1077] John (Leander) Jones OSB.
[1078] William Laud.
[1079] Walter Montagu.

knew all thos passages. Certaynely (sayd she agayne) the cardenal[1080] haith told him. As I did signifie unto you in my former, the author of the booke in defense of the oath[1081] had not that successe which he did expect in regard that he was not soe malicious but the king was as mercifull, and I doe assure you that if his Majestyes clemency did not exceed Prestons passion it had gone very hard with Catholiques. Ther haith been an answere written to this defense by one M[r] Curtney, a lay gentleman but very learned.[1082] It was feared that this answere should have much incensed his Majesty sed misericordia eius est supra omnia eius. The written copye is suppressed and noe more sayd. Fa[ther] Leander[1083] is now in this towne. He writte unto his Grace of

[1080] Presumably Cardinal Francesco Barberini. See Foster, 'Walter Montague, courtier, diplomat and abbot, 1603–77 – I', pp. 95–96.

[1081] Preston, *A Patterne of Christian Loyaltie*. See *Letter 60*.

[1082] The reference here is, in fact, to the Jesuit Edward Leedes. He was subsequently arrested (in late October 1634) for writing against the oaths of allegiance and supremacy in refutation of Roland (Thomas) Preston OSB; Foley, I, pp. 251–268; Hibbard, *CI*, pp. 68–69; VA, PD, fo. 39r. Gregorio Panzani was informed, on his arrival in England, by Robert Philip that Leedes had initially satisfied the privy council that he was justified in writing his reply to Preston, 'ma perchè dopoi l'istesso venne in contesa per lettere con certi altri preti sopra l'istessa materia, essi preti havevano procurata la sua carceratione'; *ibid*, fos 39r–40r. (On 7 January 1635 Windebank informed Panzani of the royal displeasure at Leedes's attack on Preston, although by early February Windebank was, according to John Southcot, softening his criticism of Leedes, allowing that he in conscience believed that Preston's book should not have been published; *ibid.*, fos 62r, 73r.) John (Leander) Jones OSB wrote against Leedes's opinions on the oath; Foley, I, p. 253; Sitwell, 'Leander Jones's mission to England, 1634–5', pp. 148–149. See AAW, A XXVII, no. 176 (Leedes's 'discourse to M[r] [Roger] Widdrington' of 24 November 1634, followed by an account of the 'conference' between them on 26 November); AAW, A XXVII, no. 179 (Leedes's declaration of 6 December 1634); AAW, A XXVII, no. 180 (another declaration, of 7 December, by Leedes). Leedes's 'discourse' of 24 November rejected a number of opinions attributed to him. In particular, he denied that he had ever 'maintained either as a matter of certaintie or matter of myne owne opinion the popes definitive power to depose or deprive soveraine princes by decreeinge a king to be no king'. Instead he affirmed that the deposing power was 'uncertaine and problematicall' and therefore 'not to be practised lawfully', but not to be 'certainely forsworne' either. However, he claimed that 'in cause of necessitie for defence of religion' the pope can use his 'spirituall power' to 'excite and commaund princes to use theire temporall swordes'. Leedes alleged that he made these, and other arguments, 'to distinguish poynts of religion for which wee refuse this oath from matter of alleadgeance' and also 'to prevent a generall premunier [*sic*] which was then expected to ensue upon the doctrine of M[r] Howards booke, if my booke should happen to be seene of the State, which nevertheles I intended not'. For the imprisoned Leedes's correspondence with Windebank, see Foley, I, pp. 255–263. In October 1635 Arthur Brett, appointed as Henrietta Maria's envoy to Rome, was instructed by Charles to 'press earnestly for some exemplary punishment to be inflicted' upon Leedes 'for daring so presumptuously without licence from that See to awaken that subject which of late hath been prudently laid asleep'; *ibid.*, p. 259. The Venetians obtained copies of some of the declarations and statements which passed between Leedes and Widdrington; *CSPV, 1632–1636*, pp. 311–313. See also AAW, A XXVIII, no. 220 ('Propositions in M[r] Courtney's discourse'); Lunn, *EB*, p. 56.

[1083] John (Leander) Jones OSB.

Canterbury[1084] (whos scoole fellow he was formerly)[1085] to have leave
to come over and the bishop did acquainte the king with his letter,
and order was given to the secretary[1086] to write for him, which he
did. And alreadie he haith been with the secretary as also with the
b[ishop] of Canterbury who haith entertayned him very curteously
3 severall tymes, and his Grace did much discourse about the oath
and the lawfulnes of it.[1087] All this I knew last Saterdaye and since I
have not heard any thing, onely that he is much visited by Preston and
Mr Price,[1088] and they have often dyned together, which maketh me
suspect noe good. The Jesuists have made meanes to a great person,
a counceller of state, to assure the king that they have receaved an
order from ther generall neither to write nor dispute against the oath;
and this haith been signifyed unto his Majesty. You see in what a
world we doe live. And believe it. Ro[me] is the cause of all thes
disorders that will not constitute a head amongst us here. The French
ambassadeur[1089] had a very gratious audience yesterdaye at Tyballs,
and ther was with him the Holland ambassadeur[1090] who tooke the
queens dwarfe[1091] for the young prince and made a speech unto him
which made the king and queen laugh.[1092]

Sweet Jesus be with you. July 12 1634.

The tyme of the progresse I shall be out of this towne, which will be
for 6 weekes.

[on p. 465]

Endorsed: Within this pacquett are letters from Fa[ther] Ph[ilip] and
Fa[ther] Viett.

[on p. 466]

Addressed: A Monsieur Monsieur [sic] Fitton a Rome.

Endorsed: Roberts. 12 Julye.
About order given to the Jesuitts not to dispute against the
oath.

[1084] William Laud.
[1085] See Foley, I, p. 254.
[1086] Sir Francis Windebank.
[1087] For John (Leander) Jones's discussions with Laud, particularly concerning whether an
accommodation could be reached over the oath of allegiance, see Sitwell, 'Leander Jones's
mission to England, 1634–5', *passim*.
[1088] William (Benedict) Jones OSB.
[1089] Jean d'Angennes, marquis de Pougny. See *CSPV, 1632–1636*, p. 247.
[1090] Albert Joachimi.
[1091] Geoffrey Hudson.
[1092] See *CSPV, 1632–1636*, p. 251.

65. [George Leyburn] to [Richard Smith], 1 October 1634

[*AAW, A XXVII, no. 171, pp. 521–522*]

Most honored sir,

The messenger of this weeke is not as yett arrived, soe that I have not any of yours to answere. Neither I have [*sic*] much to write. On Sundaye and Mundaye I was at Hampton Court wher our good friends did remember you in all harty manner, but not any newes of an informer. I perceave clearely that all this summer some friendly correspondence betwixt Rome and us haith been about to be setled, but as yett it hangs somewhat doubtfully and has not that wish[e]d success as was expected. The party[1093] imployed in this is the man uppon whos relation (if he chance to come over) the wish[e]d conclusion of our affayres doe [*sic*] depend.

3 dayes aggoe the busines of Sir John Winter and Sir Basile Brookes et[c] was heard before the king and councell, and they are absolutely cast and lye at the kings mercy. I was told by a great person that the busines was found soe foule that not any durst open ther mouthes in ther behalfe. I am verily persuaded that they will be utterly ruined unlesse her Majesty in regard of ther religion doe obtayne some favor for them.[1094] I protest unfainedly it doth infinitely grieve me that they are Catholiques, to scandalize ther religion by ther unworthie

---

[1093] Gregorio Panzani.

[1094] In summer 1634, Sir John Winter (nephew of the earl of Worcester, and future secretary to Henrietta Maria) and Sir Basil Brooke (Smith's opponent in the approbation controversy), were fined for encroachments on royal forests. As the Venetian ambassador, Francesco Zonca, related it, the earl of Holland, 'superintendent and general judge of a large part of the forests of this kingdom', had understood that 'an immense quantity of trees were being felled clandestinely' in the Forest of Dean which was 'under his jurisdiction in the county of Gloucester, from which alone the best timber is obtained for the royal ships'. Holland 'had the damage estimated and condemned four offenders', namely Brooke and Winter, and Lord Treasurer Portland's secretary, John Gibbon and Brooke's associate, Sir George Mynne, 'sentencing them to pay over 60,000ᶫ sterling, as damages for the harm done and as a fine for their breach of the law'; *CSPV, 1632–1636*, pp. 263–264, 293; Alexander, *CLT*, pp. 194–197; Hibbard, *CI*, p. 62. For Edward Rossingham's accounts of the case, see PRO, C 115/106/8427, 8428, 8436, 8437, 8443. Rossingham noted on 3 October 1634 that 'upon Sunday last the king was pleased to heare the whole businesse of the Forrest of Deane'. 'Sir Basill Brooke had in his petition to the king cast some assertions upon the proceedings of the justice seate.' After 'a full heareing', 'order was given by the boord that a bill should be exhibited into the court of star chamber' against Brooke 'for his scandalous petition'; PRO, C 115/106/8436.

As Kevin Sharpe points out, however, the fines levied were not what was actually paid into the exchequer. Sir John Winter was adjudged to forfeit £20,230, but this was cut to £4,000. Brooke and Mynne had their fines reduced, and simply surrendered their ironworks, Sharpe, *PR*, pp. 119, 243. (For Winter's reasons why the damages found against him should be waived, see *CSPD, 1635*, p. 100; PRO, C 115/106/8436. For Brooke's reasons, see *CSPD*,

proceedings, and also to wrong and scandalize soe good a prince of whom we are not worthie.¹⁰⁹⁵ Is it not strang[e]? The Catholiques who were the contrivers of the gunpowder plott were all the Jesuists gostly childeren, and now agayne all our Catholique projecteurs against whom the whole kingdome cryeth fearefully are all the Jesuists childeren directed by them. It were good that the sadle were sett upon the right horse and that all other Catholiques should make a publique disclaime from thes foule proceedings of the Jesuists and thers. I doe assure you faithfully I doe not speake this out of any the least malice but out of a true zeale to make appeare to our king and country that the Catholique religion will not approve such proceedings. Who can now wonder that thes men were the cheef opposers of episcopall authority? I feare that the hand of God doth hang over them for that very act. For other occurences I doe remitte you to the inclosed. The French ambassadeur¹⁰⁹⁶ haith alreadie lost him selfe. He will never be able to doe the least good. Foster is continually in his co[a]ch with him. I am very sorrie for him for he is a vertuous good man, and if he would have been advised he might have done better.

Your obedient servant.

Octob[e]r 1 [*word deleted*] 1634.

I will be myndfull of your niece¹⁰⁹⁷ at the next opportunity.

[*on p. 521*]

Endorsed: This inclosed I receaved from your best lady¹⁰⁹⁸ who doth remember her selfe in all harty manner.

1635, pp. 253, 262, 308, 309.) Holland had been put under house arrest in the previous year after the king had intervened to prevent a duel between him and Jerome Weston, the son of the lord treasurer; Sharpe, *PR*, pp. 176–177. The Forest Eyre thus served Holland, even if indirectly, as a means of revenge. The Jesuit Robert Jenison interpreted this episode as a sign that the king cared little for Catholics, treating them merely as a source of revenue, 'et che hora vuol togliere certa foresta ad alcuni Catholici baroni'; VA, PD, fo. 51r.

¹⁰⁹⁵ Leyburn seems to be picking up here on the anti-Catholic *obiter dicta* coming out of this case. Rossingham had reported on 1 August 1634 that Sir John Finch had said 'in his pleadinge [...] that in '88 the Spanish designe was (in case there invincible armada were overthrown) how they might destroy the Forrest of Deane, from whence our navie was supplyed', and that the principal ravagers 'of this forrest at present were papistes'; PRO, C 115/106/8427. On 3 October Rossingham recorded that Archbishop Laud 'spake home in the businesse' and said that 'it is not the abuse of destroying the forrest alone which wee must looke after, but the parties that have done yt', and 'of what religion they are'; PRO, C 115/106/8436.

¹⁰⁹⁶ Jean d' Angennes, marquis de Pougny.

¹⁰⁹⁷ Mary Gildon.

¹⁰⁹⁸ Anne (Philipson), Baroness Arundell.

[*on p. 522*]

Addressed: Pour mon maistre a Paris.

Endorsed: Sir Basil Brooke.

66. [George Leyburn] to Louis Ameryn [Richard Smith], 19 November 1634[1099]

[*AAW, A XXIV, no. 206, pp. 747–748*]

Most honored sir,

This morning I have yours of 16 of November. Humfrey parted with your neece[1100] two dayes aggoe, and I hope that they will be with you before this. As for Mr Clerk[1101] he doth absolutely <u>refuse the</u> authority which Mr Norton had. Mr Colleton was very earnest with him, as also my selfe. I have seen here one of Mr Chambers booke[s] concerning premotion. His brother[1102] ther may doe good offices for he haith great power with Signor Georgio,[1103] and his relation will be credited sooner than an other by the cardenal protector,[1104] and he doth <u>constantly corresp</u>onde with Fa[ther] Ph[ilip]. I am sorie for that confusion in Arras Colledge, and more sorie that the moneys due unto that house are not better imployed. As concerning Sir Basil,[1105] his hearing daye was to have been yesterdaye, but it is deferred to the begining of the next moneth. It is certayne that it will goe very ill with him. This weeke a letter[1106] was writte to the cardenal protector in such manner as you desired and we gott Fa[ther] Ph[ilip] to second it unto Signor Georgio and to enclose in his not any newes of the informeur. I writte unto you in a former that Mr Courtney[1107] was areyned at the King['s] Bench barr, but it was not soe. He had onely the two oathes tendered. It is generally thought that he shall be areyned. Notwithstanding, I am of opinion that he will not. Ther was lately brought unto his neece[1108]

[1099] This letter is dated 19 November 1631 in the AAW, A series catalogue.

[1100] Mary Gildon.

[1101] John Southcot.

[1102] See Allison, RSGB, I, p. 362.

[1103] George Con.

[1104] Cardinal Francesco Barberini.

[1105] Sir Basil Brooke. See *Letter 65*.

[1106] Presumably AAW, A XXVI, no. 175 (a letter dated 6 November 1634 from the English secular clergy to Cardinal Francesco Barberini, lamenting the silence which greets their petitions to the Holy See, and that Rome is now a stepmother rather than a mother to them).

[1107] Edward Leedes SJ. See *Letter 64*.

[1108] This may be a reference to John Leedes's daughter, Magdalen.

her lodging a great pacquett addressed unto him, and his brother, Mr Alexander Courtney, being ther did open it, and found a good big pacquett of papers sealed w*i*th this superscription, 'a Couling card for Courtney'. He, imagining some trick or other, did presently repayre unto Secretary Winnebanck, and presented unto him this pacquett w*hi*ch he, opening, found it subscribed by George Machell.[1109] This doth shewe a great violence. Preston of the Clinke, Mr Preston of the Mannor Withrington,[1110] Howard,[1111] Father Leander,[1112] Father Price,[1113] [and] Machell doe meet very often together. Believe it, all the cheef monckes are for the oath. Fa[ther] Leander and Price are constantly w*i*th Howard, and Fa[ther] Leander sayes Masse in his chamber uppon the Sundayes. I can assure you now th*a*t Father Leanders comming was onely about the oath, and I am privately informed th*a*t the archbishop of Canterbury[1114] haith promised them th*a*t if they can persuade the Catholiques of England to take the oath th*a*t then the king will declare them good subjects and capable of all sorts of offices, and after th*a*t a parlament shall be called. Poore men. I feare much th*a*t they will be deceaved. Shillingworth,[1115] of whom you have formerly heard, haith now begunne a new sect, and has his followers, and they are called Succinians,[1116] and ther cheef principall <is> th*a*t, wher the holy Scripture may be interpreted two or more wayes, a man may lawfully adhere unto any.

This is all, onely my best wishes for y*ou*r happines. November 19 1634.

Mr Clerke did deale about sending y*ou*r trunckes. He can best certifie you concerning them. I sent at the same tyme a rundelett of sack for Mrs Salesbury.

[on p. 748]

Addressed: A Mons*ieu*r Monsieur [*sic*] Louis Ameryn marchant demeurant en la Place Maubert a Paris.

Endorsed: Monks for the oathe.

[1109] For the priest George Machell, see Anstr., II, pp. 206–207. In AAW, A XXVIII, no. 68, he is named as a supporter of Roland (Thomas) Preston OSB. He is also said to have been expelled from the seminaries at Rome and Douai, and is accused of leading a dissolute life in taverns.

[1110] i.e. the Northumberland gentleman Roger Widdrington, under whose name Roland (Thomas) Preston OSB wrote.

[1111] William Howard.

[1112] John (Leander) Jones OSB.

[1113] William (Benedict) Jones OSB.

[1114] William Laud.

[1115] William Chillingworth.

[1116] Socinians.

67. 'Reasons to perswade the Court of Rome that a Catholick Bishop in England is not offensive to the king and State', 1634

[AAW, A XXVII, no. 204, pp. 717–724]

Considering that his Majesty hath no small number of subjects in his realme of England who professe the Catholick Roman Religion, and that it is not his Majest[i]es pleasure to have them oppressed or extirpated, but rather preserved, as is evident both by his Majest[i]es naturall inclination to clemency and by sundry particuler examples thereof, [and] considering also the multitude of priests both secular and regular that are sent hither in mission from time to time to direct the consciences of the said Catholicks in matters spirituall; and that the State useth to distinguish betweene priest and priest and betweene Catholick and Catholick, holding the secular clergy and their adherents for men more disinteressed and of a truer zeale towards their king and countrey, there semeth to bee noe question but that the king and State doe judge it safer for them selves that the said Catholicks and priests should be subject to a spirituall superiour of their owne profession residing ordinarily within the realme than permitted to live confusedly without order or governement amongst them. Neither would any superiour under the degree of a bishop serve for this purpose, or any authority lesse than episcopall be respected by so great a multitude, as the notable inconveniences that followed upon the archpriests[1117] governement doe sufficiently prove when priests and Catholicks were perhaps not so many as now they are.

Fower thinges therefore seeme fitt to be supposed in a Catholick bishop sutable to the present times in England. 1. That he be a man of a temperat disposition in respect of State matters and zealously affected to his prince and countrey. 2. That he take an o[a]th of fidelity and obedience to the king such as shalbe expressed at the end of these reasons. 3. That his authority be only spirituall and over Catholicks only. 4. That the execucion of his authority be without noise or forme of tribunal. And that such a bishop is not thought by the king and State to be hurtfull, but rather helpfull and usefull to them, may bee gathered by many particulers.

First they know very well that episcopall governement is the naturall and ordinary governement of the Catholick Church in all places, and, seing the king and State pretend not to punish Catholickes for any point of their religion, it may well be presumed that they will not be offended that the Catholicks of England be governed according to

---

[1117] See *NAGB*, introduction.

the principles of their religion, and in the same manner as all other Catholickes in the world are usually governed.

They knowe also and observe that no harme hath hitherto befallen the State from Catholickes since it pleased King James, his Majest[i]es father, to give way to the restoring of this governement,[1118] nor that the State hath any way bin prejudiced by the like governement in Ireland, where notwithstanding there are severall Catholick [*p. 718*] bishops, and those not titular only (as now in England) but proper diocesans of the place, whereas it is yet fresh in their remembrance what hath been attempted by some ill advised English Catholickes guided in conscience by such as are the greatest opposers of episcopall authority against the king and State in former tymes when there was noe bishop yet ordained to governe them.

It hath bin the observation and ingenuous confession of many wise and moderat Protestants that these late troubles and dissensions amongst Catholickes doe shewe apparently how behoofull it is, even in regard of the State it selfe, that they should be governed by a well settled episcopall authority. For the State, well seing the great opposition and tumult which hath bin raised through the popular conduct of so many severall guides against a Catholick bishop, although hee were lawfully sent to governe them, and they by the principles of their religion bound to admitt him or at least not to oppose him, doe thence argue and judge how easily the same men might be induced, upon the like groundes, to cause an insurrection alsoe against their temporall prince when the tymes and circumstances should be answerable to their expectacion therein.

They know likewise that they who are reputed to be the chiefe authors of this opposition against a Catholick bishop have done it out of a respect of interest, and for their owne particuler endes, the which as in this they are contrary to the generall end and spirituall good of Catholicks, so are they in the opinion of all common wealthes <men> as litle sutable to the temporall good of the State, and therefore to all prudent men it semeth very reasonable that the State, rather than favour the desighnes of those whome they account their inbred enemies, should choose to connive at a Catholick bishop, the setling of whose authority they plainely see is the only way to curb them, and to keepe them in due subjection both to the Church and State. And here to passe but lightly over the innumerable oppressions used formerly by them whilst there was no bishop to extinguish the whole clergy secular of England, or att least to bring them into a perpetuall thraledome under them selves, first by possessing their seminaries and

[1118] A reference to the appointment in 1623 of William Bishop as bishop of Chalcedon over England and Scotland.

colleges abroad, next by thrusting an archpriest insteed of a bishop upon them, and him a man[1119] that was wholy at their devotion; then by causing their lectures in Doway Colledge to be taken [*p. 719*] from them, and procuring by a speciall breve that no clergy man bredd in their seminaries should be made docto*u*r in any university w*i*thout *p*articuler leave from them;[1120] finally by using many slights to supplant the priests in England, and to turne them out of their residences; not to insist upon these *p*articulers, wh*i*ch are all noe lesse knowne to the State of England than to this court of Rome, the mayne and monstrous opposition wh*i*ch they have made, from tyme to tyme, for the space of almost forty yeares togeather, first against the creation and bringing in of a Catholick bishop, and now against his setling and the peceable enjoying of his authority, is so publickly knowne, and hath bin so well considered by the wisest men of State who [*word deleted*] <looke> w*i*th an indifferent eye and unp*re*occupated mind into the busines, as they judge that it is not w*i*thout <great> cause they are so eager and vigilant in opposing a bishop. And it was the opinion of the late most prudent prince King James that nothing wh*i*ch the State could invent to doe for the just restraint of those men would be so efficacious or so proper as to suffer a Catholick bishop with full spirituall authority to bee placed over the priests and Catholickes of o*u*r kingdome. And this was the cause why his Maj*e*sty[e]s royall predecesso*u*rs Queene Elizabeth and King James in their princely wisdomes did ever more judg it convenient to favo*u*r and protect (as farr as the times would then p*er*mitt) ~~as farre as the times would~~ the appeales and p*re*tensions of the secular clergy against the others unjust intrusions and oppressions, and King James in p*a*rticuler thought it fitt uppon this ground to give way to the making and bringing in of the former bishop[1121] into England. They conceave furthermore that a Catholick bishop, as he is supposed to have sworne fidelity and obedience to the king, so hee may powerfully p*er*swade, and (if need bee) ordaine, that all priests and Catholicks under his com*m*aund, especially they whoe are first brought into the Church, shall take the same o[a]th wh*i*ch no doubt will give the State a generall good assurance and satisfaction touching their loialty.

They conceave likewise that a prudent bishop by the example of his owne moderation, and by his pastorall care and vigilancy, may p*re*serve the Catholickes not only in peace amongst them selves but in <a> generall good temper and disposition of mind towards the State, whereby they will become lesse capable to follow novelties or to take

---

[1119] The archpriest George Blackwell.
[1120] See *NAGB*, p. 7.
[1121] William Bishop.

daungerous impressions of disloyalty from any discontented spirit.
[*p. 720*]

They see plainely that such a bishop may take away, or moderat
by his authority, many great abuses (whereby the State is insensibly
weakened) that grow amongst the Catholickes for want of spirituall
governem*e*nt, and may p*re*vent sundry practizes amongst them that
are of bad example in a State, and tend to the disturbance of the
com*m*on peace. Abuses and practises of this kynd are these: excesse
in drinking and gaming, vanity in apparell, detraction and making of
unfitt marriages, scandalous discourses, the impoverishing of wealthy
families, exorbitant transportation of monies out of the land, com-
binations, factions, gathering of hands from family to family through
out the whole kingdome, inordinat recourse to forreine ambassado*u*rs,
writing of scandalous pamphletts, publishing of da*u*ngerous doctrines
and the like.

Besides, they conceave that a Catholick bishop, being tolerated by
the State, by his gravity and authority may perswade Catholickes,
more forcibly than any other can, to graunt extraordinary contributions or benevolences when they shalbe required for the supply of
his Maj*est*[i]es ~~necessities~~ occasions.

Lastly it is conceaved that his lett*er*s and informac*i*ons to Catholick
princes abroad and his treating w*i*th their ambassado*u*rs here
concerning his Maj*est*[i]es sweete and prudent governem*e*nt, and
especially of his Maj*est*[i]es gratious proceeding w*i*th his Catholick
subjects, will have speciall creditt, and in that respect may bee not a
litle usefull to his Maj*es*ty both att home and abroad.

Neither have the Protestant bishops any peculiar reason to be
offended w*i*th a Catholick bishop coming in this nature, although
the grand opposers of episcopall governement in England have
sought to p*er*swade this court otherwise. For, seing he standeth in noe
competency w*i*th them, nor trencheth upon the livings or jurisdictions
belonging to their place, he carrying no greater port than any other
missionary preist doth, there appeareth nothing of peculiar offence to
them. Yea the wisest and most moderat of the Protestant clergy are
so farr from being offended or thinking it straunge to see Catholickes
governed by a bishop of their owne, as they rather much wonder
that the matter hath bin formerly so long neglected; and as a learned
Protestant, sometime deane of St [*p. 721*] Paules[1122] in London, tould a
Catholick that was his freind, hee wondred to see so many provincialls,
recto*u*rs and other superio*u*rs of regular orders in England, and yet
noe bishop to governe the clergy who, he said, was their true and
naturall superiour and head of all ecclesiasticall hierarchy.

[1122] Presumably a reference to John Donne.

By that which hath bin said it may sufficiently appeare that not-withstanding the bishops enemies doe continually labour to perswade this court of Rome that a Catholick bishop is most odious to the king and State in England, and that the setling of him in his authority would cause a new and greevous persecution not only against himself but against the Catholicks also for his sake, yet the king and State are worthily presumed to be farr otherwise affected, and <not> unwilling to connive and tollerat him, supposing the conditions of the mans person and clayme to be such as hath been ~~formerly~~ formerly declared.

An Apendix touching the bishop of Chalcedon.

Now concerning the present bishop of Chalcedon,[1123] howsoever by the lowd cryes and calumnious writings of his adversaries hee hath bin publickly traduced to the State, which hath caused twoe proclamations to be sent forth against him,[1124] yet information having bin since given by the mediacion of her Majesty, and of some forreigne princes ambassadours, of the naturall disposicion of the bishops person and of the verity of his clayme, those that have seene and attentively considered the said information doe confesse ingenuously that the bishop hath bin very much wronged and the State egregiously abused by his adversaries, he being found both for his person and clayme in all points really answerable to the conditions of a bishop above mentioned. For first, touching his person, they find that hee is generally averred, by the confession of all that knowe him thoroughly, to bee a true and constant lover of his naturall prince and country and by nature averted from all practizes and writings, not only against the State in generall but against any that beare authority and rule in the common wealth. And albeit his adversaries, being destitute of better meanes to defend a bad cause withall, have bin faine to fly (as their manner is) to bitter invectives against his person, and to have endeavored to possesse all those whose eare they have that hee is a man of a violent and turbulent spirit, yet have none of them [p. 722] till this day bin able to verify their accusation therein by any perticuler action or speech of his, for although hee hath pursued the right of his cause with zeale and courage (which his angry adversaries perhaps call violence) yet hath hee never don any thing therein but with apparent moderation both of tongue and minde (as his letters and all his other writings in this controversy doe well shewe) and with a due submission also to the sense and sentence of his superiours, the which hee hath bin ever ready to obay. And who soever shall indifferently

---

[1123] Richard Smith.
[1124] AAW, A XXII, no. 153; Larkin, *SRP*, no. 104; AAW, A XXIII, no. 93; Larkin, *SRP*, no. 109.

consider the extreame provocations which he hath had through the outragious proceedings of his adversaries against him, which are such as never before have bin knowne to proceed from Catholicks, living in such estate, against a bishop of their owne profession, lawfully sent unto them, by whome they were never yet prejudiced in any thing, and shall compare his comportment with theirs, will quickly see the difference of their spiritts, and that with farr more ground of reason hee might retort their crimination of turbulency and violence upon them selves, who were the assailants, the bishop and his clergy being only defendants. But for one testimony amongst many others that might be produced of his unfained love to his prince, his Majesty hath bin informed allready that besides the offering which he useth to make weekely of one Masse att least, and many other particuler praiers daily for both their Majest[i]es while hee was in England, hee gave speciall order to all preists and Catholicks to pray perticulerly for his Majest[i]es prosperity, for which cause having bin brought into obloquy by some of his chiefe opponents, one Doctor Filesac,[1125] a Sorbonist, tooke occasion to write a speciall treatise in defence of the bishops action called Apologia Smitheana, wherein he sheweth that it was ever held a laudable custome to pray for the prosperity of our naturall prince notwithstanding hee professed not the same religion with us.[1126] And how tender the bishop is of his Majest[i]es honour and good repute abroad, his Majesty hath bin given to understand in part and will further appeare by the sundry good informations which the bishop both by himself and by his clergy from tyme to tyme hath given in divers places, [p. 723] and particulerly in this court of Rome, of his Majest[i]es most eminent vertues, and of his prudent and clement governement in generall, but especially of his mild and mercifull proceeding with his Catholick subjects in particuler, notwithstanding the rigour of the lawe standing still in force against them. Finally it hath bin suggested to the king how that the bishop is ready on his part, whensoever it shall please his Majesty to require <it>, to take an oath of fidelity and obedience to his Majesty, eyther according to the forme hereunder written or according to any other forme which Catholick bishops have used heretofore in England, or which other Catholick bishops use abroad.

[1125] For Jean Filesac, dean of the Sorbonne, who was in charge of the committee which examined and condemned Matthew Wilson's and John Floyd's polemical tracts against Matthew Kellison, see Allison, RSGB, I, pp. 333–334.

[1126] On 27 January/6 February 1637 Richard Smith noted that he had shown to the earl of Leicester 'D. Filesacs apologie for my praying for the king and also the testimonie of the chapter in behalf of the k[ing] and queene made [in] 1635 and he desiered a copie which I wil give him'; AAW, A XXIX, no. 9, p. 19.

Next as touching the bishops clayme: the king hath bin allready certified that he is but a titular bishop ordained and sent hither for a spirituall end, having noe clayme to any bishoprick or benefice in England, nor pretending the exercise of any temporall power over any of his Majest[i]es subjects, but only spirituall, and that not over any Protestant, but over Catholickes only. His Majesty hath been advertised also that it is a meere fiction, which his adversaries have sett on foot to make him odious with the State, that he ever went about to erect a tribunall or court of Arches to prove wills, exact tithes, or the like.[1127] Nor can it be shewed wherein he ever yet exceeded that spirituall authority which was graunted unto him, either in the matter or in the manner. Furthermore it hath bin advertised that if the bishop pretend any spirituall coercitive power over the priests and Catholickes committed to his charge, it is but the due which every bishop hath by Christ his institution, being graunted for noe other end or use but that by feare of ecclesiasticall censures his flock should the better bee contained in their duety both to God and the king, and never to be exercised but in urgent occasions either for punishment or prevention of notorious scandalls.

The Oath[1128]

[I] A.B. doe truely acknowledge, professe, testify and declare in my conscience before God and the world that our soveraigne lord king [*p. 724*] Charles is lawfull and rightfull king of this realme and other his dominions and countries and I will beare faith and true allegeance to his Majesty, his heires and successors, and him and them will defend to the uttermost of my power against all conspiracies or attempts whatsoever, which shalbe made against his or their crowne and dignity, and doe my best endeavour to disclose and make knowne to his Majesty his heires and successors, or to their officers for the tyme being, all treasons and traiterous conspiracies which I shall knowe or heare to bee intended against his Majesty or any of them. And I doe make this recognition and acknowledgement hartily, willingly and truely uppon the true faith of a Christian, soe helpe me God.[1129]

Endorsed: Reasons for a bishop 1633, 1634.

[1127] Gregorio Panzani's 'Relazione' made it clear, however, that the secular clergy anticipated that a restored bishop would 'claim tithes' from the laity; VA, Barberini MS LVI, 136, fo. 42v (transcript and translation at ABSJ).

[1128] Panzani's diary records the suggestions of Catholics such as William Howard, John (Leander) Jones OSB, Sir Tobie Mathew, and the 2nd Baron Baltimore that a variant of the oath of allegiance could be formulated which would be acceptable both to Rome and to the king; VA, PD, *passim*.

[1129] See also AAW, A XXVII, no. 207 ('Reasons wherfore a bishop should not be more molested than provincials and superiors of regular orders' [in John Southcot's hand]). This develops the argument in the eleventh paragraph of this present document (AAW, A XXVII,

68. [George Leyburn] to [Richard Smith], 21 January 1635

[AAW, A XXVIII, no. 2, pp. 5–6]

Most honored sir,

I have receaved yours of the 17 of Jan[uary] and I am glad that at last my letters come safe to your hands which I did thinke had been intercepted or miscarryed. I confesse that your expences are great, and if you please to command a summe from hence it shall goe hard but that I will cause you to be furnish[e]d according to your desire.

no. 204). It claims, for example, that a bishop would prevent both disorders and conspiracies among Catholics. 'Seditious bookes' would be suppressed, 'such as Doleman, Corona Regia, Pacenius, and the like hatched heretofore by such as professed the names of Catholicks, though not by a bishop or any willing to be subject to a bishop'. Also, 'as the State and Church of England have ever thought it fitt to maintaine hierarchicall government against the puritans, so may it be thought lickwise behoofull, in regard of safty, to permitt the Catholicks to have their hierarchie also supported by a bishop against the opposers thereof'; AAW, A XXVII, no. 207, p. 731. AAW, A XXVII, no. 210 is another draft, or perhaps final version, of AAW, A XXVII, no. 207, incorporating the name of the notorious Jesuit Juan de Mariana among the writers of 'seditious bookes'. AAW, A XXVII, no. 211 ('That episcopall authoritie may be in such a subject as it wilbe no way prejudiciall to his Majestie or State of England, but rather manie wayes usefull') expands some of the arguments in AAW, A XXVII, no. 204 about the political fidelity of the bishop. In particular, it argues (pp. 741–742) that episcopal authority among Catholics will be conducive to the good of the State and the sovereign. 'If anie object that by permission of episcopall authoritie the number of Catholikes would be too much increased, I answere that the number of Catholikes cannot be much more increased by episcopal authoritie than by preistly [authority], because Catholikes are made by preaching and reconciling, which power is common to preists. But episcopall authoritie is proper to keep those who are Catholikes in good order and discipline. And seing his Majestie seemeth not desirous to extinguish Catholikes but to keep them in due subjection and order, episcopal authoritie would concurre with his desire'. Furthermore, (in a section entitled 'That episcopal authoritie in the handes of one sure to his Majestie may be usefull to his Majestie'), it is argued that this is so because episcopal power is 'devine authoritie instituted by Christ and the holie Ghost for the good of al mankinde, and therefore such as God is like to concurre with for their good, and blesse them that uphould it. Secondly because his Majesties wise father our late souveraigne K[ing] James was wont to say, as appeareth by the conference at Hampton Courte, "no bishop, no king", and therefore procured bishops to be made in Scotland; which though he sayed and did of Protestants [*sic*] bishops, yet no doubt is proportionably true of Catholikes.' Also 'K[ing] James did wincke at the 1st bishop of Chalcedon, and, as hath been reported, sayed he would have one who should answere for all ~~Catholikes~~ papists'. Finally, 'nether could anie zealous puritan finde fault with such permission by his Majestie than the earnest puritans of Holland finde fault with the States for tolerating the Catholike archbishop of Philips [Philip Rovenius, archbishop of Philippi]'.

See also AAW, A XXVII, no. 216 ('Concerning the bishop of Chalcedons authority' [in Peter Biddulph's hand]); AAW, A XXVIII, no. 67 ('Briefe reasons howe and why a Catholicke Bishop in England may be safely tolerated by his Majesty'); AAW, A XXVIII, no. 75 ('Motives inducing the State to connive at a Catholicke Bishop'); AAW, A XXVIII, no. 78 (For the establishing of a Catholike Bishop or Bishops in England which may not be offensive to the king or State [. . .]').

Humfrey continueth close prisonner and soe <u>also Mr Medcalfe</u>[1130] without being called to his tryall. I have weekely acquainted you with all passages concerning the Italyen stranger.[1131] I doe like <him> every daye better and better. I doe assure you faithfully that he haith proceeded hitherto <u>very discreetly and prudently</u>; and two nights aggoe[1132] he did imparte him selfe most freely and with great zeale, lamenting the <u>indirect proceedings</u> of the Jesuists on one syde and the monckes of an other, clearly seeing that, wanting just grounds to hinder the setling of episcopall authority, they doe <u>violently stirre</u> the State, the Jesuists by meanes of Sir Toby Mathews friend, and the monckes by meanes of Fa[ther] Leanders friend, in soe much that now his labor is not to informe him selfe any more <u>of the affections</u> of Catholiques toward episcopall authority, whom [sic] for the most part, he clearly perceaveth, desireth nothing more but to rightly possesse the State with good and solid reasons wherfore it is most convenient to ~~admitt~~ permit a bishop or bishops <for he feareth that his Holynes will nor [sic for not] doe any thing in this kind without a tacit liking of the State>, and if you can thinke of any good reasons in this kinde I praye send them in the next letter.[1133] I much wonder that you heare

[1130] This appears to refer to Peter Metcalf, who had been Richard Smith's secretary in Paris since 1633. He had come to England in 1634 and had been arrested; Anstr., II, p. 219.

[1131] i.e. Gregorio Panzani, for whom Leyburn in late December 1634 had found a residence opposite the New Exchange; VA, PD, fo. 51r. For Panzani's mission to and arrival in England (on 12/22 December 1634), a journey arranged in part to try to resolve the differences between regulars and seculars, see Lunn, *EB*, p. 126; Hibbard, *CI*, pp. 44–45. He was favourable towards the seculars. For Panzani's appointment by the pope and Cardinal Barberini to report on the state of Catholicism in England, see his diary; VA, PD, fos 1r–2r. On 19/29 March Panzani was briefed by Cardinal Bernardino Spada on the dispute in England over Richard Smith; *ibid.*, fos 4r–5r. Panzani was told that he should be impartial and not lean 'più ad una parte che ad un'altra, o almeno che non dimostrassi il mio sentimento'; *ibid.*, fo. 5r. Via the queen, he was to insinuate himself into the king's good graces, and inform him, *inter alia*, that the pope desired English Catholics should for protection look to Charles, and not to France or Spain. Panzani was also instructed to see if he could come to some compromise over the issue of the oath of allegiance. He was to tell Charles that his formal mission was to suppress the controversy among the English clergy, but he was to find out whether Charles would object to the presence of one or more Catholic bishops in England; *ibid.*, fos 6r–7r.

[1132] Panzani's diary records visits from Leyburn on 18 January and on 21 January but not on 19 January, the day implied by Leyburn in this letter; *ibid.*, fo. 68r.

[1133] Panzani recorded in his diary the stream of clergy who came to call on him soon after his arrival. These included Sir Tobie Mathew and John (Leander) Jones OSB. Mathew advised Panzani that 'il vescovo con autorità somma et universale non si potrà sopportare dalli nobili ricchi perchè se vorrà visitare la casa, o la capella, o il prete, il nobile non vorrà per paura delle leggi, poichè appena si fidano delli figli, molto meno di un vescovo, il quale andarà con qualche comitiva'. It would be even worse if the bishop were to try to remove a gentleman's chaplain. The pope himself, alleged Mathew, could not authorize such a visitation. Jones advised a compromise agreement between the clergy over the powers of the bishop. But he said it had been a mistake to create so many archdeacons; and, like

nothing of <u>your trunck nor</u> rundelett.[1134] They were left at Calais with M[r] Evered, a marchant, <u>who undertooke</u> to send them carefully. I doe here inclose a letter to M[rs] Salesbury. Herafter I shall not send any others. Fa[ther] Talbotts[1135] newes of sincking 3 Holland shippes is false. Y<i>our</i> best lady[1136] will shortly write unto you as you desire. I <u>have presented</u> yo<i>ur</i> remembran[c]es as you wish[e]d [<i>word deleted</i>] unto the grand almener[1137] and Mon<i>sieur</i> Ph[ilip] who doe returne thers in all harty manner. On Sundaye last, <u>good Mr Broughton</u> departed this life[1138] after th<i>a</i>t he had performed the office of the daye. He went away like a snuffe of a candle sitting in his cheare saying his prayers and [the] company w<i>i</i>th him perceaving nothing untill he was dead. <u>His mistris</u>[1139] <u>haith prom</u>ised to take noe new servant in his place without my advise, and now she haith given me order about one.[1140] She is much solicited by others.

Sweet Jesus be with you. In hast. Jan[uary] 21 1634.

No address.

[<i>on p. 6</i>]

Endorsed: Panzani of Jesuits.

69. 'Short Instructions',[1141] 1635[1142]

[<i>AAW, A XXVIII, no. 6, pp. 25–28</i>]

1 Concerning the Kings Person

The king is a prince of a most milde and sweet disposicion, mercifull and loving to his subjectes; not addicted to any enormous vice, and

---

Mathew, he opposed the powers of visitation claimed by Smith; <i>ibid.</i>, fos 45r–6r, 49r. Mathew continued to visit Panzani regularly in order to brief him against the English secular clergy leadership. Lord Cottington told Panzani on 26 March 1635 that everything which Mathew had said, he (Cottington) had instructed him to say; <i>ibid.</i>, fos 85r–6r.

[1134] See <i>Letter 66</i>.

[1135] William Talbot SJ.

[1136] Anne (Philipson), Baroness Arundell.

[1137] Jacques le Noël Du Perron.

[1138] Richard Broughton died on 18 January 1635.

[1139] Frances (Cary), wife of George Manners, 7th earl of Rutland. In the previous month Gregorio Panzani had met Viscount Dunbar's eldest son, John Constable, at the countess's house in London, where she and Constable vigorously defended Richard Smith; VA, PD, fo. 52r.

[1140] Thomas Green wrote, on 16 February 1635, to William Clifford that Broughton's 'place they tell me is reserv[e]d for you'; AAW, A XXVIII, no. 8, p. 32.

[1141] On stylistic grounds, it appears this memorandum may have been prepared by George Leyburn.

[1142] Suggested dating in the AAW, A series catalogue.

endewed with all sort of morall vertues which maketh all his people
to admire, love and honour him above all expression. These great
ornamentes of God and nature doe in a manner foretell that one day
he shall restore this countrey to its former happines, and him selfe
become the most glorious and the most renowned monarch that ever
did governe over us.

2 Concerning the Queenes Person

The queene is a princesse on whome God and nature have bestowed
most rare gifts. Her Majest[i]es sweete and vertuous carriage, her
religious zeale and constant devotions have purchased unto her selfe
love and admiracion from all the court and kingdome, and unto the
Catholique religion (which she piously professeth) great respect and
honor. She is *una beata de casa*; for whose sake Heaven I hope doth
intend many blessinges toward our countrey.

3 Concerning Persecution

Although the king out of some politick ends doe suffer to be put in execucion the penall lawes made by his Majest[i]es predecessors against
recusantes, notwithstanding he ought not neither can he justly be stiled
a persecutor because he hath never sought or permitted the effusion
of blood or exercised any rigor against any of his Catholique subjectes
out of hatred or malice towardes the religion it selfe, as he hath often
professed unto the queene when he hath perceaved her much afflicted
for the penal mulcts of Catholiques. And his Majest[i]es clemency and
moderacion is such that the Catholiques at this present doe enjoye a
farr greater quietnes and liberty for the exercise of their religion than
ever before during the raignes of Queen Elizabeth and of King James
his royall father.

The Jesuites in forrayne partes and cheefely at Rome doe style
his Majesty the greatest persecutor that ever was, but how much
this proceeding of theirs is indiscreet and full of spleene to the great
prejudice of other Catholiques, lett any indifferent man judge.

4 Concerning the Church of England

It cannot be denyed but that the present doctrine of the Church of
England is farr different from that of former tymes. It now alloweth
of altars and of a civil reverence due unto them. It commaundeth
bowing at the holy name of Jesus, it teacheth the reall presence, seven
sacramentes, meritorious workes necessary to salvacion, possibility of
fulfilling Godes holy commandmentes etc. It mantayneth the pope of
Rome to be cheefe and supreame pastor. It desireth much a reconciliation with the Church of Rome but in a particular waye of its owne
which will not easily be avoided. Yet God who doth sweetely dispose

of all thinges, and who hath inkindled this desire of a reconciliation, can (when it shall seeme fitting to his divine goodnes) perfect what soe happily is begunne. In the meane tyme it will not bee dishonorable to his Holynes, but an heroicall act of infinit charity, to seeke unto them who on [*sic*] their owne accord desire to meet with him, to apply and accommodate himself unto them, who in all appearance doth beare an unfained respect toward him, and a litle to condescend unto their weakenes whome unhappy errors have made infirme. St Gregory did yeeld some what to the Britans before he could worke their conversion.

5 Concerning the Oath of Alleageance

It were a most great happines if his Majesty might receave content and satisfaccion in this matter of the oath. He hath declared at severall tymes that by it he intended onely an assurance of his subjectes fidelity and loyalty towards him. And his Catholique subjectes are [*p. 26*] most ready to give assurance of their fidelity by any oath that ever was proposed by any king to the subjectes of this kingdome, or by the kinges of France or Spaine or by any other princes in the Christian world who live in union with the Sea of Rome, notwithstanding this doth not give wished satisfaccion unto his Majesty because he doth stand precisely upon the words of this oath as they lye. His Majest[i]es reasons are conceaved to be theis. First because the said oath made by the parlament is a lawe, and therefore not to be altered or changed without a parlament. Secondly his Majesty is enformed that his Catholique subjectes doe refuse to sweare unto the wordes of the oath as they lye, meerely because his Holynes hath by a publick breve forbide[n] them, and not because the wordes themselves conteyne the least thing contrary to faith, religion or conscience, and that before the popes breves not any did refuse to take the said oath as it doth lye. Thirdly his Majesty is enformed that his Holynes may if he please, without the least scruple, recall his breves and permitt the taking of it, supposing [*sic*] the declaracion of his Majest[i]es sincere intention.

If meanes could be found to possesse his Majesty: first that by vertue of his prerogative he may justly dispense with the altering of the forme of this oath, [and] secondly that his Catholiques [*sic*] subjectes doe not refuse to sweare unto the wordes of the oath as they lye because forbidden by his Holynes briefe, but because in the word[s] them selves are contained many things contrary to religion and conscience, and, before ever the Sea of Rome did publish her breves, the said oath of alleageance was generally condemned by all learned divines as unlawfull – if meanes, I say, might be made to possesse his Majesty with the particulars, without doubt meanes also would bee found to give his Majesty content and satisfaccion by an other forme of an oath that should give a farr better assurance of his subjectes fidelity than this doth.

6 Concerning the present Difference between the Bishop and Regulars

From the unhappy opposition of episcopall jurisdiccion have proceeded many foule scandals and disorders to the infinit dishonor of the Catholique cause in this kingdome. This opposicion hath made Catholiques a laughin[g] stock to all Protestants, and hath begott the greatest confusion that ever was seene amongst them. Her Majesty, out of her princely charity at severall tymes for present remedy of these many evills, hath solicited his Holynes by her gracious letters to send forthwith a bishop, a head such as God hath instituted for the governement of his Church, seeing noe other meanes to comfort the afflicted and agree soe many disagreeing members.

The reasons inducing his Holynes to deferre the setling of this so necessary a governement in all apparence are theis: first the feare of a dangerous shisme which the great violence of the opposers did often threaten. The second, his desire to gayne his Majest[i]es consent whome the opposers had in some sort gained by [t]her unjust and wrongfull informacions, signifying to his Majesty that a bishop of necessity was to erect a tribunall, examine wills etc., to the prejudice of his Majest[i]es spirituall courtes.

The regulars, cheefely the Jesuites, were moved to oppose against episcopall authority, in regard onely that they were affrayd that such an authority would carry too great a sway, would much obscure and eclipse their power, would bring them under, and correct vice as well in them as others, if there were just occasion for it. Reader [*sic for* Rather] than to permitt this eclipsing of their power and subjection of themselves they did judge it better to deprive the lay Catholickes of the governement by God instituted in his Church, as also of the holy sacrament of confirmacion by Christ ordained to give strength in the profession of his true faith, which sacrament cannot be esteemed but most necessary in a countrey *ubi fides continuo periclitatur*. [*p. 27*]

7 Concerning Signor Gregorio Panzano his Person

He is a man greatly to be esteemed for his many vertues, religious life and great zeale and industry for the advancement of the Catholique cause in this country. Ever since his arrivall, he hath used so discreet a moderacion in the managing of all his affaires that his person is gratfull not onely to her Majesty, who doth greatly respect him, but also to the king himself. In the present controversy betwixt the bishop and regulars he hath carried himself with the greatest indifference that could bee expected from any man, notwithstanding he hath not had the fortune to gaine the good opinion of the Jesuits who seeke to traduce him in every place[1143] as also to hinder [h]is religious designes and proceedings as much as lyeth within their reach.

8 The Reasons wherefore the Jesuits are become soe odious to the King and State

The first is: Father Parsons, the cheefe of all the Jesuittes in former tymes, composed a certaine booke intituled Doleman[1144] where he attempted to disgrace and cut of[f] the title of the most glorious queene of Scotes and her royall issue to this kingdome of England and to prove the crowne onely to apperteine unto the king of Spaine.

The second: the unfortunate treason intended by gunnpowder for which some of theirs did suffer death. And albeit that the State never had any demonstracion convincing the Jesuits to be accessary unto that ungodly treason, notwithstanding they have ever thought them selves to have a convincing presumption, because all those knights and gentlemen of the said foule conspiracy, not children but also understanding men, were all gostly children to none excepting the Jesuites, and at their deathes they did declare that, if they had been persuaded that either [sic for the] conspiracy had been a veniall synn, they could never have attempted it.[1145]

[on p. 28]

Endorsed: Informacions for agent at R[ome].
    Of the state of the Protestants Church and divers other things
    of consequence.

70. Roberts [George Leyburn] to Lewys Amerine [Richard Smith], 8 April 1635[1146]

[AAW, A XXVII, no. 139, pp. 427–430]

Most honored sir,

I have receaved yours of the 4 of Apr[il]. I can assure you that Signor Gregorio[1147] as yett haith not spoken with the archbishop,[1148]

[1143] See *Letter 72*.

[1144] R. Doleman [*pseud.*], *A Conference about the Next Succession to the Crowne of Ingland* (Antwerp, 1594); ARCR, II, no. 167. For the authorship of the tract, see L. Hicks, 'Father Robert Persons SJ and *The Book of Succession*', *RH*, 4 (1957), pp. 104–137; ARCR, II, no. 167.

[1145] John Gerard SJ's narrative of the plot claimed that the Jesuit chaplains of the plotters had not known about the conspiracy and therefore they had been unable to counsel them against it; John Gerard, *The Condition of Catholics under James I: Father Gerard's Narrative of the Gunpowder Plot*, J. Morris (ed.) (London, 1871).

[1146] Misdated in the AAW, A series catalogue to 1634.

[1147] Gregorio Panzani.

[1148] William Laud. On Panzani's arrival in December 1634, he had almost immediately enquired of Robert Philip, concerning Laud, 'si potesse guadagnare'. Philip replied that

and as concerning his demands I am certayne that as yett he haith <u>not made any</u> unto his Majesty. Thos reports proceedeth from the Jesuists who, not acquainted with his proceedings here, maketh many conjectures both out of feare and jealosie and doe publish them for truthes. Mr Bennet is exspected here this tearme. Notwithstanding, I cannot persuade <u>my selfe that</u> the monckes will make peace unlesse the clergie here will yeeld more unto them than <u>is convenient.</u>[1149] They stand now more upon ther poyntes than ever, first in regard of ther power and creditt with the secretarie[1150] and the archb[ishop]; secondly in regard they are greatly <u>incensed against</u> the clergie being informed from thos partes that the b[ishop] of Calcedoyne[1151] and his priests ther doe speake very broadly against Fa[ther] Leander[1152] and doe publish him for a great favorer <u>of the oath, which</u> doth greatly truble him, for it seemeth that in Flanders and Ro[me] he would be esteemed a great opposer of the oath, and by the State here a favorer of it.[1153] I knowe well what I saye, although I dare not <u>saye what I knowe</u>. Poore man. The State here will in the end perceave his duble dealing and then he will be neglected on all syds. In the meane tyme he and his cannot afford a good word to the b[ishop] of Calcedoine and they are infinitely incensed against Monsieur Fountayne.[1154] And many complayntes have be[en] made against him unto the State but without any <u>true or just cause</u>. If thes men would be quiett I am confident that the Catholiques of this country would be happie in a short tyme, for I doe assure you that ther was never soe great hope of wish[e]d tymes as now ther are. Our king is a most vertuous and just prince, and I beseech God that the Catholiques of this country may be made worthie of him. I writte unto you, in my former, how Doctor <u>Duppar was made</u> tutor unto our prince. On Goodfriday, the daye after that he was sworne,

---

Laud was 'troppo astuto et fino, ondo più presto guadagnara, che fù guadgnato'; VA, PD, fo. 42r. Back in late January 1635, Sir Tobie Mathew had advised Panzani to arrange, via Windebank, an interview with Laud (on the pretext of wishing to see his library); *ibid.*, fo. 69r, but on 7 March Walter Montagu called on Panzani to say that Laud could not yet grant an interview since there were 'certe spie di Protestanti' who might inform Windebank; *ibid.*, fo. 83r. On 27 May Panzani wrote to Cardinal Francesco Barberini that some of the secular clergy had come to see him to beg him to visit Laud so that, if Urban VIII were to restore a bishop to rule over the English Catholics, Laud might not oppose him; PRO, 31/9/17B (transcript of Panzani's letter to Barberini).

[1149] See AAW, A XXVII, nos 163–170, for the moves in September–October 1635 towards an accord between the seculars and the Benedictines over the question of episcopal authority.

[1150] Sir Francis Windebank.

[1151] Richard Smith.

[1152] John (Leander) Jones OSB.

[1153] Back in July 1632, Smith had reported to Biddulph that 'some write that F[ather] Leander is much dejected in mynde, perhaps becaus his writing for the oathe is not wel taken in your parts'; AAW, B 27, no. 101.

[1154] George Leyburn.

he preach[e]d before his Majesty and tooke occasion to speake of
the breache or seperation made by Harry the Eight from the Sea
of Rome, and he did call it an unhappie breach, and wish[e]d the
king to take into his consideration the reuniting of this kingdome
with the Romaine Church. And also he tooke occasion to speake of
<the> Catholiques and <of> [*p. 428*] this country and he sayd that
many of them were very good, and did instance in the b[ishop] of
Calcedoine who, when the queen was first with child, caused a prayer
to be generally sayd for her safe delivery, as also commanded all
Catholiques to praye for his Majesty['s] prosperity, for which act the
Jesuists did complaine of him at Ro[me]. I do assure you that this is
very true.[1155]

Other occurrences are not many. The lady duchesse of Buckinghame[1156] is marryed unto the Lord Donluce.[1157] Although the king
haith given his consent, being greatly importuned, notwithstanding
he is not well pleased. The Lady Feilding at Venise is dead.[1158] Your
best lady[1159] is expected here this night. The Jesuists give out that you
have placed one Smith[1160] to be confessarius to the new Monesterie,[1161]
a lude man, this to disgrace that house. And thes reportes are believed
notwithstanding that this Smith <is> a falne Jesuist and teacheth
scoole now in Coven[t] Garden and did <the Jesuist> teach before
that monestery did beginne. Mr Brooke <the Jesuist>,[1162] who doth
live with Sir Charles Smith,[1163] sayd publikely at the table that in Italy
marryed men would sooner send ther wifes to a ba[w]dy house than

---

[1155] For Brian Duppa, see *Letter 74*; Knowler, *ESLD*, II, p. 57. For his 'Arminianism', as
suggested by his enthusiasm in enforcing a non-traditional altar policy in Chichester diocese,
see Tyacke, *AC*, p. 206. For the sermon, see Hibbard, *CI*, p. 51.

[1156] Katherine (Manners), widow of Sir George Villiers, duke of Buckingham. (Smith
reported in October 1633 that she had 'leave of the k[ing] to heare Masse publikly with the
q[ueen]'; AAW, B 27, no. 131.) She had converted back to Catholicism after the duke was
assassinated.

[1157] Randal MacDonnell, Viscount Dunluce, the future 2nd earl of Antrim. See J.H.
Ohlmeyer, *Civil War and Restoration in the Three Stuart Kingdoms* (Cambridge, 1993), pp. 29, 30.

[1158] For the death in Venice of Anne (Weston), wife of Lord Basil Fielding, see Alexander,
CLT, p. 218; *CSPV, 1632–1636*, p. 347.

[1159] Anne (Philipson), Baroness Arundell.

[1160] Anthony Smith.

[1161] The new foundation of Augustinian canonnesses at Paris, sponsored by Richard
Smith.

[1162] Identity uncertain, but probably John Price SJ (rather than either Henry Hawkins SJ,
alias Brooks, or Thomas Poulton SJ, alias Brooks). Panzani mentions that Price used the
alias of Brooke. He described him as 'assai bono huomo'; VA, PD, fo. 89r.

[1163] For Sir Charles Smith of Wootton Wawen, Warwickshire, see *CSPD, 1634–1635*,
p. 97. He was executor to the countess of Buckingham. Susan Fielding, countess of Denbigh,
petitioned successfully in mid-1634 for a protection for him from proceedings concerning
his recusancy.

suffer them to goe to confession unto any <u>secular priest</u>. Bonnam,[1164] the lady treasurers[1165] Jesuist, sayd that all seculer priest[s] did live <u>unchastely here in</u> England and th*a*t de facto they were soliciting his Holynes for dispensation <u>to marrie, and</u>, sayd he, I thinke it were not a misse th*a*t his Holynes should grant it, rather than th*a*t they should <u>live as they</u> doe.[1166] Ignoscat illis Deus quia nesciunt quid faciunt.

Sweet Jesus send you all happines in hart.

Y*our* most obedient servant,

Roberts

Apr[il] 8 1634 [*sic* for 1635].

[*on p. 430*]

Addressed: A Mons*ieu*r Monsieur [*sic*] Lewys Amerine, marchant de-meurant dans la Place Maubert.

Endorsed: Jesuits humors.

71. R[ichardus] C[halcedonensis] [Richard Smith] to William Laud, 15/25 April 1635[1167]

[*AAW, A XXVIII, no. 13, pp. 43–46*]

[*on p. 45*]

May it please your Grace,

The high ranke of favour and esteeme which your Grace most deservedly houldeth with both their Majesties, togeather with the renowne of that excellent temper of mind with which your Grace is com*m*only knowne to be indued, have embouldned me at this present, after some essaies in the like kind made upon occasion to others of his Ma*je*sties most honorable privie councell hertofore, to plead my innocencie in theise few lines before your Grace <and therin most humbly request that, through y*our* Graces> powerfull mediation, the sincerity of my hart may be truly represented to his Ma*je*stie with an

[1164] John Alexander Evison SJ.

[1165] Frances (Waldegrave), second wife of Richard Weston, 1st earl of Portland. See Alexander, *CLT*, p. 29.

[1166] Smith had relayed this story to Biddulph in January 1634; AAW, B 27, no. 114.

[1167] This letter is undated. The compiler of the AAW, A series catalogue has annotated this letter's entry in the catalogue – 'date from another damaged copy' – but does not indicate the location of the copy.

unfained expression of my fidelity and alleageance to his highnesse,
being ready at all tymes to confirme the same with any oath that ever
bishop of the Catholick profession tooke in England or that bishopps
use to take in Catholick cuntries abroad.

It is not unknowne unto your Grace how much I have bin opposed
theise yeares lately past by some domesticke (as I may terme them)
adversaries of myne, antihierarchists, and no frends to bishops, who
have sought not only to disgrace me in forraine parts but to make me
suspected and hatefull to my king and country at home by casting
most injurious aspersions both upon my person and clayme. And
whereas, amoungst other imputations concerning my person, it hath
bin objected that I ame wholy at the devotion of the French, I humbly
beseech your Grace to beleive, and when occasion serveth to assure
his Majestie in the word of a bishop, that my devotion and affection
is so truly English and my hart so deeply imbued with a naturall love
and zeale towards my king and country, that no obligation or tye
whatsoever from any forreine nation hath power to alter it, professing
to rely so wholy uppon his Majesties royall clemencie and goodnesse,
as that I desire to receive no favour either from Spaine, France or
other potentate ~~but~~ but what may stand with his Majesties pleasure
and good liking. And, as for the claime of that episcopall authority
which hath bin conferred upon me for the good of English Catholicks,
your Grace well knoweth how conformable it is to the practise of our
religion in all places, and how necessary for the preservation of peace
and holy discipline, both among preists and laicks, which cannot
but by consequence redownd to his Majesties greater service. And
although, for my owne particular, as I never sought the place so is it
to mee indifferent whether I retaine the same still or resighne it unto
some other of the secular clergy as shalbe thought by others most
conducing to God Almighty his honor and to his Majesties service.
Yet to shew that the authority which I or any other in my steed may
clayme or exercise by vertue of this place over his Majesties Catholick
subjects cannot be justly offensive to his Majestie or hurtfull to the
State, but rather usefull to both, I make bould to tender to your
Graces view theise few reasons, amoungst many others that might be
alleadged, which I have here breifly set downe in a paper a part,
humbly beseeching your Grace in the prudentiall ballance of your
impartiall judgment, and with your accostomed pietie and moderation
of mind, to ponder the same, not doubting but that in your Graces
most judicious and deepe understanding they shalbe found to have
dew weight by meanes of your Graces most gratefull hand, they shall
be honored [p. 46] with his Majesties view also, and find that allowance
which is so much desired not only by myself but by the far greater
and more dutifull part of all his Majesties Catholick subjects. And

as by this so gratious a favour both I and they shall remaine most deeply obliged in duty to pray to Allmighty God for the encrease of your Graces power and greatnesse in this world, and for your eternall happinesse in the next, so shall it be with all Catholick princes abroad no smale addition of immortall honor and praise dew to your Graces memory, above all your predecessors, for so many great and magnanimous exployts hitherto achived to the admiration of the Christian world, both in advancing the universall good of the English nation, and his Majesties service generally, as most particularly in the suppressing or reducing to dew obedience the refractory spirits of those who have ever bene noted to be disloyall both to the Church and State.

And so with a most lowly and dutifull submission of my self to your Grace, craving pardon for this bouldnesse, I rest, your Graces most humbly ever at command,

R[ichardus] C[halcedonensis]

Paris 1635

Endorsed:[1168] My lords letter to my lord bishop of Canterbury, 1635.[1169]

[*on p. 43*]

Addressed: Al molto illustrissimo Signor Octavio. Prati.

Endorsed: Lettre of the bish[op] of Calcedon to the arch[bishop] of Canterburie.

72. Roberts [George Leyburn] to Leuys Amerine [Richard Smith], 8 May 1635

[*AAW, A XXVIII, no. 17, pp. 81–82*]

Most honored sir,

I have receaved yours of the 2 of Maye. Mr Bennet did not come up according to his appoyntment in soe much that the treaty of a peace with the munckes is deferred untill the next tearme. I am verely persuaded that it will not have any good successe; for the munckes now

---

[1168] In John Southcot's hand.

[1169] See also AAW, A XXVIII, no. 14, part of a draft of another letter from Smith to Laud, without date, thanking Laud for the 'honour your <Grace> did me in the favourable acceptance of one of myne which some tyme agoe I directed unto you', and praising the 'prudent moderation by which things are carried in our contrie', under the rule of the 'clement' and 'gracious' Charles, 'especially since [...] your Grace [had] the deserved honour to stand and command at the sterne'. Smith has endorsed it 'not sent'; *ibid.*, p. 47.

doe carrie ther heads high, relying upon ther power with the b[ishop]
of Canterbury[1170] and the secretary,[1171] and therfore will thinke to droe
the clergie unto ther owne conditions, but they may deceave them
selves. The b[ishop] of Canterbury some 10 dayes aggoe did aske of
Fa[ther] Leander[1172] what was the definition of a bishope and whether
the bishops of this country, albeit marryed, might not enjoye ther
bishopricks, wifes and notwithstanding be promoted to holie orders.
I have now gott a true copie of Fa[ther] Leanders answere unto
Mr Curt[ney's] 20 arguments.[1173] I have lett Mr Clerk[1174] have it to
copie out and you shall receave it by Mr Plantyn.[1175] He doth deale very
cunningly although with litle solidity. The Jesuists every daye more and
more doe showe ther passion against Signor Gregorio,[1176] and say that
his negotiation is the cause of this persecution,[1177] which I doe assure
you faithfully as yett doth not appeare more than at other tymes. Onely
I feare that the Spanish resident[1178] and cheefely Mr Tayler,[1179] sett
on by the Jesuists, doe dissuade Catholiques from comming unto ther
houses for feare of the pursevants who to my knowledge have not
any commissions.[1180] It is true that two priests have been of late taken

---

[1170] William Laud.

[1171] Sir Francis Windebank.

[1172] John (Leander) Jones OSB.

[1173] For Jones's reply to Edward Leedes's opinions on the oath, see Sitwell, 'Leander Jones's
mission to England, 1634-5', pp. 148-149.

[1174] John Southcot.

[1175] Lawrence Platt.

[1176] Gregorio Panzani. In a letter of 13 June 1635, to Urban VIII, Panzani complained
that 'the Jesuits' gave it out that 'he [Panzani] was not sent by the pope, but by Cardinal
Richelieu', and, although he had 'given them more encouragement and tokens of confidence
than to any others', they spread 'idle and personal reflections, casting my horoscope, and
pretending to be privy to all the particulars of my life'. In particular, Robert Jenison SJ
'attacked me so briskly on account of partiality in their disfavour' that Panzani was 'obliged
to make use of the strongest asseverations to silence him'; Berington, *The Memoirs of Gregorio
Panzani*, p. 175. Panzani's diary frequently records messages from secular priests who claimed
that the Jesuits were denouncing him to Rome; VA, PD, *passim*. In late October 1635, Panzani
confronted Sir Tobie Mathew with these stories of Jesuit malice; PRO, 31/9/17B (transcript
of Panzani's letter to Barberini of 31 October 1635).

[1177] On 24 April 1635 Panzani reported to Cardinal Barberini that the Jesuits were doing
all they could to prove that the Catholics in the realm were suffering persecution. Sir
Tobie Mathew had claimed that the privy council had decided to give the high commission
pursuivants a free hand, though Windebank and Cottington absolutely denied it. Panzani
confessed that there was undoubtedly not yet a liberty of conscience in England but
conditions for Catholics were milder than they had ever been; PRO, 31/9/17B.

[1178] Juan de Necolalde.

[1179] Henry Taylor.

[1180] See AAW, A XXVIII, no. 18 (a paper dated 12 May 1635 and endorsed 'Declaratio
Capituli circa Clementiam Regis', the copy of a formal document given under the hand
of the dean and the seal of the chapter). This declaration denies the reports circulated
abroad that Catholics were most grievously persecuted in England, and claims that they

and dismissed agayne,[1181] and Secretary Windebancke [a] few dayes aggoe sent for one of the pursevants and did ~~word~~ chid[e] him fearefully.

M[r] Clerke will accquainte you with the successe of the letter unto [the] b[ishop] of <u>Canterbury,</u>[1182] and hereafter we shall knowe more for he desire[s] to speake with the ambassadeur[1183] who sent it unto him, and this daye the ambassadeur intendeth to goe and M[r] Plantyn is to be his interpreter. Long aggoe I did congratulate the grand ausmonier[1184] from you as soon as I did understand for certayne that he had receaved his breife from the king to be bishop of Anguileme.[1185] The letter sent unto the kings agent[1186] ther was from M[r] Mountegue.[1187] I wounder that you write not any one word of <u>warre declared against</u> Spane; with which newes the ambassadeurs here have long aggoe acquainted the king. Our navie is shortly to sett forward and to keep upon the narrow seas as it is probably conjectured. Ther is also order <u>given all over England</u> that every family <u>shall prepare armes</u> and have them in readines.

The puretans doe <u>feare a change in</u> religion. The <u>Jesuists are fearefully</u> out with the bishop of Canterbury and says [sic] now that his Grace, to make him selfe more <u>popular,</u> doth greatly complye with the puretans and doth intend to change his course and herafter to run with them. I hope that M[r] Car[1188] is with you before this.

now enjoyed, under the rule of King Charles, greater quiet, peace and liberty everywhere as regards the exercise of their religion than in former times was permitted to them.

[1181] Panzani names them as a Franciscan, Walter (Christopher) Coleman, and a Benedictine, Dunstan Everard. Panzani, however, records that they were kept incarcerated; PRO, 31/9/17B (transcripts of Panzani's letters to Barberini of 15 July, 22 July, 16 September, and 28 November 1635). Panzani said that John Wragge (appointed to carry out the duties of the recently deceased Humphrey Cross) made these arrests in order to demonstrate his zeal. Windebank assured Panzani that Archbishop Laud had had nothing to do with it, and that he, Windebank, would investigate. But they were arrested, so the Jesuit John Clarke had assured Panzani, because they had said publicly that Laud was a crypto-Catholic, while others claimed that it was because they had said that if the gunpowder plot had succeeded it would have been a good thing.

[1182] See *Letter 71*.

[1183] John Scudamore, 1st Viscount Scudamore. See *CSPV, 1632–1636*, pp. 425–426.

[1184] Jacques le Noël Du Perron.

[1185] See Bergin, *Making of the French Episcopate*, p. 616; PRO, 31/9/127, p. 45.

[1186] Either Henry de Vic (see *CSPD, 1635*, p. 88) or Réné Augier.

[1187] Walter Montagu left for Rome in the autumn; VA, PD, fo. 115r. On 30 January/ 9 February 1636 Peter Biddulph recorded Montagu's arrival in Rome. Cardinal Barberini lodged him in 'his owne pallace'; AAW, A XXVIII, no. 99, p. 367.

[1188] Miles Pinckney.

I ame glad to understand by yours to my lord that the contract is in so good forwardnesse and that the founder[1196] is so favorable still. I pray God continew it ever, and send a good conclusion of the whole buissenesse quickly.[1197]

I hope there is sufficient order taken for the sending of schollars at the tyme appointed, and I suppose you yourself have taken order to provide a maister for them, as also for those that <shall> have ended their philosophy. Here our buissinesse goeth on but slowly by reason of opposition from all sides, and now lately some lay Catholicks (as they call them selves) have given up to Gregorio a very spitefull and shamefull information against the having of a bishop or any bishops officer,[1198] wherof I intend to send you a coppy, if not now at least by the next opportunity, that you may see what adversaries we have, and assist us with your notes and advise to answer it. At the reading therof some of our freinds were so full of just indignation that at our last consult a motion was made to article publickly before the Sea Apostolick against the true authors of these commotions, seeing there is no hope of prevailing otherwise against them, wherupon certaine articles were drawen, wherof I send you here a coppy desiring you to keep <them> privat to your self till such time as we are compleatly furnished with proofs, and to assist us with as many particulers as you can towards the prooving of every one in particuler, and, if you think this forme not so fitting, advise us otherwise for, if we proceed this way, we must be wary what we say, and in what manner.[1199] Lett your answer to this be wholy addressed to me and to no other. For newes, we have only this in generall that our fleet [p. 106] is ready and expecteth nothing but a wind to sett forth. The intent of it is not knowen, but the common ghesse is that it is to take possession of the narrow seas, and

[1196] Pedro Coutinho, a wealthy Portuguese gentleman who assisted with the foundation of the English seminary at Lisbon (the college of Saints Peter and Paul). See John Kirk and William Croft, *Historical Account of Lisbon College* (Barnet, 1902), pp. 3–4.

[1197] Coutinho had stipulated that the seminary should remain under the control of the English secular clergy. Cf. AAW, A XXVII, no. 57 (William Clifford to Richard Smith, 4/14 May 1633, concerning the problems of the Lisbon seminary). Eamon Duffy comments that the Lisbon college, 'a fully Tridentine seminary in its dependence on the bishop', became 'the principal centre for the propagation in England of Counter-Reformation ideals of a reformed priesthood'; Duffy, 'The English secular clergy', p. 225.

[1198] On 14 May Panzani noted that he had given George Leyburn 'le proteste contro il vescovo', so that he might examine the signatures. Sir Basil Brooke had given permission for this on 12 May; VA, PD, fos 79r, 92r, 93r.

[1199] See AAW, A XXVIII, no. 19 ('Capita quaedam a nonnullis Angliae Nobilibus Catholicis scripto proposita et oblata admodum Reverendo Domino Gregorio Panzani', 15 May 1635); AAW, A XXVIII, no. 20 ('Responsio ad capita [...]', an answer to no. 19). The 'capita' were presented to Panzani on 16 May by Sir Thomas Shirley, Sir John Simeon (on behalf of himself and Sir Henry Neville, 2nd Baron Abergavenny), William Perle (on behalf of himself and the 2nd Baron Baltimore), and a Catholic physician; VA, PD, fo. 93r.

I wish you all happines who am your most obedient ser

Roberts

May 8 1635.

Crosse[1189] the pursevant is dead, a Catholique.[1190]
    The Jesuists give out that the king is greatly incensed aga
Gregorio and that he hath commanded the secretary to w
[de]part the kingdome, but not a word true.

[on p. 82]

Addressed: A Monsieur Monsieur [sic] Leuys Amerin, march
            meurant dans la Place Maubert a Paris.

Endorsed: F[ather] Leander.

73. Clerk [John Southcot] to [William Hargrave],[1191] 26 May 1635

[AAW, A XXVIII, no. 22, pp. 105–106]

Sir,

I had yours of the 14 April, by which I understand you receaved or
of mine, but you specified not the date as I wish you ever to doe. I sav
also yours to my lord,[1192] which I liked very well and I delivered your
Latin letter to Signor Gregorio <Panzani>[1193] who saieth that he will
send it to the Congregacion de Propaganda and desire them to give
their answer to M[r] Fitton.[1194] We wil commend your invention therin
and thank you for your paines most hartely, not doubting but that it
will do us good, and we shall desire M[r] Strong[1195] to do the like for as
much as concerns the second part about sending over priests to labour
in this vineard. M[r] Colleton receaved your last common letter to the
deane and chapter but gave no order yet for the answering of it in
common, neither have we yet a secretary for the purpose. I remember
not the date, nor have the letter now by me; but I well remember
(being present at the reading of it) that it gave good content to all.

[1189] For Humphrey Cross, see NAGB, pp. 43, 77, 89, 218–219.
[1190] Panzani repeated to Cardinal Barberini this rumour about Cross's conversion; PRO, 31/9/17B.
[1191] See Anstr., II, p. 146; CRS, 1, p. 108; Letter 74.
[1192] Richard Smith.
[1193] Panzani recorded that Southcot had visited him on 24 May; VA, PD, fo. 94r.
[1194] Peter Biddulph.
[1195] Matthew Kellison.

to make all straungers vale bonnets to us; also to keep the French and Hollander in aw[e], in case they should attempt any thing on Flanders side. Some say they are to joine with a Spannish fleet. We also here stand uppon our guard, his Majesty having <given> order that all the traine bands shalbe in a readinesse, inquiries also being made in all places of the number of able men from sixteen to threescore etc.

Our times are still calme, God be thanked, and our good king. No more but with all woonted respects, I rest. 26 May 1635.

Yours,

Clerk

Mr Tho[mas] Taylor died on the 24 of this May of a burning fever. Pray for him, as here we all doe.[1200]

No address or endorsement.

74. [John Southcot] to Louys Ameryn [Richard Smith], 27 May 1635

[*AAW, A XXVIII, no. 23, pp. 107–108*]

[Sir,]

Bycause I wrote lately by Mr Plantin,[1201] who went not from hence till yesterday, I have the lesse to trouble you now withall. By him I sent you certaine articles which in consult were mentioned to be putt up to the Sea Apost[olic] against the Molinists[1202] by the secular clergy of England wherin your advise and <u>furtherance is</u> humbly demaunded, and it is desired that the matter may be carried wit<u>h dew secresy till</u> the buissinesse be ripe. I sent you before the coppy of a most spitefull informacion given up by their followers to Gregorio,[1203] which he would have us to answer thoroughly, and therfor your assistance was also demaunded therin by the whole consult. I sent also by Mr Plantin the <u>clergies attestation in behalf of the</u> queen <u>to be shewed</u> there as you please for the queens honor and the clergies good.

Now as concerning my lord of Canterb[ury's] answer,[1204] although it be not altogeather so good as I had wrote in that letter, for I spake

---

[1200] See Anstr., II, p. 315. Thomas Taylor was the son of Robert Taylor (who had served as an interpreter for the Spanish ambassador in London) and brother of the Jesuits' friend, Henry Taylor, the infanta's agent in London.

[1201] Lawrence Platt.

[1202] Jesuits.

[1203] Gregorio Panzani. See *Letter 73*.

[1204] i.e. William Laud's reply to Richard Smith's letter of 15/25 April 1635. See *Letter 71*.

my self two daies agoe with the French ambassador[1205] who tould <it> me ~~that~~ a little otherwise than I had understood it by Mr Plantin, yet it may justly give my lord[1206] occasion to [*word deleted*] acknowledg his favor,[1207] wh*i*ch by the advise of freinds here is thought will better be expressed in a particuler letter to <u>Mr Doctor Dupper</u>, tutor to the prince (<u>to whom my lor</u>d <u>is much</u> obliged for the honorable mention he made of him in a publick sermon before the king on Good Friday last),[1208] than to Canterbury him self, and therfor it is wished by all <u>meanes that my lord would ca</u>use a good letter to be written to the saied Doctor Dupper, both to give him thankes for that favour and to acknowledge to him the gratious answer wh*i*ch my lord of <u>Canterb[ury] made by word of</u> mouth to the French ambassador etc,[1209] and to desire the doctor to lett my lord of Canterb[ury] know ~~how true and faithful a servant he is to his Majesty~~ so much. Withall, to send th<u>e doctor a coppy</u> of those reasons <u>for a b*i*sho*p* and to entreat him</u> to propose them privatly to the State for the greater good of the kingdom and service of the king. O*u*r freinds here conceave that such a letter from my lord to Doctor Dupper, who is a moderat man, and a creature of my lord of Canterb[ury] and favoured by the king, would do my lord much good.

This being all that occurreth for the present I humbly rest.

27 May 1635.

I make bould to send the enclosed[1210] this <u>once for Mr Hart</u>.[1211]

[1205] Either Jean d'Angennes, marquis de Pougny, or Henri de Ferté Nabert, marquis de Senneterre.

[1206] Richard Smith.

[1207] An undated letter from Panzani to Urban VIII noted that Smith had written to Laud, offering that his jurisdiction should be modified. According to Panzani, Laud had gone so far as to say that he actually admired Smith, and that he had shown Smith's missive to Charles; Dockery, *CD*, pp. 44–45. Panzani's 'Relazione' also records Smith's letter to Laud; VA, Barberini MS LVI, 136, fos 45v–6r.

[1208] See *Letter 70*.

[1209] Panzani's 'Relazione' mentions that Laud had told the 'French ambassador that he greatly respected' Smith, and had referred the matter, favourably, to the king and claimed that 'he had always helped him'; VA, Barberini MS LVI, 136, fos 45v–6r (transcript and translation at ABSJ). However, Walter Montagu had told Peter Biddulph in early 1636 that 'the king for the present will nott permitt a b*i*sho*p* in England, and [...] the b*i*sho*p* of Canterburye tould the queen plainely, when she spake to him about it, that he would oppose it as much as he could'; AAW, A XXVIII, no. 98, p. 365.

[1210] *Letter 73*.

[1211] William Hargrave. He had been appointed president of the college of Saints Peter and Paul at Lisbon in 1634; Anstr., II, p. 146.

On Trinity Sunday at night Mr Thomas Taylor, the agents brother, died of a burning fever.[1212] The poor will have a great losse in him. We all pray for him as for a brother.

[on p. 108]

Addressed: A Mons*ieur* Monsieur [*sic*] Louys Ameryn marchant de-m[eurant] dans la Place Maubert a Paris.

Endorsed: Canterb[ury] of the bishop.

75. [John Southcot] to Fitton [Peter Biddulph], 14 August 1635

[*AAW, A XXVIII, no. 32, pp. 131–134*]

Sir,

The post is not yet come this week, and so we have receaved noe letters from you since that short one of July the 18 to Mr Roberts[1213] wh*ich* you sent by Paris, [and] the last wh*ich* we had by the way of Bruxelles bearing date the 7th of the same month.

This day fortnight being the last of our July I wrote unto you concerning a secrett buissenesse lately here resolved uppon, wh*ich* is to send a lay agent to Ro[me] out of hand, but I understand that the Hollanders met with the post at sea and robbed him of all his letters. Yet I repeated somwhat about the same subject the week following, and I hope those letters will come safe to yo*u*r hands. As yet there is no more donn in that buissenesse than what I signified there, and so I have now the lesse to say.

With these you shall receave a coppy of Sig*n*or Panzanos test-imoniales, wherby you may controll those reproachfull speeaches [*sic*] that you heare there of him in that kind. I send you also the forme of an oath[1214] wh*ich* is like to be proposed here by the Catholicks to give the k[ing] satisfaction concerning their alleageance. It is verbatim almost the same with the oath of alleageance, the second and fift se*c*tions only excepted, as you <may> see by comparing them togeather. But you must know that this forme is originally proposed not by the clergy or any freind of theirs, but by a freind[1215] and speciall dependant of

---

[1212] See *Letter 73*.

[1213] George Leyburn.

[1214] See AAW, A XXVIII, no. 33 (two forms of allegiance oath proposed for English Catholics, 14 August 1635); AAW, A XXVIII, no. 34 (translation of no. 33).

[1215] Cecil Calvert, 2nd Baron Baltimore.

the Molinists,[1216] by occasion of some troubles that he is otherwise like to fall into. And although he will not seem to have acquainted those his freinds with it, yet it may well <be> presumed they knew of it, but would faine have it ~~come to light~~ proposed by the clergy first, the better to save them selves in that court in case it should be disliked, and so the [*p. 132*] party interested shewed it first privatly to M[r] Roberts, and wished him to shew it to Fa[ther] Phil[ip] and to know his advise; but Fa[ther] Phil[ip] will not meddle in it, one way or other. Yet he is of opinion (and so are divers others here) that it would be dissembled at Rome if it were once sett on foot here. I pray certify what you think therof by your next letters, but take no notice to any there as yet, unlesse you find they have heard of it already otherwaies, and then be sure to lett them know ~~that~~ from whence it comes originally.

Here we say that the treaty of mariage is concluded between the k[ing] of Poland and the Lady Elizabeths daughter,[1217] and that my lord martiall[1218] is deputed to bring over the lady in September next, that the king may take her from hence as a daughter of England, but methinkes we should first heare of a dispensation from thence.[1219]

It is determined lately in councell that 45 shipps shalbe made ready against next spring with eleven thousand men. The charge will amount to 218[m] pounds sterling to be generally levied throughout the kingdome.

Our king is much disgusted both with the French and Hollanders for some affronts and abuses which they have lately offered to us at sea, and it is saied that our admirall hath order to pay them for it, if he meet with them fairly. Yet my Lord Scudamore is gonn over as ledger into France,[1220] and shortly my Lord Aston shall go in like sort

---

[1216] Jesuits. For Baltimore's complex relationship with the Jesuits, see Hughes, *HSJ*, pp. 355–359.

[1217] Princess Elizabeth, daughter of Elizabeth, Princess Palatine. See *CSPV, 1632–1636*, pp. 305, 316, 332, 379, 384, 416, 425, 456, 465, 466, 469; Berington, *The Memoirs of Gregorio Panzani*, p. 209; Laud, *Works*, VII, pp. 270–271; AAW, A XXVIII, no. 83 (Biddulph's letter to Southcot of 2/12 January 1636, concerning the marriage).

[1218] Thomas Howard, 2nd earl of Arundel.

[1219] In January 1635 Windebank had asked Panzani to make representations to Rome to facilitate the marriage; VA, PD, fo. 67r.

[1220] *CSPV, 1632–1636*, pp. 425, 426. On 30 December 1635/9 January 1636 Smith noted that 'I was with our embass[ador]', Scudamore, 'to give him the new yeare who received me very kindly as he doth al Cath[olics] and also priests and told me he heard that in England the Rhemes Testament was received by Prot*estants*'; AAW, A XXVIII, no. 81, p. 325. On 10/20 February 1636 Smith retailed that he was 'as welcome the second time to the embas[sador] as the first', but he, Smith, 'must not go too often for feare of jealousie of this State', since the French 'fear some breach with England'; AAW, A XXVIII, no. 92, p. 351. On 23 May/2 April 1636, however, Smith complained that Scudamore's wife had been at the Jesuit William Talbot's sermon, although 'so muffled as she wold not be knowne', whereas before she had been present at a sermon preached by Smith's friend,

into Spaine, although the king be not well pleased with the Spaniard for excluding the palatin[1221] in the peace ~~of~~ <with> Saxony.

I heare Sir Basil Brook and Sir John Winters lands are both extended for payment of those monies to the king ~~for~~ which may be [*p. 133*] both their undoings in a short time.[1222] Yet Sir Basil putteth a good countenance on the buissenesse outwardly. The rest to Mr Roberts.

Adieu. 14 Aug[ust] 1635.

It is intended to appropriat this oath wholy to our own king and his successors, and so that clause concerning the doctrin of murthering etc[1223] is to be qualified and restrained to our own prince.

To Mr Webster.[1224]

Sir,

You will understand by what I write to Mr Fitton that our letters miscaried a fortnight agoe.

[*on p. 131*]

Addressed: To Mr Fitton.

[*on p. 134*]

Endorsed: About an oath of alleageance which Catholicks may take.

Miles Pinckney; AAW, A XXVIII, no. 106, p. 385. (In July–October 1637 Biddulph sent a series of newsletters to Scudamore; PRO, C 115/109/8861–70.)

Smith tried in mid-1636 to establish good relations with the new English ambassador at Paris, Robert Sidney, earl of Leicester, and offered to visit him. Smith's first offer 'was nether accepted nor refused'; AAW, A XXVIII, no. 125, p. 433. However, in January 1637, Smith referred, in a letter to Southcot, to a toleration tract which he, Smith, had published in 1603/4 (*Epistola Historica de Mutuis Officiis inter Sedem Apostolicam & Magnae Britanniae Reges Christianos, Anglice olim Scripta, ad Seren. M. Britanniae Regem Iacobum* (Cologne [imprint false; printed at Paris], 1637); ARCR, I, no. 1094), and reported that 'my l[ord of] Lecester saieth the epistle to K[ing] James which was given to him hathe much wit and good Latin'; AAW, A XXIX, no. 5, p. 9. And, on 27 January/6 February 1637, Smith could enthuse that 'the other day the earl of Lecester came to visit me very courteously' to congratulate Smith on the grant to him, by his patron Richelieu, of the Benedictine abbey of St Sauveur at Charroux; AAW, A XXIX, no. 9, p. 19; Allison, RSGB, II, pp. 250–251. On 18/28 February Smith was invited to dine with Leicester; AAW, A XXIX, no. 15, p. 31. On 3/13 March 1637 Smith was pleased to record that Leicester had sent for him again, though Smith was too ill to go; and the countess of Leicester 'sent our nunnes [at the new Augustinian convent in Paris] some Lenten provision'; AAW, A XXIX, no. 18, p. 39.

[1221] Charles Louis, Elector Palatine of the Rhine.

[1222] See *Letter 65*.

[1223] This is a reference to the clause in the 1606 oath of allegiance which stated 'I do from my heart abhor, detest and abjure as impious and heretical this damnable doctrine and position that princes which be excommunicated and deprived by the pope may be deposed or murdered by their subjects or any other whatsoever'; J.P. Kenyon, *The Stuart Constitution* (Cambridge, 1966), pp. 458–459.

[1224] Anthony Champney.

76. Clerk [John Southcot] to [Peter Biddulph], 20 November 1635

[*AAW, A XXVIII, no. 46, pp. 175–176*]

Sir,

The last week I wrote not to you, neither have we had any letters these two weekes from you or Mr Champney, no post being come from those parts by reason of the contrary windes. These I write chiefly to informe you of the agreement which we made and sighned mutually on Tewsday last in the afternoon <being St Hugh of Lincolns and St Gregory Turronensis^{1225}> at <u>Gregorios</u>^{1226} chamber with the monkes and friars; and here I send you <a coppy of> the instrument, as also of the promises which were made before the subscription ore tenus. The buissenesse passed very fairely and freindly. When all the parties were come togeather we satt round in a ring by the fire side without any ceremony of place or order, and, Gregorio sitting with us, I began to read the promises, which being read, Gregorio demaunded of us one by one if we consented therunto, and every one answered yea. Which being donn I read the Instrument, and then Gregorio demanded in like manner one by one for their consent therunto, which was graunted by every one. Then we proceeded to the sighning, and three coppies were sighned authentically by every one that were present, and afterwards delivered to eather ~~party~~ part and to Gregorio, which, being donn, we saluted one an other freindly and so departed. The Carmelite was not present, but gave his voice to Mr Price^{1227} and at his next coming to town will subscribe as the rest have donn, with his own hand.^{1228}

---

^{1225} St Gregory of Tours.

^{1226} Gregorio Panzani.

^{1227} William (Benedict) Jones OSB.

^{1228} See AAW, A XXVIII, no. 41 ('Exemplar articulorum pacis et concordiae initae saeculares inter et regulares sacerdotes in Anglia in presentia [...] Domini Gregorii Panzani', 17 November 1635); Lunn, *EB*, pp. 125–126. (Panzani recorded that the Carmelite provincial came on 23 November to add his signature; VA, PD, fo. 120r.) A summary of the Accord described it as consisting 'in three things especially'. The first was 'to lay aside all former disagreements, and to cooperat hereafter joyntly to the advancement of Catholick religion in our country'. The second was to prevent the pope being 'misinformed' about 'the affayres of the Catho[lic] religion in our country', and the third was to 'defend and preserve [...] the honour and reputacion of both their Majesties and of the State especially abroad'. The same document claimed that the Jesuits tried to disrupt the making of the Accord; AAW, A XXVIII, no. 59, p. 227. On 30 January/9 February 1636 Biddulph reported from Rome that 'the regulars who are agreed with us have allso sent up this week a Manifestation to satisfye the Jesuitts that they did nott intend any thing against them by this Accord'. This infuriated Biddulph because the seculars were given no notice of it, and the document stated that the religious were to exercise their faculties 'without depending upon the bishop of Chalcedon'. The Benedictines' agent at Rome, Richard (Wilfrid) Selby OSB, had given

In the doing of the buissenesse, there came a Jesuitt[1229] to speak with Gregorio who went out to him to the next chamber and tould him what we were doing, inviting him to come in and joine with the rest. The Jesuitt replied that if they ~~should be~~ <were> invited they would perhaps joine with us also, but I doubt they would hardly joine although they were invited formally.[1230] And no doubt they will cavill and complaine there of our joining in this union without them. But we are all resolved to answer uniformely that none were particulerly invited but that the friars, hearing that the clergy and the monkes were treating of a peace, did offer them selves voluntarily to joine with them, which being notified to the clergy they accepted of their offer, wherfor the Jesuitts, knowing [*p. 176*] of this buissenesse, may offer them selves if it please them to joine with the rest in it, as others ~~of~~ <have> donn.[1231] This is the answer we are agreed uppon in case they complaine they are excluded, besides that there is an expresse clause in the instrument to invite both them and others. But the truth is the Jesuitts are so far from offering them selves that they have sought by all meanes to hinder this union, and wished Panzano not to be present at it, as Panzano tould me a good while since. I hope this agreement will produce much good in time, and be a strong bridle to the afflicted both here and there.

I have written a few lines to you by Arthure Brett to commend him to your care and assistance uppon his first arrival.[1232] He is not yet gon

the document to Monsignor Boccabella; AAW, A XXVIII, no. 99, p. 367. According to Smith, in November 1636, Boccabella agreed with Thomas Fitzherbert that Smith had fully resigned his authority, and hence the English secular clergy had no immediate superior; AAW, A XXVIII, no. 195, p. 617. Southcot appears to have sent this document to Smith in January/early February 1636; AAW, A XXVIII, no. 89, p. 345; no. 92, p. 351, though, on 9/19 March, Smith requested a copy of it from Southcot again; AAW, A XXVIII, no. 102, p. 377. On 6/16 April he thanked Southcot for his letter of 23 March 'with the Manifest of the regulars wherin they manifestly wrong you'; AAW, A XXVIII, no. 109, p. 391.

[1229] Robert Jenison SJ. See CRS, 75, p. 178.

[1230] Panzani noted this incident in his diary; VA, PD, fo. 119r; Dodd, III, pp. 133–134.

[1231] For correspondence between the Jesuit provincial Richard Blount and Panzani over the articles of the agreement, see AAW, A XXVIII, no. 47 (Dodd, III, pp. 134–135); AAW, A XXVIII, nos 49, 50, 53, 85. The Jesuit general, Muzio Vitelleschi, concluded in January 1636 that the Jesuits had been deliberately excluded from the agreement; ARSJ, Anglia MS I/iii, fo. 428v.

[1232] For Arthur Brett, see Albion, CI, pp. 154, 157; AAW, A XXVIII, no. 80, p. 323; Dodd, III, p. 72. Windebank believed Brett to be inadequate for his allotted diplomatic mission; PRO, 31/9/17B (transcript of Panzani's letter to Barberini of 31 October 1635); Albion, CI, p. 157. On 20 February/1 March 1636 Biddulph reported that Walter Montagu, who was still in Rome, wanted news of Brett before he departed the city; AAW, A XXVIII, no. 95, p. 359. By 28 February/9 March, Biddulph understood, via a letter of 15 January 1636 from Southcot 'concerning the packett of letters delivered to Mr Price [William (Benedict) Jones OSB] to be sent to Mr Brett, that the Benedictines will have the greatest hand in him, and therefore it behooveth us to keep them our friends'; AAW, A XXVIII, no. 98, p. 365.

but hath all his dispatches expecting only the shipp which is not yet ready for Livorno. He carrieth with him two men, but no secretary, hoping to meete with one there, and, if you can, I pray procure him a fitt one against his arrivall which I feare will not be before Candlemas, seeing he goeth by sea. Signor Panzani was earnest with me to give him a short caracter of him which although I would have excused, as not knowing the party well nor the family, yet uppon his importunity I gave him this which I here I [sic] send you a coppy of, to your self only.[1233] The instructions which Fa[ther] Philip gave him from the queen were these, that he should carry a <good> respect to all ecclesiastikes both secular and regular, and that he should particulerly favor the bishop and the clergy when occasion served. And, as for a bishop, that he should tell the pope she had written severall times to Rome in behalf of the bishop of Chalcedon[1234] and that she wished one or rather more bishops in England for the good of religion, and would be loath that England in that respect should fare worse since her coming than it did before. That the king liked the bishop of Chalced[on's] person and thought him an honest man, but for the present would have no bishop here. This was the summe of all, which you may do well to putt him in mind of as you see occasion hereafter.[1235] Our main labour now must be to solicit <there> for the confirmation of our deane and chapter, and for recovery of the English college there.

I referr occurrences to Mr Roberts,[1236] and rest. 20 Novemb[e]r 1635.

Soli soli. The monks have gott Secret[ary] Windebank to write by Brett to their agent[1237] there, and to tell Brett that he might be confident with him.[1238] Take no notice to [sic] him nor any of theirs.

[1233] Brett had visited Panzani on 7 October and on subsequent occasions; VA, PD, fos 115r, 116r, 117r, 118r. On 13 November Brett called in on Panzani just before he left to take ship at Dover; ibid., fo. 119r.

[1234] Richard Smith.

[1235] For the issues which Arthur Brett, as agent, was directed by the king (though he went as the representative only of the queen) to deal with principally – the question of the appointment of a bishop, and the oath of allegiance, see Albion, CI, pp. 155–156.

[1236] George Leyburn.

[1237] Richard (Wilfrid) Selby OSB.

[1238] On 18/28 April 1636 Richard Smith wrote to Southcot regretting Arthur Brett's recent death 'but I hope as good wil succeed him especially if Mr [Charles] Wal[de]grave get his place'; AAW, A XXVIII, no. 111, p. 395. Back in September 1635, Southcot and Waldegrave had visited Panzani, and Panzani noted that 'il detto Carlo [Waldegrave] si disegna mandarlo a Roma'; VA, PD, fo. 113r. (Charles Waldegrave appears to have been the East Anglian gentleman of that name who subscribed to a declaration of local gentry, dated 22 August 1632, in favour of Smith; AAW, A XXVIII, no. 15, p. 76. If Waldegrave is correctly identified as the former seminary student at Douai and son of Sir Edward Waldegrave of Stanninghall, Norfolk, then he was a relative by marriage of the Whites of Hutton, the Southcots, and Lord Treasurer Weston; Metcalfe, The Visitations of Essex, I, p. 514; BL,

No address.

[*on p. 175*]

Endorsed: Clerk. Nov[ember] 20 1635.
About the agreement.
About instructions given to Mr Brett.

77. Laborne [George Leyburn] to [Richard Smith], 9 December 1635

[*AAW, A XXVIII, no. 54, pp. 195–198*]

Most honored sir,

This week I have receaved two of yours, one of the 21 November and the other of the 5° of December. They are deceaved who thinke that Mr Mountegue shall be agent, albeit I am certayne that he will be of more authority than he[1239] who is gone, for any busines that shall concerne our queen. I beseech God to speed him well for I hope that his example will doe much good with many here, but the Jesuists doe much decrye amongst the Catho[lics] here. It is not true that his Majesty putteth Catholiques to the oath. I much feare least the Jesuists and their freinds have noe good meaning in making our king in foraine partes a great persecuteur. As concerning what you saye Mr Chambers told you, part of it is true, and part is not. It is true that his Majesty told the queen that he had a good opinion of you. But for any expresse order to deale for a b[ishop] I doe not believe [it]. It is very true that he haith order to signifie unto his Holynes that her Majesty haith ever had an earnest desire for the setling of episcopall authority, and that she continueth still in this her good desire notwithstanding she doth leave the busines wholy unto his Holynes to doe as he shall thinke good.

Additional MS 5524, fo. 156r; CRS, 10, pp. 84, 188. Charles Waldegrave's daughters, Anne and Frances, were professed, respectively in 1647 and 1648, at the Augustinian convent in Paris, which had been founded with the aid of the leading English secular clergy (see *Letter 46*). They had previously been pupils at the foundation's school. See Cédoz, *Un Couvent de Religieuses Anglaises à Paris*, pp. 32–33. I am grateful for this information to Caroline Bowden.) On 4 April 1636, Southcot recommended Waldegrave to Panzani as the best replacement for Brett, though Sir William Hamilton was appointed instead; VA, PD, fo. 133r. Panzani informed Cardinal Barberini that he had told Robert Philip about the objections to Brett. Panzani advised that Philip should recommend Waldegrave to the queen; PRO, 31/9/17B (transcript of Panzani's letter to Barberini of 31 October 1635).

[1239] Arthur Brett.

As concerning our agreement with the regulars and what haith passed since, I doe referre you to the inclosed by which you shall perceave that the Jesuists for all ther former faire florish have now refused absolutely to come into the agreement[1240] which I thinke will not be much to the[ir] honor, for I doe assure you that many are infinitely [p. 196] scandalized. And I am much scandalized at their last letter unto Signor Gregorio full of lyes.[1241]

Yesterdaye was our queens chappell at Somerset House holowed. Her Majesty was ther the fornoone and afternoone and, with the greatest demonstration of devotion that can be imagined, Monsieur Anguelame[1242] did sing Masse and preach which he did performe above all expression.[1243] I doe assure you faithfully that he is a rare man and one who truly respecteth you and yours here.[1244] I have acquainted him with all proceedings and with Fa[ther] Blunts last letter[1245] at which he was much astonished, and maketh the greatest express[ion] of his affection towards you and the cler[gy] that can be imagined. I beseech you to write unto him and lett him knowe what you [word illegible] and procure Monsieur Botelyer[1246] or some powerfull man to write unto him what they heare from you concerning him.

I cannot furnish you with any new occurrences. Onely it is much woundered at here that the French should refuse to give the title of prince elector unto the palsgrave and yett promise the[ir] assistance for the restoring of him; and the Spaniards, from whom litle assistance is to be exspected in that kinde, doe willingly style him prince elector.

[1240] On 26 November 1635, Gregorio Panzani had recorded that Robert Jenison SJ 'mi porto l'istrumento di ratificatione della Concordia fatta con questi sacerdoti', and that Jenison called again on 29 November to discuss the Accord, but on 10 December, when Jenison was with him again, the Jesuit absolutely rejected it; VA, PD, fos 120r, 121r, 122r.

[1241] Panzani had noted on 2 December 1635 that John Southcot had sent him 'le animadversioni alla lettera mandatami dal provinciale de' Giesuiti'; ibid., fo. 121r.

[1242] Jacques le Noël Du Perron (bishop of Angoulême). See Birch, CT, II, pp. 313–314; Bergin, The Making of the French Episcopate, pp. 615–616.

[1243] Panzani recorded that he was present, and 'si esposero le 40 hore con bellissimo apparato'. The queen received communion at Whitehall and then proceeded to Somerset House 'ove stette alla gran Messa cantata solennemente dal Signor Abbate du Perron, et a servirla erano l'ambasciatori di Francia ordinario, e straordinario, et quel di Venetia. Vi fu straordinario concorso di popolo'. The queen later attended vespers. Du Perron, in his sermon, rejoiced with her 'che havesse ottenuto la fabrica di detta capella dal re, dicendo molte cose in sua lode, et lodò anche il re'; VA, PD, fo. 122r. On 30 December 1635/9 January 1636, however, Smith informed Southcot that he 'shold be sorrie that the k[ing] shold dislike the bishop of Angulems sermon'; AAW, A XXVIII, no. 81, p. 325.

[1244] See Knowler, ESLD, I, p. 505.

[1245] Leyburn is probably referring to Richard Blount SJ's letter of 4 December 1635 (Dodd, III, p. 135), 'la riposta del P. Blondò' as Panzani called it, which criticized the Accord reached by the secular clergy and the religious orders (except the Jesuits), and which Robert Jenison SJ brought to Panzani on 5 December; VA, PD, fo. 121r.

[1246] Léon Bouthillier, comte de Chavigny, French secretary of State.

Fa[ther] Fisher,[1247] <u>who is wi</u>th <u>my</u> lady duchesse[1248] for some tyme, did crye out to Mr Boisse[1249] against the meeting of the clergie and other regulars, saying th*a*t it was onely to yeeld unto the oath, to give the king satisfaction and by th*a*t meanes to procure a bishop.[1250] Y*our* best lady[1251] doth present her respects unto you. She will not entertayne John[1252] before th*a*t she heare from you.

I wish you all happines who am y*our* most obedient servant. December 9 1635.

God send you read what I have written for I was never in more hast.

No address.

[*on p. 198*]

Endorsed: M[r] Laborne. Letters of Dec[ember] date. The k[ing] for Chalced[on] and Jes[uits] refuse agre[ement].

78. Relation of Thomas Green[1253] from Essex (1635)

[*AAW, A XXVIII, no. 62, pp. 239–242*]

Quis sit numerus sacerdotum tam secularium quam regularium.

Regulares sunt novem, omnes Jesuitis. Seculares 7.

Quis sit numerus Catholicoru*m* laicoru*m*.

Of earles and [*word deleted*] lords, there be 3 besydes the dutches of Buckingham,[1254] the countess of Portland,[1255] whose estates lye in Essex;

[1247] John Percy SJ. In August 1635 he had been released from prison at the instigation of the queen (an event which, said Panzani, astonished the whole of London); VA, PD, fo. 109r; PRO, 31/9/17B (transcripts of Panzani's letters to Barberini of 15 July and 26 August 1635).

[1248] Katherine (Manners), widow of George Villiers, 1st duke of Buckingham, who had recently married Randal MacDonnell, Viscount Dunluce. See *Letter 70*. She had attended the first day of the famous three-day debate (in May 1622) in front of James I between John Percy and several Church-of-England divines, a debate held for the benefit of her mother-in-law, the countess of Buckingham. Percy subsequently became the countess's chaplain. Panzani recorded in February 1635 that Percy was confessor also to Frances (Waldegrave), second wife of Sir Richard Weston, 1st earl of Portland; VA, PD, fo. 77r.

[1249] George Boyce. See Anstr., II, p. 33.

[1250] Three days after this letter was written, Percy was summoned before the privy council and ordered to leave the realm; *CSPD, 1634–1635*, pp. 352–353.

[1251] Anne (Philipson), Baroness Arundell.

[1252] Presumably either John Galmarch or John Legat, both of whom are mentioned in *Letters 81, 82*.

[1253] Thomas Green served as chaplain to the Bendlow family at Brent Hall, near Finchingfield in Essex. See Anstr., II, p. 138.

[1254] Katherine Manners.

[1255] Frances (Waldegrave), second wife of Sir Richard Weston, 1st earl of Portland.

and the old Lady Morley.[1256] Of knights, esquires with their ladyes and widdows, some 26. Of gentlemen and younger brothers, some 20. Of the inferiour rancke, some 50 families. What the severall number of these are ~~are~~ <is> not easily gathered, there being many in each family, as well children as servants.

Quot sunt notarii et officiales.

One archdeacon, your self, one rurall deane, my self, and one notary, Mr Bar[ker].[1257]

Si pauperes evangelizentur etc.

The poore for the most part are very ignorant, and rather want fitting instruction than the helpe of the sacraments. The cause is their poverty, they being not able to mentayne preists for themselves. As for such p[riests] as live with the ritcher sort, they cannot well assist their necessity. 1. because ther patrons are unwilling to have them to visitt them, fearing thereby the discovery of ther houses. 2^{ly} If their p[riest] doe assist them, it is but seldome and with much hast, without tyme and leasure to instruct them. The way to helpe this inconveniency must be to make a purse amongst the ritcher sort, to mentayne particular p[riests] [p. 240] for the poore. This way hath bene formerly used by good benefactours, of whose worth there is still a memory in two severall places ~~but not~~ <in this shire> who, for this end, allotted certayne yearly rents to continew for ever; but by <through> [sic] the avarice of the Jes[uits] those rents are eyther ceased or, as it is <more> probably thought, continued ~~in their~~ <to them> and by them onely collected, without any succour of the poore. It is true Mr Kele the Jes[uit][1258] calls him self the poore mans p[riest] and takes at tymes a long circuite, but yet performeth not well that office. 1. because his stay with them is but short, and usually upon working dayes, soe as the poore can neyther have leysure to receave the benifitt, nor he tyme to preach unto them. Where capacityes are but slender <and> rude, ~~and~~ there is neede of often instructions. And where there is scarcity of corporall foode it fitteth not to take away from them their tyme of labour, which must needs be done when on the working days onely they are called for help. 2. because his fashion of habitt suteth not with ~~the~~ <Gods> poore, he being well horst and apparrelled, they being on the other syde ragged and contemptible; and these two sute

---

[1256] Elizabeth, daughter of Sir Thomas Tresham, who had married William Parker, 13th Baron Morley and Monteagle (d. July 1622).

[1257] Thomas Barker. See Anstr., II, p. 16.

[1258] Thomas Keel SJ. See CRS, 75, pp. 219–220.

not well togeather in the eye of strangers.[1259] To conclude, the poore mans p[riest] must be a foote man, of an apostolicall spirit, zealous of soules, greedy of labours, no lover of his back or belly, dilligent to instruct, etc.

Quis sit status persecutionis

The greatest persecution is the 12^d the Sunday,[1260] which none soe much feele as the poore for of them it is oftentymes exacted with rigour. Some troubles arise upon christning of children, which also are most of all executed upon the poore. [*p. 241*]

Concerning the qualityes of p[riests]

Mr Gooch[1261] was but a philosopher, yet of noble renowne, being 7 tymes arrayned at the barr, and as often condemned. He hath brought into the Church many noble families in Norfolke, Suffoke and Essex. His tallents of preaching very good and of great fame. His age 63. 2. Mr Wilks[1262] heard his divinity at Roome, <laboravit in Anglia 11 [*altered from* 10] annis; aetatis 43>.[1263] M^r Gr[een][1264] the like in Spayne, and had two publick acts, in each science; <aetat[is] 37; labora[vit] 11>. 4. Mr Bar[ker] the like in Sevill ~~and had publick act of his divinity~~. 5. Mr Hues[1265] came out of his 2^d yeare of divinity from Roome. 6. Mr Medcalfe[1266] is unknowne to me. 7. Mr Thorowgood[1267] heard but ~~one yeare~~ his grammar at St Omers, and at Roome after his logicke went to cases, in which study he was imployed divers years, and soe sent to us. A man of vertuous lyfe, but of weake parts and naturall judgment; aetatis 28; labor[avit] 3.[1268]

[1259] For further complaints about Keel made by Thomas Green, in particular concerning Keel's abuse of the Spiritual Exercises to insinuate himself into the exercitant's house as a chaplain and confessor, see AAW, A XXVIII, no. 15, pp. 66–67.

[1260] A reference to the one shilling fine imposed by the 1559 Act of Uniformity for absence from church on Sundays and holy days; G. Elton, *The Tudor Constitution* (Cambridge, 1972), p. 403.

[1261] Thomas Gooch. See Anstr., II, p. 132. Gooch signed an attestation in favour of Richard Smith in September 1631; AAW, A XXIV, no. 160, p. 619.

[1262] Robert Holtby, alias Ducket, Brett, and Wilkes. He was a nephew of the Jesuit Richard Holtby; Anstr., II, p. 161.

[1263] On his own account, however, Robert Holtby was aged thirty-seven; CRS, 54, p. 303.

[1264] Thomas Green, the writer of this 'Relation', was born about 1600. See Anstr., II, p. 138.

[1265] Edward Hughes. See *ibid.*, p. 164. He entered the English college in Rome in October 1626, and came to England in April 1633. He was named in Edward Bennett's will; AAW, A XXVII, no. 11, p. 40.

[1266] This may be Peter Metcalf. See Anstr., II, p. 219.

[1267] James Thoroughgood. See *ibid.*, p. 319. Anstruther suggests that he was probably a chaplain to the Mannock family at Gifford's Hall, Stoke-by-Nayland in Suffolk.

[1268] See CRS, 55, p. 383.

For the regulars they are not knowne to us. Onely thus much I can say of Mr Moore,[1269] he is a good getter of monyes. ~~Ten~~ 9 yeares agoe I heard him say that for his part he had gotten 2000^l, since he arrived into England, for St Omers colledg. Mr Keele hath the like fame.

[on p. 242]

Endorsed: Relation of M^r Th[omas] Green. Essex 1635.

79. 'Instruction concerning the present state of the Protestant Church of England, May 1636'

[AAW, A XXVIII, no. 119, pp. 413–420]

Albeit the generall face of the Protestant Church of England be the same at this day both for doctrine and discipline which it was in the raigne of Queene Elizabeth and King James, for as much as they professe to retaine still the 39 Articles and the same forme of government as before, yet some changes are noted to have bin brought in of late yeares which doe shewe not only lesse aversion in the professours thereof from Catholick religion, and a greater moderation generally, but a certeine disposicion also, or preparing of mynd on their partes, to unite this Church againe to the Church of Rome both in faith and manners. The chaunges which have been chiefly noted in this kynd both for doctrine and practise are these which followe. First concerning doctrine or matter of faith, besides that they have ever agreed with the Catholick Church in the higher misteries of the Blessed Trinity, and the incarnacion of Christ our Saviour, and professe to receave the 3 generall creedes, as also the fower first ecumenicall councells, they seeme now (as may appeare by some of their late printed bookes and sermons) to have left of[f] that fundamentall article of the Protestant beleefe concerning justificacion by faith alone, and doe hould a necessity of good workes for justificacion in a Catholique sense. The like chaunge is also observed concerning the doctrine of grace and free will, <u>the number and efficacy of the sacramentes</u>, the reall presence of the body and blood of Christ in the sacrament of the altar, the nature of the sacrifice and some other pointes which may be gathered more particularly out of their said late printed bookes and sermons. Next concerning their practise of religion, they have brought into use againe the termes of holy Church, holy tradicion, pennance,

---

[1269] Henry More SJ. In January 1636 Smith noted that More 'lived at my L[ord] Pet[re's]'; AAW, A XXVIII, no. 81, p. 325. See Hibbard, *CI*, p. 41.

satisfacc*i*on, holy vestmentes, holy altar and the like, and in the late edition of their s*e*rvice booke they have chaunged the word *Minister* into *Priest* through out the whole booke. They cloath their tables like altars and place them againe at the upper end of th*e* chancell as they stood in Catholick tymes. In some cathedralls they sett great wax tapers upon the altar, and in the great east windowe they sett up againe in large and sumptuous forme the picture of the crucifix. At their coming into the church they bowe to the altar, w*i*th their faces to the ground, and com*m*end the same devotion to the people. They bowe reverently at the name of Jesus and stand up (turning towardes the East) at the *Gloria Patri* and the Creed. Their sermons for the greater p*a*rt, in court and chiefe audiences of the Citty, tend to vilify and confute the creditt and authority of *Luther* and *Calvin*, yea the famousest of their owne reformers in divers tenetes, especially touching Antichrist and the word of God interpreted against Church authority and tradic*i*on. Some of them, in their printed bookes and prayers afore sermon, doe not only make honorable menc*i*on of o*u*r Blessed Lady, the martyrs and other s*a*int*e*s (w*i*th whose pictures also, as also w*i*th th*e* crucifix, they adorne their chambers) but in plaine termes pray God to have mercy on all faithfull soules dep*a*rted. They com*m*end much the great need and benefitt of sacramentall confession and penance, and some of them take paines to instruct themselves in the Cathol*i*q*ue* formes of confession and absolution, acknowledging that no Church or religion can well subsist w*i*thout it.[1270] They acknowledge th*e* bishop of Rome for the b*i*sho*p* of the first sea, Patriark of the West, and St Peters successo*u*r, and that noe Church can demon̄strat it selfe to be apostoliq*ue*, or a member of it, w*i*thout a lyneall succession of b*i*sho*p*s from St Peter derived to the Church of England as they affirme by the Sea of Rome, notw*i*thstanding the statute of 2° Elizabethae, w*h*ich makes it high treason to extoll or com*m*end by word or writing the popes authority in cases ecclesiasticall.[1271]

[1270] In January 1634 Richard Smith reported that 'one minister [recently] preached confession before the k[ing]'; AAW, B 27, no. 114. On 8 March 1635 Robert Philip informed Gregorio Panzani that on the previous Friday (6 March) a sermon was preached in the Chapel Royal commending confession. The preacher argued that no other sacrament had so much warrant in the gospel. Philip had spoken to a puritan lady at court, and she commented that for Protestants to have confession it would be necessary for their ministers to be unmarried, for otherwise they would reveal all to their wives. The sermon found favour at the court, where it was noted that since, in the Church of England's 'Rituale', confession was ordered at death, it could not be otherwise than good during life; VA, PD, fo. 83r. Cf. Davies, *Caroline Captivity*, pp. 23–24. See also Albion, *CI*, pp. 174–175; *CSPV, 1636–1639*, p. 217.

[1271] i.e. the fourteenth branch of 1 Elizabeth c. 1 (An Acte restoring to the Crowne thau*n*cyent Jurisdiction over the State Ecclesiasticall and Sp*i*ritu*a*ll, and abolyshing all Forreine Power repugnant to the same'), *Statutes of the Realm*, IV, pp. 353–354.

By these chaunges and approaches to the Catholique faith and practize, and by other their sayinges and proceedinges, it seemeth to bee evident that an union or reconciliation with the Church of Rome is not only desired but alsoe aymed at <by> them; which perhaps the better to bring to passe, or rather to slide into [*p. 414*] it with lesse touch to their credites, they not only seeke to introduce the aforesaid doctrines and practizes by degrees, but would have it generally beleeved as a ground that there are noe fundamentall or essentiall differences in religion betweene the Church of Rome and them. Whereupon as they doe not hould themselves guilty of schisme or heresy, but true members of the Catholique Church, condemning their predecessors, the first Protestantes of England, whome they confesse ingenuously to have gon too farr in their pretended reformacion of the English Church, soe they desire to be accounted no other by the Roman Church, which they avouch to bee the mother of other Churches, and hould all other Churches adhering to her to be true members of the Catholique Church. And as for other differences they thinke them not to bee of that reckoning as to devide them in faith from the Roman Church, judging them to be either in the manner of speaking, or if it be greater in the thing it selfe yet that it is not (as their phrase is) in the fundamentalls of faith necessary to salvacion and therefore thinke it not unreasonable for the Church of Rome to tolerate them in those differences, alleaging the example of the Florentine Councell, by which the Grecians were tolerated in many particular rites and opinions disagreeinge from the Latines. Moreover, many of them have beene heard in their private conferences with some learned Catholickes to expostulate why the bishop of Rome doth not invite and exhort the kinge and bishops here to the procuringe of an union, alleadging the example of Pope Eugenius to Paleologus the emperour, with the bishops of Greece,[1272] seing Brittaine is not a smalle portion of Our Lordes flock, nor are there a fewe or unlearned bishops in it, and would easilier perhaps be united in a perfect union, and, being united, would more firmely adhere, for they hould themselves to be true bishops and truly derived from the Sea Apostolique. And this seemeth to be the true state of the Protestant Church of England at this day.

Nowe the puritans who dissent from the Protestantes both in doctrine and discipline doe utterly condemne all the aforesaid doctrines and practizes of superstition, idolatry and the like, bearing noe lesse (if not more) aversion and malice against this sort of Protestantes

---

[1272] A reference to the agreement between Pope Eugenius IV and the Emperor John Palaeologus at the council which opened at Ferrara in January 1438; Pastor, *HP*, I, pp. 315–316.

than they doe against the Catholiques. And these being in number most (because all citties, townes and corporacions are generally full of them), in minde refractory, and in power mighty, it is evident that one of the greatest impedimentes to the foresaid union or reconciliation proceedeth mainely from them, whose power therefore, if it were diminished, there would bee farr better hopes not only of effecting this union both sooner and easilier but also that Catholickes would in the meane tyme be gentlyer dealt withall by the State. For, while the State, that is the kinge and the more moderate councellours, are to struggle against the puritanes, it must bee that many impedimentes will happen to hinder soe great a good.

From that which hath been said, it may be gathered that the present cause of the English Protestantes seemeth to be farr different from the cause of the first Protestantes, and also from the cause of the Lutherans, Sacramentaries, Socinians, Calvinists, Anabaptists etc. from whome our moderne English Protestantes differr very much.

Seing therefore they pretend soe earnestly to their supposed right in Godes Church, not in that large sence wherein other sectaries rather usurpe than use it but in a Catholique sence, which argues manifestly that they doe desire a perfect and unquestionable union, such as would fully quiett and satisfy their consciences the better to correspond to this good desire in them, and the better to helpe towardes this union on both sides, some thinges seeme necessary to be advertized and observed on the part of Rome. [*p. 415*]

First it seemeth requisitt that these Protestantes should be dealt withall more fairely and mildly than their predecessors or the professors of other erring Churches, who shewe not soe good a disposicion to reconciliacion and union with the Church of Rome.

Secondly that nothing should be permitted to be done or written (not necessary for the defence of Catholique religion) which may alienat or exasperat them, much lesse make them despaire of a reconciliation.

Thirdly that all acrimony and bitternes in writing be eschewed, especially against the persons and states of men, seing that more are made worse than better affected to the Catholick faith by such manner of writing.

Fourthly that all manner of writing aswell private as publick by any of the kinges subjects concerning the extent of the regall jurisdiccion be strictly forbidden. For wee see by experience that such treatises offend the kinge and State, and, although the authors thereof bee but particular men, yet the Catholique cause in generall suffers much prejudice thereby aswell in the opinion of the State as of other moderate men.

Fiftly for as much as many learned and moderate Protestantes have been heard to complayne, and seeme to bee much distasted thereat, that divers matters yet controverted and in opinion (as they say) betweene the Catholique devines themselves are by the precipitacion or over much fervour of some of our men, or for some extrinsecall respect, obtruded (as they say) upon the consciences of the faithfull as matter of faith, whereof much use is made to the disadvantage of religion by the Socinians and others, who thereupon are bould to say that faction prevailes soe farr amongst us as that points of faith are cryed up by voices, and consequently many indifferent and judicious men left perplexed what is truly Catholick, what not.

This being soe, it seemeth a thing not unworthy of consideracion what meanes were fitt to bee used in this case, both to satisfy the moderate Protestant thus perswaded in his understanding, [and] to take away the roote of any such persuasion in him, by restrayning the precipitat or indiscreet zeale of such men of ours, whoe by their writing or otherwise have perhaps ministred occasion thereof, and it importeth soe much the more to give desired satisfaccion in this point by howe much it appeareth that the learned and moderate Protestantes doe take this for a great stumbling block in their way to union, having severall tymes complayned thereof with great feeling, whereupon some of them spare not to say in plaine termes that religion is not taught amongst us and union sought with that sincerity it ought, abstracting from interestes, partiall respectes and affeccions.

Lastly it is to be observed that those whoe are designed to the functions of the apostolique mission nowe in England ought not to thinke them selves sufficiently furnished with those disputacions or argumentes wherewith heretofore the errors of Lutherans, Sacramentaries and the like are ventilated in our schooles. For against our English Protestantes wee are to fight with other armes, especially with the tradicion of the auncient Church and the solid testimonies of authenticall doctors, for to these nowe doe they yeald soe much credit and reverence as that they professe simply they are ready to admitt any tenett which may be sufficiently shewed by those meanes to be necessary to be beleeved for eternall salvacion.

[*p. 419*]¹²⁷³

---

¹²⁷³ Page 416 is blank, except for an endorsement which reads 'Instructions from Ingland'. Pp. 417–418 repeat material found on pp. 413–415 with a few alterations, notably the claim (p. 417) that 'in some partes they exact of the clergy to say over the whole service every day, and divers of them say the Romane breviary privately of their owne devocion. Some of them professe that at their pretended consecracion they elevate the B[lessed] Sacrament as high as they dare for offence, and say secreately the wordes of the Masse for the oblacion of a sacrifize.' The text of pp. 419–420 is also to be found in AAW, A in the form of a separate piece entitled 'Information touching the present state of the Cath[olic] Church in Ingland [May] 1636'; AAW, A XXVIII, no. 118.

There were better hopes of good for religion in England if in Rome they were made to understand rightly the condicion thereof, and what course they might for their parte take to advance it, which the diversity and peradventure the contrariety of informacions hath hetherto much hindered because there hath still wanted some person of quality, judgment and indifferency that could and would enforme trueth impartially and without respect to persons, parties or private endes. This inconvenience may (wee hope) be now redressed by the employment of so noble and Catholique a gentleman[1274] from the queene (not as wee presume without the kinges allowance) to his Holynes, whose obligacion therefore it wilbe to informe rightly the true present state of religion and Catholickes here, with the cheefe impedimentes of the progresse thereof, for which it wilbe necessary that he consider religion, first in respect of the professed Catholiques themselves; 2^{ly} in respect of the kinge and State; 3^{ly} in respect of the Protestant clergy, especially those that are in dignity amongst them; 4^{ly} in respect of the rest of the people. In the first respect it rather prospereth than decayeth (as wee conceive) for the professours thereof rather encrease than decrease in number, aswell lay people as priestes. For priestes encreasing, fewe or none there are to whome God Allmighty presents not some occasion of converting some, and many more are daily converted than fall. This also proceeds from the clemency of the kinge partly, and partly from the moderacion of the cheefe men of the clergy. Lastly infinite multitude of sectes and opinions have even wearied them, and made understanding men discerne the inconvenience of rejecting the authority of the Church which bounded this liberty of broaching new opinions. Yet disunion amongst Catholiques themselves and some other occasions have somewhat cooled their primitive zeale and fervour, especially their wonted brotherly and charitable correspondence amongst themselves, which coldnes hath originally proceeded from the divisions and distractions amongst the priestes, and these from emulacion which inconvenience is partly begun to bee remedied by a late Accord etc.[1275] But this cannot be perfected till the occasions of this emulacion betweene the twoe greater bodies be taken away. Religion considered in the second respect is also rather bettered in condicion than deteriorated. For, first, the king is a clement and mild prince and of his owne disposicion not willing to

---

[1274] Sir William Hamilton. In May 1636 Hamilton went to Rome as an agent to represent Henrietta Maria (in place of the deceased Arthur Brett); *CSPV, 1632–1636*, pp. 547, 550, 555; Albion, *CI*, pp. 151f; VA, PD, fo. 139r. As Gordon Albion points out, Hamilton was brother of the earl of Abercorn, and a relative of the marquis of Hamilton, the duke of Lennox, and the king himself; Albion, *CI*, p. 157.

[1275] See *Letter 76*.

force the consciences of his Catholique subjectes. His wantes indeed doe in some sort compell him to take money of Catholiques by way of composicion for their recusancy, and although it be true that the burthen of these paimentes be great and heavy, especially to the poorer sort, yet there want not consideracions of ease and benefitt that may in some sorte seeme to countervayle the burthen. This will appeare to such as knowe from the penalties of what statutes they are freed by their composicion. This is the only generall molestacion of Catholiques for recusancy, and these paymentes are commonly racked very high by the diligence of the comissioners, partly out of aversion in some of them from religion, but principally out of a desire in all of them to advance the kinges profitt. Besides this generall molestacion there are many particular men and women in severall shires molested by informers, some also questioned (though not many) for marrying, and some for christning. The penalty of 12ᵈ a Sunday is also in some places exacted, but all this is rather done by the officiousnes, covetousenes or malice of some inferiour officers than by order from the State, which cannot bee allwayes prevented while the lawes remayne in force. Pursivantes also have still comissions, yet Catholiques are not generally so much molested by them either in citty or countrey as they have beene, for they are not soe much countenanced by the State as they were wont to bee, nor hath any of them had comission by order from the State,[1276] and as an acte of State, these 3 yeares, for though some of the lordes be very averse from religion yet there be alsoe some of the cheefest councellours that are moderat men who would be content as occasion serves [*p. 420*] to further union and reconciliation, wherof there is so much the more hope <conceaved>, both for that the kinge is of a disposicion apt to be obliged and wonn by reall curtesies receaved from princes abroad, and because he loveth the queene tenderly, by whose power, diligence and zeale the said union or reconciliation is principally to bee wrought in this court, and wee hope that there would not want persons of worth and power to second her Majest[i]es endeavours and to serve her willingly in so good a busines.[1277]

The condicion of religion in respect of the principall men in the Protestant clergy is allready insinuated in their moderacion and the

---

[1276] On 15 May 1636 Gregorio Panzani met at court with Sir Francis Windebank and Robert Philip to discuss the problem of the pursuivants, and afterwards spoke to the queen on the matter; VA, PD, fo. 138r. Panzani's diary records how Windebank and Cottington were lobbied constantly to take action against the agents of the high commission; *ibid., passim.* On 19 May Panzani learned that Charles had delegated the problem to Laud, Coventry, Coke, and Windebank; *ibid.,* fo. 139r.

[1277] The passage 'wherof there is so much [. . .] so good a busines', inserted on p. 420 after the main body of the text, replaces a similar passage in the text at the top of p. 420 which the copyist has failed to strike out.

experience they have of the great inconvenience of the late liberty to dogmatize whatsoever novelty any fanaticall spirit doth fancy. But of this point there wilbe peradventure requisite a discourse by it selfe.

The people lastly are not so generally averse as they were wont to bee, for they alsoe observe a great change in the clergy and some in the State. The cheefe reason of this change is that whereas nothing hath more hindered the progresse of religion, and hath made indeed the profession thereof odious, than this opinion both in State and people that religion (as it is at least taught by the missionary priestes) doth alienate the affeccions of the subjectes from the prince and imbue them with opinions dangerous and pernicious to the kinge and State, in this matter both prince and people are better satisfied of late of the affeccions of Catholiques towardes their kinge and countrey, wherein if wee could fully prevaile the cause were halfe gained. One good medium for this end is the settlinge of good intelligence and correspondence betweene the State and his Holynes, for this of it selfe will take away all jealousy and suspicion of any practizes in that court against this State, which was the only pretended cause of putting priestes to death heretofore, for they were not punished for being priestes, ministring the sacramentes etc. precisely, but for returning into the land being made priestes[1278] with traiterous intention (as they termed it) of alienating the heartes of the subjectes from their obedience to their soveraigne, which they understood to be implyed in the reconciling or reducing to the obedience of the Sea of Rome, and therefore to be reconciled or to perswade any other to be so, whether he was priest or layman that did it, was made high treason 23 Eliz[abeth].[1279]

80. Laborne [George Leyburn] to [Richard Smith], 3 July 1636

[*AAW, A XXVIII, no. 134, pp. 455–456*]

Most honored sir,

I have receaved yours with divers inclosed which I have carefully disposed according to your owne desire. Mr Clifford[1280] doth not goe to

---

[1278] In the version of this text in AAW, A XXVIII, no. 118 (p. 412) there are added at this point the words 'in the seminaries erected by the pope and kinge of Spaine then enemies to the queene'.

[1279] For the two statutes, of 1571 (13 Elizabeth c. 2) and 1581 (23 Elizabeth c. 1), which dealt with the offence of reconciling to Rome, see Elton, *The Tudor Constitution*, pp. 418–424.

[1280] William Clifford. See Anstr., II, p. 63.

Mrs Stoners[1281] but to Mr Sanders,[1282] a place which he desireth above
all other him selfe in regard it is not far distant from his friends. M^r
Musk[et][1283] hath desighned Mr Hyde[1284] for Mrs Stoners, but he is not
at this present to be found and the place is voide. I send you here an
answere of yours to Mr Gage.[1285] I perceave that he hath yeelded to
your proposition and will be shortly in thes partes, onely I heare that
he ex[sp]ecteth your answer agayne. I had sent it the last Thursdaie
if I had been in the towne and divers others of thes which now I send.
Your friends at River Parke[1286] doe exspect you with much impatience.
It may fayle out that I shall wayte on you thither if I may have notise
before 3 or 4 dayes.

I have presented your remembrances unto your best lady[1287] and
Mr Harrington,[1288] who had presented you in theirs, and your lady
wisheth me in every letter to present her respects unto you. She is a
litle sorrowfull at this present for the death of my Lord Baltamoores
onely sunne.[1289] Signor Georgio[1290] is daily expected here[1291] and he

[1281] It is not certain which member of the Stonor family (of Oxfordshire) is indicated
here, but for the connection between the Cliffords and the Stonors, see Davidson, 'Roman
Catholicism', pp. 99–100.
[1282] In c.1628 an informer reported that the priest John Bosvile 'did lately keep with
Mrs Sandars at Wellforde in Northampton shire'; PRO, SP 16/529/94, fo. 146r.
[1283] George Fisher.
[1284] This may be a reference to William Bayaert, alias Hyde. He returned from Douai in
1636 and took up residence with Sir Walter Blount (at Sodington in Worcestershire), who
was regarded by Richard Smith and his friends as a patron and supporter; Anstr., II, p. 19;
AAW, A XXVIII, no. 128, p. 439. (Alternatively it might be a reference to the Hampshire
priest Humphrey Hyde; *Letter 35*; Anstr., II, p. 166.)
[1285] George Gage. See *ibid.*, pp. 121–124.
[1286] The Browne family's residence at Tillington, West Sussex. It appears from *Letter 84*
that, at this time, the ailing Edward Bennett was resident there.
[1287] Anne (Philipson), Baroness Arundell.
[1288] Mark Harrington. See Anstr., II, p. 147.
[1289] The 2nd Baron Baltimore, Cecil Calvert, had married Anne Arundell's daughter,
Anne, in early 1628. They lived at Hook House in the parish of Donhead St Andrew, near
Wardour; J. Anthony Williamson, *Catholic Recusancy in Wiltshire 1660–1791* (London, 1968),
p. 185. Their first son, George, born in 1634, died in June 1636; GEC, I, pp. 393–394.
[1290] George Con.
[1291] On 26 April 1636, Biddulph wrote to Southcot that 'it is determined here to send
Signor Giorgio [Con] into England, and I think he will depart from hence within these 10
or 12 dayes'; AAW, A XXVIII, no. 112, p. 397. For an assessment of Con, see Hibbard,
CI, pp. 38–39, 46–48. Con was a Scottish cleric who rose to prominence in the household
of Cardinal Barberini, secretary of State in Rome, and had previously been a secretary
to Cardinal Montalto, whom the seculars regarded as a friend; *NAGB*, p. 194. He sailed
for England from Dieppe on 16/26 June 1636; Albion, *CI*, pp. 117, 159; *CSPV, 1636–1639*,
p. 303. Con was far more sympathetic to the Jesuits than Panzani had been; Hibbard, *CI*,
pp. 47–48. But initially the seculars believed that he would be favourable to them. (Smith
regarded Barberini as one of his supporters. In March 1637 he recorded that Biddulph had
relayed the news that Barberini 'professed much to honor and respect me'; AAW, A XXIX,

hath power to doe us good, an[d] Fa[ther] Ph[ilip] told me in private that he was obliged to doe us good.[1292] But this to your selfe. Warres, plague and famine are very hott in foraine partes, and his Majesty had letters that the French had defeated 3000 Spaniards nere unto Milane, surprised a strong place and taken 50 officers prisonners, and the prince of Coundy hath hath [sic] beseeged Dole in Burgundy.[1293] It seems that they intend to prisse the Spaniard this summer. The Spanish ambassadeur is expected howerly here.[1294] Here is come an ambassadeur from Ruschia. The earle of Arundell hath had audience of the emperor, and good hopes.[1295] My humble service unto your most noble lady, with my best wishes to your selfe.

In hast, your harty obedient servant, Laborne.

July 3 1636.

If my cosen Sanford[1296] be there I beseech you to remember my respects. I have a letter for her sister of some importance and I knowe not wher she is.

No address.

[on p. 456]

Endorsed: 1636.
Mʳ Laborn of the 3 of July answered the 8 of the sam[e].

no. 18, p. 39.) On 18/28 May, Smith informed Southcot that the Jesuit William Talbot 'had letters from R[ome] that Signor Georgio was comming downe and that he could not sleep that night he first heard of it'; AAW, A XXVIII, no. 117, p. 409. On 7/17 May 1636 Biddulph warned Southcot that Con would 'set forth from hence within these 10 days', and that he would 'have commission to gett the king his consent for a bishop, butt this must be kept very secrett'; AAW, A XXVIII, no. 114, p. 401. In June, Smith was repeating Biddulph's boasts that the seculars would achieve 'their desire' by Con's means; AAW, A XXVIII, no. 128, p. 439.

[1292] On 30 July/9 August 1636 Biddulph reported to Southcot that he supposed Con would by now have arrived 'safe there, and so I intend to answeare one of his letters by this post which I receaved from him at Paris, and withall I will send him a short writeing touching our pretension of a bishop which writeing you may be pleased to take notice of when you see him, and desyre him to shew it you that you may conferr of it together, that he may accordingly deale with his Majestye aboute it'; AAW, A XXVIII, no. 147, p. 489.

[1293] See PRO, C 115/105/8244; CRS, I, p. 109. For Viscount Scudamore's account of the siege, see PRO, SP 78/101, fo. 264r.

[1294] The ambassador, Iñigo Ladron Velez de Guevara y Tassis, count of Oñate and Villa Mediana, arrived in July 1636; CSPV, *1636–1639*, p. 24. On 9 August 1636 Southcot informed Edward Bennett that George Fisher and 'Mʳ Worthington [. . .] were to kisse the new Spanish embasadors hands'. Southcot would have gone with them if he had been well enough; AAW, A XXVIII, no. 148, p. 494.

[1295] For the earl of Arundel's unsuccessful embassy to Vienna in April 1636, see Hibbard, *CI*, p. 73.

[1296] This individual may be a relative of Robert Ducket, alias Francis Samford (who came from Westmorland, as did Leyburn); Anstr., II, p. 90.

81. J[ohn] Lovel [Southcot] to Edward Hope [Bennett], 26 August 1636

[*AAW, A XXVIII, no. 154, pp. 515–518*]

Deer cosen,

I have yours now of John <Legat> of the 22 August and uppon Wednesday in the afternoon I had a former packett from you of the 18. If this lat[t]er had come to my hands a day sooner I could have sent yours to Mr Layborne by John Galmarch, who went back to his maister this day with divers letters that I sent by him. I can not think anything amisse which is resolved on by your advise and direction. Otherwise I could have thought it somewhat straunge to see our former determination altered so sodainly concerning Mr Layborns going to Rome presently, and cannot but think still that it ~~was~~ is a made buissenesse, how cun*n*ingly soever contrived. Yet methinkes an other kind of stile would have better become that lord and would have effected his desire (if it be indeed his own desire) as soon and with lesse offence to others, which he giveth by this letter surely without cause or ground. Howsoever, I cannot but submitt to better judgments in this and all other things. If it be so indeed that Mr Fitton[1297] wilbe contented to stay there all this winter the daunger is the lesse in forbearing till spring. But the lord that is so earnest against his going now is like to be no lesse at spring, and I dare lay a good wager that the buissenesse will so fall out that from spring it wilbe further differed to the fall of the leaf. Since I requested that letter from you to Mr Button I heare Mr Fittons father is dead, in which respect I imagin it wilbe the easier to persuade Mr Fitton to stay this winter. And I wish you had written a few lines to him your self which would have had more authority than our letters, and I pray you do it yet and send it me by the next occasion. I ame glad you had so good satisfaction from the superior of the friars, and so many kind words from Mr Gray.[1298] Ne crede, he is one of the subtilest foxes they have. It is well that Mr Gage wilbe the secretary.[1299] I pray God he performe it well. Mr George Fenwick[1300] wrote lately to me to offer his humble service to you, and is [*p. 516*] willing to be employed by you in any service in these parts and surely he would do much ~~here~~ <good> were he employed, for he is very active, diligent and humble, and one thing particulerly he were good for which is to keep a dew correspondence

---

[1297] Peter Biddulph.
[1298] Lawrence Anderton SJ.
[1299] i.e. secretary to the episcopal chapter. See Anstr., II, p. 122.
[1300] George Warwick; see *ibid.*, pp. 340–341.

at home with the vicars and archdeac[ons] who complayne much for waunt of intelligence concerning the common affai[res] and therfor are so loath to contribute or collect monies for the common use wherof we stand more in need now than ever, both for Lisbon[1301] and for the agent at Rome. Wherfor he that is secretary here must needs undergo this tasque to keep once in three weekes or a month correspondence in all countries with the vicars and archdeacons, else our affaires will go on but slowly.

M[r] Ghilmett[1302] is come from Lisbon lately and left M[r] Eldrington[1303] procurator in his place. He saieth the college beginns to flourish extraordinarily, and M[r] Hart is respected there as an oracle. But it greeves him much that from hence the pension is not dewly payed, according to promise, wherwith he is so much disgusted sometimes (at our unkindnesse, as he interpreteth it) that it hath caused him some sicknesses. For the love of God therfor lett some effectuall course be taken for the dew setling of this pension that it may be dewly payed, collected and sent at the two great termes.

I know no better way than that every archdeacon should be writt unto to moove the priests of their district to contribute every one something more or lesse as they have donn in Yorkshire and Lancashire already. And it were good for example sake to send into every quarter a coppy of what others of [sic for have] donn and to ~~prefix~~ add the names of those that give greater sommes, beginning with your own and M[r] Muscots.[1304] There are letters from Lisbon, but we cannot yet come by them, being still in the shipmaisters hands. Still the founder[1305] demaunds a clock. This week the bill of the sicknesse hath 429 but I hope [p. 517] when the weather groweth coulder it will decrease as fast as it encreaseth now. M[r] Southworth followeth his task stoutly and is much commended even by some of the French.[1306] M[r] Muscot and I spake to the superiour of the Capucins to depute one of theirs,

[1301] The college of Saints Peter and Paul at Lisbon.
[1302] Henry Shirley; see Anstr., II, p. 295. He had been appointed procurator at Lisbon in 1634. See also Duffy, 'The English secular clergy', pp. 226–227.
[1303] Edward Elrington. See Anstr., II, p. 94. He was vice-president at Lisbon from 1636 to 1637, when he was dismissed by the cardinal protector. He was later expelled from the college.
[1304] George Fisher.
[1305] Pedro Coutinho, founder and benefactor of the college of Saints Peter and Paul at Lisbon.
[1306] While Richard Smith urged John Southcot to avoid London and the plague, recognized that it presented a propaganda opportunity. On 9/19 September 1635 he wrote that he was 'exceding glad' that the secular priest 'Mr [John] Southworth undertaketh that heroical work' of tending plague victims. 'He escaped one martyrdome' (in 1628, when he was condemned at Lancaster) 'and now he is in danger of an other'; AAW, A XXVIII, no. 161, p. 535. Southworth's activities in ministering to plague victims brought accusations that he was using the epidemic in order to proselytize; Anstr., II, p. 306.

but it seemes by the answer that the queen will not give them leave.
There is one Mors[e] a Jesuitt deputed also, but <I> do not heare
what visitt he hath made yet.¹³⁰⁷ I pray cause all our friends in those

For other instances of the secular clergy's use of the plague to publicize how seriously
they took their pastoral duties, see George Fisher's report of 5 August 1625 to Thomas Rant
(AAW, B 47, no. 160) that 'London is now a mapp of misery left desolate' by the plague, but
'I am here to attend the sicke and cheifly to releive the necessity of the poore'. There was 'an
other of ours apointed by my l[ord] [Richard Smith] to visit them'. 'We ar[e] called uppon
daily. The number of the sicke is so greate.' The 2nd Viscount Montague's manuscript
tract ('An Apologeticall Answere [...]', completed in 1628 in support of Smith), asked of
the regulars, 'will they yet be pastours cum honore with the exemptions and priviledges
thereof, and not cum onere, with the burthen and charge thereunto belonginge? Who did
in the tyme of the last plague discharge the tender care of pastours to the sicke and whole
in this towne? Concear[n]inge the sicke, the care was through the charitable provision of
my lord bishop, and with noe smale charge undertaken by one of the archdeacons with
an other of the cleargie, and one only [sic for only one] Benedictine whose labours for
about five monthes were exceedinge greate in that good worke, without any healpe of the
fathers of the Societie, notwithstandinge promis made for two of them to helpe in this
kinde.' One Carmelite had been involved in tending plague victims. Montague did not
deny that 'some other regulars might have remained in their owne particular residences
about this towne [London] and some others mo[r]e might also have resorted theither
to some particular freind'. But there were many others, resident in London, who had
'many honorable and wealthie dependents'. And they left 'the poore infected persons in
theire soe greate extreamitie', even while Smith's archdeacon 'was inforced severall tymes
to ride into the cuntrie to visite the infected there who were under the charge of the
fathers of the Societie'; Anthony Maria Browne, 2nd Viscount Montague, 'An Apologeticall
Answere [...]' (Gillow Library manuscripts, on microfilm at the West Sussex Record Office),
pp. 127–129. In October 1636 Southcot and George Fisher signed and published a
'declaration' 'to the Catholickes of England' to urge them to relieve plague victims. They
stressed that 'the example of the Protestants, both in the citty and the countrey (which
is well knowne to all) may bee no small inducement unto Catholicks to imitate their
care, providence, and bounty in this behalfe'. For 'if those who acknowledge no merit in
good workes, out of a generous minde, or naturall compassion are so ready to assist their
distressed brethren so plentifully; it may seeme that no lesse, but rather much more, should
bee expected at the hands of Catholicks who, professing to believe the doctrine of merit,
have thereby a farre higher motive than Protestants have to performe workes of charity
and to open the bowells of mercy, especially in a time of so generall and pressing necessity,
towards their poore and desolate brethren, who have no expectation of hope or reliefe from
any, but from them alone'; AAW, SEC 16/1/10 (formerly AAW, A XXVIII, no. 165).
    For puritan usage of the plague as a polemical weapon to emphasize the superiority of
some ministers' pastoral ministry over that of others, see P. Slack, *The Impact of Plague in
Tudor and Stuart England* (Oxford, 1985), pp. 233–236.
    ¹³⁰⁷ The Jesuits, especially Henry Morse, were swift to exploit plague as a means of
demonstrating the quality of their own ministry. In late January 1635, two Jesuits told
Gregorio Panzani that there was no need in England for bishops and parish priests, and,
in addition, 'si pigliorono sopra di loro ad assistere alli appestati'; VA, PD, fo. 70r. (In April
1635 Matthew Wilson SJ had arranged with the seculars that they would each appoint one
representative to see to the needs of those unfortunate Catholics who were struck down by
the disease; Dockery, *CD*, p. 43.) On 18 May 1636 Panzani asked the Jesuit Robert Jenison to
request the Jesuit provincial, Richard Blount, to assign some London Jesuits to tend plague
victims, although, Panzani claimed, Jenison made no direct response, 'anzi si lamenti delli

parts to pray for Mr Fittons fathers soule lately departed.[1308] It is an office we ow[e] to him for his sonns sake so well deserving and I promised to procure so much.

I ame glad you resolve to send up the jubily[1309] almes to be devided betwen the college and the poor here, for there is need in both. I have ventured to lend the house 200^l which lay dead in my hands till Michelmas terme, being the mony of one of our brethren.[1310]

Mr Ghilmett wisheth us to send xx^l for a token to Mr Hart, by this shipp that now goeth, to encourage him the better, having sent him nothing since he went thither, and I like the motion well. But I assure you our rents for the present are not able to spare it nor to afford half the mony. Yet I tould him that, if Mr Muscot or Mr Curtese[1311] could procure the mony, I did hope in Michelmas terme to make it good, as soon as my rents come in. I gave 5^l to Mr Ghilmett by the advise of our brethren here, and have promised him 5^l more when we have it in part of recompence for his paines there. We must of necessity

secolari che pensano a questo, quasi che usurpino giurisdittione'; PRO, 31/9/17B. On 16/26 September 1636 Smith enquired of John Southcot how John Southworth was faring and whether 'any Jesuit really assist the infected'; AAW, A XXVIII, no. 163, p. 541. However, on 6 October 1636, Southworth and Henry Morse SJ issued a joint appeal to English Catholics for money to assist plague victims, *To the Catholickes of England* (London, 1636); ARCR, II, no. 726.

[1308] On 25 June/5 July 1636 Peter Biddulph had written to Southcot that he understood that 'my father is exceedingly decayed of late, and for that reason I desyred to returne into England as soone as may be, but now I feare I shall nott have the comfort to see him by reason of my stay here this summer, which is likely to be very prejudiciall to mee, for you must know that as yett he hath nott settled anything upon mee and I doubt nott butt the Jesuitts doe what they cann to hinder him from leaving mee anything'. Biddulph asked Southcot to get Richard Button, archdeacon of Staffordshire, to deal with Biddulph Snr 'in my behalf', since his father would not live long, and he believed that 'it may be he is much incensed at my being here in Rome, butt I am sure he hath no reason if he consider what I have negotiated here, for no Catholike cann chuse butt rejoyce at this resolution of the pope his sending one [George Con] into England, and the queens keeping another [Sir William Hamilton] [...] here, in regard of the greate good that must needs follow upon it'. Biddulph believed that 'if I had nott sett this business first on foote here and sollicited the sending of Panzani it had nott been effected'; AAW, A XXVIII, no. 135, pp. 457–458. On 24 September/4 October Biddulph acknowledged Southcot's notice of Biddulph Snr's death 'which news I had receaved before from the Jesuitts here. I cann now only desyre you to pray for his soule. As for the meanes left mee by my father I know nothing, because my brother in his letter doth only give mee a bare notice of his death'; AAW, A XXVIII, no. 177, p. 571. On 2/12 October 1636 Biddulph wrote to Southcot that he was content to stay in Rome for the winter, 'and indeed the chiefest motive of my returne is taken away by my father his death, whom I desyred to see before he dyed', though Biddulph wanted to leave Rome 'at the end of March' 1637; AAW, A XXVIII, no. 169, p. 553.

[1309] See AAW, A XXVIII, no. 137 ('Conditions for the gaining of the present jubily granted by his Holynesse the xi of July 1636').

[1310] See Allison, RSGB, II, pp. 246–247.

[1311] Peter Curtis. See Anstr., II, pp. 78–80.

gratify our freinds, though we streatch our selves farther than we are well able.

I have wearied my self and you also, I feare. Pardon my scribling. My service to all there.

Your most affectionate cosen and servant,

J[ohn] Lovel

26 Aug[ust] 1636

[on p. 518]

Addressed: To my honoured cosen M[r] Edward Hope.

Endorsed: M[r] Lovells of the 26 of Aug[ust] answeared the 29.

82. Jo[hn] Clerk [Southcot] to Edward Farrington [Bennett], 2 September 1636

[AAW, A XXVIII, no. 156, pp. 521–522]

Dear cosen,

I have but a short warning to write unto you by this bearer John Galmarch and therfor must be brief. I wrote unto you my mind at large by John Legatt, but that was in confidence to yourself. I send you here enclosed M[r] Fittons[1312] letter which hath bin shewen to Fa[ther] Philip who promiseth to speake to the queen effectually about it. What newes is at court I suppose M[r] Layborne will informe you by this bearer. Other newes I have none but what I signified in my last from Lisbo[n][1313] brought by M[r] Ghilmett[1314] who is gonn down on foot into Norfolk, and by the way I wished him to call uppon our brethren in Essex and Suffolk and gett their names to a paper of contribution for Lisbo[n] to which [I s]ett down mine ~~first~~ for five pounds yearly as I promised at first. I hope they will all help a little. Otherwise we shall not be able to make good the nine score pounds which we have promised during the founders[1315] life. I feare our letters from Lisbo[n] are lost by the negligence of the shipman that brought them, for as yet we heare nothing of them. These enclosed M[r] Ghilmett gave me, who remembers his service to you and desires you to send that to

---

[1312] Peter Biddulph.
[1313] The college of Saints Peter and Paul at Lisbon.
[1314] Henry Shirley.
[1315] Pedro Coutinho.

Christ Church Colledge.[1332] Signor Georgio did onely see
ere he was much honored by both the king and queens
ne[s][1333] who did earnestly invite him to sitt with them which
And at the comedy at St Jhons Colledge their Majesties, not
their, sent a gentleman to enquire for him.[1334] He hath been
red by all the nobility about the court.[1335] And on Sundaye
dstock he did conferre almost an hower in private with the
5] at which many did wounder, but to your selfe this, for
s passage is knowne, as also the manner of the archbishops
im, notwithstanding I would not have us publish them, for
ries will take advantage against us upon every litle busines.
ure you faithfully that I am confident that Signor Georgio
e to doe great good here if he doe setle a firme corres-
which is that he doth ayme at, but to yourselfe this. And
yne that he desireth noe thing more than 3 or 4 bishops
ntry, but I doe see that my lords returne[1336] will not be
d unlesse it may appeare gratful to his Majesty. Yett before
to Rome nothing will be done. Howsoever I have desired
ilip to move her Majesty to some present order unto Sir
amleton[1337] to deale about bishop[s], that his Holynes may
Majesty is still myndfull of the busines.

y was William Cartwright's *The Royal Slave*. See Taylor, 'Royal visit', pp. 157–
rchbishop Laud', pp. 151–152. Laud complained to the vice-chancellor that
was unwilling to contribute to the cost of the entertainment at Christ Church;
, p. 144.
d chamberlain of the household was Philip Herbert, 4th earl of Pembroke.
ria's chamberlain was Edward Sackville, 4th earl of Dorset.
Panzani did not attend the play performed at St John's college, allegedly be-
nted to avoid seeming too forward in seeking royal favour; Albion, *CI*, p. 161.
contacts which Con was making among the nobility at this time, see *ibid.* He
d by Bishop Juxon, and the earl of Holland invited him to meet the marquis
and other leading Catholics at Holland's own residence in Hyde Park; *ibid.*,

roposed return of Richard Smith to England.
Smith reported to Southcot on 25 May/4 June 1636 that he had spoken
m Hamilton as he passed through Paris. Smith gave him 'instructions such
ood', and Hamilton told Smith that Henrietta Maria had commanded him
consult Smith; AAW, A XXVIII, no. 121, p. 423. Smith believed that Hamilton
te at Rome on their behalf, though, as Smith learned in August 1636, Hamilton
so without specific instructions from the queen; AAW, A XXVIII, no. 151,
9 July 1636 Biddulph reported that Hamilton had been well received by the
made a very good impression in Rome. Cardinal Barberini had 'presented
very faire horses for his coach'. Hamilton kept correspondence with Secretary
nd, as Brett had done, used the Benedictine agent in Rome, Richard (Wilfrid)
y his letters; AAW, A XXVIII, no. 139, p. 467. On 24 September/4 October
d that Hamilton was 'our trew friend and affected to our business as well as
, A XXVIII, no. 177, p. 571. The secular clergy supported Hamilton out of
nancial resources. On 4 January 1638 Champney remarked to Biddulph that

---

M[r] Pugh[1316] when you send into Walles next. M[r] Layborne is come to
Richmond, where I wish you were also that we might sometimes meet
togeather to conferr about our affaires. We have nothing of moment
from my lord.[1317] This from M[r] Fitton I desire you to send me back
againe by the next.

My service to all with you, and in hast I rest. 2 Septemb[er] 1636.

Yours ever being but to serve you ever,

Jo[hn] Clerk

Lett us have that Latin letter againe I pray which was written in your
name to the Span[ish] ambassador[1318] lately that we may putt it uppon
the register as we use to doe.

[*on p. 522*]

Addressed: To my much honoured cosen M[r] Edward Farrington in
Sussex or elsewhere.

Endorsed: 1636.
    M[r] Lovells of the 2 of September.

83. Laborn [George Leyburn] to Farrington [Edward Bennett], 3 September 1636

[*AAW, A XXVIII, no. 157, pp. 523–528*]

Most honored sir,

You had heard from me long before this if I could have been
furnish[e]d with any convenient opportunity to convey my letters unto
you. The plague continuing and increasing in London taketh away
all meanes of correspondence, in soe much that I am enforced to
send at this tyme my owne servant to give you an accoumpt of all
passages since my departure from you.[1319] On Weddensday last I
parted from Oxeford with Signor Georgio[1320] and Signor Panzano[1321]

[1316] This may be a reference to the priest Stephen Pugh. See Anstr., II, p. 374.
[1317] Richard Smith.
[1318] Presumably a reference to Iñigo Ladron Velez de Guevara y Tassis, count of Oñate
and Villa Mediana.
[1319] See *Letter 81*.
[1320] George Con.
[1321] Gregorio Panzani. Panzani's diary records his visit to Oxford. He arrived there on
19 August, and met the Benedictine provincial, Robert Sherwood, and also William
(Benedict) Jones OSB. On 20 August he visited All Souls, the Schools, and Bodley's
library, and then, after meeting Leyburn and Christopher Davenport OFM, he went to see

and on <u>Thursedaye night we arrived at</u> Hampton towne <u>a myle from Hampton Court wher they intend to</u> continue untill it <u>shall please God to free London</u> of the sicknes.[1322] Their Ma*j*esties parted also the same daye, the king towards New Forest, and the queen towards Otelands. Wher [*sic*] and [at] Hampton <u>Court she intends to continue thes 2 moneths</u> or longer if the plague do not cease. They were most gloriousely receaved at Oxeforde.[1323] They were mett two myles from the towne by the cheef citizens, aldermen, batchlers of divinity, doctors of phisike, doctors of divinity in their scarlett roabes, bishops, mayor and chancellor (viz the archbishop of Canterbury), all w*h*ich ridde in great state before their Ma*j*esties coache unto Christ Church Colledge wher they were lodged, and after supper intertayned wi*th* a new comedy called the Passions Calm*e*d, or the Floating Iseland,[1324] in w*h*ich was represented a king whos name was Prudentius (you may imagine our most prudent prince) and an Intellectus Agens, a person active and wise (you may imagine his Grace of Canterbury); by the passions you may understand the puritans and all such as are opposit to the courses w*h*ich our king doth run in his goverment. Thes passions were very unrulye and disobedient unto Prudentius['s] goverment in soe [*p. 524*] much th*at* they resolved noe longer to ~~endure~~ <suffer> him to be their king, w*h*ich the Intellectus Agens, perceaving, persuaded Prudentius to yeeld his crowne quietly, w*h*ich he did. Thes disordered passions, having now the crowne, consulted together on whom they should bestowe it, and election was made of Lady Fancy, under whos goverment they fell into bitter discords and discentions amongst them selves, plotting to kill each other. At length, beeing wearie of thes differences, they resolved to aske counsell of Desparato what to doe,

St John's. Over the next couple of days he saw another twelve colleges. Following a trip to the court at Woodstock, Panzani returned to Christ Church to see the rehearsals for William Strode's *The Floating Island* which Leyburn describes in this letter; VA, PD, fos 146r, 147r; PRO, 31/9/17B.

[1322] On 30 May Panzani had noted in his diary that he went to reside at Hampton, where he could both avoid the plague and visit the court regularly, and see, among others, Jacques le Noël Du Perron, Robert Philip, and Leyburn; VA, PD, fo. 139r. He negotiated, in June, with Windebank, for two rooms at the palace; PRO, 31/9/17B (transcript of Panzani's letter to Barberini of 17/27 June 1636).

[1323] For this event, see K. Sharpe, 'Archbishop Laud and the University of Oxford', in H. Lloyd-Jones, V. Pearl, and B. Worden (eds), *History and Imagination* (London, 1981), pp. 146–164, at pp. 150–152; Sharpe, *Criticism and Compliment*, p. 48.

[1324] See William Strode, *The Floating Island: A Tragi-Comedy, Acted before His Majesty at Oxford, Aug. 29. 1636. By the Students of Christ-Church* (London, 1655); B. Dobell (ed.), *The Poetical Works of William Strode [...] to which is added The Floating Island a Tragi-Comedy [...]* (London, 1907), pp. 137–263. Strode was the Public Orator in the university. The play had been written at Laud's own prompting. Leyburn's account of the performance gives us a different perspective from the description in Sharpe, 'Archbishop Laud', pp. 156–157, 160. Panzani had been taken to see a rehearsal of the play on 26 August; VA, PD, fo. 147r.

who would make noe answere bu...
knyfes and roapes. They were not...
thought good to advise with Intelle...
submitte them selves unto Pruden...
unto him, w*h*ich counsell, beeing...
embrace. Prudentius receaved the...
and accepted of their submission...
foule errors and made a speech un...
th*at* the courses which he ran in his...
and as for the navy it was to defend...
was represented a puritan ministe...
their Ma*j*esties laugh[ed] hartely. H...
was marryed to Concupiscence. W...
tender his submission to Prudentiu...
King, I kneele not to thee but to th...
adore thee.[1326]

The next daye their Ma*j*esties...
Canterbury at St Jhons Colledge...
entertainement as ever I did see i...
him selfe most noble, kept 14 tables...
and one table for the queen, almer...
the cheef French who they should b...
the grand almener by Sir Jhon Tuns...
Grace durst not invite Sig*n*or Geor*g*...
come he should be hartely welcom...
for at] dynner. And Panzano[1329] and...
I doe assure you th*at* I never see [*s*...
fish and sweet meates as was at th*at*...
the French fashion.[1330] This manne...
much please, more than if he had b...
their Ma*j*esties was [*sic*] entertayned...
Loves Hospitall[1331] which gave great...

[1325] See Dobell, *Poetical Works*, p. 234. This...
already expressing criticism of the Ship Money...

[1326] *Ibid.*, p. 235 ('I kneel not/To thee, but to...
thee').

[1327] Jacques le Noël Du Perron.

[1328] Albion says that Laud's invitation was sent...

[1329] See VA, PD, fo. 147r.

[1330] See A.J. Taylor, 'The royal visit to Oxf...
Oxoniensia, 1 (1936), pp. 151–158, at p. 157.

[1331] Laud informed the vice-chancellor on 15 J...
production of this play, written by George Wilde...
visit', p. 157; J.L. Funston (ed.), *A Critical Edition o*...
patronage of Wilde, see *ibid.*, iv.

an other a...
the first w...
chamberla...
he refused...
seeing him...
much hon...
last at Wo...
king, [*p. 5*...
although I...
inviting o...
our adver...

I doe a...
will be al...
pondence...
I am cer...
for this c...
much urg...
his returr...
Fa[ther] I...
William I...
see that h...

[1332] This p...
158; Sharpe...
the universi...
Laud, *Works*...

[1333] The le...
Henrietta M...

[1334] Con a...
cause they w...

[1335] For th...
was entertai...
of Winchest...
p. 162.

[1336] i.e. th...

[1337] Richa...
with Sir Wi...
as I though...
(Hamilton)...
would nego...
would not...
p. 509. On...
pope, and h...
him with tw...
Windebank...
Selby, to co...
Biddulph n...
cann be'; A...
their scarce...

Signor Georgio as also Panzano doe present their respects unto you and will be glad to see you, and I desire that it may be as sodainely as your occasions will give you leave, for Fa[ther] Price[1338] and the superior M[r] Sherwood[1339] have been alreadie with him as also Fa[ther] Francis,[1340] and Father Roberts[1341] from the superior of the Jesuists,[1342] as I went to him from you. Fa[ther] Price and Fa[ther] Sherwood did promise to write unto Fa[ther] Jhon[1343] their agent at Rome about the Accord[1344] and to cause him to goe to our protector[1345] and to signifie the generall consent and acceptance of all the Benedictines here in England. The increase of the plague is a great hindrance unto all our affayres. If M[r] Lane[1346] and you doe resolve to come to Hampton I will meet you wher you please, but I would not have you come unlesse you [word obscured: can (?)] make 2 dayes jorney of it, for it is too far for you in one daye. The superior of the Benedictines[1347] did please Signor Georgio very much in that he did showe great willingnes and readines to remitte himselfe to his Holynes in all poyntes.[1348] This is all, onely humble respects and best wishes for your happines. You may communicate with M[r] Lane thes contents. He will be secrett.

My best respects. Sep[tember] 3 1636.

Richard Worthington 'will write unto you about the 1000 crownes taken up there long since of the colleges pension for the use of Sir William and not yet repayd, to the great hurt of the howse, wherfore I pray you secure a letter from him to his agent here to pay the money to M[r] Jhon Morgan who shall present the letter'; AAW, A XXIX, no. 38, p. 151. See also AAW, A XXIX, no. 37 (a note of 4 January 1638 from Richard Worthington to Biddulph concerning Hamilton's money).

[1338] William (Benedict) Jones OSB.

[1339] Robert Sherwood OSB was a chaplain to the Browne family at Kiddington; Lunn, EB, p. 228; idem, 'Benedictine opposition', pp. 8–9. He had in 1628 'sayd to the bishops [i.e. Richard Smith's] face, and in the presence of his owne superiour, that he would sinke, yea die rather than aske the bishops approbation'; AAW, A XX, no. 159, p. 602.

[1340] Christopher Davenport (Francis a Sancta Clara) OFM.

[1341] Robert Jenison SJ.

[1342] Richard Blount SJ.

[1343] Richard (Wilfrid) Selby OSB.

[1344] See Letter 76.

[1345] Cardinal Francesco Barberini.

[1346] Probably the priest Richard Lane (see Letter 23), but possibly Valentine Harcourt, alias Lane, who was a cousin of Peter Biddulph. Harcourt had returned to England from Rome in 1634; Anstr., II, p. 144.

[1347] This seems to be a reference to Robert Sherwood OSB (cited already in this letter under his own name), who had been the Benedictine provincial of Canterbury since 1633; Lunn, EB, p. 232; Letter 84.

[1348] Biddulph, however, reported back to Southcot on 24 September/4 October 1636 that 'the Benedictines are the men who doe [. . .] hinder us of haveing a bishop by averting my lord of Canterbury and Secretarye Windebank from it, although they make to us a faire shew to the contrarye'; AAW, A XXVIII, no. 177, p. 571.

I have noe tyme to read my letter over, and therfore I beseech you to make good sense of it as you can.

[*on p. 524 in margin*]

I beseech you to present my humble service unto noble Mr Fortescue. I thinke th*a*t I shall be able to make an end of his troublsome busines according to his desire. After he was gone from Sherborne, Petites wife came to the Vyne[1349] to speake w*i*th me wh*i*ch she did before Mr Sands, Mrs Atkins and Mrs Savage.

[*on p. 525 in margin*]

I had the honor to speake w*i*th my lord of Carnarvon[1350] twise, once at Woodstock and an other tyme at Oxeford. I did see also his two brothers and Mr Dormer of Peeterley who did aske kindly for you and will be glad to see you.

[*on p. 528*]

Addressed: To his most honored friend Mr Farrington present thes. Ryver Park.

Endorsed: Mr Laborn 1636 the 3 of Sept[ember].

84. R[oberts] [George Leyburn] to [Richard Smith], 7 September 1636

[*AAW, A XXVIII, no. 158, pp. 529–530*]

Most honored sir,

I have receaved none from you since I writte my former by the last weekes post. I presented y*ou*r remembrances to Sig*no*r Georgio[1351] and y*ou*r good friends in the court who returne theirs w*i*th harty thankes. Such occurrences as thes tymes doe afforde are signifyed in the inclosed to Mr Mountegue wh*i*ch you may please to peruse and

---

[1349] The Vyne, Hampshire, residence of the Sandys family. See N. Pevsner and D. Lloyd, *Hampshire and the Isle of Wight* (London, 1967), pp. 634–638. For Fortescue, see *Letter 92*.

[1350] Sir Robert Dormer, 1st earl of Caernarvon. The Dormer family were prominent patrons of the secular clergy. In July 1632 Smith had sent on two packets of letters from Biddulph in Rome to the earl; AAW, B 27, no. 101. Allegedly Caernarvon disliked Strode's *Floating Island*, and 'sayd it was the worst that ever he sawe but one that he sawe at Cambridge'; Taylor, 'Royal visit', p. 156.

[1351] George Con.

after seale it. Fa[ther] Ph[ilip] did move her Majesty to give order to Sir William Hamleton as was desired in M[r] Fittons[1352] letter, but she wish[e]d him to exspect yett for some litle tyme. I perceave that noething will be done before a firme correspondence be setled, which I hope will be very shortly; and after that I am confident that our affayres shall succeed prosperousely. Two dayes aggoe I mett with Fa[ther] Price[1353] and we had much speech concerning the Accorde[1354] which, as Signor Panzani told me yesterdaye,[1355] is generally approved at Rome, and they [sic for the] Jesuists ther dare not speake against it. He and his superior, Father Sherwood, have writte unto Father Jhon[1356] their agent to stand firmely for it, and that, in case he hath sayd any thing to the cardenall protector[1357] by which his eminence may have occasion to suspect that their order is devided in the approbation of it, to unsaye it agayne. And he told me that both his judgement and power shall fayle him if Father Rudisinde[1358] shall be able to hinder it, and wish[e]d me to signifie thus much to M[r] Bennett. I see clearely that the moncks and fryers here doe desire nothing more than union with the clergie, for they see that the Jesuists doe but comply with them for their owne ends. This daye I have receaved a letter from Ryver Parke to acquainte me that M[r] Bennett is falne very sick, and not without some danger of death, for which I am hartilie sorie, for if he should dye it would be a great losse unto us. I have delivered M[r] Hanmors[1359] letter to Signor Georgio. But as yett I have not gott his answere. To morrowe I intend to be with him, and then I will not fayle to urge him. When I have his answere I will write unto him.

I wish you all happines who am your most obedient servant,

R[oberts]

September 20 1636.

No address.

[on p. 530]

Endorsed: Accord with monks.

[1352] Peter Biddulph.
[1353] William (Benedict) Jones OSB.
[1354] See *Letter 76*.
[1355] VA, PD, fo. 148r.
[1356] Richard (Wilfrid) Selby OSB.
[1357] Cardinal Francesco Barberini.
[1358] William (Rudesind) Barlow OSB.
[1359] William Claybrook. He had been rector of Pwllcrochan, Pembroke (1628) and of English Bicknor in Gloucestershire (1630). He was tonsured in Rome in March 1637, though he did not enter the English college there. He was later involved in the conversion to Catholicism of Godfrey Goodman, bishop of Gloucester; see Anstr., II, p. 61.

85. [George Leyburn] to [Richard Smith], late October/ early November 1636

[*AAW, A XXVIII, no. 211, pp. 655–658*]

Most honored sir,

I have yours of the 17 of October and I have presented your respectfull remembrances as you wish[e]d me. I am certayne that the monkes in England will never recall the agreement,¹³⁶⁰ but as for Fa[ther] Rudicind¹³⁶¹ and Father Clement,¹³⁶² who governe thos on the other syde, I knowe not what to saye nor thinke. D[octor] Kell[ison] doth write unto me that they doe in a kind oppose, notwithstanding Fa[ther] Price¹³⁶³ wish[e]d me (as I writte unto you in a former letter) to assure Mʳ Benett from him that Fa[ther] Rudicind should never be able to hinder or hurt the sayd agreement. What I writte concerning Sir Jhon Thimbleby his servant ther hath been noe more speech made of it; and Sir Jhon hath been with the king and graciousely used publiquely before many of the lords of the councell, for he kissed the kings hands att the breaking up of the councell. Yett the poore man continueth prisonner in the Tower and peradventure shall come to his tryall as well [as] the fryer.¹³⁶⁴ Ther have been great complaintes made to Signor [*p. 656*] Georgio¹³⁶⁵ concerning my cosen Holdens conclusions,¹³⁶⁶ and as I probablely [*sic*] conjecture, by Fa[ther] Knott¹³⁶⁷ or Fa[ther] Blunt.

---

¹³⁶⁰ See *Letter 76*.

¹³⁶¹ William (Rudesind) Barlow OSB.

¹³⁶² Clement Reyner, who had been president of the English Benedictine congregation since 1635 (in succession to John (Leander) Jones), and was now at Douai. See Lunn, *EB*, pp. 171–172, 232; Sitwell, 'Leander Jones's mission to England', p. 135.

¹³⁶³ William (Benedict) Jones OSB.

¹³⁶⁴ Sir Thomas Puckering was informed on 28 September 1636 that 'a poor man, Bumsted by name, sometime serjeant to Sir John Thimlebee, was sent a prisoner from Oatlands to the Tower of London [. . .] for saying he would cut off the king, or the king must first be cut off'; Birch, *CT*, II, p. 250; CRS, 1, p. 109. For the 'fryer', Arthur McGeoghan, see *Letter 53*.

¹³⁶⁵ George Con.

¹³⁶⁶ Henry Holden had been a member of the English secular clergy's writers' institute in Paris, the Collège d'Arras, and in mid-1625 was offered a post in the household of Michel de Marillac, Richelieu's minister of finance. At some point shortly before the end of 1635 he left the Collège d'Arras and went to England to join his friend Thomas White who was residing with his own patron, Sir Kenelm Digby. In March 1636 Holden and White came back to Paris, and Holden returned to the college; Allison, 'An English gallican', pp. 323–324. On 4/14 November 1636 Richard Smith wrote to John Southcot that 'this is noted that D[octor] Holden spake far more freely against Jes[uits] since he returned out of Engl[and] than before and said that the [secular] clergie was tyranized over, and manifest wrong was done to me, which kind of speches he never uttered befor but rather reprehended men for such'; AAW, A XXVIII, no. 186, p. 595. In December 1637 Holden left for Rome.

¹³⁶⁷ Matthew Wilson SJ.

He thinketh that they will be displeasing at Rome and give some litle advantage to our adversaries. I replyed that I thought that ther was noe error in poynt of doctrine contayned in the conclusions. Agayne, they were the act of a privat man, and therfore, ~~and therfore~~ if not soe discreetly done, and with that respect and foresight of thes corrupted tymes in which we live, it is not to be imputed to the whole body of the clergie. I feare that in tyme we shall not dare to entertayne a good opinion of episcopall jurisdiction least the regulars (who are not to be offended for their multitudes) be displeased. I also had speech with Signor Georgio concerning the report of his proceedings in the busines of the oathe,[1368] and he had <u>been inform[e]d</u> that it should <u>come from</u> you, but I did give him good satisfaction by showing him your owne letter to the contrarie. [*p. 657*] He knew well that the Jesuistes had reported a litle before his comming over that he was sent from Rome to receave our king into the Catholique Church.[1369] Thes speeches are given out on purpose to make him odious to the [*word omitted*: State (?)]. But I am persuaded that the authors of them will misse of their marke. Concerning the Jesuist prefect of the mission[1370] and the promise made unto him, M[r] Lovell[1371] will endevour to enforme him selfe very exactely. I had also speech with Signor Georgio about a report concerning your supposed renunciation, of which he was made the author. And he did protest unto me seriousely that he never did signifie to any since his comming into England that you <u>had renoun</u>ced and that his Holynes had accepted it. But he told me how planely he had delt in his dis<u>course with y</u>our selfe in privat. I perceave <u>both</u> by him and Signor Gregorio[1372] that in this poynte they desire to walke clarisis oculis, and that it should not be touch[e]d upon. I told [*p. 658*] them both planely that, in case it should be called in question, that [*sic*] our friends w<u>ould menta</u>yne it and stand for <u>it as pro aris</u> et foris. And I did alledge many reasons which I doe suppose M[r] Clerk[1373] will signifie unto you. By occasion of this discourse we fell into an other concerning the breve[1374] procured by the regulars which was the most dishon<u>orablest act</u> that ever was done by the Sea Apostolique quot

---

[1368] On 7/17 October 1636 Smith informed Southcot that 'we heare here' in Paris 'that M[r] Con [. . .] hath perswaded our k[ing] that the oathe of alleageance [of 1606] is unlawful for Cath[olics] to take, and that there is hope it shall no more be proposed to Cath[olics]. But nether you nor M[r] Font[aine] [George Leyburn] write any such thing, which maketh me suspect it as a rumour for to disgrace M[r] Con with the k[ing]'; AAW, A XXVIII, no. 171, p. 557.

[1369] See Hibbard, *CI*, pp. 47–48.

[1370] Thomas Fitzherbert SJ.

[1371] John Southcot.

[1372] Gregorio Panzani.

[1373] John Southcot.

[1374] Urban VIII's breve *Britannia* (29 April/9 May 1631).

verba tot injuriae illatae clero et cleri episcopo. I am of opinion that Mr Fitton[1375] did greatly prejudice us in not presenting the exceptions, I meane the supplication[1376] which is an excellent peece, and I perceave thus much by the discourse that I have. This is all, onely I am to present unto you your best ladyes[1377] respects and to imparte a busines which concerning [sic for concerns] her ladiship. When Sir Jhon Gage,[1378] our good friend, was upon his deaths bed, a proposition was made unto him of a marriage between his eldest sonne[1379] and one of her ladiships doughter[s]. He did very greatly relish the proposition, as Mr Anderton[1380] knowes, and although he thought it not fitting to marrie his sonne soe young, notwithstanding he wish[e]d Mr Anderton to lett his sonne knowe, when he should attayne unto riper yeares, that it was his desire that he should match ther if soe be he could affect the gentlewoman and she him. That noble family was ever true to the clergie and peradventure if we should louse him in his marriage we should louse him [word deleted] <altogether>. And I perceave that my lady his mother hath a designe to provide a wyfe for [word omitted: him], as also some of the executeurs. They have a designe and thinke to keep him ther very long for their owne ends.[1381] Wherfore your best lady and our best desireth your advise how to bring this busines about. I have writte to Mr Car[1382] and Mr Plantyne[1383] to the same effect, with whom you may be confident. And as for the young gentlewomen [sic], I knowe not in England more hansome or more vertuous. And for a portion ther will be noe dispute.

[in margin of p. 657, and continued on top of p. 658]

I beseech you send a copie of Mr Mountegue[s] letter for Fa[ther] Ph[ilip] doth much desire to see it. Thes inclosed [are] to himselfe. I have seen D[octor] Mayler. He is now with my Lord Mountegue[1384]

[1375] Peter Biddulph.

[1376] The 'Humillima Supplicatio' (6/16 July 1631), the secular clergy's petition to Urban VIII to delay publication of the breve *Britannia*. See AAW, A XXIV, no. 127; *Letter 1*.

[1377] Anne (Philipson), Baroness Arundell.

[1378] Sir John Gage (d. 4 October 1633). For his will, see PRO, PROB 11/164, fos 433v–4v, and for his inquisition post-mortem, see PRO, C 142/500/35.

[1379] Sir Thomas Gage, who succeeded his father as 2nd baronet.

[1380] Perhaps this is a reference to George Gorsuch, who used the aliases of Talbot and Anderton. He was a supporter of Richard Smith. See Anstr., II, p. 134.

[1381] In the event Sir Thomas Gage married Mary, daughter of John Chamberlain (of Shirburn Castle in Oxfordshire) and Catherine Plowden; Davidson, 'Roman Catholicism', p. 115. For the marriage settlement (dated 29 January 1638), see ESRO, SAS/G19/27.

[1382] Miles Pinckney.

[1383] Lawrence Platt.

[1384] Francis Browne, 3rd Viscount Montague. Mayler would almost certainly have met Francis Browne in Spain in 1623. Browne had been sent to stay at the Spanish court while

who hath bestowed a good house on him and, as I am privately informed, would willinglie give him 100ˡⁱ per annum to staye with him if he though[t] that they should agree together.¹³⁸⁵ I thinke that he cannot have a greater portion in any noble Cath[olic] family. I beseech you to take this busines to hart.

[on p. 655]

Endorsed: About the breve to the bishop of Chalced[on] in relation to the contest between him and regulars.

[Hen]ry Mayler.

86. [George Leyburn] to Leuys Amerine [Richard Smith], 2 November 1636

[*AAW, A XXVIII, no. 179, pp. 577–580*]

Most honored sir,

By the last weekes post I commended unto you a pacquett with others inclosed to Mʳ Mountegue and Mʳ Car.¹³⁸⁶ And I shall [be] very glad to understand of the receipte of it in respect I did touch on divers businesses of some importance. Since, I have <had> more serious discourse with Signor Georgio¹³⁸⁷ concerning the breve as also the supposed renunciation.¹³⁸⁸ As for the first he mentayneth the proceedings of the court of Rome, and greatly complayneth of the

the negotiations for the proposed Anglo-Spanish dynastic treaty were in progress, while Mayler was actually involved in the negotiations; James Wadsworth, *The English Spanish Pilgrime* (London, 1629), pp. 48–49; Anstr., I, p. 224; *Letter 17*.

¹³⁸⁵ On 16/26 September 1636 Smith had written to Southcot that 'this day sevennight Mʳ D[octor] Mailer' came to bid Smith farewell, as he prepared to go to England on the following day, but 'I heare he intendeth not to staye unles he finde entertainment to his liking and perhaps he wil speak with the k[ing]'; AAW, A XXVIII, no. 163, p. 541.

¹³⁸⁶ Miles Pinckney.

¹³⁸⁷ George Con.

¹³⁸⁸ On 14 October 1636 Leyburn had issued a circular letter concerning a rumour that 'it is certified from Rome lately [. . .] not only that my lord bishop of Chalcedon hath resighned up his authority', but also that the pope 'hath accepted of the resignation'. Con was thought to be the author of the rumour, 'although wee doe not easily beleeve it'; AAW, A XXVIII, no. 170, p. 555. On 22 October/1 November Peter Biddulph notified John Southcot that he had recently written to Leyburn that Thomas Fitzherbert SJ, the rector of the English college in Rome, 'told mee that he would nott address any more priests that goe from hence to Mʳ Bennett or any other in England, because he sayeth they have no more authoritye over the priests, because by the bishop of Calcedon his resignation all their authoritye allso expired'. (Since mid-1633 Fitzherbert had been sending priests from Rome 'with this clause that they shold obey the archpriest'; AAW, B 27, no. 123.) Biddulph recommended that a memorandum should be sent to Cardinal Barberini to desire him to declare that the authority of Richard Smith's officials should 'continue over the secular priests without

clergies negligence and bacwardnes in their informations at that tyme. I did acquainte him with the true reasons of this neglect, but withall told him plainely that this negligence would not excuse the unjust proceedings of the court of Rome in that busines, which both in honour and justise was obliged not to decree altera parte inaudita. Moreover in that decree the cheef poynt of the controversie was not determined but divers other poyntes which were never called in question, most injuriousely and to the great prejudice of the b[ishop] and clergie. For whosoever shall read that decree (unlesse he be particular[ly] acquainted with the b[ishop's] proceedings) shall be made to believe that the b[ishop] his designe was to invalid[at]e confessions heard or to be heard by regulars without his approbation, as also to infringe their priviledges et[c]. Moreover he shall be made [*p. 578*] to harbour a hard opinion of the appellants in former tymes, whom Clement the 8 did justifie by a speciall briefe,[1389] and of whom some were glorious martyres. I doe assure you faithfully that I cannot speake of thes passages without great griefe and truble of my mynd. As for the second, I told him the author of that report; notwithstanding he did seriousely protest unto me that he did never speake any such wordes as that the b[ishop] had renounced and that his Holynes had accepted his renunciation. I told him freely the many inconveniences which would happen if his Holynes either by word of mouth or any other act should give an occasion wherby the regulars might informe the Catholiques of this country that the b[ishop] had renounced his authority and that his Holynes had accepted it, and therfore wish[e]d him in his next letters to touch somewhat upon that poynt to prevent further inconveniences, and I knowe he will. Signor Panzani is not as yett certayne when to beginne his jorney because he hath not receaved the letters which contayneth his bills and order to returne. I am certayne that we shall find him a true friend to his power and readie to assist in our affayres.[1390]

I cannot furnish you with any occurrences, onely that the king and queen are come to Hampton Court, but I feare that they will make noe long stay ther, for this night I heare that there is a howse shutt up at Hampton towne, a myle from the court and wher many of your courtyers are lodged. And it is thought that the plague will encrease much this week at London.

meddling with the regulars or laitye for the interim untill the controversye be ended'; AAW, A XXVIII, no. 178, p. 575.

[1389] For Clement VIII's breve (of October 1602), see *NAGB*, p. 5.

[1390] Gregorio Panzani took his leave of the queen on 10 December. He left London on 15 December. On 13/23 and 17/27 January he saw Richard Smith in Paris, although he went to visit the leading Jesuits there as well; VA, PD, fos 154r, 156r.

I wish you all happines who am your obedient servant. All Soules daye.

[p. 579]

The lady abbesse[1391] busines of Brussells hath been much commended unto Signor Georgio, as also to Sir William Hamleton, in soe much that I hope that it will be ended shortly and to her ladiships desire;[1392] and then I hope M[r] Champney may be spared ther to attend unto other affayres of greater importance.[1393]

[on p. 580]

Addressed: A Monsieur Monsieur [sic] Leuys Amerine dans la Place Maubert a Paris.

Endorsed: Of the breve and the bishop.

87. G[eorge] Fountayne [Leyburn] to Leuys Amerine [Richard Smith], 24 November 1636

[AAW, A XXVIII, no. 194, pp. 613–616]

Most honored sir,

I have receaved yours of the 14 of November and I will not fayle to acquainte M[r] Lovell[1394] and M[r] Musk[et][1395] with your great expences for

---

[1391] Mary Percy, daughter of Thomas Percy, 7th earl of Northumberland.

[1392] For an account of the troubles at the Convent of the Glorious Assumption at Brussels, see Guilday, *The English Catholic Refugees on the Continent*, pp. 259–264; Lunn, *EB*, pp. 200–201; Arblaster, 'The infanta and the English Benedictine nuns', pp. 512, 525 nn. 4, 17, 18; AAW, A XXVIII, no. 188, p. 599. The nuns at the convent in Brussels had once used the services of a Jesuit chaplain, but when the gallican Anthony Champney was appointed in 1628 as a replacement for the resident secular priest now in post, some of the nuns refused to accept him; Allison, 'The English Augustinian convent', p. 457. Nineteen of the fifty-five nuns would not submit to his direction; Lunn, *EB*, p. 200. In June 1632 John Pory had retailed the salacious rumour that in the dispute between the 'English nunnes' and 'their abbesse', they 'threw her downe a payer of stayers', and when the archbishop of Mechlin subsequently arrested the miscreants he 'found many of them bigg with childe'; JPN, p. 279. On 19/29 November 1636 Champney remarked that Mary Percy was wholly relying on Sir William Hamilton 'to move the cardinall in her sute'. Southcot had advised her to commend her cause to Panzani who himself was returning to Rome; AAW, A XXVIII, no. 196, p. 619. On 7/17 January Biddulph confirmed to Southcot that he had received letters from him, in the name of the chapter, in which Southcot recommended Mary Percy's cause. Biddulph himself was supporting her at Rome, but 'the Jesuitts doe now seek to gett the queen to write in behalfe of the separated nunns, and therefore diligence must be used there that they gett no surreptitious letter from her Majestye'; AAW, A XXIX, no. 4, p. 7.

[1393] Anthony Champney became dean of the secular clergy's episcopal chapter in succession to Edward Bennett (who died in November 1636) and returned to England. This allowed the rebel nuns to go back to their convent; Lunn, *EB*, p. 201.

[1394] John Southcot.

[1395] George Fisher.

letters. But I doe assure you faithfully that I never knew us in a worse
estate for moneys. Litle summes comes [*sic*] in, and thos Lisboa[1396]
doth devoure. Now our cheef friends never thinke of procuring any
charityes for the discharge of common expences; and M[r] Fitton[1397]
haith been mentayned w*i*th the moneyes of Dow[ay] thes two yeares
together and not any satisfaction as yett made. Our ruine is the want
of a superior amongst us. Sweet Jesus send us one of thos two you
mention, and as for D[octor] Stratford[1398] he is greatly desired by the
cheefe Catholiques of this country and a man against whom there
<are> not any exceptions. Whatsoever M[r] Benett writte unto you I
am certayne that Sig*n*ore Georgio[1399] gave him wish[e]d content, and
in the poynt of jurisdiction to be setled in this country. And assure
you[rself] that you are wrong[e]d in y*ou*r information concerning his
Holynes designe to give us an archpriest, albeit you saye that you
have it from a good ground. And some of our best friends here are
to blame to be jealous of Sig*n*ore Georgio before ever they have seen
him or spoken w*i*th him, giving too much creditt to M[r] Price[1400] his
informations; who to my knowledge, w*i*th thos who run the same
courses w*i*th him, as Fa[ther] Francis[1401] [and] Preston,[1402] have done us
more hurt since they begunne [*sic*] to tamper w*i*th the State than ever
the Jesuists did, and now most violently under hand oppose the setling
of ordinarie jurisdiction. Moreover it may be that the sayd party and
his [*p. 614*] adherents doe knowe that the sea of Rome doe dislike
their courses and proceedings, and are jealous that Sig*n*ore Georgio
doth [*word deleted*] <likewise> soe, and dispaire of working him as
they have wrought Sig*n*ore Panzani. If this be true our cheef friends
have noe great reason to give creditt to the sayd partyes informations.
Howsoever I knowe this to be true, that by their meanes <and>
through the secretary[1403] his power w*i*th Panzani (who hath a great
opinion of him) if Panzani be asked by his Holynes whether he doth
judge it expedient to grant bishops, rebus sic stantibus, he will answere
negative, notw*i*thstanding Sig*n*ore Panzani is a good friend of the
clergies and hath done good offices, but he hath been infinitely fooled
by thes meanes to my knowledge, and hath medled wher he had noe
order to medle. And it was never his Holynes intention that he should
aske the secretary of State here whether the king would be drone to

---

[1396] The college of Saints Peter and Paul at Lisbon.
[1397] Peter Biddulph.
[1398] Edmund Lechmere.
[1399] George Con.
[1400] William (Benedict) Jones OSB.
[1401] Christopher Davenport (Francis a Sancta Clara) OFM.
[1402] Roland (Thomas) Preston OSB.
[1403] Sir Francis Windebank.

suffer bishops. His order was to deale with the queene and medle noe farther. I knowe what I saye, and many other passages which I dare not committ to writing; and I beseech you not to imparte what I write to any one friend. And I shall advise our friends in their proceedings here as conveniently as I can. But thes passages and many more are imparted to me with such secrecy that I dare not communicate [them] as yett <by writing>. [*three lines deleted*] <When the plague will suffer [*word deleted*] us to returne to London I shall give some light to our cheef friends how to proceed. But the want of a superior is very prejudiciall unto us.> I am confident for all this that our affayres will succeed happely if we will proceed discreetly. Some thing will be done for the present for our content and assurance of more hereafter. As [*p. 615*] concerning the report with which Mr Lovell[1404] acquainted you formerly, I doe assure you that Signore Georgio hath often tymes since protested unto me that he never spoke such words to Mr Price.[1405] Since, on purpose, he hath discoursed with him about bishop[s] and told him that he could not imagine wherfore he and his adherents should refuse to admitt of bishops. Mr Price replyed that ther were bishops alreadie in England and they would not suffer any. He answered that now the ministers doe style themselves priests, therfore noe priests must be in England. Then Fa[ther] Price answered that the State <u>would not</u> suffer bishops, and withall protested that if his Holynes should send a bishop with ordin<u>arie jurisdiction</u> that he should not make him obey him. He would first l[eave] England and <u>retyre him selfe</u> into his monestery. I could acquainte you with many passages and with the rest to [*sic for of*] their discourse, but I am unwilling to write thus much least my letter should miscarrie. <u>Father Knots booke</u>[1406] hath given great disgust to the State and will doe the Jesuistes m<u>ore hurt</u> than they can imag[i]n. The secretary hath delt with Signore Georgio about it who doth m<u>uch condemne</u> Knott for his indiscretion. But all thes passages to your selfe. The king and queen went yesternight to Richmond, and this daye they are gone to Greenwich with intention to returne at

[1404] John Southcot.

[1405] William (Benedict) Jones OSB. On 20/30 November 1636 Peter Biddulph wrote to Southcot that he was suprised by the news about Con, for Biddulph had received a letter from him in which he showed himself very 'reall for the [secular] clergye', 'and indeed I cannott upon small grounds be persuaded to the contrarye, since he is governed altogather by F[ather] Philip; and therefore I would not wish the clergye to give any shew of mistrust in him unless they see very manifest arguments of it'. 'If the Jesuitts have really any hand over him it will be worse for him, especially if the queen and his Majestye should perceave any such thing'; AAW, A XXVIII, no. 197, p. 621. See also AAW, A XXVIII, no. 201 (Biddulph to Southcot, 27 November/7 December 1636).

[1406] Matthew Wilson SJ, *A Direction to be Observed by N.N. if Hee Meane to Proceede in Answering the Booke intituled Mercy and Truth, or Charity maintained by Catholiks &c* (np [printed secretly in England], 1636); ARCR, II, no. 820.

night to Richmonde, but they would take Somersett House on their waye, and to morrowe they are to come to Hampton Court agayne.

I write in hast. God grant that you may read my hand. Sweet Jesus send you all wish[e]d happines.

Your obedient servant,

G[eorge] Fountayne

November 24 1636.

[on p. 616]

Addressed: A Mons*ieur* Monsieur [*sic*] Leuys Amerine dans la Place Maubert a Paris.

Endorsed: About Price and Knot.

88. [George Leyburn] to [Richard Smith], 27 December 1636

[*AAW, A XXVIII, no. 212, pp. 659–660*]

Most honored sir,

I writte unto you by the last post a very long letter[1407] wherin I did signifie divers passages concerning Sig*n*or Georgio,[1408] and if I were with you I could acquainte you with many more. I have reason to imagine that M[r] Clerke[1409] hath sent you informations contrarie to myne, for he hath ben credulous to Fa[ther] Price[1410] his discourses, and I feare continueth soe. Also M[r] Blun[t][1411] frequenteth too much Fa[ther] Francis.[1412] I perceave also th*at* the foresayd persons, M[r] Price and Fa[ther] Francis, doe see th*at* they cannot worke Sig*n*ore Georgio as they <u>wrought Panzani</u> and therfore they desire to carrie the clergie w*ith* them in opposition against him. I doe protest before my B[lessed] Saviour that I doe intimate thus much onely to prevent many inconveniences w*hich* will happen unto us if we doe proceed according to M[r] Clerks <u>informations. Notwi</u>thstanding I doe not wish you to believe my informations, nor our friends here, onely

[1407] *Letter 87.*
[1408] George Con.
[1409] John Southcot.
[1410] William (Benedict) Jones OSB.
[1411] Identity uncertain; but see Anstr., II, pp. 30, 370.
[1412] Christopher Davenport (Francis a Sancta Clara) OFM.

kes greatly in the court and [*p. 13*] [is] most proper for thes tymes, nd it will be gratfull at Rome.¹⁴³⁰ Fa[ther] Ph[ilip], the grand almener nd all *your* friends did showe a great joye for the grace the king had one you and Mons*ieur* Almener wish[e]d me to present his humble rvice and signifie how glad he was, as also that you were to be his eig[h]bour. I sent one of *your* bookes unto a doctor of divinity,¹⁴³¹ sole haplaine to our prince, and he gave me great thankes and protested at the bishop of Calcedoyne was a brave man. As concerning M*r* Clerke¹⁴³² I doe protest unfainedly before my Blessed Saviour I esire as much to gayne his affection and give him content as I desire ny earthlie thing. He was first displeased with me because I did not goe to Ro[me] and cheefly in regard of a letter that *your* best lady¹⁴³³ writte at that tyme, w*hich* was very sharpe, and therin he did declare hat he would never give his consent that I should goe, and M*r* Clerk hought him selfe touched in that letter because he <u>did attribute</u> my going to some of our cheef men. I doe assure you faithfully that I was most ignorant of that letter and, if I had imagined that *your* best lady and her husband would have taken my going as they did, I would not have taken my leave with them rather than to have disappoynted our friends. But afterwards all were against my going untill the spring, and then *your* best lady told me that she would give way and helpe to my maintainetance [*sic for* maintenance], as I acquainted both M*r* Benett (who was also much against my going then by reason of Signore Georgio his coming) and M*r* Clerk. For my parte whither soever you shall commande me to goe or runne, I doe assure you faithfully I will not refuse, although all the friends I have in this world dissuade me.

This is all, onely my best wishes, w*hich* I present in all harty manner who [am] *your* most obedient servant,

Rob[erts]

Jan[uary] 19 1637

No address

[*on p. 14*]

Endorsed: The bi*s*hops booke.

¹⁴³⁰ It is not clear which of Richard Smith's works is meant, but it could well have been his *A Brief Inquisition into F. Nicholas Smith his Discussion of M.D. Kellison his Treatise of the Ecclesiasticall Hierarchie* (Douai, 1630), attacking Matthew Wilson SJ's tract against Kellison. However, on 10/20 February 1636, Smith, in Paris, had asked Southcot to send him some copies of Smith's own *Prudentiall Ballance of Religion* (St Omer, 1609), as well as other books; AAW, A XXVIII, no. 92, p. 351.
¹⁴³¹ This is, presumably, a reference to Brian Duppa, who was the prince's tutor. See *Letters 70, 74*. I am grateful to Kenneth Fincham for advice on this point.
¹⁴³² John Southcot.
¹⁴³³ Anne (Philipson), Baroness Arundell.

my desire is that they may prevaile soe far as to make us deale warely, that is to complye with Sig*nore* Georgio howsoever we doe imagine him to be Jesuited and not to decrye him before we have greater grounds of his disaffection towards us.¹⁴¹³ You cannot imagine how he was trubled at M*r* Chambers letter wherin [*word deleted*] <were> mentioned divers speeches of yours concerning him. But I am confident <u>that he is well satisfy</u>ed now, and th*at* he doth not impute it a falt to you but to *your* informers whosoever they were, for you did speake onely what you heard. For Fa[ther] Ph[ilip], first you may please to knowe th*at* I doe noething <u>without him. And he</u> hath the same opinion of Sig*nore* Georgio that I have, besyd[e]s by occasion of what M*r* Chambers writte concerning *your* speeches. He tould me in these words: I am of opinion that if <u>you have any good done it must</u> be by Sig*nore* Georgio his meanes and therfore doe not louse him. But I wonder who informeth you th*at* Sig*nore* Georgio hath a designe to make the clergie to qu<u>itte ~~your~~ <the> b[ishop's] authoritie and</u> not to stand for it. I doe assure you faithfully that after th*at* I had given him many reasons wherfore it was necessarie to menta<u>yne *your* authority, he wr</u>itte to the cardinal protector¹⁴¹⁴ that he thought it convenient that you <u>should be mentayned in</u> *your* authority alleadging the reasons. But to deale planely with you I perceave by Sig*nore* Georgio <u>that it was held generally at Ro</u>me th*at* you had resigned, th*at your* resignation was accepted, and that the clergie kn<u>ew soe much, and that they would</u> not stand upon th*at* poynt. And therfore he blameth much Panzani who never did intimate to Rome as th*at* the clergie did stand for the b[ishop's] authority. I am in hast. The earle of Arundell is com[me]d.¹⁴¹⁵ 10 27 1636. M*r* Lovell¹⁴¹⁶ is sickelie still.¹⁴¹⁷

¹⁴¹³ On 28 January/7 February 1637, Peter Biddulph notified John Southcot that he had received two or three letters from Leyburn 'who doth still continue in good conceate' of Con. Leyburn hoped that by Con's means the dean and chapter would be confirmed, 'which would be a greate establishment to our clergye; butt in this buisness wee must entreate Sig*nor* Giorgio to deale with the card*inal* [Francesco Barberini] as from himself, for so it will be obtained sooner, and the negotiation will be kept more secrett than if I should deale [with] it here in the name of the clergye'; AAW, A XXIX, no. 10, p. 21. Smith, however, opined to Richard Lascelles at Rome in a letter of 13/23 March 1638 that, 'as for the hope you have of confirming the chapter, I know not what good will come therby to the clergy' because 'I think thereby they shall have but the archpriest and assistants changed into the names of a deane and canons'; AAW, B 27, no. 136.
¹⁴¹⁴ Cardinal Francesco Barberini.
¹⁴¹⁵ The earl of Arundel returned from the Hague on 27 December 1636/6 January 1637; *CSPV, 1636–1639*, p. 126.
¹⁴¹⁶ John Southcot.
¹⁴¹⁷ Back in March and April 1636 Smith had several times warned Southcot to take care of his health; AAW, A XXVIII, no. 102, p. 377; no. 104, p. 381; no. 106, p. 385.

No address.

[*on p. 659 at top of page*]

For the <love> of God be secrett in what I write, neither lett Mr Clerke knowe any thing. I have delt planely with him and I thinke he will be of an other opinion. And he is very friendlie to me and I desire not to take notise of anything [?].

[*on p. 660*]

Endorsed: Signor Con for the b*isho*p.

89. Rob[erts] [George Leyburn] to [Richard Smith], 19 January 1637

[*AAW, A XXIX, no. 6, pp. 11–14*]

Most honored sir,

I have receaved yours of the 18 of Jan[uary] and I have imparted to Fa[ther] Ph[ilip] and Mr Conne what you writte concerning [*sic*] and they were <u>both well satisfy</u>ed for they had receaved letters at the same tyme from Mr Chambers to the same effect. I am very hopefull, <u>as also Fa[ther] Ph[ilip]</u>, that some good will be done by his meanes as I have signifyed in my former letters. He continueth very gracious both with the king and queen with whom he is daily. I am sorrie that <u>none of our cheef friends</u> would ever yett make a jorney to Hampton to see him. The superiors of all other religious have often visited him ther, especially Father Blunt, Fa[ther] Price[1418] and Fa[ther] Frances[1419] who, as I heare, is made superior in Father Perkins[1420] place. The court will now be shortly here at London and then I hope that we shall make amends for all this neglect. I doe not wounder if Sig*n*ore Gregorio[1421] did speake coldely of episcopall authority, and the reasons I have intimated in my former letters. And I doe assure you faithfully that he told Sig*n*ore Georgio (if he be to be believed), fearing least he should harken too much <u>to the clergie</u> (by reason of Fa[ther] Ph[ilip]) whom he knew for the most part neither to approve Fa[ther] Leanders[1422] proceeding nor Fa[ther] Frances, first that I was <u>a good man</u> but he was not to heed my informations because they were not good, secondly

---

[1418] William (Benedict) Jones OSB.

[1419] Christopher Davenport (Francis a Sancta Clara) OFM.

[1420] John Gennings OFM. See Anstr., I, pp. 128–129; *NAGB*, pp. 108, 111; Dockery, *CD*, p. 36.

[1421] Gregorio Panzani.

[1422] John (Leander) Jones OSB.

---

that Mr Muskett[1423] was a collericke and passionate m[an] to my knowledge he had spoken before). Thirdlie [ ] was a turbulent man. And is it not strange he us[ ] me sometymes, but never when Fa[ther] Frances wa[ ] Fa[ther] Price? Thes two complye greatly with Sig[ ] will never gayne him as they gayned the other. He w[ ] between him and the secretary[1425] when he has any [ ] goe himselfe rather when he hath any busynes with t[ ] not use any to breake it unto his M*ajest*[i]e but him[ ] [*p. 12*] Price some 6 dayes aggoe, complying muc[h] Georgio, and knowing well that he had taken s[ ] Sig*n*ore Panzani, tooke occasion to speake of him, [ ] that he (Panzani) was a proude man, a malench[ ] <u>a simple man.</u> This I doe protest unto you, before [ ] Saviour, <u>Sig*n*ore Georgio</u> tolde me with his owne mo[ ] any man trust such an one? And one daye Sig*n*ore [ ] occasion, before Panzani, to speake unto him[1426] ab[ ] jurisdiction, and asked him wherfore he thought it n[ ] to admitt of bishops, and he replyed that ther were bis[ ] By that reason, replyed Sig*n*ore Georgio, you should n[ ] priests, for the ministers doe stile them selves priests. [ ] told him that the State would not permitt bishops, as Pa[ ] can witnes, whom I carryed to the secretary, who declar[ ] mynde in that poynte. But, sayes he to Sig*n*ore Georgio, d[ ] it convenient? For my parte (says he) if his Holynes shou[ld] bishop with ordinarie jurisdiction I <u>would returne</u> to my[ ] before that I would obey him. With many such passag[ ] could acquainte you if I were with you. This Fa[ther] P[ ] Fa[ther] Francis, are very gratious with the secretary[1427] a[nd] the court very often and, to my knowledge, endevour to d[ ] bad offices, and strive to gayne freinds on the French syde, [ ] freinds will be advised, they shall never be able to hurt us. [ ] love of God keep to y*our* selfe all thes passages w*hi*ch I have [ ] Otherwise I shall suffer prejudice.

I have presented the grand almener[1428] and the superi[ ] Capucins[1429] with one of y*our* bookes as from you. It is a w[ ]

[1423] George Fisher.

[1424] John Southcot.

[1425] Sir Francis Windebank.

[1426] i.e. William (Benedict) Jones OSB's contacts with W[ ]

[1427] For Christopher Davenport (Francis a Sancta Clara) OFM, see Dockery, *CD*, *passim*.

[1428] Jacques le Noël Du Perron.

[1429] Jean-Marie Trélon. See Hibbard, *CI*, p. 56.

90. Rob[erts] [George Leyburn] to Leuys Amerine [Richard Smith], 23 February 1637[1434]

[*AAW, A XXVIII, no. 94, pp. 355–358*]

Most honored sir,

I have yours of the 20 of Febr*uary* for w*hich* I humbly thank you. Thos good offices you doe in favor of our English are well taken here. What you writte concerning Mr Yates[1435] I did cause it to be signifyed to his father who is in this towne exspecting to heare of the <u>enlargement</u> of his sonne. He sent unto me this morning, the post beeing com[me]d. Notwithstanding, as yett I have not receaved any letters. Many here are glad that the king and his brother[1436] are soe <u>well accorded</u>. It will be advantageous to the present designes of this State, for I perceave great signes of a future breache with Spane. If Mr Fitton[1437] will not staye any longer, some one of the clergie to succeed will be necessarie, for I would not have it appeare at <u>Ro[me] that we are</u> soe unfurnish[e]d with men that we are enforced to employ a secular and soe young as he is. We did suffer noe litle prejudice by leaving[1438] Mr Skynner.[1439] But in this busynes I doe remitte you to Mr Clerke.[1440] If ther be any faith in Mr Conne he meaneth well towards us. He told me the other daye that he never mett yett with any Jesuist who would saye that they thought it not <u>fitting to have bishops</u> in thes tymes. I confesse they complye mightely with him. Before, in their speeches to Sig*nor* Panzani, noething was soe frequent in their mouthes as persecution, hard conditions of Catholiques, and the kings rigour against them; but now they sing a contrarie song, for Fa[ther] Blunt in his letter [which] he writte lately in waye of satisfaction for Knotts booke[1441] dothe greatly <u>extolle the</u> kings clemency, and speaketh much of the ease and quietnes w*hich* Catholiques now enjoye in respect of former tymes, and, as for the booke, he and his doe disclaime from it <u>as ignorant of the writing</u> of it.[1442] This proceeding is much against their owne principals w*hich*

[1434] Dated 23 February 1636 in the AAW, A series catalogue.
[1435] See *Letter 91*.
[1436] Louis XIII and Gaston, duke of Orleans.
[1437] Peter Biddulph.
[1438] i.e. losing.
[1439] See *Letter 32*.
[1440] John Southcot.
[1441] Wilson, *A Direction to be Observed [. . .]*.
[1442] In margin of p. 355: 'I beseech you to acquainte Mr Fitton with thes passages <u>because I dare not</u> write unto him. I wounder that he gives us noe better informations from that great city. He might give us great light how to proceede here if he would but learne our passages. His letters are alwaise very maigre. I praye write to him soe, for I doe intend [*subsequent words concealed in binding of volume*]'.

are to mentayne whatsoever they doe although never soe bad. But this will not suffice. The secretary[1443] doth much urge to have him banished, to which they [*word illegible*] [*p. 356*] and they tell Signore Georgio[1444] that he is a sickelie man and therfore if he doe commaund him out of England his blood shall lye on him, and Signore Conne is too yeelding to favour them in thes wayes which, as I have often told him, will make the State here jealous of him if he doe not prevent [it], and also make him incapable to doe good for the Catholique cause. For believe it that [*sic*] they are much hated by the State, as also Sir Tobye Mathew, for they and he cheefely have done bad offices in the emperors courte which they now strive to excuse, and doe use Signore Conne to deale for them, which I, understanding, advertized Fa[ther] Ph[ilip] and wished him to deale roundly with Signore Conne and tell him that if he did embarke him selfe in their quarrells he would louse him selfe. Some days before, Fa[ther] Ph[ilip] spoke unto him about confirming of the d[ean] and ch[apter] and alleadged new reasons for the necessity of it, and he told me that he found him as willing to performe that act as any one of us could be. I have delivered a sylver bazin an[d] eure unto M^{ris} Salesbury and I wish that it were better, and truly your best lady[1445] would have made it more rich if I had not dissuaded her ladyship, for I am confident that this is as good as you will desire.[1446] I cannot acquainte you with more occurrences than I have alreadie signifyed in my former, onely here is newly published a declaration of the faith of [the] Palsgraves churches[1447] soe contrarie to the religion professed in the Church of England that I wounder that such a worke should be permitted here. Your best lady wishes me to present unto you her best respects as also your friends at the court.

And thus with my best wishes, I rest, who am your obedient servant,

Rob[erts]

February 23 1636.

[*p. 357*]

[1443] Sir Francis Windebank.

[1444] George Con.

[1445] Anne (Philipson), Baroness Arundell.

[1446] On 9/19 March 1636 Smith had noted that Anne Arundell would 'entertain' Edward Bennett, the new dean of the episcopal chapter in England; AAW, A XXVIII, no. 102, p. 377.

[1447] *A Declaration of the Pfaltzgraves: concerning the Faith and Ceremonies professed in his Churches* (London, 1637); CRS, I, p. 110.

I wish that Mr Mallyer[1448] were ther agayne. This country is not for him. I doe assure you that he will disgrace him selfe and us. He is soe addicted to company. But to your selfe this. Onely conferre with my cosen Houlden[1449] how to gitt him over agayne.

[*in margin of p. 356*]

Concerning affayres at Dow[ay] I did showe Mr Plantyne[1450] divers letters from Mr Strong[1451] and M^r D[octor] Stratford[1452] and he undertooke to informe you truly. This inclosed is from Mr Strong.[1453]
Humfry is com[me]d. I have sent away Mr Bolds pacquett for Mr Ireland.[1454] I beseech you to remember my respects unto him.

[*on p. 358*]

Addressed: A Monsieur Monsieur [*sic*] Leuys Amerine marchant dans la Place Maubert a Paris.

Endorsed: Jesuits for a bishop and Knots booke.

91. Roberts [George Leyburn] to Louys Amerine [Richard Smith], 19 May 1637

[*AAW, A XXIX, no. 21, pp. 47–50*]

Most honored sir,

I have receaved yours of the 21 of Maye, and I have presented your respects to our best lady[1455] who was most glad to heare from you as also to understand what you writte concerning Sir Thomas Gage, who I perceave by Mr Anderton[1456] writte to the executeurs that he was resolved to returne this summer into England, and they have alreadie writte backe to dissuade him. Notwithstanding, Mr Anderton told me that he would wish him to continue in his resolution to returne, by reason a jorney into Italy at this tyme is very dangerous.[1457]

[1448] Henry Mayler.

[1449] Henry Holden was a relative of George Leyburn; Anstr., II, pp. 158–159; Allison, 'An English gallican', p. 320.

[1450] Lawrence Platt. He must have recently arrived in England, though Smith had noted on 13/23 January that Platt would 'goe to England after Easter'; AAW, A XXVIII, no. 89, p. 345.

[1451] Matthew Kellison.

[1452] Edmund Lechmere.

[1453] This sentence is in Anthony Champney's hand.

[1454] Edmund Dutton. For Richard Lascelles, alias Bold, see *Letter 91*.

[1455] Anne (Philipson), Baroness Arundell.

[1456] A reference, perhaps, to George Gorsuch.

[1457] According to Smith, on 27 January/6 February 1637, Gage had been imprisoned in the Bastille, for an unspecified offence, at the same time as one Mr Yates (whom Smith

Mr Anderton told me also and wish[e]d me to acquainte you that
he and the executeurs are much trubled that Garnett, Mr Peeters
man, was suffered to treate with Sir Thomas soe much as they heare
he did, for he was expressely sent over by his sister Peeters[1458] att
the entreaty of the padres,[1459] with whom she is gracious and they
with her, to move a marriage between him and the Lord Peeters
doughter and a great portion is offred. If Sir Thomas doe come
over this summer, as I hope by your meanes he will, it will behove
Mr Plantyne[1460] to carrie the busynes discreetly and secretly, for if his
sister Peeters and my lady his mother[1461] gett notise they will applye
all their forces to droe him their owne wayes. I writte unto you in
my former of my Lord Peeters death.[1462] I doe heare credibly that
he hath left to the Jesuists [*word deleted*] 15 thousand pound[s], and
some saye that he hath left amongst secular priests 500^{li} but I see
noething given as yett. Monsieur Anguilaime will be with you before
this, for we have understood of his arrivall at Deepe.[1463] Good [*p. 48*]
Mr Clerk[1464] is now past all hopes. Father Symons the Jesuist[1465] and his
owne father,[1466] as thos who were about him saye, have in a <u>manner
killed him</u>. For, upon Sunday last in the afternoone, they did assaulte
<u>him (Symons cheefely)</u> most furiousely prissing him upon his salvation
to repent him selfe of his proceedings and urging his obligation to
be a Jesuist.[1467] They preach[e]d unto him noething but damnation
for the space of one hower and more in soe much that he was

described first as a son of Sir Thomas Yates and then of Sir Edward Yates) was similarly
incarcerated, as it was reported to England, for coining. The English ambassador, the earl
of Leicester, had made representations on behalf of both of them; AAW, A XXIX, no. 9,
p. 19; no. 12, p. 25. Sir Thomas Puckering was informed on 14 February 1637 that the Jesuit
William Talbot had 'sent his despatches' to Spain 'sometimes by Sir Thomas Gage, and
othertimes by Mr Yatts, besides the suspicion of Yatts's rounding of pistoles'; Birch, *CT*, II,
p. 280.

[1458] Probably Sir Thomas Gage's sister, Ann, who married Henry Petre, 5th son of William
Petre, 2nd Baron Petre. See Berry, *Sussex*, p. 295.

[1459] Jesuits.

[1460] Lawrence Platt.

[1461] Penelope, third daughter and co-heiress of Thomas Darcy, 1st Earl Rivers; Berry,
Sussex, p. 294.

[1462] William Petre, 2nd Baron Petre died on 5 May 1637; *CSPD, 1637*, p. 71.

[1463] See *ibid.*, p. 22.

[1464] John Southcot.

[1465] Henry Floyd SJ.

[1466] John Southcot Snr (the eldest son of the judge of the Common Pleas, of the same
name, who died in 1585). He was known to be a favourer of the Society. Smith wrote to John
Southcot Jnr in October 1636, 'God forgive your father who I think is a laye Jesuit'; AAW,
A XXVIII, no. 171, p. 557. Southcot Snr's will, made in June 1615, names Baron Petre, a
great patron of the Jesuits, as a trustee for some of his property; CRS, 1, p. 114.

[1467] See also *Letter 93*. Southcot may originally have had some inclination towards the
Society. Back in June 1614, Anthony Champney reported from Paris to Thomas More that
'Mr Southecoates alias Daniell ys thought to be retired to some religious [house ?] for he

absolutely spent in answering them, and tould them that they had killed him, howsoever he <u>was resolved to</u> dye in perfect obedience to <u>his lawfull superior</u> the bishop. And with that they parted. The daye after, he tould me that <u>never such cruelty was</u> used towards any in the <u>like extremity, and</u>, as for his beeing a Jesuist formerly, he <u>protesteth that it is</u> a calumnie. Did ever living crea<u>ture heare of such</u> proceedings?[1468] Thes inclosed are from Fa[ther] Ph[ilip]. I cannot acquainte you with any occurrences, onely the prince elector and his brother <u>are to staye</u>. Ther are hopes that the <u>busynes concerning</u> the palatynate shall <u>be accommodated</u>. Madame St George[1469] her two sonnes are newly arrived here.

And thus with my best wishes, I rest, who am y*our* most obedient servant,

Roberts

19 Maye 1637.

It is resolved th<u>at Mr Bolds</u>[1470] shall goe to succeed Mr Fitton.[1471] I beseech you to remember my respects unto him and to worthie Mrs Salesbury, y*our* nephew[1472] and good Mr Car.[1473]

hathe beene absent these 5 or 6 dayes', and 'yt ys like he ys with the Jesuites'; AAW, A XIII, no. 127, p. 323.

[1468] For a longer account of the treatment of Southcot in his last illness by his father and the Jesuit Henry Floyd, see AAW, A XXIX, no. 23. The first page (p. 55) is in Richard Smith's hand, the second (p. 56) in another's. See also *Letters 92, 93*. Following Southcot's death, there circulated 'A coppy of a *lettre*, written by D[octor] Southcott, upon his death-bead, unto his brother, M^r Ed[ward] Southcott, concerninge the due obedience to bee yealded by Catholickes unto b*ishops*'; AAW, A XXIX, no. 27.

[1469] Mary (Grey), wife of John St George, of Hatley St George, Cambridgeshire. Their second son, William, entered Douai in 1610 and was ordained at Arras in 1614. He briefly entered the Society at Liège in 1615 but returned unwell in late 1616. He became a supporter of Richard Smith; Anstr., II, p. 275; CRS, 75, p. 189.

[1470] Richard Lascelles. He returned from Rome in 1638 in order to enter Cardinal Richelieu's entourage. On 4 January 1638 Anthony Champney wrote, from England, that Smith had sent word that 'Cardinall Richlieu hath called Mr Lassells back into France intending to imploy him there and that Mr Lassells will accept thereof'; AAW, A XXIX, no. 38, p. 151. See also AAW, A XXVIII, no. 207, p. 645 (Smith's warning to Lascelles of 5/15 December 1637 that Richelieu was intending to take him into his service).

[1471] Peter Biddulph.

[1472] Thomas Smith. See Anstr., II, p. 301. On 31 March/10 April 1636 Richard Smith asked John Southcot to advance a loan to his nephew, who 'yesterday [...] parted from hence for England'; AAW, A XXVIII, no. 108, p. 391. On 26 May/5 June 1636 Smith remarked that his nephew (whom he complained about having to maintain financially; AAW, A XXVIII, no. 125, p. 433) had arrived in Paris two days before with Miles Pinckney; AAW, A XXVIII, no. 121, p. 423; and, on 12/22 August, Smith noted that his nephew had 'departed yesterday', with Thomas White and Mrs Salisbury, 'for England'; AAW, A XXVIII, no. 151, p. 509. Thomas Smith had evidently lived with Mrs Salisbury while he completed his not entirely conventional education; AAW, A XXIX, no. 18, p. 39.

[1473] Miles Pinckney.

I beseech you to make much of Mr Touchett.[1474] He is a vertuous gentleman. I could wish that after that [sic] he had been ther some tyme he would goe to Dow[ay], and to goe forward ther.

Humfry will bring your truncke. I could gitt noething to passe with Madame Peroune.[1475] The French are fearefull. I caused Fa[ther] Ph[ilip] to [word illegible] as also for 2 for Mr Cars house.

[on p. 50]

Addressed: A Monsieur Monsieur [sic] Louys Amerine dans la Place Maubert a Paris.

Endorsed: F^r Floids [word obliterated].
          Mr Lovel.[1476]

92. Roberts [George Leyburn] to Leuys Ameryne [Richard Smith], 26 May 1637

[AAW, A XXIX, no. 22, pp. 51–54]

Most honored sir,

Yesterdaye I receaved yours of the 29 of Maye, and was glad to heare of good Father Vietts[1477] safe arrivall as also of your bulles. I would not wish you to goe in person to take possession, the tymes beeing soe dangerous. For as I heare the Croates doe greatly infest thos quarters of France wher your abbey is.[1478] As concerning the report of his Majesties proceedings in the busynes of Mr Mosse[1479] a Jesuist, I thinke that I have alreadie in a former letter mentioned as particulars: he was not condemned, onely areigned; it was not a private judge but the lord cheef justice[1480] who was to pronounce sentence of condemnation, and had done it if the king had not sent to hinder him. He is not put out of his place. It is true his Majest[ie] did checke him for areigning him without first advising with him; to which he replyed that before he came upon the bench he did not knowe that ther was a priest to be

---

[1474] This may be a reference to George Touchet, who in 1643 was professed as a Benedictine.

[1475] Henrietta Maria's midwife. See CSPD, 1635–1636, p. 279; ibid., 1636–1637, p. 124; ibid., 1637, pp. 71, 112, 143.

[1476] John Southcot.

[1477] Pierre Viette, Oratorian chaplain to Henrietta Maria.

[1478] The Benedictine abbey of St Sauveur at Charroux. See Allison, RSGB, II, pp. 250–251; PRO, C 115/105/8212; Letter 75.

[1479] Henry Morse SJ. See Anstr., II, p. 227.

[1480] John Bramston, lord chief justice of King's Bench since April 1635.

areigned, and this is the truth of the busynes. I am sorie that ther are noe better signes of a generall peace. The busynes of the Palatinate is the greatest hinderance, and this will enforce our king to joyne with France though much against his will, and breake with Spane, for the Spaniards doe continue to feed him with good words without any reall effects. Good Mr Lovell[1481] on Mundaye last in the ~~afternoone~~ <evening> about 8 of the clocke departed to the great greife of all his friends. He never held up his head after that Father Symons[1482] the Jesuist and his owne father did use that great cruelty towards him as in my former I have expressed.[1483] He made a very blessed end, calling upon Jesus and our B[lessed] Lady even to the last gaspe. I beseech you to cause [*p. 52*] him to be remembred by our friends ther. Two dayes aggoe I commended thither, at the entreaty of Sig*no*re Conne, a falne priest.[1484] He was of Valdelide,[1485] and as soone as he came into England he marryed and soe continued for divers yeares, non [*sic for* not] prejudicing any but him selfe. Now at leng[t]h it hath pleased God to touche his hart and to make him penitent. Sig*no*re Conne his desire [is] that he may be restored to the altar and spend some yeares ther living on his Masses in w*hi*ch he desireth yo*u*r charitable assistance. Our friends here were very unwilling to medle with him in regarde he was made and sent by the Jesuistes, thinking it fitting that thos who made and sent him should relieve him. Wherupon I made a proposition to Sig*no*re Conne that hereafter such men should returne to the places from whence they [*word deleted*] came: a Jesuist to the Jesuistes, a fryer to the fryers, a moncke to the monckes, a secular priest of Dow[ay] to the colledge of Dow[ay], a secular priest of the Romane colledge to the Romane colledge et[c]. And he hath promised to procure that such an order may be made, judging it very unreasonable that the poore clergie enjoying but one colledge should be charged with all the drugges [*sic for* dregges] of other orders and other colledges where the Jesuistes are superiors. And if such an order be procured it will be to good purpose. Our cheife adversaries have informed principall persons of this State that the secular priests doe take an oath of fidelity to the b[ishop] of Calcedoine[1486] prejudiciall to his Ma*j*est[i]e. Notw*i*thstanding, I doubt not but, when the truth shall appeare, their malice will be discovered and his Ma*j*est[i]e [*p. 53*] well satisfyed. Howsoever you may see by this proceeding that the b[ishop]

[1481] John Southcot.
[1482] Henry Floyd SJ.
[1483] See *Letters 91, 93*.
[1484] Anthony Smith.
[1485] E. Henson (ed.), *Registers of the English College at Valladolid 1589–1862* (CRS, 30, 1930), pp. 107–108.
[1486] Richard Smith.

of Calcedoine is still feared by them. God forgive them. This is all, onely I have presented all your remembrances to your best lady[1487] and friends in the court. I doe keepe your sylver bazen untill Mr Fortescue doe returne.[1488] Mr Touchett is very vertuous and if he were at Dow[ay] I thinke that he would proceed to the ends of the colledge, and many of his friends desire that he would take such a course. I praye assist him with your best advise and present my respects unto him.[1489]

And thus with my best wishes to your most honored selfe, I rest, your obedient servant,

Roberts

Maye 26 1637

[in margin of p. 52]

Mr Carpenter,[1490] Fa[ther] Blunts kinsman whom Mr Fitton[1491] commended from Rome is falne and showeth great malice.[1492]

I send you here inclosed a letter from a lady[1493] with whom formerly you have lived. She speaketh much good of you.

[on p. 54]

Addressed: A Monsieur Monsieur [sic] Leuys Ameryne dans la Place Maubert a Paris.

Endorsed: Of Mr Lovels death.

[1487] Anne (Philipson), Baroness Arundell.

[1488] George Fortescue was a friend of the secular clergy. He employed John Jackson as a confessor-chaplain, and corresponded with, among others, the priest Nicholas Strickland; AAW, A XXIX, no. 30, p. 71; Anstr., I, p. 187. (Fortescue was also a correspondent of Galileo Galilei, Gregorio Panzani, and Cardinal Francesco Barberini. Some of his letters survive in the secular clergy's Roman agent's papers.) He had been at the English college, Douai, and the English college in Rome (until 1614). In August 1633 Smith recorded that the Paris nuncio, Bichi, had sent to Rome a long letter written to him by Fortescue in favour of the restoration of bishops in England. But, Smith noted, Oliver Burke OP had told him that 'in R[ome] Mr Forscue is called a castrato'; AAW, B 27, no. 125.

[1489] See Letter 91.

[1490] Richard Carpenter. See Anstr., II, pp. 45–46. He was a nephew of Richard Blount SJ and had been converted to Catholicism by the Benedictine Peter Wilford.

[1491] Peter Biddulph.

[1492] In January 1636 Smith had recorded that Carpenter, using the alias of Dacres, had arrived in Paris from Rome, short of money; AAW, A XXVIII, no. 81, p. 325, and that he was 'thought to be a true sec[ular] preist'; AAW, A XXVIII, no. 84, p. 329. There is a copy in the secular clergy's Roman agent's papers of a letter by Carpenter describing his motives for his change of religion; AAW, A XXV, no. 75.

[1493] Identity uncertain. For Smith's itinerary when he was in England in the later 1620s, see Foley, I, p. 138.

93. Roberts [George Leyburn] to [Richard Smith], 14 June 1637[1494]

[*AAW, A XXIX, no. 26, pp. 61–62*]

Most honored sir,

I have this daye receaved yours of the 19 June with the inclosed for M[r] Webster[1495] which I have delivered. Good man, he taketh very great paynes. This inclosed is a copie of a letter written by M[r] Lovell[1496] to his brother some 2 or 3 monethes before his death, but was not to be sent untill after his death, and as yett it is not delivered in regarde his executeurs have a litle busynes with his father in respect of his debt which as soon as it shall be ended then it shall be delivered unto his brother signed with his owne hand. It is well composed and will be a strong argument against Symons[1497] his proceedings who pretendeth onely this excuse that M[r] Lovell told him some yeares aggoe (beeing putt in mynde by him of his proceedings against the Jesuistes, who as he says was a Jesuist) that he would not dye as he lived. Of which speech he beeing informed some 10 dayes before his death did protest that he was calumniated. More particulars I knowe not, onely that Symons did often presse him upon his salvation to repent him selfe of his former proceedings and become a Jesuist; and did soe laboure him in that weakenes as also his father that, not able to replye any longer, perceaving his spirits to fainte, [he] desired them both to speake noe more unto him for, says he, you have killed me, and after that he never held up his head. And D[octor] Turner, comming to see him immediately after this conflict, and perceaving in him soe great an alteration, and understanding how it came, sayd planely that they had killed him. Your best lady[1498] continueth infirme, afflicted with a cancer in her brest. Both she and M[r] Mountegue, as also Fa[ther] Ph[ilip], doe often remember you. I doubt not but that M[rs] Salesbury her truncke will come safely thither in regarde of my Lord Sturton his sunne.[1499] [*p. 62*] As concerning your newes reported by a Capucin I dare sweare it was very false both for the number of Catholiques as also for the number of coaches. I wounder that such reportes should

[1494] Dated 19 June 1637 in the AAW, A series catalogue.
[1495] Anthony Champney.
[1496] John Southcot.
[1497] Henry Floyd SJ.
[1498] Anne (Philipson), Baroness Arundell.
[1499] A reference, presumably, to Sir William Stourton. See *Letter 22*.

be published ther. I shal not fayle to put Mr Lane and Mr Cape[1500] in mynde as you wish me. Signore Conne had an order from Rome (as I writte in a former letter) to suppresse Knots booke[1501] as also to correct him; and he hath delt with the provinciall about both, who hath written a circular letter unto all the Jesuists to suppresse the booke, and he him selfe hath commaunded Knott not to come to this towne without his leave, and, since, he hath onely been once here with his leave. This palliated correction doth not give satisfaction. Our occurrences here are that our State is like to make a league offensive and defensive with France, but, although I heare that the articles are signed by the king of France, they are not as yett signed by our king.[1502] The prince elector beginneth his jorney towards Holland with his brother on Mundaye next.[1503] Yesterdaye Prymme,[1504] Burton[1505] and an other archpuretan[1506] were censured in the starre chamber first to paye 5000^li a peece, secondly to loose their eares, but, wher as Prymme had lost his eares before, he is to be marked with a hott yron in the forehead and in both sides of his face with an S and an L, signifying slanderous libeller. Thirdly they are to be perpetually imprisoned in 3 divers corners of this kingdome.

This is all, onely my best wishes for your happines who am your most obedient servant,

Roberts

June 14 1637

My best respects to good Mrs Salesbury, Mr Bolds[1507] and Mr Handsome.[1508] The Lord Mountegue is to be marryed the next weeke with the Lady Elizabeth Somersett. They are fully agreed, 1000^l portion, and 1500^l joynture.[1509]

No address.

Endorsed: Of Knotts book[s] condem[nation].

[1500] For the Cape family, who were retainers of the Browne family of Cowdray (Viscounts Montague), see A.F. Allison, 'Franciscan books in English, 1559–1640', *BS*, 3 (1955), pp. 16–65, at pp. 46–47, 48–49.

[1501] See *Letters 87, 90*; Wilson, *A Direction to be Observed [...]*.

[1502] See *CSPV, 1636–1639, passim*.

[1503] See *ibid.*, pp. 234, 237, 247, 248.

[1504] William Prynne.

[1505] Henry Burton.

[1506] John Bastwick.

[1507] Richard Lascelles.

[1508] Thomas Smith, alias Hansom.

[1509] The marriage licence was dated 6 July 1637; Berry, *Sussex*, p. 354.

94. Roberts [George Leyburn] to Leuys Amerine [Richard Smith], 9 August 1637

[*AAW, A XXIX, no. 29, pp. 69–70*]

Most honored sir,

The last letter that I receaved from you was written the 31 of July and, since, I have <u>not receaved</u> any. Neither Mr Anderton[1510] nor Mr Plantyne[1511] have ever sent unto me to excuse their proceedings concerning Sir Thomas.[1512] But now I feare that they shall misse of their marke. For the Lord Stafford is newly dead, and I doe assure my selfe that the earle of Arundell who had the wardship of the young lord, and now agayne of his sister, will marrie her to his second sunne Sir William Howard, especially if the king will suffer the honor to go with the doughter.[1513] Men propose, and God disposeth. I am hartely sorrie and soe are many more for the losse of the young lord, for in him is a most noble Catholique family extinguished. I have receaved letters from Mr Fitton[1514] of the 18 of July wherin he says that the popes sicknes hath been the cause of the delayes in our affayres. But his Holynes is now recovered, soe that I shall beginne to hope well agayne. This daye morning I was with Sig*no*re Conne as also Mr Mountegue who presenteth their respects. The first is sure (as it is believed by thos who should knowe) of a red cappe. I am myndfull of my [*p. 69b*] <u>ladyes[1515] legasie and</u> I am confident that, although <u>I feare</u> I shall not gitt what was intended, notw*i*th<u>standing I</u> shall procure a good part. God knowes my lord[1516] now will not be governed and I much feare that he will marrie agayne. Here are not any new occurrences at the court. The king is gone his progresse towards Salesbury and the queen continueth at Otelands.

[1510] George Gorsuch.

[1511] Lawrence Platt.

[1512] Sir Thomas Gage.

[1513] Henry Stafford, 5th Baron Stafford, died on 4 August 1637 at Ankerwyke in Wraysbury, Buckinghamshire. Con reported that he 'met death like an angel'. His wardship had been granted to the earl of Arundel in November 1625. Mary, his sister, inherited the family estates and was created Baroness Stafford in 1640; GEC, XII/i, p. 187. For her marriage to Sir William Howard, fifth but second surviving son of the earl of Arundel, see *ibid.*, pp. 187, 189. Sir William Howard, created Viscount Stafford after the marriage, was executed in 1680.

[1514] Peter Biddulph.

[1515] Anne (Philipson), Baroness Arundell. She had died on 28 June 1637.

[1516] Thomas Arundell, 1st Baron Arundell.

And thus with my best wishes for y*our* happines I rest who am y*our* obedient servant,

Robertse [*sic*]

Aug[ust] 9 1637

This inclosed I receaved since I writte this. Her ladiship[1517] writte a most kinde letter to me. I beseech you to doe her all the honor you can and provide a place for her sunne.[1518] For she will relye on you. I will write to M[r] Carre[1519] by her ladiship because I desire that he may have the spirituall care of the young lord.

[*on p. 70*]

Addressed: A Monsi*eu*r Monsieur [*sic*] Leuys Amerine dans la Place
          Maubert a Paris.

Endorsed: La[dy] Warders[1520] legacie.

95. Webster [Anthony Champney] to Clarkson [Richard Smith], 22 February 1638

[*AAW, A XXIX, no. 44, pp. 165–168*]

Most r*evere*nd and my very good lord,

Yesterday (w*h*ich was the first tyme I stirred out of my chamber these 6 weekes) M[r] Hammon,[1521] M[r] Musket,[1522] <M[r] Layborn> and my self were w*i*th S*i*g*n*or Con and sayd unto him thus: Sir, we are come to you in the name of the rest of our bretheren to complayn of wrong and injury done not agaynst our p*er*sons (for then <we> would by patience and humility <have> indeurred to have made our p*r*ofit of it) but agaynst our order and function w*h*ich we cannot w*i*th <but> [*sic for* but w*i*th] the offence of God suffer. This wrong hath beene done us <by> the exhibiting of a scandalouse and, as we are tould by

---

[1517] This appears to be a reference to Elizabeth (Howard), widow of William Knollys, 1st earl of Banbury and now the wife of Edward Vaux, 4th Baron Vaux. See GEC, XII/ii, p. 225.

[1518] The countess of Banbury's eldest son, Edward, born on 10 April 1627, in the lifetime of the the countess's husband, the earl of Banbury, but known by the name of Vaux; *ibid.*

[1519] Miles Pinckney.

[1520] i.e. Anne (Philipson), Baroness Arundell.

[1521] John Jackson.

[1522] George Fisher.

some that were present, a lascivious play composed by Mr Flecknoe
<preist> and acted [*word deleted*] <upon> the publike theatre by the
ordinary comediantes of the towne, the whole [*word deleted*] howse
knowing before hand that it was a preistes play and inquiring of on[e]
the [o]ther where is the preist the author of [*word deleted*] this play? Is
he not to be seene? And he him self haveing invited many personages
of ~~both~~ either sex to see it (as <of> his compasinge) and to some
he had read all or part of it before it was acted. And the relation
hereof being made to the king he sayd, what have preistes no ~~other~~
better imploymentes for them selves than to make playes? The wrong
therefore done unto us seminge so great (he being reputed one of
ours^{1523} and, as we are tould, hathe sayd unto your self, in excuse of
his fact, that he was forced through necessity to doe it, the seculer
clergy haveing not provided him any residence where to live) we doe
declare unto you and desire that you will declare it unto him and also
to those to whome he pertaynes that he is none of ours nor ever wilbe
admitted as one of ours. For neither was he preferred to preisthood
by us nor sent into Ingland by those of our body but by the Jesuites,
haveinge first made his noviship at Watten and after studied and [*sic
for* at] Liege, and after five or sixe yeares was dismissed and so came
into Ingland without either testimony of his mission or of his life and
manners and therfore was rejected for his faculties by Mr Muskett two
or three severall tymes. This was the summ of our complaynt.^{1524}

Whereunto he answered that we <had> great reason to complayn
[of] the wrong being done to our order and function. That he had
already told him that he could <not> serve both the stage and the
alter and that he had tould the Jesuites who gave him testimony for his
life and manners (whereupon he gave him faculties) that he deserved
not only to lose his faculties but also to be suspended from the alter.
What he will doe in the end I knowe not. We shall see in tyme and, as
we have occasion, he shall heare from us.

We seyd further unto him that upon this occasion we desired to lett
him knowe the greife we hadd to see our body so quite neglected by our
pastor that after so long sute and so great expense we could not have

---

^{1523} i.e. of the secular clergy.

^{1524} In March 1638 Richard Smith passed this information about Richard Flecknoe to
Richard Lascelles and added that George Fisher refused faculties to Flecknoe 'becaus
he wold not acknowledg my authoritie'. Flecknoe then obtained faculties from George
Con, 'and now lately hath made a lascivious and scandalous playe which he caused to be
publikely used, and now seeketh to be of our bodie', a request which Anthony Champney
had refused. For he was 'no seminarie priest'; AAW, B 27, no. 136; Anstr., II, pp. 112–113.
For Flecknoe's philological interests, see D. Katz, 'The Language of Adam in seventeenth-
century England', in Lloyd-Jones, Pearl, and Worden, *History and Imagination*, pp. 132–145,
at pp. 141, 142.

any answer at all but [*word deleted*] <remayn> still as a body without a head and <as> a scorn to all others. He answered that he was [*p. 166*] as sensible thereof as our selves, but <it> lay not in his powre to help it though he had not omitted any thing; and other words, as often tymes before. Whereupon we asked of him, what then, must we dispayre of any remedy from the Sea Apostolique? He answered, noe. The last letters I had, sayd he, signifyed that after the popes recovery (whose sicknesse hindred all things) Monseignior Boccabella,[1525] who is president of the Congregation of our Inglishe affayres, fell dangerousely sick which continued so long that the cardinall ordayned that another prelate should be chosen in his place for the dispatch of our businesse and that Cardinall Balneo[1526] was sent for <to Rome> for the same purpose. We asked him of what date these letters were. He answered, of January. We replyed that this putt us in some hope that wee were not wholly forgotten. You are not only <to> hope, saythe he, but you may be assured of the grant of your businesse and if I live but two monethes I hope to see it. These were his words. What wilbe the event, God knowethe. We will have patience for these two monthes more. And, if nothing come, I shall dispayre of all good from Rome but not lose my trust and hope in God qui in altis habitat et humilia respicit. I see our pore body groweth weake and decrepid every way. Our colleges <abroad> goe to ruine. Our clergy at home is without life and spirit as it seemeth to me. Wherefore our only hope must be in the goodnesse of God to revive in us his spirit which I wishe hartely but my hands are to[o] weake to help it up. Other things I leave to others to write.

And with due respect take ~~lease~~ <leave> this 22 of Feb[ruary] 1638.

Your lordships ever at command,

Webster

After I had writen this I received yours of the 26. Mr Price[1527] shall knowe what you write. And I ame gladd he had noe occasion to complayn. For I had rather suffer wrong than doe wrong. And though I think it litle prudence to be very confident yet I would not have them think us so opposit as that we cannot or will not live in good peace with them. For Mr Hammon there is small or no meanes to force him to do more than he shall be willing to doe by persuation, which hath prevayled with him thus farr as that he hath given up [*p. 167*] bands of

---

[1525] For Boccabella, see Dockery, *CD*, p. 74.
[1526] Cardinal Giovanni Francesco Guido del Bagno.
[1527] William (Benedict) Jones OSB.

1800^{li} reserveing 500 for the use which he saythe the fownder[1528] hath his hand for. So that the 800 above the 1000 is for the frutes of the first capitall which he sayth was only 1000 for the end of Arras Colledge, thother 500 being for an nother [sic] end. This will not enrich the clergy otherwayes than to help to bring up ~~men~~ able men for the clergy so farr as I can conceive.[1529] What is become of Mrs Mary Ward and hers?

[on p. 168]

Addressed: For Mr Clarkson. Parise.

No endorsement.

96. Rob[erts] [George Leyburn] to Louys Amerine [Richard Smith], 15 March 1638[1530]

[AAW, A XXIX, no. 19, pp. 41–44]

Most honored sir,

I have yours of the 10 of March with the enclosed to Mr Thomas Roper[1531] which is carefully delivered as also the gazett which is contradicted by the Spanish party, and all letters from Brussells doe speake of Duke Bernards defeat. Some two dayes more will manifest the truth.[1532] Signore Conne doth now seem to admire the [word deleted] slowe proceedings of the court of Rome as well as wee. The French ambassadeur[1533] told me that he had written to the cardenall[1534] and

---

[1528] Thomas Sackville, fourth son of Thomas Sackville, 1st earl of Dorset. See NAGB, pp. 85–86.

[1529] For the foundation of the Collège d'Arras, see ibid., passim. For its troubles at this time, see Allison, 'An English gallican', pp. 320–324. Allison notes both the incessant quarrelling among the members and also the problems created by the war with Spain. The college was leased from the Abbey of St Vaast in the Spanish Netherlands and was seized by the French crown as enemy property. For a time there were threats of distraint against the English clergy occupying the college.

[1530] Dated 15 March 1637 in the AAW, A series catalogue.

[1531] For Thomas Roper (son of Sir William Roper, and cousin of the secular clergy's former agent in Rome, Thomas More), see NAGB, p. 254. Roper was still active at this time in lobbying for the restoration of a Catholic bishop in England; VA, PD, fo. 91r.

[1532] For Bernard of Saxe-Weimar's military victories in early 1638, and notably his defeat of Johann von Werth at Rheinfelden, see CSPV, 1636–1639, pp. 388, 393; C. Burckhardt, Richelieu and his Age, 3 vols (London, 1970), III, pp. 194–195.

[1533] Pomponne de Bellièvre.

[1534] Cardinal Richelieu.

to your selfe. He hath but poore councelleurs here. Mr Hammon is very ill in the night often tymes and is affrayd least he may dye sodainely as his brother Mr Volentyne[1535] did, but I hope it is onely a strong apprehension and that ther is noe just cause. I heare that now he hath delivered up 800^l more which maketh in all 1800^l and this is all the accompt that he is like to make of all the rents of 1500^{li} for soe many yeares togeather receaved by him. I doe wounder that Fa[ther] Talbott hath been suffered soe long to continue in thos partes. The countesse of Banbury intendeth to be ther shortly after Easter as also the countesse of Newport.[1536] The puretans in Scotland are very obstinate and turbulent, and I heare that they have possessed themselves of the two cheef castles, Sterling and Edenborough.[1537] A great disaster lately happened in our court. Archy[1538] is deprived of his fooles coate and discarded for calling the bishop of Canterbury[1539] trayter.

This is all, onely my best wishes which I present unto you in all hartie manner who am your most obedient servant,

Rob[erts]

March 15 1637

The earle of Northumberland[1540] is made admirall of England untill the duke of Yorke come to his full age.

[on p. 44]

Addressed: A Monsieur Monsieur [sic] Louys Amerine dans la Place Maubert a Paris.

Endorsed: D[octor] Laborn of moneys given up.

[1535] Hammond was the usual alias of John Jackson. I assume that, here, 'Hammon' denotes Jackson's brother, the Franciscan, Bonaventure Jackson and, in the text, the term 'his brother Mr Volentyne' refers loosely to his Capuchin (Franciscan reform movement) confrere William (Anselm) Valentine, who had died in 1634; Bellenger, *EWP*, p. 117. (Bonaventure Jackson was imprisoned in Newgate in 1633; Dockery, *CD*, p. 22.) For Valentine, see *CSPD*, *1633–1634*, p. 315; Foley, I, p. 519; AAW, A XXVIII, no. 10, p. 36.

[1536] For the conversion in 1637 of Anne (Boteler), wife of Mountjoy Blount, 1st earl of Newport, see Hibbard, *CI*, pp. 55, 57; Albion, *CI*, pp. 208, 212, 227.

[1537] See P. Donald, *An Uncounselled King: Charles I and the Scottish Troubles 1637–1641* (Cambridge, 1990), pp. 129–130.

[1538] Archibald Armstrong, court jester.

[1539] William Laud.

[1540] Algernon Percy, 10th earl of Northumberland.

97. Ro[berts] [George Leyburn] to Louys Amerine [Richard Smith], 10 May 1638

[*AAW, A XXIX, no. 58, pp. 203–204*]

Most honored sir,

I have been holden with a feaver for a 12 dayes togeather which hath been the occasion of my silence. At the same tyme my Lady Shrewsbury[1541] was visited with the small poxe. God be praised both of us are upon recovery. I have been free thes 4 dayes. Your last letter, as also the former, I delivered unto M[r] Webster[1542] and wish[e]d [him] well to consider with our other friends of the cheef poyntes therin contayned, espetially concerning the setling of Arras house.[1543] But M[r] Blacloe[1544] hath onely receaved a 1000 of thos moneyes, and I see noe hopes of [any] more. M[r] Hammon[1545] says that the other 500[l] belongeth to him to dispose, and, as for the profitt of thes moneyes for soe many yeares, I dispayre of any. I doe assure you unfainedly I am hartely ashamed at his proceedings. Your letter to the embassadeur[1546] I sent unto one of his gentlemen. He and his whole family are in the country about Richmond soe that I have not as yett re[c]eaved any answere. About an hower aggoe M[r] Mountegue was here to see me who presenteth his respects unto you. He telleth me that Pere Joseph[1547] is dying. If it be true, your friends will find the ambassadeur more curteous hereafter. This morning we have newes that Don Pedro[1548] is dead and that he hath provided well for the house which will be some ease to our friends here.[1549] The stirres in Scotland continue very bad. Now the Marquis Hamleton is going thither with some other of the Scotch nobility sent from our king to compose all differences, but I see litle signes of any good. They are soe insolent, and lately they have deposed divers ministers, some for speaking in his Majesties behalfe, others for giving the communion to the people kneeling. My humble service to my most noble lady the countesse of Bannbery, and noble Sir Kenelme[1550] if he be ther. I doe omitt to write because I am

[1541] Frances (Arundell), second wife of John Talbot, 10th earl of Shrewsbury.
[1542] Anthony Champney.
[1543] The Collège d'Arras.
[1544] Thomas White.
[1545] John Jackson.
[1546] Presumably the French ambassador, Pomponne de Bellièvre.
[1547] François Joseph le Clerc du Tremblay.
[1548] Pedro Coutinho.
[1549] For Coutinho's death in April 1638, see Kirk and Croft, *Historical Account of Lisbon College*, p. 15.
[1550] Sir Kenelm Digby.

weake, and I heare that he is exspected here sodainely. My lord of Northumberland,[551] as it is thought, will not escape this sicknes. My respects to good Mrs Salesbury whose letter is delivered to Mr Blunt who was with me yesterdaye and sayd he would answere. Also to Mr Car[552] and Mr Hansome.[553]

And my best wishes for your happines, who am your most obedient servant,

Ro[berts]

May 10 1638

Sir Thomas Roe is to goe ambassadeur into Germany and it is reported that we shall joyne with France and Swed[en] for the recovery of the Palatinate.[554]

[on p. 204]

Addressed: A Mons*ieu*r Monsieur [*sic*] Louys Amerine dans la Place Maubert a Paris.

Endorsed: M. Lovel.[555]
    Of 1000^l to M. Blaclo.

---

[551] Algernon Percy, 10th earl of Northumberland.
[552] Miles Pinckney.
[553] Thomas Smith, Richard Smith's nephew.
[554] See *CSPV, 1636–1639*, pp. 401, 405, 410, 411, 429, 431; Hibbard, *CI*, p. 79.
[555] 'Lovel' had been John Southcot's alias. The endorser of this letter, Richard Smith, meant to refer to George Leyburn.

Mʳ Pugh[1316] when you send into Walles next. Mʳ Layborne is come to Richmond, where I wish you were also that we might sometimes meet togeather to conferr about our affaires. We have nothing of moment from my lord.[1317] This from Mʳ Fitton I desire you to send me back againe by the next.

My service to all with you, and in hast I rest. 2 Septemb[er] 1636.

Yours ever being but to serve you ever,

Jo[hn] Clerk

Lett us have that Latin letter againe I pray which was written in your name to the Span[ish] ambassador[1318] lately that we may putt it uppon the register as we use to doe.

[on p. 522]

Addressed: To my much honoured cosen Mʳ Edward Farrington in Sussex or elsewhere.

Endorsed: 1636.
            Mʳ Lovells of the 2 of September.

83. Laborn [George Leyburn] to Farrington [Edward Bennett], 3 September 1636

[AAW, A XXVIII, no. 157, pp. 523–528]

Most honored sir,

You had heard from me long before this if I could have been furnish[e]d with any convenient opportunity to convey my letters unto you. The plague continuing and increasing in London taketh away all meanes of correspondence, in soe much that I am enforced to send at this tyme my owne servant to give you an accoumpt of all passages since my departure from you.[1319] On Weddensday last I parted from Oxeford with Signor Georgio[1320] and Signor Panzano[1321]

[1316] This may be a reference to the priest Stephen Pugh. See Anstr., II, p. 374.

[1317] Richard Smith.

[1318] Presumably a reference to Iñigo Ladron Velez de Guevara y Tassis, count of Oñate and Villa Mediana.

[1319] See Letter 81.

[1320] George Con.

[1321] Gregorio Panzani. Panzani's diary records his visit to Oxford. He arrived there on 19 August, and met the Benedictine provincial, Robert Sherwood, and also William (Benedict) Jones OSB. On 20 August he visited All Souls, the Schools, and Bodley's library, and then, after meeting Leyburn and Christopher Davenport OFM, he went to see

and on Thursedaye night we arrived at Hampton towne a myle from Hampton Court wher they intend to continue untill it shall please God to free London of the sicknes.[1322] Their Majesties parted also the same daye, the king towards New Forest, and the queen towards Otelands. Wher [sic] and [at] Hampton Court she intends to continue thes 2 moneths or longer if the plague do not cease. They were most gloriousely receaved at Oxeforde.[1323] They were mett two myles from the towne by the cheef citizens, aldermen, batchlers of divinity, doctors of phisike, doctors of divinity in their scarlett roabes, bishops, mayor and chancellor (viz the archbishop of Canterbury), all which ridde in great state before their Majesties coache unto Christ Church Colledge wher they were lodged, and after supper intertayned with a new comedy called the Passions Calmed, or the Floating Iseland,[1324] in which was represented a king whos name was Prudentius (you may imagine our most prudent prince) and an Intellectus Agens, a person active and wise (you may imagine his Grace of Canterbury); by the passions you may understand the puritans and all such as are opposit to the courses which our king doth run in his goverment. Thes passions were very unrulye and disobedient unto Prudentius['s] goverment in soe [p. 524] much that they resolved noe longer to ~~endure~~ <suffer> him to be their king, which the Intellectus Agens, perceaving, persuaded Prudentius to yeeld his crowne quietly, which he did. Thes disordered passions, having now the crowne, consulted together on whom they should bestowe it, and election was made of Lady Fancy, under whos goverment they fell into bitter discords and discentions amongst them selves, plotting to kill each other. At length, beeing wearie of thes differences, they resolved to aske counsell of Desparato what to doe,

St John's. Over the next couple of days he saw another twelve colleges. Following a trip to the court at Woodstock, Panzani returned to Christ Church to see the rehearsals for William Strode's *The Floating Island* which Leyburn describes in this letter; VA, PD, fos 146r, 147r; PRO, 31/9/17B.

[1322] On 30 May Panzani had noted in his diary that he went to reside at Hampton, where he could both avoid the plague and visit the court regularly, and see, among others, Jacques le Noël Du Perron, Robert Philip, and Leyburn; VA, PD, fo. 139r. He negotiated, in June, with Windebank, for two rooms at the palace; PRO, 31/9/17B (transcript of Panzani's letter to Barberini of 17/27 June 1636).

[1323] For this event, see K. Sharpe, 'Archbishop Laud and the University of Oxford', in H. Lloyd-Jones, V. Pearl, and B. Worden (eds), *History and Imagination* (London, 1981), pp. 146–164, at pp. 150–152; Sharpe, *Criticism and Compliment*, p. 48.

[1324] See William Strode, *The Floating Island: A Tragi-Comedy, Acted before His Majesty at Oxford, Aug. 29. 1636. By the Students of Christ-Church* (London, 1655); B. Dobell (ed.), *The Poetical Works of William Strode [...] to which is added The Floating Island a Tragi-Comedy [...]* (London, 1907), pp. 137–263. Strode was the Public Orator in the university. The play had been written at Laud's own prompting. Leyburn's account of the performance gives us a different perspective from the description in Sharpe, 'Archbishop Laud', pp. 156–157, 160. Panzani had been taken to see a rehearsal of the play on 26 August; VA, PD, fo. 147r.

who would make noe answere butpresented unto them many naked knyfes and roapes. They were not pleas[e]d with this, wherupon they thought good to advise with Intellectus Agens who persuaded them to submitte them selves unto Prudentius and returne the crowne agayne unto him, which counsell, beeing in this extremity, they did willingly embrace. Prudentius receaved the crowne agayne from the passions and accepted of their submission with an acknowledgement of their foule errors and made a speech unto them full of sweetnes, signifying that the courses which he ran in his goverment was [sic] for their good, and as for the navy it was to defende them and the kingdome.[1325] Ther was represented a puritan minister who made very good sport, and their Majesties laugh[ed] hartely. His name was Malancholico and he was marryed to Concupiscence. When he came with the passions to tender his submission to Prudentius, he kneel[e]d doune and sayd, O King, I kneele not to thee but to the [sic for thy] power, neither doe I adore thee.[1326]

The next daye their Majesties were feasted by his Grace of Canterbury at St Jhons Colledge and [p. 525] ther was most great entertainement as ever I did see in all my life. His Grace did shew him selfe most noble, kept 14 tables, as many as are kept in the court, and one table for the queen, almener,[1327] Fa[ther] Philip and some of the cheef French who they should bring with them. His Grace invited the grand almener by Sir Jhon Tunstall who did signifie also [that] his Grace durst not invite Signor Georgio. Notwithstanding, if he would come he should be hartely welcome,[1328] soe that he was ther ad [sic for at] dynner. And Panzano[1329] and I went with Fa[ther] Philip and I doe assure you that I never see [sic for saw] such store of flesh and fish and sweet meates as was at that table and all curiousely drist after the French fashion.[1330] This manner of inviting Signor Georgio did much please, more than if he had been invited directly. After dynner their Majesties was [sic] entertayned with an other new comedy called Loves Hospitall[1331] which gave great content and, after supper, with

[1325] See Dobell, *Poetical Works*, p. 234. This was a reproof directed at those who were already expressing criticism of the Ship Money levies.

[1326] *Ibid.*, p. 235 ('I kneel not/To thee, but to thy power; I kneel to thee/But not adore thee').

[1327] Jacques le Noël Du Perron.

[1328] Albion says that Laud's invitation was sent via Du Perron; Albion, *CI*, p. 161.

[1329] See VA, PD, fo. 147r.

[1330] See A.J. Taylor, 'The royal visit to Oxford in 1636: a contemporary narrative', *Oxoniensia*, 1 (1936), pp. 151–158, at p. 157.

[1331] Laud informed the vice-chancellor on 15 July 1636 that he undertook to pay for the production of this play, written by George Wilde; see Laud, *Works*, V, p. 147; Taylor, 'Royal visit', p. 157; J.L. Funston (ed.), *A Critical Edition of Love's Hospital* (Salzburg, 1973). For Laud's patronage of Wilde, see *ibid.*, iv.

an other at Christ Church Colledge.[1332] Signor Georgio did onely see the first where he was much honored by both the king and queens chamberlaine[s][1333] who did earnestly invite him to sitt with them which he refused. And at the comedy at St Jhons Colledge their Majesties, not seeing him their, sent a gentleman to enquire for him.[1334] He hath been much honored by all the nobility about the court.[1335] And on Sundaye last at Woodstock he did conferre almost an hower in private with the king, [*p. 526*] at which many did wounder, but to your selfe this, for although his passage is knowne, as also the manner of the archbishops inviting of him, notwithstanding I would not have us publish them, for our adversaries will take advantage against us upon every litle busines.

I doe assure you faithfully that I am confident that Signor Georgio will be able to doe great good here if he doe setle a firme correspondence, which is that he doth ayme at, but to yourselfe this. And I am certayne that he desireth noe thing more than 3 or 4 bishops for this country, but I doe see that my lords returne[1336] will not be much urged unlesse it may appeare gratful to his Majesty. Yett before his return to Rome nothing will be done. Howsoever I have desired Fa[ther] Philip to move her Majesty to some present order unto Sir William Hamleton[1337] to deale about bishop[s], that his Holynes may see that her Majesty is still myndfull of the busines.

[1332] This play was William Cartwright's *The Royal Slave*. See Taylor, 'Royal visit', pp. 157–158; Sharpe, 'Archbishop Laud', pp. 151–152. Laud complained to the vice-chancellor that the university was unwilling to contribute to the cost of the entertainment at Christ Church; Laud, *Works*, V, p. 144.

[1333] The lord chamberlain of the household was Philip Herbert, 4th earl of Pembroke. Henrietta Maria's chamberlain was Edward Sackville, 4th earl of Dorset.

[1334] Con and Panzani did not attend the play performed at St John's college, allegedly because they wanted to avoid seeming too forward in seeking royal favour; Albion, *CI*, p. 161.

[1335] For the contacts which Con was making among the nobility at this time, see *ibid*. He was entertained by Bishop Juxon, and the earl of Holland invited him to meet the marquis of Winchester and other leading Catholics at Holland's own residence in Hyde Park; *ibid.*, p. 162.

[1336] i.e. the proposed return of Richard Smith to England.

[1337] Richard Smith reported to Southcot on 25 May/4 June 1636 that he had spoken with Sir William Hamilton as he passed through Paris. Smith gave him 'instructions such as I thought good', and Hamilton told Smith that Henrietta Maria had commanded him (Hamilton) to consult Smith; AAW, A XXVIII, no. 121, p. 423. Smith believed that Hamilton would negotiate at Rome on their behalf, though, as Smith learned in August 1636, Hamilton would not do so without specific instructions from the queen; AAW, A XXVIII, no. 151, p. 509. On 9/19 July 1636 Biddulph reported that Hamilton had been well received by the pope, and had made a very good impression in Rome. Cardinal Barberini had 'presented him with two very faire horses for his coach'. Hamilton kept correspondence with Secretary Windebank, and, as Brett had done, used the Benedictine agent in Rome, Richard (Wilfrid) Selby, to convey his letters; AAW, A XXVIII, no. 139, p. 467. On 24 September/4 October Biddulph noted that Hamilton was 'our trew friend and affected to our business as well as cann be'; AAW, A XXVIII, no. 177, p. 571. The secular clergy supported Hamilton out of their scarce financial resources. On 4 January 1638 Champney remarked to Biddulph that my desire is that they may prevaile soe far as to make us deale warely, that is to complye with Sig*no*re Georgio howsoever we doe imagine him to be Jesuited and not to decrye him before we have greater grounds of his disaffection towards us.[1413] You cannot imagine how he was trubled at Mr Chambers letter wherin [*word deleted*] <were> mentioned divers speeches of yours concerning him. But I am confident that he is well satisfyed now, and th*a*t he doth not impute it a falt to you but to y*ou*r informers whosoever they were, for you did speake onely what you heard. For Fa[ther] Ph[ilip], first you may please to knowe th*a*t I doe noething without him. And he hath the same opinion of Sig*no*re Georgio that I have, besyd[e]s by occasion of what Mr Chambers writte concerning y*ou*r speeches. He tould me in these words: I am of opinion that if you have any good done it must be by Sig*no*re Georgio his meanes and therfore doe not louse him. But I wonder who informeth you th*a*t Sig*no*re Georgio hath a designe to make the clergie to quitte ~~you~~ <the> b[ishop's] authoritie and not to stand for it. I doe assure you faithfully that after th*a*t I had given him many reasons wherfore it was necessarie to mentayne y*ou*r authority, he writte to the cardinal protector[1414] that he thought it convenient that you should be mentayned in y*ou*r authority alleadging the reasons. But to deale planely with you I perceave by Sig*no*re Georgio that it was held generally at Rome th*a*t you had resigned, th*a*t y*ou*r resignation was accepted, and that the clergie knew soe much, and that they would not stand upon th*a*t poynt. And therfore he blameth much Panzani who never did intimate to Rome as th*a*t the clergie did stand for the b[ishop's] authority. I am in hast. The earle of Arundell is com[me]d.[1415] 10 27 1636. Mr Lovell[1416] is sickelie still.[1417]

[1413] On 28 January/7 February 1637, Peter Biddulph notified John Southcot that he had received two or three letters from Leyburn 'who doth still continue in good conceate' of Con. Leyburn hoped that by Con's means the dean and chapter would be confirmed, 'which would be a greate establishment to our clergye; butt in this buisness wee must entreate Sig*no*r Giorgio to deale with the card*ina*l [Francesco Barberini] as from himself, for so it will be obtained sooner, and the negotiation will be kept more secrett than if I should deale [with] it here in the name of the clergye'; AAW, A XXIX, no. 10, p. 21. Smith, however, opined to Richard Lascelles at Rome in a letter of 13/23 March 1638 that, 'as for the hope you have of confirming the chapter, I know not what good will come therby to the clergy' because 'I think thereby they shall have but the archpriest and assistants changed into the names of a deane and canons'; AAW, B 27, no. 136.

[1414] Cardinal Francesco Barberini.

[1415] The earl of Arundel returned from the Hague on 27 December 1636/6 January 1637; *CSPV, 1636–1639*, p. 126.

[1416] John Southcot.

[1417] Back in March and April 1636 Smith had several times warned Southcot to take care of his health; AAW, A XXVIII, no. 102, p. 377; no. 104, p. 381; no. 106, p. 385.

No address.

[*on p. 659 at top of page*]

For the <love> of God be secrett in what I write, neither lett Mʳ Clerke knowe any thing. I have delt planely with him and I thinke he will be of an other opinion. And he is very friendlie to me and I desire not to take notise of anything [?].

[*on p. 660*]

Endorsed: Signor Con for the bishop.

89. Rob[erts] [George Leyburn] to [Richard Smith], 19 January 1637

[*AAW, A XXIX, no. 6, pp. 11–14*]

Most honored sir,

I have receaved yours of the 18 of Jan[uary] and I have imparted to Fa[ther] Ph[ilip] and Mʳ Conne what you writte concerning [*sic*] and they were <u>both well satisfyed</u> for they had receaved letters at the same tyme from Mʳ Chambers to the same effect. I am very hopefull, <u>as also Fa[ther] Ph[ilip]</u>, that some good will be done by his meanes as I have signifiyed in my former letters. He continueth very gracious both with the king and queen with whom he is daily. I am sorrie that <u>none of our cheef friends</u> would ever yett make a jorney to Hampton to see him. The superiors of all other religious have often visited him ther, especially Father Blunt, Fa[ther] Price[1418] and Fa[ther] Frances[1419] who, as I heare, is made superior in Father Perkins[1420] place. The court will now be shortly here at London and then I hope that we shall make amends for all this neglect. I doe not wounder if Signore Gregorio[1421] did speake coldely of episcopall authority, and the reasons I have intimated in my former letters. And I doe assure you faithfully that he told Signore Georgio (if he be to be believed), fearing least he should harken too much <u>to the clergie</u> (by reason of Fa[ther] Ph[ilip]) whom he knew for the most part neither to approve Fa[ther] Leanders[1422] proceeding nor Fa[ther] Frances, first that I was <u>a good man</u> but he was not to heed my informations because they were not good, secondly

[1418] William (Benedict) Jones OSB.
[1419] Christopher Davenport (Francis a Sancta Clara) OFM.
[1420] John Gennings OFM. See Anstr., I, pp. 128–129; *NAGB*, pp. 108, 111; Dockery, *CD*, p. 36.
[1421] Gregorio Panzani.
[1422] John (Leander) Jones OSB.

that Mr Muskett[1423] was a collericke and passionate man (which indeed to my knowledge he had spoken before). Thirdlie that Mr Lovell[1424] was a turbulent man. And is it not strange he used to confesse to me sometymes, but never when Fa[ther] Frances was in company or Fa[ther] Price? Thes two complye greatly with Signore Georgio but will never gayne him as they gayned the other. He will employe them between him and the secretary[1425] when he has any busynes. He will goe himselfe rather when he hath any busynes with the king. He will not use any to breake it unto his Majest[i]e but him selfe. Fa[ther] [*p. 12*] Price some 6 dayes aggoe, complying much with Signore Georgio, and knowing well that he had taken some disgust at Signore Panzani, tooke occasion to speake of him, and told him that he (Panzani) was a proude man, a malencholie man and a simple man. This I doe protest unto you, before my B[lessed] Saviour, Signore Georgio tolde me with his owne mouth. How can any man trust such an one? And one daye Signore Georgio tooke occasion, before Panzani, to speake unto him[1426] about episcopall jurisdiction, and asked him wherfore he thought it not convenient to admitt of bishops, and he replyed that ther were bishops alreadie. By that reason, replyed Signore Georgio, you should not admitte of priests, for the ministers doe stile them selves priests. With that he told him that the State would not permitt bishops, as Panzani says he can witnes, whom I carryed to the secretary, who declared the kings mynde in that poynte. But, sayes he to Signore Georgio, doe you thinke it convenient? For my parte (says he) if his Holynes should send in a bishop with ordinarie jurisdiction I would returne to my monestery before that I would obey him. With many such passages as thes I could acquainte you if I were with you. This Fa[ther] Price, as also Fa[ther] Francis, are very gratious with the secretary[1427] and frequent the court very often and, to my knowledge, endevour to doe us many bad offices, and strive to gayne freinds on the French syde, but, if our freinds will be advised, they shall never be able to hurt us. But for the love of God keep to your selfe all thes passages which I have signifyed. Otherwise I shall suffer prejudice.

I have presented the grand almener[1428] and the superior of the Capucins[1429] with one of your bookes as from you. It is a worke that

[1423] George Fisher.
[1424] John Southcot.
[1425] Sir Francis Windebank.
[1426] i.e. William (Benedict) Jones OSB.
[1427] For Christopher Davenport (Francis a Sancta Clara) OFM's contacts with Windebank, see Dockery, *CD, passim*.
[1428] Jacques le Noël Du Perron.
[1429] Jean-Marie Trélon. See Hibbard, *CI*, p. 56.

takes greatly in the court and [*p. 13*] [is] most proper for thes tymes, and it will be gratfull at Rome.[1430] Fa[ther] Ph[ilip], the grand almener and all y*our* friends did showe a great joye for the grace the king had done you and Monsi*eur* Almener wish[e]d me to present his humble service and signifie how glad he was, as also that you were to be his neig[h]bour. I sent one of y*our* bookes unto a doctor of divinity,[1431] sole chaplaine to our prince, and he gave me great thankes and protested that the bishop of Calcedoyne was a brave man. As concerning M*r* Clerke[1432] I doe protest unfainedly before my Blessed Saviour I desire as much to gayne his affection and give him content as I desire any earthlie thing. He was first displeased with me because I did not goe to Ro[me] and cheefly in regard of a letter that y*our* best lady[1433] writte at that tyme, w*hi*ch was very sharpe, and therin he did declare that he would never give his consent that I should goe, and M*r* Clerk thought him selfe touched in that letter because he <u>did attribute</u> my going to some of our cheef men. I doe assure you faithfully that I was most ignorant of that letter and, if I had imagined that y*our* best lady and her husband would have taken my going as they did, I would not have taken my leave w*i*th them rather than to have disappoynted our friends. But afterwards all were against my going untill the spring, and then y*our* best lady told me that she would give way and helpe to my maintainetance [*sic for* maintenance], as I acquainted both M*r* Benett (who was also much against my going then by reason of Sig*no*re Georgio his coming) and M*r* Clerk. For my parte whither soever you shall commande me to goe or runne, I doe assure you faithfully I will not refuse, although all the friends I have in this world dissuade me.

This is all, onely my best wishes, w*hi*ch I present in all harty manner who [am] y*our* most obedient servant,

Rob[erts]

Jan[uary] 19 1637

No address

[*on p. 14*]

Endorsed: The b*isho*ps booke.

[1430] It is not clear which of Richard Smith's works is meant, but it could well have been his *A Brief Inquisition into F. Nicholas Smith his Discussion of M.D. Kellison his Treatise of the Ecclesiasticall Hierarchie* (Douai, 1630), attacking Matthew Wilson SJ's tract against Kellison. However, on 10/20 February 1636, Smith, in Paris, had asked Southcot to send him some copies of Smith's own *Prudentiall Ballance of Religion* (St Omer, 1609), as well as other books; AAW, A XXVIII, no. 92, p. 351.

[1431] This is, presumably, a reference to Brian Duppa, who was the prince's tutor. See *Letters* 70, 74. I am grateful to Kenneth Fincham for advice on this point.

[1432] John Southcot.

[1433] Anne (Philipson), Baroness Arundell.

INDEX

Names are given in the form in which they are most commonly written. Only the aliases which are actually cited in the text are listed in the index.

episcopal court at 75, 76
Gibbon, John 232
Gifford, William, Archbishop 13
Gildon, Mary 7, 116, 233, 234
 uncle of *see* Smith, Richard
Ginetti, Martio, Cardinal 57, 60, 62, 89,
 138
Gloucester, bishop of *see* Goodman,
 Godfrey
Godbolt, Mr
 brother and sister-in-law of 159
 conversion and death of 159–160
Gondi, Jean François de, Archbishop
 185
Gondomar, count of *see* Acuña, Diego
 Sarmiento de
Gonzaga, Charles, duke of Mantua,
 marriage of 175
Gooch, Thomas 154, 271
Goodman, Godfrey, Bishop 220, 293
Goodman, John, SJ 220
Gore, George, OSB 155
Goring, George, duel with Lord Basil
 Fielding 169
Goring, George, 1st Baron Goring
 169
Gorsuch, George, alias Anderton, alias
 Talbot 152, 296, 309, 310, 317
grace, doctrines of 272
Grandison, 1st Viscount *see* Villiers,
 William
Gray, Andrew 128
 daughter of *see* White, Anne (née
 Gray)
Gray, John 212
Green, Henry 152
Green, Thomas 154, 245
 as chaplain of Bendlow family 269
 memorandum of 16, 97, 269–272
 scandalous cases, compiled by 171
Greenfield Abbey, Jesuit school at 47
Greenwich, court at 221, 301
Greenwood, Christopher, SJ 171
Gregory I, Pope 247
Greville, Robert, 2nd Baron Brooke 22
Grosvenor, John, SJ, alias Altham 97, 148,
 179
Guevara y Tassis, Iñigo Ladron Velez de,
 count of Oñate and Villa Mediana
 287
 arrival in England of 281
gunpowder plot 50, 92, 105, 161, 233, 249,
 256

Gussoni, Vicenzo 158, 205, 208, 215
 and William Warmington 135
Gustavus Adolphus, King 47, 55, 86, 100,
 167, 168, 178

Haddington, 1st earl of *see* Hamilton,
 Thomas
Hall, Joseph, Bishop, and puritanism 181
Hallier, François, book of, *Defensio
 Ecclesiasticae Hierarchiae [. . .]* (1632) 65,
 83, 103, 138
Hamilton, James, 2nd earl of Abercorn 24,
 277
Hamilton, James, 3rd marquis of Hamilton
 24, 55, 177, 277, 323
 expedition to Germany of 55, 91, 100
Hamilton, Sir William, as Henrietta
 Maria's envoy to Rome 24, 267, 277,
 285, 290–291, 293, 299
Hamilton, Thomas, 1st earl of Haddington
 55
Hamnet, Mrs 222
Hampden, John 22
Hampshire
 Arminian minister in 99
 English Catholic clergy in 99, 155
 Irish clergy in 172
 puritans in 99
Hampton 288, 291
Hampton Court 232, 288, 298, 302, 304
Hampton Court conference 243
Hanford, Mrs 179
 son of 179
Harcourt, Valentine, alias Lane 291
 cousin of *see* Biddulph, Peter
Hare, Robert 41, 56, 64, 117–118, 135
Harewell, William 3, 182
 as chaplain of Elizabeth Knollys 81
 as secretary of William Bishop and
 Richard Smith 81
Hargrave, James, SJ 106
Hargrave, William, alias Hart
 as chaplain of Henry Parker, 14th Baron
 Morley and Monteagle 42
 newsletter to 257
 as president of the college of Saints Peter
 and Paul at Lisbon 43, 260, 283, 285
Harrington, Mark 280
Harris, Francis 208, 220
 apostasy of 208
Hart, Mr *see* Hargrave, William
Haselwood, James 62
 as chaplain of 1st Viscount Stafford 62